The Lion of Princeton

B. B. Warfield as Apologist and Theologian

The Lion of Princeton

B. B. Warfield as Apologist and Theologian

Kim Riddlebarger

STUDIES IN HISTORICAL AND SYSTEMATIC THEOLOGY

LEXHAM PRESS

The Lion of Princeton: B. B. Warfield as Apologist and Theologian
Studies in Historical and Systematic Theology

Lexham Press, 1313 Commercial St., Bellingham, WA 98225
LexhamPress.com

Print ISBN 978-1-57-799588-3
Digital ISBN 978-1-57-799589-0

Lexham Editorial Team: Lynnea Fraser, Katie Terrell
Cover Design: Jim LePage
Typesetting: ProjectLuz.com

Contents

Acknowledgments

One writer states, “It is a deep privilege to salute mentors and friends who made the academic pilgrimage so meaningful.” My own pilgrimage began inauspiciously one night many years ago in a burger joint, when I engaged in my first-ever theological discussion with a real live theologian. The challenge given that night—that someone undertake a look at the relationship between the Princeton apologetic and Scottish Common Sense philosophy—ultimately culminated in this effort. And so it is Dr. Rod “Dad” Rosenbladt, esteemed professor and now beloved friend and colleague, to whom this effort is sincerely dedicated.

I have enjoyed sitting at the feet of several masters, most notably Dr. John Warwick Montgomery and Dr. W. Robert Godfrey. I certainly owe a word of thanks to Dr. D. G. Hart, Dr. William Harris, Dr. Brad Gundlach, Dr. James Bradley, Dr. Donald Hagner, Professor John M. Frame, and Dr. Mark Noll for all their suggestions, corrections, and help with sources. My dear friend Michael Horton also contributed much in the way of encouragement and intellectual stimulation, as did Westminster Seminary California professors R. Scott Clark and Steve Baugh. I also want to thank the consistory of Christ Reformed Church (URCNA) in Anaheim, CA, for all their gracious support and encouragement. Thanks to all of you! But a special note of gratitude must go to my dissertation advisor, Dr. Richard A. Muller, whose knowledge, wisdom, and counsel proved invaluable.

Thanks also go to Deborah Barackman for her editorial work in turning a Ph.D. dissertation into a more readable format, and to Brannon Ellis of Lexham Press for encouraging me to finally update and publish that which had been sitting in my computer’s hard drive in the form of electronic “1’s” and “0’s” for too many years.

How do you thank your wife and family for all of the countless sacrifices they have made during the years that this project was underway? To my wife, Micki, I can only offer a heartfelt thank you for all of the support and love that you have given me. To my sons, David and Mark,

I tell you once again how proud I am of you both, and I am sorry that B. B. Warfield deprived you of your father's full attention on far too many occasions in your youth. Perhaps the publication of *The Lion of Princeton* will make the sacrifice seem a bit more worthwhile.

Introduction

During his 34-year reign as the ranking theologian at Princeton Theological Seminary, Benjamin Breckinridge Warfield (1851–1921) exerted tremendous influence upon much of American Presbyterianism. His lucid pen and passion to defend the Westminster Standards left little doubt as to where Warfield stood on most every subject. Even this many years after his death, mere mention of his name in certain circles sparks a strong reaction—either positive or negative. Many view Warfield either as a brilliant, but nevertheless obscurantist, fundamentalist[1] or as a thorough-going rationalist,[2] who supposedly invented the notion of biblical inerrancy. Seen from this perspective, Warfield's detractors claim that his legacy skews the nature of biblical authority. His work fuels the heated controversy over this issue that has dominated American Presbyterian circles in the latter part of the 19th century. Others view Warfield as an apologist and polemicist *par excellence*, a valiant fighter standing in the breach between the fading memory of Protestant orthodoxy and the rise of Protestant liberalism. All agree that B. B. Warfield is a man with whom one must reckon.

In John Updike's novel *In the Beauty of the Lilies*, a central character, the agnostic Presbyterian minister Clarence Wilmot, encounters Dr. Warfield during his student days at Princeton Theological Seminary. Updike describes Warfield as "erect as a Prussian general, with snowy burnsides—whose *Introduction to the Textual Criticism of the New Testament* ... should have fortified [the struggling Clarence Wilmot] against [Robert] Ingersoll's easy sneers."[3] Photographs of Warfield taken during his later years at Princeton and recollections of his former

1. James Barr, *Beyond Fundamentalism* (Philadelphia: Westminster Press, 1984), 141.
2. Alister McGrath, *A Passion for Truth: The Intellectual Coherence of Evangelicalism* (Downers Grove: InterVarsity Press, 1996), 169.
3. John Updike, *In the Beauties of the Lilies* (New York: Alfred A. Knopf, 1996), 14.

students show that Updike has indeed quite accurately captured the essence of the man.

Not everyone sees this portrait of Warfield as flattering, however. In *The Authority and Interpretation of the Bible*, Jack Rogers and Donald McKim argue that B. B. Warfield reduces theology to a mere technology. They assert that Warfield's uncritical dependence upon Scottish Common Sense philosophy moved him outside the mainstream of Reformed orthodoxy.[4] Although they argue Warfield defended the faith with "great passion and technical expertise," Rogers and McKim conclude that Warfield's efforts in "reinterpreting Calvin in light of Aristotelian assumptions ... would have been alien to the Reformer."[5] Others are even more outspoken. For example, University of Durham New Testament scholar James D. G. Dunn has gone so far as to label Warfield's position on biblical inspiration and authority "exegetically improbable, hermeneutically defective, theologically dangerous, and educationally disastrous."[6] One diatribe against the supposed evils of scholastic Protestant theology rails that "ever since the days of the Princetonians (Warfield, Hodge, Machen, et al.), American non-charismatic evangelicalism has been dominated by Scottish common sense, by post-Enlightenment, left-brain, obsessive compulsive, white males."[7] Astonishingly, these words come not from a liberal scholar but from Daniel B. Wallace, a professor of New Testament at a "fundamentalist" institution: Dallas Theological Seminary.

The most surprising criticism of Warfield issues from the apologetics department of Westminster Theological Seminary—the very institution founded by Warfield's most prominent *protégé*, "old-school" Presbyterian J. Gresham Machen. Since many of the founders of that institution learned to defend the faith directly at the feet of Warfield himself, it is surprising that there is such an outspoken rejection of his apologetics. This stems from the seminary's embrace of the apologetical methodology of Cornelius Van Til, who attended Princeton several years after Warfield's death in 1921. Van Til, who was a student at Princeton during the Machen years, decisively spurned Warfield's

4. Jack B. Rogers and Donald K. McKim, *The Authority and Interpretation of the Bible* (San Francisco: Harper & Row, 1979), 323–79.
5. Ibid., 333, 348.
6. James D. G. Dunn, *The Living Word* (Philadelphia: Fortress, 1988), 107.
7. Daniel B. Wallace, "Who's Afraid of the Holy Spirit?" *Christianity Today* (September 12, 1994), 38.

method, choosing instead a modified version of the apologetics of Dutch theologian Abraham Kuyper.[8] Van Til saw Warfield's apologetic as an unfortunate capitulation to incipient Thomist and Arminian principles, which attempt to defend the faith by exalting nature over grace and reason over revelation. Such a defense actually left the faith defenseless, in Van Til's opinion.

B. B. Warfield's legacy is not always regarded with disdain. Leon Morris, himself a man of great exegetical skill, calls Warfield a "great exegete" deserving of serious study.[9] The late Hugh T. Kerr, who served as Warfield Professor at Princeton, and was no champion of Warfield's doctrine of biblical inerrancy, nevertheless stated that "Dr. Warfield had the finest mind ever to teach at Princeton Theological Seminary."[10] Many of Warfield's own contemporaries and colleagues generally held him in highest regard. He was seen as a fearless defender of Reformed orthodoxy, pious and devout, and a formidable presence in his classroom.[11]

The contemporary interpreter of Warfield, then, must navigate between the perilous shoals of strongly held and diametrically opposed interpretations of Princeton Theological Seminary generally, and of B. B. Warfield in particular. Of late there has been a "Warfield renaissance" of sorts. Noted American church historian Mark Noll has edited a fine anthology and critical introduction to the Princeton theology,[12] while David Wells' *Reformed Theology in America*[13] provides a useful treatment of Warfield and the other major Princetonians. A number of recent and significant doctoral dissertations have dealt with various

---

8. Cornelius Van Til, *The Defense of the Faith* (Grand Rapids: Baker Book House, 1967), 265.

9. Leon Morris, *The First and Second Epistle to the Thessalonians*, The New International Commentary on the New Testament (Grand Rapids: Eerdmans, 1964), 226.

10. Recounted in personal correspondence of February 25, 1995, from William O. Harris, Librarian for Archives and Special Collections at Princeton Theological Seminary.

11. See Oswald T. Allis, "Personal Impressions of Dr Warfield," in *The Banner of Truth* 89 (Fall 1971).

12. Mark A. Noll, ed., *The Princeton Theology, 1812–1921* (Grand Rapids: Baker Book House, 1983).

13. David F. Wells, ed., *Reformed Theology in America: A History of its Modern Development* (Grand Rapids: Eerdmans, 1985). This volume has subsequently been re-printed by Baker Book House as a three-volume set. For this revised treatment of Warfield and Old Princeton, see David F. Wells, *The Princeton Theology: Reformed Theology in America* (Grand Rapids: Baker Book House, 1989).

aspects of Warfield's thought in the broader Princeton context.[14] Despite all of the interest in his life and work, however, Warfield's views are still often misunderstood. Noll laments, "Evangelicals still await a treatment of Old Princeton that is as sophisticated and as refined as the work of the Princetonians was itself."[15]

This book will investigate the theological, apologetical, and polemical writings of perhaps the key figure of the Princeton tradition, Benjamin Breckinridge Warfield. To paraphrase George M. Marsden's designation of Warfield as the aging lion of Presbyterian orthodoxy, Warfield is well-lauded as the "Lion of Princeton." Chapter 1 will give a thumbnail biographical overview of Warfield's life, highlighting his devotion to his invalid wife, Annie, and how this impacted Warfield's career and productivity.

Chapter 2 provides an introduction to one of the two streams of thought which exert significant influence upon Warfield's theological and apologetic method, Scottish Common Sense Realism (SCSR). The other source is a long-standing tradition of Reformed dogmatic texts, which stress internal and external evidences for the truth of Christianity, as a means through which the Holy Spirit bears witness to the veracity of Jesus' bodily resurrection from the dead, and the truth of Holy Scripture. This latter stream will be discussed in Chapters 4, 5, and 7.

Chapter 3 will begin with the virtually overlooked fact that during Warfield's early career as professor of New Testament at Western Theological Seminary, a number of his theological and apologetic methodological emphases began to crystallize. Here we first see Warfield using the critical tools provided by the emerging science of textual criticism to bolster his doctrine of biblical inerrancy.

Chapter 4 will describe Warfield's apologetic method and epistemology. It will also evaluate important fundamental structures in Warfield's overall theology. These include his evidential apologetic, his

14. See, for example, the dissertations by: Peter Maarten van Bemmelen, "Issues in Biblical Inspiration: Sanday and Warfield" (Ph.D. diss., Andrews University, 1987); James Samuel McClanahan, "Benjamin B. Warfield: Historian of Doctrine in Defense of Orthodoxy" (Ph.D. diss., Union Theological Seminary, 1988); and Bradley J. Gundlach, "The Evolution Question at Princeton, 1845–1929" (Ph.D. diss., University of Rochester, 1995).

15. Mark A. Noll, *The Princeton Theology*, 43. Fred Zaspel's 2010 volume is certainly a big step in the right direction. See Fred G. Zaspel, *The Theology of B. B. Warfield: A Systematic Summary* (Wheaton, Ill.: Crossway, 2010).

subjective-objective epistemological formulation, his doctrine of the witness of the Holy Spirit, and his understanding of apologetics as the prolegomena (or foundational basis) for theological systems. Warfield focuses on Christian evidences as a defense of special revelation. Since it is all too common for Warfield's critics to describe him as something of a Thomist, it is important to note his apparent disinterest in classical theological argumentation.

Chapter 5 turns attention to Warfield's work in the field of systematic theology. Although Warfield did not produce his own systematic theology, he produced several important essays which addressed the task, nature, and right of systematic theology, carefully building upon his prior work in the field of New Testament. Warfield clearly saw himself standing in the long line of Reformed scholastic theologians.

Chapter 6 evaluates Warfield's polemical writings. Since B. B. Warfield served for over 30 years as professor of didactic and polemical theology, and produced literally hundreds of important book reviews and significant journal articles dealing with the controversies of his day, this is a rich field to excavate his views. This chapter will consider his response to such Arminian dogmaticians as John Miley, as well as his rather harsh treatment of the emerging fundamentalist movement. Warfield's polemical response to mysticism emerged in his critique of several of the works by the English mystic, Evelyn Underhill. He also dealt firmly with the "Ritschlite" variety of rationalism then making significant inroads into Protestant circles.

Chapter 7 traces the growing appreciation for Warfield's thought by contemporary Reformed thinkers. It makes a case for re-evaluating natural theology and the role of evidences in Warfield's apologetic. The charges of innovation on Warfield's part will be shown to be unfounded, placing him firmly within a broad and well-established Reformed apologetic tradition.

This book endeavors to clarify some of the confusion that surrounds Warfield's life and work. His methodology remained remarkably consistent over the course of his career, and his arguments are clearly and cogently framed. The divergence of opinion about him, lies, I believe, precisely in the fact that he *was* eminently clear. It is the unpopular nature of his views on inerrancy, the relationship between faith and reason, and the role that he assigned to Christian evidences that incite protest.

The "Lion of Princeton" defined his terms with great detail and consistency and was willing to challenge all comers. Those who consider themselves his theological heirs revere his memory. Those who still bear the brunt of his pointed criticism find his work distasteful and his legacy troubling. Therefore, it is important to take a fresh look at the work of this great scholar, who in many ways is the most significant American apologist, polemicist, and theologian of his age.

1

The Heir to the Princeton Tradition

"THE PUGILIST"

Princeton College alumni who remembered B. B. Warfield's student days at Princeton recall that on November 6, 1870, the young Warfield and a certain James Steen "distinguished themselves by indulging in a little Sunday fight in front of the chapel after Dr. McCosh's afternoon lecture." Warfield, it seems, "in lieu of taking notes" during Dr. McCosh's lecture, took great delight in sketching an "exceedingly uncomplimentary picture of Steen," which was subsequently circulated among the students.[1] The resulting fist-fight between the two young men ultimately didn't amount to much, but it earned Warfield the nickname—"the pugilist."[2]

B. B. Warfield's earliest days at Princeton, as well as his last, were characterized by a passionate defense of his personal honor. Princeton Seminary colleague, Oswald T. Allis, tells the story about Dr. Warfield's encounter with Mrs. Stevenson, the wife of the Seminary president, shortly before Warfield's death and during the height of the controversy at Princeton over an "inclusive" Presbyterian church. When Mrs. Stevenson and Dr. Warfield passed each other on the walk outside the Seminary, some pleasantries were exchanged, and then Mrs. Stevenson reportedly said to the good doctor, "Oh, Dr. Warfield, I am praying that everything will go harmoniously at the [General] Assembly!" To which Warfield responded, "Why, Mrs. Stevenson, I am praying that there may be a fight."[3] As the late Hugh Kerr, formerly Warfield Professor of

1. Hugh Thomson Kerr, "Warfield: The Person Behind the Theology." Annie Kinkead Warfield Lecture for 1982 at Princeton Theological Seminary (ed. William O. Harris, 1995), 21.
2. Ibid., 21–22.
3. O. T. Allis, "Personal Impressions of Dr Warfield," in *The Banner of Truth* 89 (Fall 1971), 10–14.

Theology at Princeton Theological Seminary, reflects, "From the very beginning to end, Warfield was a fighter."[4]

B. B. Warfield was not only a fighter, he was also a theological giant, exerting significant influence upon American Presbyterianism for nearly 40 years. John DeWitt, professor of church history at Princeton during the Warfield years, told Warfield biographer Samuel Craig that:

> ... he had known intimately the three great Reformed theologians of America of the preceding generation—Charles Hodge, W. G. T. Shedd and Henry B. Smith—and that he was not only certain that Warfield knew a great deal more than any one of them but that he was disposed to think that he knew more than all three of them put together.[5]

Unlike many of today's "specialists," B. B. Warfield was fully qualified to teach any of the major seminary subjects—New Testament, church history, systematic or biblical theology, and apologetics.[6] One of Warfield's students and an influential thinker in his own right, J. Gresham Machen, remembers Warfield as follows: "With all his glaring faults, he was the greatest man I have known."[7] And as previously mentioned, Hugh Kerr, though critical of Warfield's "theory of the inerrancy of the original autographs," still told his own students a generation later that "Dr. Warfield had the finest mind ever to teach at Princeton Seminary."[8]

A VERY PRODUCTIVE LIFE (1851–1921)

The biographical details of Warfield's life are well-documented and quite straightforward.[9] Born in 1851 near Lexington, Kentucky, Warfield

---

4. Kerr, "Warfield: The Person Behind the Theology," 22.

5. Samuel G. Craig, "Benjamin B. Warfield," in B. B. Warfield, *Biblical and Theological Studies* (Philadelphia: P&R Publishing, 1986), xvii.

6. Ibid., xix.

7. Ned B. Stonehouse, *J. Gresham Machen: A Biographical Memoir* (Philadelphia: Westminster Theological Seminary, 1977), 310.

8. Recounted in personal correspondence of February 25, 1995, from William O. Harris, Librarian for Archives and Special Collections at Princeton Theological Seminary.

9. One of the most interesting of these is found in Kerr's essay "Warfield: The Person behind the Theology." Personal reflections by Warfield's colleagues are: Francis L. Patton, "A Memorial Address" in *The Princeton Theological Review*, Volume XIX (July 1921), 369–391; W. J. Grier, "Benjamin Breckinridge Warfield," *The Banner of Truth* 89 (Fall 1971), 3–9; Oswald T. Allis, "Personal Impressions of Dr Warfield," *The Banner of Truth* 89 (Fall 1971). Warfield's brother, Ethelbert D. Warfield, produced a short biographical essay which appears as "Biographical Sketch of Benjamin Breckinridge

came from good Puritan stock on his father's side[10] His mother was the daughter of Dr. Robert J. Breckinridge, who in the words of one writer was "an able Presbyterian Theologian and professor of theology at Danbury (Kentucky) Theological Seminary (1853–69)."[11] One of Robert's sons (and Warfield's uncle), John Cabell Breckinridge (1821–1875), was a two-term congressman and served as the Vice President of the United States during the Buchanan administration. (He later became a distinguished general and cabinet member of the Confederate States of America.)[12]

Warfield was educated by some of the finest tutors available[13] and also received education at home; Reformed piety was ingrained in the Warfield home at an early age. The Larger and Shorter Catechisms, along with the Scripture proofs were memorized by all of the Warfield

---

Warfield," in B. B. Warfield, *Revelation and Inspiration* (Grand Rapids: Baker Book House, 1981), v–ix. Also see: S. G. Craig, "Benjamin B. Warfield," in *Biblical and Theological Studies* (Grand Rapids: Baker Book House, 1968) xi–xlviii. There are also two biographical and historical essays evaluating Warfield's career: Wilber B. Wallis, "Benjamin B. Warfield: Didactic and Polemical Theologian," 2 parts, *Presbyterion: Covenant Seminary Review*, Volume III (Spring 1977), 3–20, 73–94; Stanley W. Bamberg, "Our Image of Warfield Must Go," *Journal of the Evangelical Theological Society*, Volume 34 (June 1991), 229–41. There is also a helpful biographical chapter in James Samuel McClanahan, "Benjamin B. Warfield: Historian of Doctrine in Defense of Orthodoxy, 1881–1921," (Ph.D. diss., Union Theological Seminary in Virginia, 1988), 10–67.

10. Kerr, "Warfield: The Person Behind the Theology," 4.

11. Wilber Wallis, "Warfield: Didactic and Polemical Theologian," 4. For a history of Warfield's maternal line, see Bradley J. Gundlach, " 'B' Is for Breckinridge: Warfield's Maternal Kin" in Gary L. W. Johnson, ed., *B. B. Warfield: Essays on His Life and Thought* (Phillipsburg: P&R Publishing, 2007), 13–53. See also Alfred Nevin, *The Encyclopedia of the Presbyterian Church in the United States of America* (Philadelphia: Presbyterian Encyclopaedia Publishing Co., 1884), s.v. "Breckinridge, Robert, Jefferson."

12. McClanahan, "Benjamin B. Warfield: Historian of Doctrine in Defense of Orthodoxy, 1881–1921," 13. See also Patricia L. Faust, *Historical Times Illustrated Encyclopedia of the Civil War* (New York: Harper Perennial, 1991), 78. It is important to point out that Robert Breckinridge remained a staunch supporter of the Union cause despite the efforts of his son, and Warfield himself was quite outspoken in his advocacy of civil rights for African Americans. See, for example, Warfield's two essays in this regard: "A Calm View of the Freedmen's Case," *The Church at Home and Abroad* (Jan 1887), 62–65; and "Drawing the Color Line," *The Independent*, (July 5, 1888). Both are re-printed in: Benjamin B. Warfield, *Selected Shorter Writings*, Vol. 2 (ed. John E. Meeter; Phillipsburg: P&R Publishing, 1980), 735–50. See also Bradley J. Gundlach, "Warfield, Biblical Authority and Jim Crow," in Gary L. W. Johnson, ed., *B. B. Warfield: Essays on His Life and Thought* (Phillipsburg: P&R Publishing, 2007), 136–68.

13. Kerr, "Warfield: The Person Behind the Theology," 4–5.

children; the Shorter Catechism was memorized by the sixth year.[14] At 16, the young Kentuckian made profession of faith and joined the Second Presbyterian Church in Lexington, though he appeared to have inherited from his father "a reluctance to speak of spiritual matters." His mother, on the other hand, often expressed her wishes that "her sons would preach the gospel."[15] This dream did not come true until her oldest son Benjamin, quite surprisingly, changed his vocational plans and announced his intention to enter into the Presbyterian ministry upon his return from Europe in 1872.[16]

When B. B. Warfield entered Princeton College as a sophomore in 1868, his lengthy connection to that institution was only beginning. Warfield was not, however, the only new member of the Princeton community that year. The school's new president, the fatherly Scotsman James McCosh, also undertook his new calling in 1868, and when a number of years later Warfield playfully remarked to McCosh that they both "entered Princeton the same year and that they both had achieved advanced standing," we are told that "McCosh was not amused."[17]

At Princeton College, when he was not drawing caricatures of fellow students, Warfield excelled at mathematics and science, and upon graduation in 1871, he decided to pursue further studies at the universities of Edinburgh and Heidelberg. His younger brother, Ethelbert,[18] remembers that Benjamin's "tastes were strongly scientific. He collected birds' eggs, butterflies and moths, and geological specimens; studied the fauna and flora of his neighborhood; read Darwin's newly published works with great enthusiasm."[19] Objecting to studying Greek—since he saw no use for it—he had planned to follow a scientific career. He made perfect marks in science and mathematics, and "counted Audubon's works on

14. Ethelbert D. Warfield, "Biographical Sketch of Benjamin Breckinridge Warfield," vi.

15. Ibid., vi–vii.

16. Ibid.

17. Kerr, "Warfield: The Person Behind the Theology," 5.

18. Benjamin Warfield's younger brother, Ethelbert, had studied both in Germany and at Oxford (UK), and was a noted educator serving first as president of Miami University (Ohio) and later at Lafayette College. Ethelbert D. Warfield's own tumultuous career is described in George M. Marsden, "The Ambiguities of Academic Freedom," *Church History* Vol. 62, 2 (June 1993), 221–36. Also see, George M. Marsden, *The Soul of the American University* (New York: Oxford University Press, 1994), 301 ff.

19. Ethelbert D. Warfield, "Biographical Sketch of Benjamin Breckinridge Warfield," vi.

American birds and mammals as his chief treasure."[20] Between the time of his graduation and his departure for Europe, however, Warfield's career took an odd turn, when "he returned to Kentucky, and following in his father's footsteps, began an editorial stint with the Lexington *Farmer's Home Journal*," a kind of foreshadowing of his future career as editor of the *Princeton Theological Review*.[21] After his father talked him out of taking a fellowship to study experimental science, B. B. Warfield instead went abroad. In the summer of 1872, his family received the surprising news from Heidelberg that he had given up his previous career objectives and now intended to enter into the Presbyterian ministry.[22]

Since Warfield was apparently quite reticent to discuss his own spiritual development, we know little of his decision made, while in Heidelberg, to enter Princeton Seminary to study for the ministry. While in Europe he makes his only autobiographical comment in this regard, stating that he "realized the paramount claims of God and religion upon him."[23] His brother informs us that this decision came as a complete "surprise to his family and most intimate friends."[24] When he returned to the states in 1873, he enrolled in Princeton Theological

---

20. Ibid.

21. Kerr, "Warfield: The Person Behind the Theology," 5. Warfield bibliographers John E. Meeter and Roger Nicole note that Warfield retained a lifelong interest in the subject, especially in "short-horn cattle, in the breeding of which Warfield had a great interest." See John E. Meeter and Roger Nicole, *A Bibliography of Benjamin Breckinridge Warfield: 1851–1921* (Phillipsburg: P&R Publishing, 1974), iii–iv. Warfield's cousins recall Ethelbert Warfield's home adorned with pictures of various ancestors and short-horn cattle. See Bradley J. Gundlach, "The Evolution Question at Princeton, 1845–1929" (Ph.D. diss., University of Rochester, 1995), 291, n. 14.

22. Ethelbert D. Warfield, "Biographical Sketch of Benjamin Breckinridge Warfield," vi.

23. Cited in Grier, "Benjamin Breckinridge Warfield," 4. Dr. Kerr tells of Warfield's first European trip as one in which Warfield, while in London, "nightly visited the opera, theaters and other evil and pernicious haunts ... and when he got to Germany he took great delight in acting as referee to the Heidelberg dueling corps." Kerr describes Warfield as "a jaunty, carefree youth." (See Kerr, "Warfield: The Person Behind the Theology," 20–22). One can only imagine how all this relates to the young Warfield's sudden desire to enter the Christian ministry. In a piece written in 1916, recounting his years at Princeton College, Warfield recalls a revival occurring on campus during his junior year. A number of fellow students during his seminary years were drawn to the ministry as a result. See B. B. Warfield, "Personal Recollections of Princeton Undergraduate Life: IV. The Coming of Dr. McCosh," *The Princeton Alumni Weekly* 16, no. 28 (April 19, 1916), 653.

24. Ethelbert D. Warfield, "Biographical Sketch of Benjamin Breckinridge Warfield," vii.

Seminary; he graduated in May of 1876. The young Warfield was soon licensed to preach, but he declined to take a call in Dayton, Ohio to pursue further studies in Europe. Soon after marrying Annie Pearce Kinkead, who was also from noble stock, the newlyweds journeyed to Leipzig. Kinkead was a descendent of George Rogers Clark, the famous general of the Revolutionary War who was known as the "Hannibal of the West."[25]

During their stay in Europe, an event occurred that would forever change the Warfields' lives. While walking together in the Harz Mountains, they were caught in a violent thunderstorm. Annie Warfield suffered a severe trauma to her nervous system from which she never fully recovered. She was so severely traumatized that she would spend the rest of her life as an invalid of sorts, becoming increasingly more incapacitated as the years went by. Her husband spent the rest of his life giving her "his constant attention and care"[26] until her death in 1915. B. B. Warfield could not have foreseen just how difficult a demand this would be, nor how, in the providence of God, it would positively impact his entire career.

While still abroad, Warfield was offered a position on the faculty in Old Testament at Western Theological Seminary in Allegheny, Pennsylvania. Although previously expressing a distaste for the study of Greek, he made New Testament the primary focus of his European studies.[27] Upon the completion of his studies, he returned home and took a call to be an assistant pastor at First Presbyterian Church of Baltimore. He served a brief period, then accepted a call to Western Theological Seminary as instructor in New Testament. Beginning his new labor in September of 1878, he was subsequently ordained and appointed full professor. By 1880, he had received so much notice through his publications that he was awarded the Doctor of Divinity Degree by the College of New Jersey.[28]

The unexpected death of Warfield's friend Archibald Alexander Hodge in 1886 prompted his return to Princeton. A. A. Hodge, the son of Charles Hodge, had been Professor of Systematic Theology at Princeton,

25. Kerr, "Warfield: The Person Behind the Theology," 9.
26. Allis, "Personal Impressions of Dr Warfield," 10.
27. Ethelbert D. Warfield, "Biographical Sketch of Benjamin Breckinridge Warfield," vii.
28. Ibid.

after assuming the very chair made famous by his father upon his father's death. Francis Patton remembered the events this way.

> I remember the shock which passed through this community when word went out that Dr. A. A. Hodge was dead. ... When the question of his successor arose, our minds turned naturally to Dr. Warfield, then Professor of New Testament Criticism and Exegesis in the Western Theological Seminary, Allegheny, Pennsylvania. I recall today the delight with which Dr. C. W. Hodge welcomed his former pupil to the chair which his father and brother had successively filled.[29]

Warfield's very productive nine-year career in New Testament at Western ended and he began a tenure at Princeton that was to last another thirty-three years until his own death in February 1921.

Warfield's herculean literary accomplishments over the course of his career are remarkable. Hugh T. Kerr describes the huge volume of material that Warfield managed to produce.

> Of his printed and published work, there are ten large, and I mean large, volumes of posthumously selected and edited articles known as the Oxford edition as well as two volumes of additional essays put together by John E. Meeter, plus two volumes of handwritten scrapbooks and fifteen volumes of *Opuscula* (1880–1918), collected and bound by Warfield himself. He also wrote a major work on the textual criticism of the New Testament which went through nine editions, published three volumes of sermons, several commentaries, and a significant investigation of popular religious movements, *Counterfeit Miracles*. Yet, we are nowhere near the end of the list, for there are literally hundreds of essays, reviews and other miscellanea in dictionaries, encyclopedias, and especially in the three Princeton quarterlies over which he had editorial supervision from 1889 until the day of his death in 1921. We are talking about a theological authorship on the order of Augustine, Aquinas, Luther, Calvin and Barth.[30]

---

29. Patton, "Benjamin B. Warfield, A Memorial Address," 369–70.

30. Kerr, "Warfield: The Person Behind the Theology," 12–13. J. Gresham Machen once noted that Warfield "has done about as much work as ten ordinary men." Cited in Ned B. Stonehouse, *J. Gresham Machen: A Biographical Memoir* (Philadelphia: Westminster Theological Seminary, 1978), 220.

His tremendous energy, more than any other single factor, however, contributed to Warfield's wide reaching influence. As Kerr notes, one of Warfield's most important venues was the book review, used as an important "bully pulpit." "Book reviewing is, I think, one of the most important means of theological communication," adds Dr. Kerr. Somehow the Princetonian managed to publish over 780 of them in various publications—of which 318 were "very substantial critical reviews."[31]

Warfield's remarkable literary output is due greatly to the frail condition of his wife and his amazing devotion to her.[32] O. T. Allis recalls, "I used to see them walking together and the gentleness of his manner was striking proof of the loving care with which he surrounded her. They had no children. During the years spent at Princeton, he rarely, if ever, was absent for any length of time."[33] J. Gresham Machen remembers Mrs. Warfield as a brilliant woman to whom Dr. Warfield would read several hours each day. During his own student days Machen dimly recalled seeing Mrs. Warfield in her yard, but notes that she had been long since bed-ridden.[34] Dr. Warfield almost never ventured away from her side for more than two hours at a time. In fact, he left the confines of Princeton only one time during a 10-year period—for a trip designed to alleviate his wife's suffering, which ultimately failed.[35] As Colin Brown points out, Warfield's lectures on the cessation of the *charismata*, given at Columbia Theological Seminary in South Carolina shortly after her death, are quite remarkable and demonstrate "a certain poignancy [which] attaches itself to Warfield's work in view of the debilitating illness of his wife throughout their married life."[36] Although Warfield may have been known as a tenacious fighter, the compassion he directed toward his wife demonstrates his deep capacity for tenderness and caring.

In the mysterious providence of God, the illness of Warfield's wife also provided the greatest impetus for his massive literary output.

31. Ibid., 14.
32. David Calhoun states that "the seminary students often noted his gentle and loving care for Mrs. Warfield as they walked together on Princeton streets and, later, back and forth on the porch of their campus home." David B. Calhoun, *Princeton Seminary: The Majestic Testimony, 1869–1929* (Carlisle: Banner of Truth Trust, 1996), 315–16.
33. Allis, "Personal Impressions of Dr Warfield," 10.
34. Stonehouse, *J. Gresham Machen: A Biographical Memoir*, 220.
35. Bamberg, "Our Image of Warfield Must Go," 229.
36. Colin Brown, *Miracles and the Critical Mind* (Grand Rapids: Eerdmans, 1984), 199. See also Stanley W. Bamberg, "Our Image of Warfield Must Go," 238.

As caretaker for an invalid wife, Warfield spent many hours each day in the confines of his study. Personally vital and energetic, "he did not allow" his wife's illness "to hinder him in his work. He was intensely active with voice and pen."[37] Thus his creative energies were focused in two directions: his writing and the classroom. One friend remembers:

> He was pre-eminently a scholar and lived among his books. With the activities of the church he had little to do. He seldom preached in neighboring cities, was not prominent in the debates of the General Assembly, was not a member of any of the Boards of our Church, did not serve on committees, and wasted no energy in the pleasant but perhaps unprofitable pastime of after-dinner speaking.[38]

Thus unencumbered by administrative and ecclesiastical duties, Warfield was free to do his fighting, pen in hand. Francis Patton describes Warfield's pen as more of a sword than a battle-axe. "His writings impress me," notes Patton, "as the fluent, easy, offhand expression of himself. He wrote with a running pen, in simple unaffected English, but with graceful diction, and only a moderate display of documented erudition."[39] Dr. Kerr adds, "It must be said that he knew how to construct lucid, direct sentences, and that his meaning was always clear. He is not an easy writer to read, for he makes us work as he thinks. It is often slow going, not designed for those who would read as they run."[40]

While the book review is a significant place to mold opinion, so is the classroom. Warfield left quite a mark upon his students. "There was something remarkable in his voice. It had the liquid softness of the South rather than the metallic reason [of the North]." "He kept the calm level of deliberate speech, and his words proceeded out of his mouth as if they walked on velvet."[41] His brother observed that the professor has a certain loftiness and aloofness about him, but also possessed a genuine love for people, which was seen in "a heart open to every appeal."[42] O. T. Allis, a former student and later a colleague on the Princeton

37. Allis, "Personal Impressions of Dr Warfield," 11.
38. Patton, "Benjamin Breckinridge Warfield, A Memorial Address," 370.
39. Ibid., 371.
40. Kerr, "Warfield: The Person Behind the Theology," 17.
41. Patton, "Benjamin Breckinridge Warfield, A Memorial Address," 370.
42. Cited in Calhoun, *Princeton Seminary: The Majestic Testimony, 1869–1929*, 325.

faculty, remembers Warfield's classroom as "his domain, and his desk as his throne."[43] Years later, Allis could clearly recall:

> His favorite method of teaching was the quiz, a kind of Socratic dialogue, in which by question and answer he tested the student's knowledge of the assigned reading and his understanding of it. His aim was to open the eyes of the student to the wealth of meaning in the subject under discussion. His style was conversational. He did not pound the desk or try to browbeat the student but to help him, even if in doing so he exposed the sometimes blissful and abysmal ignorance of his respondent. Sometimes there was a gleam in his eyes and a touch of humor in his voice. I remember once, when a student was explaining to Dr. Warfield the doctrine of the Trinity and speaking of the three persons of the Godhead, he failed to make the proper distinction; and Dr. Warfield said, "So there are three Gods, are there?" The student hastened to retrieve the error. Once when the subject dealt with or involved the miraculous, and the questions and answers indicated some confusion or doubt, Dr. Warfield remarked, "Gentlemen, I like the supernatural." He said it, I think with a twinkle in his eye, and this *obiter dictum* impressed itself on my memory more than anything else in the discussion. When he had finished quizzing a student he would say, "Is there any question you would like to ask"? If, as usual, there was not, he would turn to his class and ask, "Has anyone else a question?" Then he would call up the next student on his list.[44]

Warfield's reputation as a formidable presence in the classroom was such that some years later, Donald Grey Barnhouse, himself a former Princeton Seminary student and a strong and combative personality, was remembered by his colleagues as one of the few students who dared "argue in class with the scholarly Benjamin B. Warfield."[45] Barnhouse later became a leader of the fundamentalist wing of the Presbyterian Church. Although apparently not mean or vindictive to his 2,750 students, there is little doubt that B. B. Warfield was an intimidating presence in the classroom.

43. Allis, "Personal Impressions of Dr Warfield," 10.

44. Ibid., 11.

45. C. Allyn Russell, "Donald Grey Barnhouse: Fundamentalist Who Changed," *Journal of Presbyterian History*, Volume 59 (1981), 35.

"My last glimpse of Dr. Warfield was on a mid-February afternoon fifty years ago," writes O. T. Allis. On Christmas Eve of 1920, "Dr. Warfield had suffered a heart attack and had been ill for some weeks. That afternoon I saw him walking slowly across the campus to meet his class. ... But he overtaxed his strength, had a severe relapse and passed away during the night."[46] It was the end of an era. Abraham Kuyper, the great Dutch theologian had died on November 12, 1920; Warfield died February 16, 1921, followed by another great Dutch theologian, Herman Bavinck, on July 29 of that same year. "Within the space of nine months the people of the Reformed faith were bereft of their three greatest leaders. ... These three were devoted friends. Their parting was for a very brief time; their reunion in glory was speedy."[47] With the death of Kuyper and Warfield, and with the current travail in the Presbyterian Church, it was no wonder that J. Gresham Machen so deeply lamented Warfield's death. "It seemed to me that the old Princeton—a great institution it was—died when Dr. Warfield was carried out."[48] Machen was more of a prophet than he knew.

WARFIELD'S THEOLOGICAL LEGACY

It is extremely difficult to judge the extent of B. B. Warfield's impact upon theological developments after his death, but there are several important indicators that highlight Warfield's powerful influence upon the current American theological scene.[49] One key legacy is that Warfield himself was responsible for the primary theological training of nearly 3,000 students during his tenure at Princeton.[50] His influence can be seen most clearly in the work of his heir of sorts, J. Gresham Machen, and the eventual split in the Presbyterian Church which led to the founding of Westminster Theological Seminary. While Machen was the most notable theologian trained by Warfield, his influence upon a whole generation of clergymen and academics kept his legacy alive.

46. Allis, "Personal Impressions of Dr Warfield," 14.
47. Grier, "Benjamin Breckinridge Warfield," 4.
48. Stonehouse, *J. Gresham Machen: A Biographical Memoir*, 310.
49. See Sydney E. Ahlstrom, *A Religious History of the American People* (New York: Image Books, 1975), Vol. 2, 284; *Theology in America: The Major Protestant Voices from Puritanism to Neo-Orthodoxy* (Indianapolis: The Bobbs-Merrill Company, 1967), 45-48; and Lefferts A. Loetscher, *The Broadening Church: A Study of Theological Issues in the Presbyterian Church Since 1869* (Philadelphia: University of Pennsylvania Press, 1954), 136 ff.
50. Noll, *The Princeton Theology*, 19.

Another factor is that most of Warfield's books and his collected essays and sermons have continually remained in print.[51] The sheer number of references made by evangelicals in the years after Warfield's death to his defense of the inspiration and authority of the Bible, his attempt to ground the Christian faith upon the objective facts of revelation, and his incisive criticisms of anti-supernaturalism, rationalism and mysticism keep his views alive in the present. Subsequent evangelical theological reflection has largely been conducted in his shadow. To adequately approach the subject, both defenders and foes must address his thought.[52]

Another indicator of the importance of Warfield's legacy is his prominence in several recent treatments of the history and development of American evangelicalism. According to Mark Noll, Warfield was responsible for the "most learned defense" of biblical inerrancy. Noll argues that his distinctive views on the relationship between creation, providence, and evolution figure quite prominently in the development of a distinctly "evangelical mind."[53] George Marsden has evaluated Warfield's influence upon the evangelical movement's attempt to deal with the challenges of modern science.[54] Detractors Jack Rogers and Donald McKim, whose *The Authority and Interpretation of the Bible*[55] pointedly criticizes Warfield's conception of inerrancy, still indicate

---

51. The details of Warfield bibliography are set out in Meeter and Nicole, *A Bibliography of Benjamin B. Warfield, 1851–1921*.

52. This is evident in several attempts to relate contemporary evangelical theological reflection to broader theological discussion. For example, both Clark Pinnock and Stanley Grenz repeatedly speak of the need to overturn or otherwise mitigate Warfield's influence upon contemporary evangelical theology. See Clark H. Pinnock, *Tracking the Maze: Finding our Way through Modern Theology from an Evangelical Perspective* (San Francisco: Harper & Row, 1990), and Stanley J. Grenz, *Revisioning Evangelical Theology: A Fresh Agenda for the 21st Century* (Downers Grove: InterVarsity Press, 1993). On the other hand, there are evangelicals who see much in Warfield that is useful. See Richard Lints, *The Fabric of Theology: A Prolegomenon to Evangelical Theology* (Grand Rapids: Eerdmans, 1993; J. I. Packer, "Is Systematic Theology a Mirage? An Introductory Discussion," *Doing Theology in Today's World* (ed. John D. Woodbridge and Thomas Edward McComiskey; Grand Rapids: Zondervan, 1991), 17–37.

53. Mark A. Noll, *The Scandal of the Evangelical Mind* (Grand Rapids: Eerdmans, 1994).

54. See George M. Marsden, *Understanding Fundamentalism and Evangelicalism* (Grand Rapids: Eerdmans, 1991); and *The Soul of the American University*.

55. Jack B. Rogers and Donald K. McKim, *The Authority and Interpretation of the Bible* (San Francisco: Harper & Row, 1979).

that much of contemporary evangelical theological reflection is conducted in Warfield's long shadow.

One of the most contentious debates involving the Warfield legacy is the "Hatfield and McCoy" style dispute within the confessional Reformed tradition over apologetic methodology. Polarized into two camps are the evidentialists, who claim to self-consciously follow Warfield and Old Princeton,[56] and the presuppositionalists, who are the followers of Cornelius Van Til of Westminster Theological Seminary and who reject Warfield's apologetic.[57] The debate remains a divisive point within many Reformed circles.

Dr. Walter Lowrie most succinctly describes Warfield's theological legacy: "He was Princeton."[58] That a distinct "Old Princeton" theological tradition continues to influence much of contemporary evangelicalism is due, in large measure, to the very productive life of B. B. Warfield.

56. R. C. Sproul, John Gerstner, and Arthur Lindsley, *Classical Apologetics: A Rational Defense of the Christian Faith and a Critique of Presuppositional Apologetics* (Grand Rapids: Zondervan, 1984).

57. See the two volumes by John Frame, Van Til's successor and now professor of apologetics at Reformed Theological Seminary in Orlando: *Apologetics to the Glory of God: An Introduction* (Phillipsburg: P&R Publishing, 1994); and *Cornelius Van Til: An Analysis of His Thought* (Phillipsburg: P&R Publishing, 1995).

58. Cited in R. W. Cousar, "Benjamin B. Warfield: His Christology and Soteriology," (Th.D. diss., University of Edinburgh, 1954), 7.

2

The Wisdom of the Vulgar

SCOTTISH COMMON SENSE REALISM AND PRINCETON THEOLOGICAL SEMINARY

The influence of Scottish Common Sense Realism upon the intellectual life of American theological thought in the 19th century is well-documented.[1] This influence has been seen to be so pervasive that one writer described the extent of the impact of Common Sense philosophy on American life as "ubiquitous."[2] While this sentiment may be an exaggeration, there can be no doubt that Scottish Common Sense philosophy[3] did, in fact, influence much of American intellectual development

1. Sydney Ahlstrom's magisterial essay is still a definitive treatment of the subject. See Sydney E. Ahlstrom, "The Scottish Philosophy and American Theology," *Church History*, 24 (1955), 257–72. A number of significant articles have appeared on the same subject. These include: Darryl G. Hart, "The Princeton Mind in the Modern World and the Common Sense of J. Gresham Machen," *The Westminster Theological Journal* 46 (1984), 1–27; Paul Helm, "Thomas Reid, Common Sense and Calvinism," *Rationality in the Calvinian Tradition* (eds. Hendrik Hart, Johan Van Der Hoeven, and Nicholas Wolterstorff; Lanham: University Press in America, 1983), 71–89; Mark A. Noll, "Common Sense Traditions and American Evangelical Thought; The Influence of Epistemological, Ethical and Methodological Traditions," *American Quarterly* 37 No. 2, 216–38. Important book-length studies are: Theodore Dwight Bozeman, *Protestants in an Age of Science: The Baconian Ideal and Antebellum American Thought* (Chapel Hill: University of North Carolina Press, 1977); J. David Hoeveler, Jr., *James McCosh and the Scottish Intellectual Tradition* (Princeton: Princeton University Press, 1981); Herbert Hovencamp, *Science and Religion in America: 1800–1860* (n.p.: University of Pennsylvania Press, 1978); Jack B. Rogers and Donald K. McKim, *The Authority and Interpretation of the Bible* (San Francisco: Harper & Row, 1979), 265–379; and John C. Vander Stelt, *Philosophy and Scripture: A Study in Old Princeton and Westminster Theology* (Marlton: Mack Publishing Company, 1978).

2. Richard J. Peterson, "Scottish Common Sense in America, 1768–1850: An Evaluation of its Influence," (Ph.D. diss., American University, 1963), 1, 12.

3. The terms Scottish Common Sense Realism (SCSR) and Common Sense philosophy (CSP) are used interchangeably throughout the literature on the subject. Where applicable, I will use the abbreviation SCSR.

during this period, especially in regards to theological education.[4] Princeton Theological Seminary was but one institution that drew much of its intellectual vitality from the basic epistemological foundations inherited directly from the Scottish lineage of the leading light of Princeton College, John Witherspoon (1723–1794). The first theological professor in the seminary there, Archibald Alexander (1772–1851), was himself well-schooled in the distinctives of Scottish philosophy. This devotion to the Common Sense philosophy was so loyal that it persisted as an intellectual force 100 years later through the tenure of another noted president of Princeton College, James McCosh (1811–1894). It was a student of James McCosh, B. B. Warfield, who would become in his own right a noted progenitor and defender of the Princeton tradition. Indeed, Warfield's own prolific career as an apologist and theologian is to a significant degree indebted to an epistemological foundation, which is itself the product of Common Sense Realism reflected in Warfield's own variety of evidential apologetic.[5]

4. Ahlstrom's essay, written in 1955, makes this very point and marks a significant milestone in the way in which the influence of SCSR on American theology has been interpreted. Until that time, it was common to assume "that this philosophical movement was essentially a reactionary movement to shore up the ruin of orthodox theology. This view, it seems to me, requires modification." See Ahlstrom, "The Scottish Philosophy and American Theology," 257. Also see Peterson, "Scottish Common Sense in America," 10–18. Peterson describes the pervasive influence of Scottish Common Sense thought on other areas of American academic life as well, including economics, literary criticism, education, and moral philosophy. Peterson notes that moral philosophy was a course that was often taught by the college president and was considered the "apex" of a college education of the period. The textbooks used on the subject were frequently Scottish in origin, and Common Sense in orientation. Professors of moral philosophy were often Protestant ministers as well as college presidents. It is also quite interesting to note that Methodist theologians were also able to appeal to SCSR—especially Reid's view of the freedom of the will—as well. See James Hamilton, "Epistemology and Theology in American Methodism," in *Wesleyan Theological Journal*, Vol. 10, (Spring 1975), 70–79.

5. It is interesting that the only extant doctoral dissertation dealing specifically with the subject of Warfield's apologetic methodology makes no mention of the influence of SCSR in evaluating Warfield's thought on the subject. See William D. Livingstone, "The Princeton Apologetic as Exemplified by the Work of Benjamin B. Warfield and J. Gresham Machen: A Study in American Theology 1880–1930," (Ph.D. diss., Yale University, 1948). Cornelius Van Til, who is also critical of Warfield's apologetic efforts, fails to mention in his published works the influence of Thomas Reid and SCSR on Warfield's thought. Van Til attributes Warfield's views on natural theology to an incipient Romanism, but it is much more likely that Reid, McCosh, and SCSR is the source. For Van Til's evaluation of Warfield, see *A Christian Theory of Knowledge* (Nutley: P&R Publishing, 1977), especially 235–55.

THOMAS REID AND SCOTTISH COMMON SENSE REALISM

The architect of what came to be popularly known as Scottish Common Sense Realism (SCSR), and which would ultimately have such a pronounced influence on Warfield's apologetic more than a century later, is Thomas Reid (1710–1796).[6] Thomas Reid, while perhaps not as well known in America as Locke, Berkeley, or Hume, is as likely as influential in the development of 19th-century American thought as any of the English Empiricists.[7] When Reid lamented that "modern s[k]cepticism is the natural issue of the new system,"[8] he revealed the motivation behind the search to find a more sure foundation for knowledge

6. On the broader context of the philosophical, theological, and scientific world in which Reid conducted his labors, see Alexander Broadie, "Reid in Context," *The Cambridge Companion to Thomas Reid* (eds. Terrance Cuneo and René Van Woudenberg; Cambridge: Cambridge University Press, 2004), 31–52.

7. On the extent of this influence and the effects that SCSR had upon American intellectual development, see Vander Stelt, *Philosophy & Scripture*, 57–64. Reid's works are available in their entirety with critical notes and comments. See Thomas Reid, *The Works of Thomas Reid.* 7th ed. 2 vols., (ed. Sir William Hamilton; Edinburgh: MacLachlan & Stewart, 1872). Also recently available is a previously unpublished series of lectures given by Reid: Thomas Reid, *Lectures on Natural Theology (1780)* (ed. Elmer H. Duncan; Washington: University Press of America, 1981). Secondary sources dealing with Thomas Reid and the history of Scottish Common Sense Realism include dissertations by Alan Wade Davenport, "Evidence and Belief, Common Sense and the Science of Mind," (Ph.D. diss., American University, 1987); Richard J. Peterson, "Scottish Common Sense in America," and S. H. Stenson, "A History of Scottish Empiricism from 1730–1865," (Ph.D. diss., Columbia University, 1952). Important critical studies include Stephen F. Barker and Tom L. Beauchamp, eds. *Thomas Reid: Critical Interpretations* (Philadelphia: Philosophical Monographs, 1976); William J. Ellos, *Thomas Reid's Newtonian Realism* (Washington: University Press of America, 1981); S. A. Grave, *The Scottish Philosophy of Common Sense* (Oxford: Clarendon Press, 1960); O. M. Jones, *Empiricism and Intuitionalism in Reid's Common Sense Philosophy* (Princeton: Princeton University Press, 1927); James McCosh, *The Scottish Philosophy* (New York: Robert Carter & Brothers, 1875); Daniel Sommer Robinson, *The Story of Scottish Philosophy: A Compendium of Selections from the Writings of Nine Preeminent Scottish Philosophers. With Biographical Essays* (New York: Exposition Press, 1961). Important articles include: Ronald E. Beanblossom, "Introduction," Thomas Reid, *Thomas Reid's Inquiry and Essays* (eds. Ronald E. Beanblossom and Keith Lehrer; Indianapolis: Hackett, 1983); Nicholas Wolterstorff, "Thomas Reid on Rationality," *Rationality in the Calvinian Tradition* (ed. Hendrik Hart); S. A. Grave, "Common Sense" and "Reid, Thomas," in *The Encyclopedia of Philosophy*, 8 vols., (ed. Paul Edwards; New York: Macmillan, 1967). Also helpful is the article "Realism" in *The Encyclopedia of Philosophy* by R. J. Hirst.

8. Reid identified the "new system" as the rise of idealism, what Reid called the "theory of ideas," which he believed developed in earnest with the efforts of Descartes. See Reid, *Inquiry and Essays*, 110–21.

that characterized his entire life's work. "Although it [the new system] did not bring forth this monster until the year 1739, it may be said to have carried it in its womb from the beginning."[9] Reid was referring, of course, to the publication of fellow Scotsman David Hume's *Treatise of Human Nature*, which Reid believed to be nothing more than the offspring of the logical gestation of skeptical thought, conceived in the rationalism of Descartes.[10] It seems that Immanuel Kant was not the only person to be shaken from his "dogmatic slumbers" by the radical skepticism of David Hume. "The natural issue of this system is s[k]cepticism with regard to everything except the existence of our ideas," lamented Reid.[11] Thomas Reid would spend virtually all of his intellectual energy searching for a better way.

Thomas Reid was born April 26, 1710, at Strachan, in Kincardineshire, Scotland.[12] Little is known about Reid's early life, but his father, Lewis, was a Presbyterian minister for over 50 years. Many of the Reid clan, dating from the time of the Reformation, served as Protestant minsters, while others had served in government. Reid was educated at the University of Aberdeen, and at the ripe old age of 12, he entered Marischal College, under the tutelage of George Turnbull.[13] Upon graduation in 1737, Reid accepted the position of librarian—a position he may have secured because it had long been endowed by one of his ancestors.[14] During this formative period of his professional life, Reid became intimately acquainted with mathematics and Newton's *Principia*. "Reid's appreciation of Newton's efforts is reflected throughout Reid's writings."[15]

---

9. Reid, *Inquiries and Essays*, 112.

10. Ibid., 114. For a helpful discussion of Reid's opposition to skepticism, which he regarded as an absurdity, see Nicolas Wolterstorff, *Thomas Reid and the Story of Epistemology* (Cambridge: Cambridge University Press, 2001), 185–214.

11. Ibid.

12. The biographical details of Reid's life are set out by a student and follower of Reid, Dugald Stewart (1753–1828). See Thomas Reid, *The Works of Thomas Reid* (ed. William Hamilton), which contains Stewart's *Life* of Reid. Other helpful biographical treatises are: Beanblossom, "Introduction," and James McCosh, *The Scottish Philosophy*, 192 ff.

13. S. A. Grave believes that Reid probably learned from Turnbull "to regard common language as 'built on fact' and as manifesting the common convictions of mankind." See Grave, "Reid, Thomas," 118.

14. Beanblossom, "Introduction," x.

15. Ibid. William Ellos points out that unlike Hume, who made little use of Newtonian commentators in his interpretation of Newton, Reid was highly influenced by them, especially that of his mentor George Turnbull. See William Ellos, *Reid's Newtonian Realism*, 8–13. Reid also used Newton's insights into the "principle of description"

In 1737 Thomas Reid also entered the Presbyterian ministry, receiving his assignment by patronage and therefore making his arrival in the New Machar parish unpopular.[16] Any displeasure, however, apparently abated with his marriage to Elizabeth, a cousin who had earned the respect of the parishioners. Reid's energies at this time were not devoted so much to the ministry[17] as to investigating the problems of perception, and he completed his first published work in 1748, "Essay on Quantity."[18] Since Reid's vocational interests at this time were philosophical rather than pastoral or theological, the question has been raised as to whether the direction that Reid's philosophical studies ultimately turned, was the cause or the effect of an ambiguous commitment to orthodox Calvinism.

Since Scottish Common Sense Realism was to have such a marked influence upon the overtly Calvinistic thought of B. B. Warfield, Reid's own commitment to Reformed orthodoxy has been the object of scrutiny by contemporary Reformed historical analyses of the Old Princeton apologetic. Paul Helm, for one, has argued that "there is no strong reason to think that Reid was a Calvinist. Nominally, at least, Reid was a Calvinist, in that as a minister of the Church of Scotland at that period he would subscribe to the *Westminster Confession of Faith*."[19] Dale Tuggy points out that "Thomas Reid was a Christian philosopher" and was "apparently, orthodox in belief" in a broad sense.[20] From what little is known about Reid's intellectual development, it has been suggested that

---

along with his "four rules for philosophy," which Reid combined with the inductive method to form the basic methodological groundwork for "Common Sense."

16. Ibid.

17. Ibid. Beanblossom notes that "the modest and humble character of Reid is supposedly attested by the fact that he preached the sermons of Dr. Tillotson and Dr. Evans rather than trust his own powers." Anglican historians consider Tillotson to be the champion of "moderation" and that his sermons, though quite popular, were "moralistic." See Stephen Sykes and John Booty, eds. *The Study of Anglicanism* (Philadelphia: Fortress, 1988), 30, 347. However, this thesis has been disputed in William M. Spellman, *The Latitudinarians and the Church of England, 1660–1700* (Athens, Ga.: University of Georgia Press, 1993).

18. Ibid., xi. Dugald Stewart notes that this treatise was written in response to an earlier work by Francis Hutcheson, *Ethical Treatises*, wherein Hutcheson had applied mathematical formulations to ethical problems. See Noah Porter's essay, "Thomas Reid: The Man and His Work," in Robinson, *Story of Scottish Philosophy*, 120–21.

19. Paul Helm, "Thomas Reid, Common Sense and Calvinism," *Rationality in the Calvinian Tradition* (ed. Hart), 81.

20. Dale Tuggy, "Reid's Philosophy of Religion," in Terrance Cuneo and René Van Woudenberg, *The Cambridge Companion to Thomas Reid* (Cambridge: Cambridge University Press, 2004), 289.

Reid was a member of the moderate party of Hugh Blair and Principle Robertson. The moderates were primarily concerned with the rights of ministers to receive parish assignments through patronage and championed "preaching of morality rather than the evangelical truths of the *Confession*."[21] While Helm concludes that "his Calvinism is so mild as to be fairly indistinguishable from Arminianism," Reid considered his own commitment to Calvinism to be quite compatible with his involvement with the moderate party, and with his supposed "libertine" view of human freedom.[22] Thus, as a moderate with more pressing interests, it is not surprising that Reid eventually left the parish for the university.

21. Ibid. This point may be further evidenced by Reid's use of the moralistic sermons of Tillotson.

22. Ibid. While Helm cautions that "due to the lack of data much of the evidence is negative," he finds it necessary to conclude that Reid argues for "philosophical libertarianism and conced[es] that although 'God foresees every determination of the human mind' we can form no proper understanding of this." In his *Lectures on Natural Theology*, Reid states that God is the first cause of all things (p. 80) and harshly criticizes the Jesuits for "inventing" the doctrine of *scientia media*, since God's foreknowledge extends to all events, past, present, and future (p. 76). In a passage in "Essays on the Active Powers of Man," Reid again dismisses the *scientia media*, and concludes that a "scheme of necessity, appears to me much more shocking than the permission of evil upon the scheme of liberty (*The Works of*, Vol. II, p. 633.)." Yet, elsewhere, Reid sees this as quite compatible with Calvinistic convictions. "The Calvinist theologian maintains the predestination and foreknowledge of God *in conjunction* with the liberty of man. ... Acknowledging our necessary dependence upon God, he likewise vindicates to man a personal freedom, not wrested from the prerogative, but conceded by the grace, of the Divinity. ... Asserting the contingency (not the causality) of human action, he does not reduce omniscience to the foreknowledge of a necessitated order; and maintaining the universal infallibility of the divine decree, he denies that it imposes a universal necessity. Attributing to man in his *un*fallen state a full and perfect liberty to good and ill, spiritual as well as moral, he still postulates his freedom in actions of natural and civil import; and while he asserts the concourse of the Deity, he still preserves all activity proper to our personality. ... The Calvinist has been careful ... not to derogate from the perfections of the Deity as the author of our salvation ... [and] not to destroy the liberty of man as its condition (*Works of*, Vol. II, pp. 977–78)." Therefore, whatever "libertine" tendencies Reid expressed as a moderate, must be weighed in light of the more orthodox statements expressed here. Arminius, for example, seems to equivocate when discussing internal causes (in which God is the first cause), and external causes (where a volitional act on the part of the creature constitutes an "out-wardly moving cause"). Arminius also affirms the Molinist form of middle knowledge. See James Arminius, *The Works of*, vol. 2, reprint ed. (trans. James Nichols and William Nichols, Grand Rapids: Baker Book House, 1986), 342–44. Also see: Richard A. Muller, *God, Creation, and Providence in the Thought of Jacob Arminius* (Grand Rapids: Baker Book House, 1991), especially pages 155–57, and 163–66; and "Grace, Election, and Contingent Choice: Arminius's Gambit and the Reformed Response," in *The Grace of God, the Bondage of the Will*, vol.

In 1752, with only one published paper, Reid was named professor of philosophy at Kings College in Aberdeen. Dugald Stewart notes that Reid obtained the position despite a "thin" publishing record because of his robust intellectual abilities and due to the fact that Reid was highly proficient in mathematics, logic, ethics, and physics—all of which were required of the philosophy professor.[23] It was during this period that Reid helped to organize the Aberdeen Philosophical Society, which included James Beattie,[24] George Campbell, and Alexander Gerard.[25] "To that society he contributed a series of papers containing most of the views which were afterwards embodied in the work which established his reputation, *An Inquiry into the Human Mind on the Principles of Common Sense*."[26] While not published until 1764, Reid himself states that the impetus to produce the volume had come as far back as 1739, when he first became aware of Hume's *Treatise*.[27]

In 1763, Reid was called to be professor of moral philosophy at the University of Glasgow, replacing a very notable predecessor—Adam Smith. Reid had desired to use his position at the university to devote more time to writing, but fearing that this was not going to happen, he resigned in 1781. In 1785, he completed *Essays on the Intellectual Powers of Man*, and in 1788, *Essays on the Active Powers of Man*. Reid remained an active man throughout the balance of his days; he passed away in October of 1796.[28]

If any one thing were to characterize Reid's philosophical endeavors, it was his fierce and unbending opposition to the philosophical skepticism that Reid believed to be the logical consequence of the rationalism of his day. This opposition is very evident in his treatment of the historical development of the theory of ideas which Reid traces from

---

2 (ed. Thomas R. Schreiner and Bruce A. Ware; Grand Rapids: Baker Book House, 1995), 251–78. Also see the discussion of this in William Cunningham, *The Reformers and the Theology of the Reformation* (Carlisle: Banner of Truth, 1979), 471; and B. B. Warfield and A. A. Hodge, "Calvinism," in *Selected Shorter Writings*, vol. 2 (ed. John E. Meeter; Phillipsburg: P&R Publishing, 1980), 427 ff.

23. Beanblossom, "Introduction," xi.

24. Beattie's *Essay on Truth* was a popular introduction to SCSR, and unfortunately "vulgarized" Reid in the process of publicizing him. It was Beattie's works that attracted the harsh criticisms from Immanuel Kant, in *Prolegomena to Any Future Metaphysics* (ed. Lewis White Beck; Indianapolis: Bobbs-Merrill, 1950), 7.

25. Beanblossom, "Introduction," xi. Also see McCosh, *The Scottish Philosophy*, 201–03.

26. McCosh, *The Scottish Philosophy*, 202.

27. Reid, *Inquiry and Essays*, 112.

28. Beanblossom, "Introduction," xii.

Rene Descartes' rationalism to David Hume's empiricism. The change from the old system, which "admitted all of the principles of common sense as first principles, without requiring any proof of them ... and had no tendency to s[k]cepticism,"[29] to the new system, which "admits only one of the principles of common sense as a first principle; and pretends ... to deduce all the rest from it," commences with the development of the Cartesian system. "His whole system [Descartes] is built upon one axiom, expressed in one word, *cogito*."[30] Because an entire system of thought is made to rest upon consciousness:

> The natural issue of this system is s[k]cepticism with respect to everything except the existence of our ideas, and of their necessary relations, which appear upon comparing them, is evident; for ideas, being the only object of thought, and having no existence but when we are conscious of them, it necessarily follows that there is no object of our thought which can have a continued and permanent existence.[31]

Since Descartes had left the latch open to the cage of skepticism, it was simply a matter of time before the "monster" escaped to be made manifest in the writings of Locke. In Reid's analysis, with "Descartes, the theory of ideas is the view that what we immediately think about or perceive is not an actual physical object but a mental surrogate. This surrogate for Locke is an idea or image in the mind that represents the real object."[32] Locke had divided human understanding into two types. The first type was described as "notions" or "simple apprehension," and the second as "judgements." The "new system reduces them [judgments] to two classes—*ideas of sensation*, and *ideas of reflection*. ... The new system allows no part of [judgment] to be the gift of nature."[33] This idealist construct not only disallows any form of native knowledge and insists

29. Reid, *Inquiry and Essays*, 112.
30. Ibid.
31. Ibid., 114. See also 3–6.
32. Beanblossom, "Introduction," xiii. See also S. A. Grave, "Common Sense," in *The Encyclopedia of Philosophy* (ed. Edwards), 155–57; S. A. Grave, "The Theory of Ideas," in *Thomas Reid: Critical Interpretations* (eds. Barker and Beauchamp), 55–61, and Noah Porter, "Thomas Reid" in *The Scottish Philosophy* (ed. Robinson), 118–30.
33. Reid, *Inquiry and Essays*, 116. It is important to note the stress that Reid places upon these so-called "gifts of nature." They "are a part of that furniture which Nature hath given to the human understanding. They are the inspiration of the Almighty. ... They are part of our constitution; and all the discoveries of our reason are grounded upon them (p. 118)."

that all judgment is acquired through reason by comparing ideas and "perceiving their agreements or disagreements," but that this system is illogical as well, "because the second member of the division includes the first."[34] The net effect of Locke's distinction is that it does not explain how we perceive objects, making the "theory of ideas" in Newtonian terms, an "illegitimate hypothesis." A second problem is that there is simply "no evidence that such a theory is true, and, in fact, there is good reason to believe it is false."[35] Thus for Reid, the Newtonian criteria of verification proved to be serious obstacles for the "theory of ideas."

But it is in the criticism of Locke by Bishop Berkeley that:

> Reid thought that the latent paradox and skepticism in the theory began to reveal themselves. Berkeley realized that nothing could be like an idea but another idea and that it was absurd to imagine, as Locke had done, that any of the ideas we have were supposed to receive in perception from the qualities of physical objects could be like any of these qualities. Proceeding on the assumption he shared with Locke, that we could have no conception of such qualities except through ideas resembling them, Berkeley discarded as an empty fiction the notion that physical objects exist independently of our perception and allowed existence only to minds and their ideas.[36]

In Reid's view, "The Bishop undid the whole material world."[37] "Thus we see that Des Cartes and Locke take the road that leads to skepticism, without knowing the end of it. ... Berkeley shoots directly into the gulf."[38]

If Bishop Berkeley "undid the material world," it was David Hume who undid the last remaining vestige—the mind. "Berkeley had shown that these assumptions involved the reduction of matter to ideas, and the universe of matter to a universe of ideas," and it was one logical step forward to "Hume [who] had logically concluded that the mind itself is no more than a bundle of ideas, and its phenomena are but a series of impressions."[39]

According to Dugald Stewart, Reid's most "original and profound" work, *Inquiry into the Human Mind*, was written in direct response to

---

34. Ibid.
35. Beanblossom, "Introduction," xv.
36. Grave, "Reid, Thomas," 119.
37. Reid, *Inquiry and Essays*, 8.
38. Ibid., 115.
39. Porter, "Thomas Reid," 118.

Hume and reflects Reid's deep meditation on the subject for some 25 years.[40] In 1763, the year before *Inquiry*'s publication, Reid and Hume corresponded with one another. Writing first, in response to seeing an unfinished manuscript presented to him by an intermediary, Hume commented to Reid that:

> No man appears to express himself with greater perspicuity than you do. ... I shall be so vain as to pretend to a share of the praise; and shall think that my errors, by having some coherence, had led you to make a more strict review of my principles, which were the common ones, and to perceive their futility.[41]

When Reid wrote back, he spared no lack of admiration for Hume's ability, even though he vehemently disagreed with Hume's conclusions:

> I shall always avow myself your disciple in metaphysics. I have learned more from your writings in this kind, than from all others put together. Your system appears to me not only coherent in all its parts, but likewise deduced from principles commonly received among philosophers; principles which I never thought of calling into question, until the conclusions you draw from them in the *Treatise on Human Nature* made me suspect them. If these principles are solid, your system must stand; and whether they are or not, can be better judged after you have brought to light the whole system that grows out of them. ... I agree with you, therefore, that if this system shall ever be demolished, you have a just claim to a great share of the praise, both because you made it a distinct and determined mark to be aimed at, and have furnished proper artillery for the purpose.[42]

In the *Inquiry*, Reid brought out his biggest guns "against the profound skepticism of Hume, [and] protested in the name of Common Sense. Many of the arguments of both [Hume and Berkeley] he subjected to a critical revision."[43] Since the theory of ideas inevitably leads to such skepticism, allowing the more consistent idealist philosophers to deny the reality of the material world, Reid protested that he would

40. Stewart, "Life" in *Works of* (ed. Reid), 7.

41. David Hume, "Letter to Thomas Reid," February 25, 1763, re-printed in Noah Porter, "Thomas Reid," 130–32.

42. Thomas Reid, "Letter to David Hume," March 18, 1763, in Porter, "Thomas Reid," 132–33.

43. Porter, "Thomas Reid," 119.

have no part of it. "If this is wisdom, let me be deluded with the vulgar," laments Reid.[44] "I despise Philosophy, and renounce its guidance—let my soul dwell with Common Sense."[45] As a philosopher himself, Reid is certainly not renouncing his own vocation, as much as lamenting the fact that idealism had subjected the honorable discipline of philosophy to "the contempt and ridicule of sensible men."[46] The problem is that philosophy has exceeded its rightful domain, calling into question the very Common Sense foundations of legitimate philosophical inquiry.

> In this unequal contest betwixt Common Sense and Philosophy, the latter will always come off both with dishonour and loss. ... Common Sense holds nothing of Philosophy, nor needs her aid. But on the other hand, Philosophy (may I be permitted to change the metaphor) has no other root but the principles of Common Sense; it grows out of them, and draws its nourishment from them. Severed from this root, its honours wither, its sap is dried up, it dies and rots.[47]

Therefore, Hume's skepticism can exist only as a sort of intellectual parasite, because in order to deny the Common Sense foundations of reason, the skeptic must use reason, in effect, without reason. The only way out of this dilemma, Reid argues, is to see that reason itself is not basic or foundational, but that reason is part of something that is foundational in the faculty psychology of human nature.[48] Therefore:

> All reasoning must be from first principles, and for first principles no other reason can be given but this, that, by the constitution of

44. Reid, *Inquiry and Essays*, 53.
45. Ibid., 6.
46. Ibid., 7.
47. Ibid.
48. This kind of construction has overtly Theistic overtones; as Reid himself admits, human nature derives from the inspiration of the Almighty. Recently, discussions of epistemology among Reformed philosophers has again led to a re-discovery of Thomas Reid's understanding of first principles and their theological implications. See for example: William P. Alston, *Epistemic Justification: Essays in the Theory of Knowledge* (Ithaca: Cornell University Press, 1989), 15; and *Perceiving God: The Epistemology of Religious Experience* (Ithaca: Cornell University Press, 1991), 151–69; Alvin Plantinga, "The Foundations of Theism: A Reply," in *Faith and Philosophy*, vol. 3, no. 3 (July 1986), 303–06; *Warrant: The Current Debate* (New York: Oxford University Press, 1993), viii; and *Warrant and Proper Function* (New York: Oxford University Press, 1993), 50; Nicholas Wolterstorff, "Thomas Reid on Rationality" in *Rationality in the Calvinian Tradition* (ed. Hendrik Hart), 43–69; Kelly James Clark, *Return to Reason* (Grand Rapids: Eerdmans, 1990), especially pages 143 ff. As S. A. Grave notes,

> our nature, we are under a necessity of assenting to them. Such principles are part of our constitution, no less than the power of thinking: Reason can neither make nor destroy them; nor can it do anything without them. ... A mathematician cannot prove the truth of his axioms, nor can he prove anything unless he takes them for granted. We cannot prove the existence of our minds, nor even of our thoughts and sensations. A historian, or a witness, can prove nothing unless it be taken for granted that the memory and senses may be trusted.[49]

Accordingly, all knowledge that is "obtained by reasoning must be built upon first principles. Some of these are certain, others probable only."[50] These first principles are such that not only is every person a competent judge of them (hence the idea of "Common Sense"), but that any opinion which may contradict these principles is not only false, but absurd. "The consent of men of all ages and conditions is of great authority in establishing them."[51] These first principles of Common Sense are of two basic types: Those which are contingent ("probable only") of which Reid enumerates 12; and those which are necessary ("certain") of which there are 6. James McCosh summarizes them as follows:[52]

I. Principles of Common Sense Relating to Contingent Truth.[53]

1. The existence of everything of which I am conscious.
2. The thoughts of which I am conscious are the thoughts of a being which I call myself, my mind, my person.

"In Reid's doctrine the existence of common sense has theistic presuppositions. ... Reid did not maintain that belief in them depends upon belief in God; they are imposed upon us by the constitution of our nature, whatever our other beliefs. His implication is that we have to go behind common sense, *if* we are to explain its competence, to the fact that our nature has been constituted by God. We have the same sort of evidence for the existence of God that we have for intelligence and will in our fellow men: self-identifying marks of intelligence and will. The man who can see no grounds for a belief in God ought in consistency, Reid thought, to see no grounds for a belief in any mind besides his own ("Reid, Thomas," 120–21)."

49. Reid, *Inquiry and Essays*, 57–58.

50. Porter, "Thomas Reid," 126.

51. Ibid.

52. McCosh, *The Scottish Philosophy*, 217–18.

53. According to Reid, contingent truths are always dependent upon a cause, while necessary truths are true at all times and in all places, and which could not possibly be otherwise. See Ellos, *Thomas Reid's Newtonian Realism*, 71.

3. Those things did really happen which I distinctly remember.[54]
4. Our own personal identity and continued existence as far back as we remember distinctly.
5. Those things do really exist which we distinctly perceive by our senses, and are what we perceive them to be.[55]
6. We have some degree of power over our actions, and the determination of our wills.
7. The natural faculties by which we distinguish truth from error are not fallacious.
8. There is life and intelligence in our fellow-men with whom we converse.[56]
9. That certain features of the countenance, sounds of the voice, and gestures of the body, indicate certain thoughts and dispositions of the mind.
10. There is a certain regard due to human testimony in matters of fact, and even to human authority in matters of opinion.
11. There are many events depending upon the will of man in which there is a self-evident probability, greater or less according to circumstances.
12. In the phenomena of nature, what is to be will probably be like to what has been in similar circumstances.

II. Principles relating to Necessary Truths.[57]

- Grammatical; as, that every adjective in a sentence must belong to some substantive expressed or understood.
- Logical axioms; such as, any contexture of words which does not make a proposition is neither true [n]or false.[58]
- Mathematical axioms.

---

54. Reid defines memory as a reflective belief in the past existence of an object. See Ellos, *Thomas Reid's Newtonian Realism*, 2.
55. Reid makes a distinction between "observation" and "reflection." Observation provides the material for physical analysis through sensations. Reflection is our mental activity. Synthesis and analysis then follow. See Ellos, *Thomas Reid's Newtonian Realism*, 23.
56. The ability to converse is, for Reid, an aspect of the structure of the mind, which has Theistic overtones as well. See Reid, *Lectures on Natural Theology*, 45.
57. In Reid's scheme, necessary truths cannot be discovered by experience, they are the *basis* for our experience and are "objectively" true whether "discovered" or not. See Reid, *Lectures on Natural Theology*, 53.
58. These powers according to Reid distinguish humans from "brutes." See Reid, *Lectures on Natural Theology*, 32.

- Axioms in matters of taste.
- First principles in Morals; as, that an unjust action has more demerit than an ungenerous one.
- Metaphysical; as that, —
    - The qualities which we perceive by our senses must have a subject, which we call a body; and that the thoughts we are conscious of must have a subject, which we call mind.
    - Whatever begins to exist must have a cause which produced it.
    - Design and intelligence in the cause may be inferred with certainty from marks or signs of it in the effect.

This structure, while not profound, nevertheless gave Reid the epistemological framework that he needed to oppose the skepticism of Hume. "Let scholastic sophisters entangle themselves in their own cobwebs; I am resolved to take my own existence, and the existence of other things, upon trust."[59]

Reid's Theism is overtly expressed in connection with his Common Sense epistemology.[60] Since "Common Sense and Reason have both one author; that Almighty Author in all whose other works we observe a consistency, uniformity, and beauty which charm and delight the understanding," there must, Reid concludes, "be some order and consistency in the human faculties, as well as in other parts of his workmanship."[61] Expressing his inductive Theism, Reid asserts arguments for God's existence from causality, design,[62] and from human mental and moral "excellencies" which can only be analogous to a Supreme Being.[63]

59. Reid, *Inquiry and Essays*, 11.
60. Ibid., 118.
61. Ibid., 53.
62. See Reid, *Lectures on Natural Theology*, 13, 25. Reid uses a syllogistic form of this argument. (1) "That an Intelligent first cause may be inferred from marks of wisdom in the effects. (2) There are clear marks of wisdom and design on the works of nature—the conclusion is then—the works of nature are effects of a designing and wise cause. Now it is evident that we must deny the premises or admit the conclusion (p. 54)."
63. Reid, *Lectures on Natural Theology*, 13.

REID'S SCOTTISH SUCCESSORS—STEWART, BEATTIE, BROWN, AND HAMILTON

Many of these same Common Sense principles and the inductive method as articulated by Reid will re-surface again in the apologetic and theological writings of B. B. Warfield. The genealogy of Scottish Common Sense Realism in Warfield's own thought reflects two somewhat circuitous historical routes[64]—one through Reid's intellectual children in his native Scotland, and another through American Presbyterianism—both of which later converge in one person, James McCosh, who was named president of Princeton College the same year that Warfield arrived there as a student, 1868.[65]

64. This understanding of SCSR's influence on Old Princeton has generally been articulated by Vander Stelt, in *Philosophy and Scripture*, 22–89. Reid's influence was not confined to America and Scotland, as SCSR was picked up by Catholic theologians who in turn spread Reid's Common Sense into France. See Etienne Gilson, *Thomist Realism and the Critique of Knowledge* (trans. Mark A. Wauck; San Francisco: Ignatius Press, 1986), 27 ff., and Stenson, "A History of Scottish Empiricism," 2.

65. J. David Hoeveler, *James McCosh and the Scottish Intellectual Tradition: From Glasgow to Princeton* (Princeton: Princeton University Press, 1981), 275. An alternate and unorthodox proposal for understanding the influence of SCSR upon the Princeton tradition has been offered by Paul Kjoss Helseth, who contends that "the Princeton apologetic and understanding of Christian scholarship that follows from it are grounded in epistemological assumptions that are consistently Reformed," and that any dependence upon SCSR in Warfield's thought is mitigated by "subjective factors in his evidentialist apologetic." Helseth concludes "the Princeton apologetic is grounded not in one form of Enlightenment rationalism or another, but in the acknowledgment that fallen sinners are absolutely dependant on the sovereign grace of God not only for salvation, but also for the 'right' apprehension of revealed truth by which salvation is obtained and the kingdom of God is advanced." See Paul Kjoss Helseth, *"Right Reason" and the Princeton Mind: An Unorthodox Proposal* (Phillipsburg: P&R Publishing, 2010), xxiii–xxxiv. I am of the opinion that Helseth's unorthodox proposal is correct insofar as he contends that whatever rationalist tendencies are inherent in SCSR, are mitigated by the Princeton theologians' reliance upon the Augustinian, Reformed, and Puritan streams of thought also inherited and shared by Warfield (see my discussion of this in chapter 7). Helseth, however, downplays the historical context in which the Princeton theology developed—one in which SCSR was dominant. In fact, as we will see many of Warfield's methodological assumptions and apologetic arguments reflect the influence of the Scottish epistemology since Reid's arch-enemy was skepticism—a foe Warfield also found quite dangerous and in need of refutation. The SCSR arguments against the notion of ideas found in various forms in the works of Descartes, Hume, Locke, and Berkeley are quite compatible with Reformed orthodoxy and were used by a number of Reformed theologians, including Warfield.

The first of these routes was through the direct line of Reid's intellectual descendants in Scotland. The Scottish route includes both philosophical and apologetic developments. While Reid's efforts had reflected a larger change in Scottish thinking generally, by the time of his death in 1796, Common Sense[66] had "acquired with Dugald Stewart the stability of an institution."[67] Dugald Stewart (1753–1828), Reid's successor, and the man who Reid called his foremost disciple,[68] "followed Reid very closely in his methods of analysis and his accumulation of the discriminated facts of experience, but went far beyond him in the exactness and reach of his philosophical principles and method."[69] It was Stewart who modified and improved some of Reid's metaphysical terminology, substituting the term "Fundamental Laws of Human Belief" for Reid's ambiguous term "Principle of Common Sense" and replacing "Metaphysical Axioms" with the term "Principles of Human Knowledge."[70] Stewart's works, *The Elements of Philosophy of the Human Mind* and *The Philosophy of the Active and Moral Powers*, were used extensively in Great Britain and America. While Stewart succeeded in institutionalizing Reid and Scottish Common Sense Realism, he was not an original thinker and his work is "characterized by the defect that is universal in [his] writings ... discoursing of the opinions of others [rather] than defining and defending his own."[71]

If Stewart had turned Scottish Common Sense Realism into a philosophical institution, "second rate and less critical disciples" James Beattie (1735–1803) and James Oswald (d. 1793), reduced Scottish Common Sense

66. Peterson describes the eclectic nature of what came to be known as "Common Sense" and the difficulty in categorizing the Scottish philosophers as a whole. "As a school of thought it had a common faith and methodology but upon little else was there wide agreement." See Peterson, "Scottish Common Sense in America," 49. Peterson also notes that Stewart opposed the use of the terminology "Common Sense" to describe the burgeoning Scottish philosophy (41). S. H. Stenson also agrees with this caution, calling the Scottish school "Scottish empiricism"; see Stenson, "A History of Scottish Empiricism," 19 ff.

67. Grave, "Reid, Thomas," 121. See also Grave's fine article on Stewart in the same publication, *The Encyclopedia of Philosophy*, Vol. 8, s. v. "Stewart, Dugald."

68. Vander Stelt, *Philosophy and Scripture*, 29, n. 109.

69. Noah Porter, "Dugald Stewart: The Man and His Work," in *The Story of Scottish Philosophy of Common Sense* (ed. Robinson), 151. For the critical edition of the works of Stewart, see Dugald Stewart, *Collected Works*, 11 vols. (ed. Sir William Hamilton; Edinburgh, 1854–58).

70. Ibid., 152. Peterson argues that Stewart's discussion of first principles was much clearer than Reid's. See Peterson, "Scottish Sense in America," 42.

71. Ibid., 157.

Realism (in the words of one critic) to mere "religious dogmatism."[72] However, the fact that Scottish Common Sense Realism was picked up by conservative Presbyterians so quickly indicates the usefulness of Common Sense philosophy in apologetic endeavors against the kind of skepticism then popular in the writings of Hume. John C. Vander Stelt concludes that this was not always a successful endeavor, however.

> Beattie gained great fame for his Essay on the Nature and Immutability of Truth in Opposition to Sophistry and Scepticism, which appeared in 1770, and Oswald for his An Appeal to Common Sense in Behalf of Religion, which appeared two years later in 1772. By elevating mere common opinions to the high status of the self-evident and intuitive judgements of CSP [Common Sense philosophy], these two theologians and their many followers carried CSP to unwarranted extremes.[73]

While Beattie and Oswald may have brought a fair degree of disrepute to Reidianism, even provoking Kant to wrath, other Presbyterian

72. Stenson, "A History of Scottish Sense in America," 25–28 (see also footnote 22). Peterson concludes that Beattie "was more of a poet than a philosopher." See "Scottish Common Sense in America," 37.

73. Vander Stelt, *Philosophy and Common Sense*, 32. Vander Stelt concludes that the influence of SCSR upon the conservative Presbyterians "tainted" them, forcing them into neither orthodoxy nor unorthodoxy, "but in a subtle form of semi-(un) orthodoxy." This type of *ad hominem* argument does not actually deal with the basic question of whether or not Reid's schema is, in fact, necessarily incompatible with the tenants of Reformed orthodoxy, such as the Reformed understanding of the noetic effects of sin (see especially 33, n. 128). Vander Stelt makes this charge while ignoring the fact that historically, perfectly orthodox Calvinists at Princeton such as Charles Hodge and B. B. Warfield, as well as a number of Scottish Presbyterians such as John Dick, Thomas Chalmers, William Cunningham, and James Buchanan, accepted the basic epistemology of SCSR and did not reject in the slightest either the Reformed doctrine of human inability or the authority of biblical revelation by exalting the intellect over the witness of the Spirit. Paul Helm, in evaluating this very question, concludes that the relationship between SCSR and Calvinism is a "slack one." Helm rightly sees no necessary connection between Calvinism and any particular form of epistemology, nor does he conclude that Calvinism, though necessarily excluding some epistemologies, necessarily excludes the SCSR of Reid. This point is further developed in detail in chapter 7. See Paul Helm, "Thomas Reid, Common Sense and Calvinism" in *Rationality in the Calvinian Tradition* (ed. Hendrik Hart), 86–88. Recently, however, Reformed philosophers such as Alvin Plantinga have been much more open to the virtues of Reid's extensive modifications of traditional foundationalism. For example, see Kelly James Clark, *Return to Reason*, 143 ff. But as Dale Tuggy has argued, the Reformed Epistemologists do have problems with Reid's stress upon natural theology. See Tuggy, "Reid's Philosophy of Religion," 299.

theologians were much more philosophically adept in their use of Scottish Common Sense Realism. One such theologian, Thomas Chalmers (1780–1847),[74] who converted from "moderatism" to evangelicalism, and "continued to think of the natural sciences and humanities as precursory to revelation."[75] Following Reid, Chalmers was convinced that psychological arguments for God's existence were, in fact, valid. "The reason that man can feel and recognize (the laws of) virtue results from the fact that the subjective nature of his mind bears God's stamp and thereby reveals his will."[76]

Dugald Stewart's own successor was not as loyal to Reid as Stewart himself had been. Thomas Brown (1778–1820) rejected much of Reid's epistemology in favor of John Stuart Mill's "associated psychology."[77] Brown's star failed to shine in the Scottish circle largely because he was closer to the empiricism of Mill than to the realism of Reid, and therefore, he was out of step with much of the subsequent Scottish tradition. Brown's efforts were virtually eclipsed by the next major Scottish figure, who was far brighter and who rejected Brown's denial of Reid's doctrine that the objects we perceive are the external realities themselves.[78] William Hamilton (1788–1856) attained "international fame for his erudite editions of the works of Reid and Stewart."[79] Noah Porter calls

74. James McCosh once declared that Chalmers had "a greater influence in the moulding of the religious belief and character of his countrymen than any one since the greatest Scotchman, John Knox" (cited in Stenson, "A History of Scottish Empiricism," 250). Thomas Chalmers' integration of Calvinism and SCSR is found in his posthumously published *Theological Institutes*. A complete edition of Chalmers' works, including his works on natural theology and Christian evidences are found in Chalmers' *Collected Works*, 25 vols. (ed. T. Constable; Edinburgh: 1836–42).

75. Vander Stelt, *Philosophy and Scripture*, 34.

76. Ibid.

77. Ibid., 30. Since Stewart outlived Brown by eight years, he spent the last portion of his life attempting to vindicate Reid from Brown's attacks (30, n. 116). Hoeveler adds that Thomas Brown was also the "first of the Scots to take Hume positively and seriously. ... Brown wanted to limit philosophy to the immediately knowable ... all we can know is the mind itself. He therefore assumed a skeptical posture toward knowledge of the external world and acknowledged only that sensations indicate, but do not verify, the existence of a world outside the self." Such a position was anathema in the Scottish tradition. See Hoeveler, *James McCosh and the Scottish Intellectual Tradition*, 119 ff. Brown's major philosophical works include: *Inquiry into the Relation of Cause and Effect* (Andover: M. Newman, 1822); and *Lectures on the Philosophy of Mind*, 2 vols. (New York: Hallowell, Glazier, Masters & Smith, 1842).

78. Hoeveler, *James McCosh and the Scottish Intellectual Tradition*, 118–22.

79. Vander Stelt, *Philosophy and Scripture*, 30.

Hamilton "the most learned student of his time."[80] Since Hamilton had studied in Germany, he appears to have been the first of the Scotsmen to attempt a synthesis between Scottish Common Sense Realism and Kant.[81]

JAMES MCCOSH, JOHN WITHERSPOON, AND PRINCETON COLLEGE

It is with the death of Hamilton in 1856 that the mantle of the unspoken leadership of the Scottish philosophical heritage passed to one of his students, James McCosh (1811–1894).[82] McCosh had been reared in the Protestant Evangelicalism of Thomas Chalmers and the Scottish Philosophy of Reid, Stewart, and perhaps William Hamilton. Nevertheless, he was an independent thinker, "recasting older molds of thought to meet the challenges of new philosophical currents."[83] According to McCosh biographer, J. David Hoeveler, McCosh's subsequent philosophical efforts were characterized by his attempt to redirect the Scottish tradition from the divergent path taken by Hamilton. "To a large extent the reconstruction and rehabilitation of the Scottish school undertaken by McCosh was a response to the legacy of this

80. Noah Porter, "Sir William Hamilton: The Man and His Work," in *The Scottish Philosophy* (ed. Robinson), 214 ff. See also Hoeveler's treatment of the development of Hamilton's thought within the Scottish context, *James McCosh and the Scottish Intellectual Tradition*, 120–25. Hamilton's major works include: "On the Philosophy of the Unconditioned," in *Edinburgh Review*, vol. 1 (1829), 194–221; *Discussions on Philosophy and Literature, Education and University Reform* (London: 1852); and *Lectures on Metaphysics and Logic*, 4 vols. (eds. H. L. Mansel and John Veitch; Edinburgh: 1859–60).

81. Stenson calls this attempt "disastrous." See Stenson "A History of Scottish Empiricism," 96 ff. See also Porter, "William Hamilton," 216 ff., and Vander Stelt, *Philosophy and Scripture*, 30–31. Hoeveler implies that James McCosh produced his most complete philosophical treatise *Intuitions of the Mind*, in an effort to "strengthen the Scottish system" after Hamilton's effort's moved the tradition in a new direction. See Hoeveler, *James McCosh and the Scottish Intellectual Tradition*, 115. See also Andrew Seth-Pringle-Pattison's similar synthesis in *Scottish Philosophy: A Comparison of the Scottish and German Answers to Hume*, 2d ed. (Edinburgh: William Blackwood & Sons, 1889).

82. Hoeveler, *James McCosh and the Scottish Intellectual Tradition*, 114–15. McCosh had been recommended for his master's degree by Hamilton for a paper that he had written on the Stoics while at the University of Edinburgh. See Harvey Gates Townsend, "James McCosh: The Man and His Work," in *The Scottish Philosophy* (ed. Robinson), 265 ff.

83. Ibid., ix.

most ingenious of the Scottish thinkers [Hamilton]."[84] McCosh's trans-Atlantic journey from Scotland to the presidency of Princeton College marks the confluence of the Scottish line with the second stream of Warfield's intellectual heritage, the Scottish Common Sense Realism of American Presbyterianism and Princeton College.

While the Scottish philosophers Reid, Stewart, and Hamilton, were not as well known in America as the names of Locke, Voltaire, and Rousseau, the influence of the Scotsmen was much greater.[85] Scottish Common Sense Realism:

> ... provided North American theoreticians and national leaders with historically significant and culturally formative answers to the peculiar questions that the new world faced with respect to such a fundamental issue as the nature of man, society, truth and reality. Especially in Presbyterian educational circles, the main tenants of Scottish CSP were frequently appealed to.[86]

The effects of the influence of Scottish Common Sense Realism were felt upon virtually all sectors and competing ideologies of American life. Among those who could be labeled "conservatives," Scottish Common Sense Realism became the philosophical basis for "dogmatic exposition in religion, economics and literary criticism."[87] Those with more liberal interests, and who desired to preserve the virtues of the Enlightenment, readily applied Scottish Common Sense Realism to social matters. For the emerging movements of romanticism and transcendentalism, the intuitional elements of Scottish Common Sense Realism were appealing. Even the rationalists of the day, the Harvard Unitarians, also found the virtues of Scottish Common Sense Realism to their liking.[88]

Since Presbyterian higher education had become an especially important place to perpetuate the more dogmatic and apologetic virtues of Scottish Common Sense Realism, Princeton College became a bastion of the religious and dogmatic application of the Scottish Philosophy. John

84. Hoeveler, *James McCosh and the Scottish Intellectual Tradition*, 125.
85. Ibid., 4. For a dissenting opinion on the influence of the French Enlightement upon American intellectual development, see Henry F. May, *The Enlightenment in America* (New York: Oxford University Press, 1976).
86. Vander Stelt, *Philosophy and Scripture*, 48. See also Peterson, "Scottish Common Sense in America," 47 ff.
87. Peterson, "Scottish Common Sense in America," 47–48.
88. Ibid. See also Ahlstrom, "The Scottish Philosophy and American Theology," especially pages 261 ff.

Witherspoon (1723–1794),[89] who had graduated from the University of Edinburgh in 1743, and who had served as a Presbyterian minister for 23 years, left his native Scotland for America in 1768 and was named president of Princeton College.[90] Witherspoon had "brought a complete approach to Thomas Reid and the Common Sense school, at the same time actively opposing other systems of philosophy."[91] Witherspoon's mark upon subsequent Presbyterian history is indelible:

> By lecturing for some twenty-five years at this College, Witherspoon played a decisive role in setting its religious direction and in determining the theoretical focus of important Presbyterians and other future leaders. ... What has given Witherspoon's memory and reputation certain "talismanic effects" is his having transmitted and given firm rootage to the importance of Scottish Realism in North America. It was Witherspoon's basic philosophical stance that became central and permanent in the history of P[rinceton] C[ollege].[92]

Witherspoon had studied philosophy in Scotland and he was very familiar with contemporary philosophical developments of his day.[93] "One of the first things that he did after his arrival in 1768 at P[rinceton] C[ollege] was to resist and remove the influence of Berkeley's idealistic

89. John Witherspoon signed the Declaration of Independence and was actively involved with the Continental Congress. See John C. Vander Stelt, *Philosophy and Scripture*, 65 ff. For an important biographical treatment of Witherspoon, see James McCosh, *The Scottish Philosophy*, 183. ff. McCosh points out that Witherspoon was a descendent of the greatest of Scotsmen, John Knox (184–85). Mark A. Noll's work, *Princeton and the Republic, 1768–1822: The Search for a Christian Enlightenment in the Era of Samuel Stanhope Smith* (Princeton: Princeton University Press, 1989), includes a very complete and up-to-date bibliography of the "Princeton Circle" (305 ff.). Important dissertations on the development of Princeton College and Princeton Theological Seminary include: John Oliver Nelson, "The Rise of the Princeton Theology. A Genetic Study of American Presbyterianism until 1850" (Ph.D. diss., Yale University, 1935); Penrose St. Amant, "The Rise and Early Development of the Princeton School of Theology" (Ph.D. diss., University of Edinburgh, 1952); and Wayne William Witte, "John Witherspoon: An Exposition and Interpretation" (Th.D. diss., Princeton Theological Seminary, 1953).

90. Vander Stelt, *Philosophy and Scripture*, 65. Mark A. Noll points out that Witherspoon was a sort of rival to Reid, because Reid had been credited with developing "Common Sense" when Witherspoon felt that he had been its true originator. See Mark A. Noll, *Princeton and the Republic*, 189–90.

91. Peterson, "Scottish Common Sense in America," 48.

92. Vander Stelt, *Philosophy and Scripture*, 65–66.

93. Vander Stelt, *Philosophy and Scripture*, 66.

philosophy."[94] With the influence of the dreaded idealism on the wane, the Scottish philosophy did, in effect, finally and completely "supplant Berkeley" through the efforts of Witherspoon.[95]

As an educator in the Scottish tradition, Witherspoon ensured that Princeton College was the first American institution to offer and require a course on moral philosophy, taught by Witherspoon himself. It was in this course that he developed and refined his own views within the Scottish tradition, which were in turn applied to moral philosophy, anthropology, philosophy, and epistemology.[96] Witherspoon's only published philosophical work, *Lectures on Moral Philosophy*, was in many ways a polemic against the idealism of Berkeley and allowed Witherspoon to develop an insight into Common Sense epistemology that would shape much of Princeton's intellectual future:

> The evidences of mathematics and natural philosophy are of an essentially different character than those of moral philosophy; the former are not intuitive, the latter are. The kind of Newtonian precision that can be obtained in the science of natural philosophy ought also to be applied in the study of moral philosophy. Such precise knowledge presupposes a tracing of facts "upwards" in a natural science and a reasoning from metaphysical principles "downwards" in moral philosophy.[97]

Ramifications from this dualism will become readily apparent in Witherspoon's own apologetic treatment of special revelation. Because the Bible is a book that contains the "facts of revelation," it must be studied exegetically and inductively in an "upward" fashion, and not deductively in a "downward" fashion.[98] In parallel with this, apologetics as a rational theological science, should be pursued in the same manner. Revelation as given by God is rational, therefore apologetic arguments

94. Ibid., 67.
95. Ahlstrom, "Scottish Philosophy and American Theology," 262. Archibald Alexander, for example, would write a trenchant critique of Berkeley, though it was not published until 34 years after Alexander's death. See "The Idealism of Bishop Berkeley," in *Presbyterian Review*, vol. 6. no. 22 (April 1885), 301–14.
96. Vander Stelt, *Philosophy and Scripture*, 68.
97. Ibid., 70.
98. Vander Stelt, *Philosophy and Scripture*, 71.

must be constructed in an inductive and "upward" fashion, rather than in intuitional and "downward" forms.[99]

The epistemological pattern was now in place for many of the distinctive elements of the Old Princeton apologetic that would soon crystalize in the writings of Archibald Alexander.[100] Whereas earlier theologian-philosophers in the Scottish Common Sense Realism tradition had used the Scottish epistemology to establish a natural theology through inductive arguments for the existence of God, those in the Princeton tradition, such as Witherspoon, began using the same philosophical structure in defense of special revelation as well. "By trying to use natural science to establish compatibility between revelation and natural science and thus demonstrate the acceptability of revelation," the Princetonians would be able to "directly attack ... the opponents of revelation."[101]

While much of the philosophical structure underlying Warfield's apologetic system can already be seen in Witherspoon's own thought, Princeton's dependence upon Scottish Common Sense Realism was just beginning its initial phases. Samuel Stanhope Smith (1750–1819)[102] became president of Princeton College in 1794 and held that office until 1812, the year that Princeton Theological Seminary was established.

Smith had been enamored for a time with Berkeley but under Witherspoon's tutelage he had "accepted Reid's and Beattie's 'more practical and common sense view of things.' "[103] In fact, Smith went so far as to argue that Reid's work was superior to Witherspoon's, and indeed he followed Reid, rather than Witherspoon, in his polemics against the

99. These arguments as developed by Witherspoon comprise four types: "(1) Five presumptive evidences [which] support the idea of biblical infallibility ... (2) Three presumptive proofs [which] verify the truth of the Christian religion ... (3) Miracles, which by their very nature support the Christian religion ... (4) Three consequential proofs, [which] clearly demonstrate the truth of Christianity" (from Vander Stelt, *Philosophy and Scripture*, 73–74).

100. See, for example, Alexander's *Evidences of the Authenticity, Inspiration and Canonical Authority of the Holy Scriptures* (Philadelphia: Presbyterian Board of Publication, 1836).

101. Vander Stelt, *Philosophy and Scripture*, 81. Not surprisingly, the objects of these attacks were the radical empiricists (Locke and Berkeley) and the skepticism of David Hume.

102. For a very interesting treatment of the intellectual and historical development of Princeton College in the days of Smith, see Mark A. Noll, *Princeton and the Republic*, 185 ff.

103. Vander Stelt, *Philosophy and Scripture*, 75.

dreaded skepticism of Locke, Berkeley, and Hume. In perpetuation of the traditional form of Scottish Common Sense Realism, Smith re-affirmed the cherished doctrine that "external things are the direct object of our perception."[104] While Smith felt that Reid was superior to Witherspoon on some points, he did perpetuate Witherspoon's notion that philosophy served to confirm the Christian faith. The tried and true method of natural philosophy, including observation, the inductive method, and the correspondence theory of truth, all enabled the theologian to have a systematic understanding of the world.[105]

Like Witherspoon before him, Smith also assumed the duties of the chair of moral philosophy. Since both the physical world and human psychology could be explained by the Reidian method, various conclusions could be reached about the nature of the world and human character that could serve as the basis for a moral philosophy that would be in perfect harmony with revealed religion.[106] This allowed Smith to lecture on moral philosophy and to produce his own published notes on the subject, as well as to develop a text on Christian evidences almost simultaneously. Thus his apologetic arguments developed in direct parallel with his moral philosophy.[107] Almost from the beginning, the Princeton tradition placed natural theology, moral philosophy, and the apologetic arguments for the defense of special revelation, on the same epistemological footing. By building upon the values that he had inherited from Witherspoon, Smith effectually ensured that the fundamental epistemology of Scottish Common Sense Realism was passed forward

104. Noll, *Princeton and the Republic*, 189–90. Noll adds in an interesting sidelight that so strong was Smith's endorsement of Reid, that Reid's works were considered to be the favorite philosophical text at Princeton. A certain William Weeks of New England had complained that Reid's works were inherently Arminian, since they advocated a self-determining power inherent in the human will. Weeks additionally complained that the "more consistent Calvinists," Edwards, Samuel Hopkins, and Nathaniel Emmons had very little place in Princeton's curriculum (211). Vander Stelt concurs with the assessment of Mr. Weeks as to the Arminian character of Reid's view of the will. See *Philosophy and Scripture*, 79.

105. Ibid., 187.

106. Noll, *Princeton and the Republic*, 187.

107. Ibid., 118. In Smith's earlier apologetic lectures "Lectures on the Evidences of the Christian Religion (1809)," he presented a "science of divine truth." Smith, following Witherspoon, defended the Bible by arguing for the validity of miracles and prophecy through standard empirical/evidential arguments, and by "showing how 'the known and immutable principles of human nature' demonstrated Christianity's moral superiority." See Noll, *Princeton and the Republic*, 188.

into the succeeding generations of Princetonians in both the college and seminary.[108]

Samuel Stanhope Smith's successor as president of Princeton College was Ashbel Green (1762–1848), who had graduated from the college. Green, who wrote the charter for Princeton Theological Seminary, is usually given credit for the seminary's rise to prominence.[109] Following in the footsteps of those who had gone before him, Green inherited a great deal from Smith and Witherspoon. As an influential Presbyterian pastor and leader, "Green did much to enhance and institutionalize the Presbyterian tradition of philosophizing."[110] Following the methodology of S. S. Smith, Green was convinced that the way to "defend Christianity was by facts, discovered through rigorous scientific procedures and organized by the careful use of reason."[111] Green, however, had differences with Smith and even played a part in having Smith removed from the presidency of Princeton. When Green took over the chair of moral philosophy, he replaced Smith's published lecture notes with Witherspoon's class lectures from own his student days, which had now been published as a textbook. This resulted in a further entrenchment of the basic method and influence of Scottish Common Sense Realism, by one who was extremely influential in both the educational and political hierarchy of the Presbyterian Church.[112]

JAMES MCCOSH AND INTUITIONAL REALISM

James McCosh was born in Ayrshire, Scotland, in 1811, and subsequently received his philosophical training in the finest Scottish

---

108. Ibid. Vander Stelt is very critical of the "orthodoxy" of Smith and Witherspoon, stating that an allegiance to SCSR and orthodox Calvinism could be maintained only by a "compromise" of one or the other. According to Vander Stelt, one could choose between "philosophy or Scripture, Thomas Reid or the Westminster Confession (*Philosophy and Scripture*, 82)." This either/or choice is not justified historically since the Princetonians actually managed a successful synthesis of Calvinism and SCSR for over 100 years. In fact, it may be argued that the decline of Reformed orthodoxy actually *commences* with the abandonment of the SCSR epistemology in the years after Warfield's death in 1921.

109. Noll, *Princeton and the Republic*, 289–90. Green had been an extremely popular minister in Philadelphia and was a member of the board of the college from 1790–1812. He served as president of Princeton from 1812 through 1822, and then as the president of the board of the seminary until his death in 1848.

110. Vander Stelt, *Philosophy and Scripture*, 83.

111. Noll, *Princeton and the Republic*, 285.

112. Vander Stelt, *Philosophy and Scripture*, 83.

universities—Glasgow and Edinburgh.[113] Before becoming president of Princeton in 1868, McCosh had already established an impressive academic record in Belfast, Ireland, serving at Queen's College. As Hoeveler points out, it was in Great Britain that "McCosh fought the great philosophical battles of his day."[114] It was during this period of his life that McCosh produced his most important philosophical works, *The Method of Divine Government*, *The Intuitions of the Mind*, and *An Examination of Mr. J. S. Mill's Philosophy; Being a Defense of Fundamental Truth*.[115]

When McCosh assumed the chair of professor of philosophy at Queen's on January 12, 1852, the philosophical climate had changed greatly since the days of Thomas Reid. Everything cherished in the Scottish tradition was now in a state of philosophical flux. The writings

---

113. Noah Porter, "James McCosh: The Man and His Work," in *The Story of Scottish Philosophy* (ed. Robinson), 265–86. For additional biographical and intellectual history of McCosh, see J. David Hoeveler, *James McCosh and the Scottish Intellectual Tradition* (Hoeveler's volume also includes a complete bibliography of McCosh's published and unpublished works); and William M. Sloane, ed., *The Life of James McCosh* (New York: Charles Scribner's Sons, 1896). Articles include: Alexander T. Ormond, "James McCosh as Thinker and Educator," *The Princeton Theological Review* I (1903): 337–61; and John DeWitt, "Princeton College Administrations in the Nineteenth Centuries," *Presbyterian and Reformed Review* VIII (1897): 619–71. Doctoral dissertations include John Henry Gerstner, "Scottish Realism: Kant and Darwin in the Philosophy of James McCosh" (Th.D. diss., Harvard University, 1945).

114. Hoeveler, *James McCosh and the Scottish Intellectual Tradition*, 320. Hoeveler also points out that while in America, McCosh became "increasingly remote" from the philosophical struggles that were now dominating the American scene. Hoeveler attributes this both to McCosh's adherence to SCSR, which was now on the wane in America, and to the fact that much of his precious energy was devoted to his administrative duties at Princeton at a time when the college was undergoing serious organizational changes (320 ff.). Noah Porter reaches a similar conclusion: "James McCosh has been neglected in the study of American philosophy. This may be accounted for in part by the fact that he did not come to America until he was fifty-seven years old. By that time he had identified himself with the Scottish school of Thomas Reid and Sir William Hamilton. ... An additional reason for the neglect of McCosh may be that he came to America at a time when the philosophy which he taught, already outmoded, had a slightly antique flavor. Scottish realism did not find in him so much a source as a culmination." See Noah Porter, "James McCosh: The Man and His Work," 265.

115. During his time at Princeton, McCosh managed to complete another important work, *The Scottish Philosophy, Biographical, Expository, Critical, From Hutcheson to Hamilton*. Hoeveler concludes, however, that McCosh's other works completed during this time, such as *The Emotions* and *A Criticism of Critical Philosophy*, demonstrate that while McCosh was "not to be written off the American scene," nevertheless "amid a frantic administrative career at Princeton [he] was losing ground in the prolific philosophical literature of his day (p. 321)."

of Immanuel Kant were readily available and causing tremendous consternation. Kant's materialistic Idealism, wherein the laws of the mind imposed forms upon all subsequent experience of the world, presented a formidable challenge to Scottish Common Sense Realism. Thomas Brown had challenged Reidianism by formulating a theory of causality that was indebted to the infidel Hume, and although he had reached his limited popularity by the thirties, his work produced some continuing fallout. Sir William Hamilton's response to Brown had been swift and definitive according to many within the tradition, but John Stuart Mill's appropriation of Brown's insights in a more consistent system was proving to be very problematic. Mill's very stout critique of Hamilton, *An Examination of Sir William Hamilton's Philosophy*, challenged the very concept of first principles and intuitional epistemology, and Mill completely rejected the Scottish system for a more "pure" form of Empiricism. To make matters even worse, fellow Scot, Sir William Hamilton, was felt by many to have been seduced by Kant's variety of German metaphysic. Not only were there challenges from the external forces of German materialism and British skepticism, but there was now the real possibility of apostasy from within.[116] The new situation demanded a new response:

> For Reid and others the epistemological question rested on the laws of the mind and consciousness. But McCosh ... had a more critical problem to meet. For merely to prove against Hume, for example, that our notion of causality is not derived from experience was not to prove that it had any real bearing on the actual world. Hamilton ... made much use of his conviction that it did not and McCosh was left to deal with that assertion too. How can the laws of the mind, certain though we are that they do exist, in fact describe the actual constitution of the world outside, the way in which it is ordered and arranged? For the Scots it was essentially a matter of faith that they do. ... McCosh always believed that Reid was essentially correct, but he knew his ideas needed stronger fortification.[117]

The way in which McCosh responded to the situation marked a slight change in the direction of Scottish epistemology and resulted in McCosh's identification as an "intuitional realist." *The Intuitions of the*

116. Hoeveler, *James McCosh and the Scottish Intellectual Tradition*, 110–46.
117. Ibid., 118.

Mind would move the Scottish tradition from a discussion of first principles to a new footing—one based upon "intuitions" as a kind of *via media*—"which would certify the reality of the laws of the mind and their precise and conjunctive relation to the world of experience."[118] Dr. McCosh eloquently explains the philosophical problem that he planned to address:

> In this present age, two manner of principles, each of the character of a different parent, are struggling for the mastery: the one earth-born, sensational, empirical, utilitarian, deriving all ideas from the sense, and all knowable truth from man's limited experience, and holding that man can be swayed by no motives of a higher order than the desire to secure pleasure or avoid pain; the other, if not heaven-born, at least cloud-born, being ideal, transcendental, pantheistic, attributing man's loftiest ideas to inward light, appealing to principles which are discovered without the trouble of observation, and issuing in a belief in the good, instead of a belief in God. ... Those who claim to be neutral, however, being all the while unconsciously in the service either of the one or the other, commonly of the lower or earthly, just as those who profess to belong neither to God or Mammon, do in fact belong to Mammon.[119]

McCosh wanted to avoid the extremes of both the German idealists and the British empiricists. His solution is spelled out in terms of negative and positive propositions about the nature of intuitions. The "false" propositions which McCosh rejects regarding intuitions include innate mental images and representations (Plato and Locke), innate abstract or general notions (Locke), *a priori* forms imposed by the mind upon objects (Kant), and finally, that intuitions are immediately before consciousness as laws or principles (Locke and Kant).[120] "It is one of the aims of this treatise" writes McCosh, "to specify the way in which the mind gets ... ideas in the concrete and singular. But for the present I

118. Ibid., 126. Porter calls *Intuitions of the Mind* "the work which most secured for McCosh the attention of the academic world. ... In it we find his systematic philosophy. Though he lived and wrote for half an ordinary lifetime after the publication of his chief work, he spent his energies in support and defense of the dogma announced in it." See Porter, "James McCosh: The Man and His Work," 267.
119. James McCosh, *Intuitions of the Mind: Inductively Investigated* (New York: Robert Carter & Brothers, 1880), 4.
120. Ibid., 11–20.

am seeking to have rubbish removed, that there may be free and secure space whereon to lay a foundation."[121]

McCosh articulated five positive propositions that would serve as the epistemological foundation for his "intuitional realism." These primary concepts are, (1) that there actually are intuitive principles operating in the mind, (2) that the nature of the native convictions of the mind is such that they are of the nature of perceptions or intuitions, (3) that intuitive convictions rise on the contemplation of objects presented or represented to the mind, (4) that these intuitions of the mind are primarily directed to individual objects, and (5) that individual intuitive convictions can be generalized into maxims, and these are entitled to be represented as philosophical principles.[122] Noah Porter's summation is helpful:

> [McCosh] held that the intuitions of the mind are direct, immediate perceptions of a real objective order. However complex the object may be, the intuition as such is simple. It seizes its object directly, whether the object be sensory, relational, or abstract. There is no error possible at this primitive level of knowledge. Error arises out of a false association and inference, and therefore it can be corrected by additional and more careful observation. The laws of intuition are revealed in their exercise. The

121. Ibid., 16.

122. McCosh, *Intuitions of the Mind*, 20–30. There are strong similarities between McCosh's "intuitional realism" and Reid's basic structure of necessary and contingent first principles. Similarities exist in that there are "innate" or "native" abilities (not ideas) of the mind, and that what is perceived is the "object itself." Both schemes have overtly Theistic implications. For McCosh, intuitions must be self-evident. "It must be evident, and must have its evidence in the object (p. 30)." In addition, "Necessity is a secondary mark of intuitive truth. ... A proposition is true as being true, and certain propositions are seen by us to be self-evidently true. I would not ground the evidence on the necessity of belief, but I would ascribe the irrepressible nature of the conviction to the self-evidence. As the necessary flows from the self-evidence, so it may become a test of it, and a test not difficult of application (pp. 32–33)." A third aspect for McCosh echoes Reid's idea of "Common Sense" as the "wisdom of the vulgar." "Catholicity may be employed as a test. By catholicity is meant that the conviction is entertained by all men ... when the objects are presented (p. 33)." McCosh also argues that "the native principles in the soul are analogous to the physical laws operating in external nature. ... The intuitions do not depend for their operation on any voluntary determination of the human mind, and they act whether we observe them or no; indeed they often act best when we are taking no notice of them ... A greater or less number of them are working in the soul at every waking moment of our existence (p. 28)."

> exercise of intuition exhibits native human aptitudes for dealing with a real world; these are "regulative" in character and widely distributed among men. The healthy or normal mind is equipped to know in much the same sense that any other natural entity is equipped to function according to inherent characteristics or attributes.[123]

According to McCosh, intuitions can be classified as "of the nature of cognitions and beliefs, while others have the nature of judgements."[124] In true Scottish fashion, McCosh affirmed the cherished doctrine of Reid, "But whatever be their distinctive nature, as intuitions they primarily contemplate their objects as individuals. ... Intuition is a perception of an object, and of something in it or pertaining to it."[125]

McCosh's metaphysical structure follows "almost point by point, the outline of his epistemology."[126] In an important passage on the subject, McCosh spells out the inductive route along which his metaphysic would be built:

> Like every other science which has to do with facts, [metaphysics] must be conducted in the Inductive method, in which observation is the first process, and the last process, and the main process throughout; the process with which we start, and the process by which we advance all along, and at the close test all that is done; but with which, at the same time, analysis and generalization are employed as instruments, always working, however on facts observed.[127]

On this scheme, McCosh was able to explain causation in very strict Aristotelian terms, including material, efficient, formal, and final causes. "The mistake of mechanism is in supposing that because efficient causes can be shown to be always present, final causes are excluded as redundant. As a matter of fact, the two may be co-extensive, and, to this degree, independent."[128]

123. Porter, "James McCosh: The Man and His Work," 267–68.
124. McCosh, *Intuitions of the Mind*, 26.
125. Ibid.
126. Porter, "James McCosh: The Man and His Work," 269.
127. McCosh, *Intuitions of the Mind*, 282–83.
128. Porter, "James McCosh: The Man and His Work," 269.

McCosh followed Reid in holding to the correspondence theory of truth. "We have truth when our ideas are conformed to things."[129] He also anticipated the later so-called "abduction" method advocated by C. S. Peirce, in which induction and deduction were seen as complementary, rather than opposites.[130] As we will see, these are themes which will appear at many places in Warfield's apologetic efforts. There are others as well.

In his intuitional system, McCosh was able to make a distinction between "belief and knowledge," in which the two categories of faith and knowledge were seen as complementary. Belief "follows automatically from the boundaries, from the ultimate expressions, of our positive knowledge." Faith "is not the leap of mind that springs from its own ash heap; it is that toward which all powers of the intelligence build with relentless logic and force."[131] This distinction would enable McCosh to build a system that could be used to support his own evangelical convictions, and in effect, allow philosophy to once again become the handmaiden to the queen of the sciences.[132] On these terms, it was possible to move inductively from the facts that God had given in revelation and human experience, toward the "larger truths of moral reality and divine existence."[133] As we will see, this is a useful philosophical category from which to develop a doctrine of the "witness of the Holy Spirit" to the divinity of Holy Scripture, because if intuitions are merely capacities for experience, they must necessarily be restricted to experience itself, and cannot include additional data. This allows the activity of the Holy Spirit to center upon allowing the fallen will to acquiesce to

129. James McCosh, *Realistic Philosophy: Defended in a Philosophic Series* (New York: Charles Scribner's Sons, 1887), 30.

130. C. S. Peirce, *Collected Papers of Charles Sanders Peirce* Vol. V. (Cambridge: Harvard University Press, 1931–35), para. 146, 171. Peirce writes, "Abduction consists in studying facts and devising a theory to explain them. ... Deduction proves that something must be; Induction shows that something actually is operative; Abduction merely suggests something may be." Porter concludes that McCosh "found no serious difficulty in the union of induction and deduction, the understanding and reason, faith and knowledge, thought and things, *because* he made the initial assumption that our knowledge is a knowledge of objects. See "James McCosh: The Man and His Work," 269. While realism was on the wane in America, Peirce and the "critical realists" would extend its influence by a whole generation. See Elizabeth Flower and Murray G. Murphey, *A History of Philosophy in America*, vol. 2 (New York: Capricorn Books, 1977), 567 ff.

131. Hoeveler, *James McCosh and the Scottish Intellectual Tradition*, 162.

132. Ibid., 147.

133. Ibid., 128.

what the data gathered by experience through the intuitions tells the individual to be true. Therefore belief in the authority and divinity of Scripture is a distinctively supernatural activity of the Holy Spirit that allows probable truth in the mind of the believer (assent) to pass to certitude (fiducia) in his heart.[134]

Another effect of McCosh's intuitional realism is that there is no attempt in his philosophy to develop a complete natural theology as there had been in the earlier Scottish philosophy.[135] "McCosh's extension of his intuitional realism to the knowledge of God was inferential only." McCosh "admitted as much. It was inferential because whereas the philosopher had shown that the laws of the mind coincide in their operations with experienced things, with substantial reality," the conclusion must be that "he was now inferring, with respect to the intuition of the infinite, and its existence, that they must somehow coincide with some substantial being."[136] Thus, the tendency, which began in Witherspoon's efforts, to move away from establishing a complete natural theology as the best method of defending the faith had reached its apex in McCosh.

When McCosh came to America in 1868 to assume his duties as president of Princeton, much of his philosophical system had already been articulated. His qualifications as an educator, pastor, and philosopher made him the perfect candidate for the job. As president of the college, McCosh assumed the duties of professor of moral philosophy, and thus the last of the Scottish philosophers assumed the most influential of posts. McCosh's career at Princeton lasted until his retirement in 1888, when the reins passed to Francis Landey Patton (1843–1932), who was a theological conservative, and while of sound mind, was not effective as

---

134. Hoeveler, *James McCosh and the Scottish Intellectual Tradition*, 127–28. Hoeveler points out that McCosh retained his Neo-Calvinistic convictions about the falleness of man, and that McCosh never saw man's knowledge of God as "co-extensive with divine reality (pp. 159–60)." This understanding of faith and knowledge and the witness of the Holy Spirit will be developed more fully by Warfield. This point will be covered in some detail in chapter 4.

135. This is also paralleled in Warfield, whereby Warfield affirms merely in passing the validity of the classical proofs for the existence of God. See, for example, Warfield's article "God," reprinted in *Studies in Theology* (Grand Rapids: Baker Book House, 1981), 109–14. It is interesting that Warfield does not use the "proofs" in his apologetic writings, stressing almost exclusively the inductive arguments for the historicity of special revelation and the resurrection of Christ. See, for example, "The Resurrection of Christ a Historical Fact," in *Selected Shorter Writings of Benjamin B. Warfield*, vol. 1 (ed. John E. Meeter; Phillipsburg: P&R Publishing, 1980), 178–92.

136. Hoeveler, *James McCosh and the Scottish Intellectual Tradition*, 165.

an administrator of an institution struggling to liberalize in a changing world. The relative success of McCosh's presidency is difficult to judge, but the reforms instituted under his leadership moved the college to the point that by the end of Patton's stormy term in office in 1902, Woodrow Wilson, a former student and protégé of McCosh, and a much more progressive educator, was named president of Princeton College.[137]

Upon McCosh's death on Friday, November 16, 1894, the students "rang the bell at Nassau Hall to tell Princeton that Dr. McCosh was dead."[138] It was a former student of Dr. McCosh, B. B. Warfield, who informed the readership of the *Presbyterian and Reformed Review* of McCosh's death. "He was above all things a great religious philosopher," Warfield wrote.

> The present writer had the happiness of a personal acquaintance with [him]. He entered Princeton College as a student in the autumn in which Dr. McCosh took charge of its administration, and sat as his feet in the class-room for three stimulating years, which have left a permanent impression on all his thinking. The admiration of the man which began then, has been deepened by the intercourse of more mature years.[139]

Looking back at his years as a student at Princeton College some years later, Warfield remembered McCosh as a "great man and a great teacher." Indeed, Warfield recalls McCosh as an outstanding lecturer who had a tremendous influence upon his students. "He was distinctly the most inspiring force which came into my life during my college days."[140] These were more than mere kind words, for not only did Warfield admire Dr. McCosh, but his "intuitional realism" left a lasting mark upon Warfield's own efforts to defend the faith. Warfield was not only influenced by McCosh, but as the last of the "old Princetonians," Warfield helped to perpetuate his mentor's philosophical legacy. For Warfield himself stood in the long line of theologian-philosophers, including the Princeton theologians, who used certain elements of the Scottish philosophy in

---

137. This period is described in great detail in Hoeveler, *James McCosh and the Scottish Intellectual Tradition*, 312–49.

138. Ibid., 338.

139. B. B. Warfield, "Obituary Notes. James McCosh, D.D., L.L.D., and William Greenough Thayer Shedd, D.D., L.L.D." in *The Presbyterian and Reformed Review*, vol. VI (1895), 123–24.

140. Benjamin B. Warfield, "Personal Recollections of Princeton Undergraduate Life. IV. The Coming of Dr. McCosh," in *The Princeton Alumni Weekly*, 16, no. 28 (April 19, 1916), 632.

defense of the faith–especially when dealing with epistemological skepticism and the various theories of "ideas." McCosh may have been the last of the educator-philosophers, but for 30 more years, Warfield remained on the scene even as the influence of Scottish Common Sense Realism began to wane among conservative Presbyterians and evangelicals.

3

New Testament Studies

EARLY FOUNDATIONS

Benjamin Breckinridge Warfield was one of those rare professors who is qualified to teach virtually any field in the theological curricula. His reputation grew over the course of his lengthy career as professor of polemical and didactic theology at Princeton Theological Seminary. Although he is not often thought of as a "New Testament" specialist, Warfield did, in fact, begin his career in 1878 as professor of New Testament language and literature at Western Theological Seminary.[1] William Robertson Nicoll once lamented, "It was a thousand pities that Warfield did not continue to make the New Testament his chief field of study."[2] One of Warfield's biographers, Samuel G. Craig, argues that Warfield's voluminous endeavors over the balance of his life must be seen in the context of his abiding interest in New Testament studies.[3] Often overlooked, Warfield's New Testament studies are actually quite crucial to fully understand Warfield's inductive and evidential method of defending the truth of Christianity. They play a key role in his efforts to define and defend the inerrancy of the original biblical autographs.

While recent studies have correctly pointed out the tremendous influence of Scottish Common Sense Realism upon Warfield, they tend to overlook the fact that, in many ways, Warfield was also indebted to a critical methodology more associated with mainstream German scholarship. This influence, specifically upon Warfield's inductive and historical methodology, surfaces throughout his various apologetical and polemical writings. Earlier critiques of Warfield, such as that by William

1. Details of Warfield's professional career can be found in Samuel G. Craig, "Benjamin B. Warfield" in B. B. Warfield, *Biblical and Theological Studies* (Philadelphia: P&R Publishing, 1968), xi–xlviii.
2. Ibid., xiv.
3. Ibid.

Livingstone (1948), simply labeled Warfield a "rationalist," ignoring the influence of Scottish Common Sense Realism with its intuitional and inductive methodology.[4] More recent treatments, such as that by Jack Rogers and Donald McKim in *The Authority and Interpretation of the Bible* (1979), perhaps overstate the case when they argue that Warfield uncritically capitulated to the prevailing 19th-century understanding of the natural sciences. This view of the natural sciences, germinated in the work of Francis Bacon and the Scottish Enlightenment, later came to full flower in what has come to be known as Scottish Common Sense Realism.[5]

The efforts of one researcher, Theodore P. Letis, have broken important new ground in this area. His work requires serious evaluation since he overlooks critical evidence which mitigates against some of his conclusions.[6] Letis contends that Warfield's importation of critical methodology to Princeton ultimately backfired, leading to an increasing historical skepticism.

> It is my conviction that Warfield himself represents a paradigm shift at Princeton, away from the tradition of Archibald Alexander and Charles Hodge. ... Warfield's wholly new paradigm, which relegated final authority to the *autographa*, rather than to the *apographa*, left Princeton vulnerable to the fragmenting efforts of the early twentieth century biblical criticism. Warfield probably never foresaw that his quest for the historical *text* (for it is here where he would find *inerrancy*) would evolve into the quest for the historical *Jesus* at Princeton, just as it did in Britain in the eighteenth century and in Germany in the nineteenth century.[7]

4. See William D. Livingstone, "The Princeton Apologetic as Exemplified by the Work of Benjamin B. Warfield and J. Gresham Machen: A Study in American Theology 1880–1930" (Ph.D. diss., Yale University, 1948), 342.
5. Rogers and McKim, *The Authority and Interpretation of the Bible*, 323–58.
6. Theodore P. Letis, "B. B. Warfield, Common-Sense Philosophy and Biblical Criticism," in *American Presbyterians*, vol. 69, no. 3 (Fall 1991), 175–90; and "The Protestant Dogmaticians and the Late Princeton School on the Status of the Sacred Apographa," in *The Scottish Bulletin of Evangelical Theology*, vol. 8, no. 1 (Sept 1990), 16–42.
7. Theodore P. Letis, "Brevard Childs and the Protestant Dogmaticians: A Window to a New Paradigm of Biblical Interpretation," in *The Churchman*, vol. 105, no. 3 (1991), 622. The italics are in the original. Letis has argued that Warfield's quest for the inerrant original autographic text opened the doors to a form of destructive higher criticism, but he offers no support for this contention.

This chapter will identify and evaluate the influences of this critical historical methodology on Warfield's apologetic efforts. First, it will explore the often overlooked connection between Princeton Theological Seminary and the efforts of critical German biblical scholarship. Second, it will investigate Warfield's early career as professor of New Testament, where these critical influences begin to emerge in his early published writings. Third, it will evaluate Warfield's significant but overlooked efforts in the emerging field of textual criticism. This was an important endeavor for Warfield, given his concerns about the inerrancy of the original autographs and the corresponding need to recover the autographic text. Finally, it will assess several of the issues raised by Theodore Letis. These concern the connections between Warfield's arguments for the inspiration and authority of the Bible, and his parallel work in the field of textual criticism.

GERMAN CRITICAL METHODOLOGY

B. B. Warfield was not the first Princeton theologian to study critical methodology on German soil. Indeed, by the time that Warfield arrived at Princeton as a student in 1868, Princeton Seminary had already had a surprisingly long interest in the development of lower and higher criticism. Charles Hodge, perhaps in many ways the most significant personal and lasting influence upon Warfield,[8] had himself gone to Europe in 1826, spending two years traveling across the continent to study in the leading universities. During this period, Hodge developed a close and lasting friendship with the German theologian August Tholuck and heard noted German theologians E. W. Hengstenberg, Friedrich Schleiermacher, Wilhelm Gesenius, and J. A. W. Neander lecture in person.[9] It was during his time with Tholuck that Hodge's basic commitment to an objective "factual defense" of Christianity, already consistent with his previous commitment to Scottish Common Sense Realism, which he learned from Archibald Alexander, was certainly reinforced.[10] Hodge

8. See Warfield's comments in this regard in B. B. Warfield, "Dr. Charles Hodge as a Teacher of Exegesis" reprinted in *The Selected Shorter Writings of Benjamin B. Warfield*, vol. 1 (ed. John E. Meeter; Phillipsburg: P&R Publishing, 1980), 437–40.
9. Charles Hodge's years in Europe are effectively surveyed in his biography. See A. A. Hodge, *The Life of Charles Hodge* (New York: Charles Scribner's Sons, 1880), 100–201. Also see John William Stewart, "The Tethered Theology: Biblical Criticism, Common Sense Philosophy and the Princeton Theologians, 1812–1860" (Ph.D. diss., University of Michigan, 1990), 122–50.
10. A. A. Hodge, *The Life of Charles Hodge*, 141–43.

seemed to take great pride in noting that two Scots—David Hume and Thomas Reid—were highly regarded by the Germans, while the British empiricist John Locke was not esteemed by them at all.[11]

Several years later in 1833, Joseph Addison Alexander (1809–1860), the third son of Archibald Alexander and professor of oriental and biblical literature, also traveled across Germany. J. A. Alexander "heard the lectures of Schleiermacher shortly before the latter's death, and acquainted himself with leading theological scholars, including Ernest Wilhelm Hengstenberg, J. A. W. Neander, and F. A. G. Tholuck."[12] Alexander came to greatly appreciate the work of German evangelicals such as Hengstenberg, but was vehemently opposed to those whom he considered radical critics, such as David Strauss.[13] Thus, well before Warfield's arrival at Princeton as a student, the latest critical methodology had been studied firsthand, and new endeavors were reviewed as soon as possible in the *Princeton Review*.[14] In fact, to the readership of the *Review*, J. A. Alexander noted:

> The true course with respect to German labours and researches is not to look away from them or cover them with dust, but to seize upon their valuable products and convert them to our own use in the very face and teeth of those who after bringing them to light are often utterly unable to dispose of them.[15]

Thus Princeton Seminary had a lengthy history of interaction with the German theologians and, as an institution, was not entirely unappreciative of their great learning. But it was certainly the feeling of the Princetonians that while the Germans occupied the "cutting-edge" in the field of New Testament studies, one must learn to "convert" the discipline to "our own use," lest it turn and devour him.

---

11. Ibid., 122.
12. James H. Moorhead, "Joseph Addison Alexander: Common Sense, Romanticism and Biblical Criticism at Princeton," in *Journal of Presbyterian History*, vol. 53 (1975), 52.
13. Ibid., 54.
14. See Mark Noll's fine history of the *Princeton Review*, in the *Westminster Theological Journal*, vol. L, no. 2 (Fall 1988), 283–304.
15. J. A. Alexander, "Review of Kitto's Cyclopedia," in *Princeton Review* XVIII (October 1846), 561–62. Alexander also recognizes what he considers to be the extremely important contributions made by August Tholuck and E. W. Hengstenberg as German evangelicals.

Taking the advice of C. W. Hodge,[16] B. B. Warfield obtained a letter of endorsement from noted church historian Philip Schaff and subsequently enrolled in the University of Leipzig for a year of study (1876–1877), after he had completed his theological education at Princeton. Warfield set out for Germany with the intention of studying under Heinrich Merkel, only to learn unfortunately that Merkel had died several months before his arrival. Instead, Warfield took up study with two highly regarded members of the so-called Erlangen School, working with Ernst Luthardt (1823–1902) and Franz Delitzsch (1813–1890).[17] It is significant perhaps that Luthardt, a noted conservative confessional Lutheran and outspoken critic of Strauss and Renan,[18] and Delitzsch, the noted Old Testament exegete, had both completed important apologetic works shortly before the time that Warfield had arrived there—Luthardt's work entitled *Apologetische Vortäge uber die Grundwahrheiten des Christenthums* (1865), and Delitzsch's *System der christlichen Apologetik* (1869).[19] What exact influence this had upon Warfield's later apologetic efforts is difficult to determine, though Warfield certainly engaged in similar efforts. He took up the mantle of apologist and defender of Reformed orthodoxy during his own lengthy career at Princeton.[20] Warfield readily used many of the critical skills he had learned abroad to demonstrate that Christianity is *the* absolute religion.

---

16. Letter from C. W. Hodge to B. B. Warfield, June 6, 1876, papers of B. B. Warfield, Speer Library, Princeton Seminary. Cited in Letis, "B. B. Warfield, Common-Sense Philosophy and Biblical Criticism," 180.

17. McClanahan, "Benjamin B. Warfield: Historian in Defense of Orthodoxy, 1881–1921," 19.

18. Ian Sellers, "Luthardt, Christoph Ernest" in *Dictionary of the Christian Church* (ed. J. D. Douglas; Grand Rapids: Zondervan, 1981), 609.

19. Warfield specifically refers to the work of Delitzsch in his article "Apologetics," written for the noted Schaff-Herzog encyclopedia. Warfield points out that in Delitzsch's work (among others), "Apologetics is conceived ... as a special department of theological science, capable of and demanding a separate treatment." This was a point that Warfield himself regarded as an important one. See B. B. Warfield, "Apologetics," reprinted in *Studies in Theology* (Grand Rapids: Baker Book House, 1981), 19.

20. Mark Noll has also seen this connection. "It is noteworthy that almost all serious historical work on Warfield's generation at Princeton Seminary has been in the context of fundamentalism rather than the European Reformed tradition which Warfield himself considered his primary allegiance." See Noll, "Common Sense Traditions and American Evangelical Thought," 235.

WARFIELD'S EARLY CAREER

When Warfield returned to the United States after completing his studies in Europe, the field of New Testament caught his eye, though he had already been offered a position in Old Testament at Western Theological Seminary in Pittsburgh while still abroad.[21] It was not until Warfield had been home for a full year that he finally accepted the position of instructor in New Testament at Western. He was given a full professorship the following year. It is quite significant that Warfield's first five major published works were in the field of New Testament, and all of them were specially oriented toward defending orthodoxy by using the "latest" critical methodology. Amazingly, between 1880 and 1886, the prolific young professor published at least 60 additional works in New Testament studies, the vast majority of these dealing with the latest developments in textual criticism, New Testament background, word studies, and exegetical issues, as well as related Patristic studies.[22]

It is possible that Warfield's inaugural address, entitled "Inspiration and Criticism"[23] given at Western Seminary in 1880, may have been aimed at convincing the audience that the use of the new critical methodology was perfectly compatible with Reformed orthodoxy. Warfield began the lecture by unabashedly affirming his commitment to the historic Reformed standards.

> Fathers and Brothers: It is without doubt a very wise provision by which, in institutions such as this, an inaugural address is made a part of the ceremony of induction into the professorship. Only by the adoption of some such method could it be possible

21. McClanahan, "Benjamin B. Warfield: Historian of Doctrine in Defense of Orthodoxy, 1881–1921," 23.

22. See John E. Meeter and Roger Nicole, *A Bibliography of Benjamin Breckinridge Warfield 1851–1921* (n. p.: P&R Publishing, 1974), 1, 9 ff. Warfield's first published effort, a *Syllabus on the Canon of the New Testament in the Second Century* (Pittsburgh: n. p., 1881), was followed by a tract the next year entitled, *The Divine Origin of the Bible. (The General Argument). Tract no. 210* (Philadelphia: The Presbyterian Board of Publication, 1882). In 1883 Warfield completed another syllabus, *Syllabus on the Special Introduction to the Catholic Epistles* (Pittsburgh: W. W. Waters, 1883), and then a series of notes on Romans entitled, "Synopsis of Paul's Epistle to the Romans," which was initially published as an appendix to the preceding. In 1886 Warfield's first book was published, *An Introduction to the Textual Criticism of the New Testament* (London: Hodder & Stoughton, 1886).

23. B. B. Warfield, "Inspiration and Criticism," repr. in *Revelation and Inspiration* (Grand Rapids: Baker Book House, 1981), 395–421.

> for you, as the guardians of this institution, responsible for the principles here inculcated, to give to each newly-called teacher an opportunity to publicly declare the sense in which he accepts your faith and signs your standards. ... And how much more forcibly can all this be pled when he who appears before you at your call, is young, untired and unknown. I wish therefore, to declare that I sign these standards not as a necessary form which must be submitted to, but gladly and willingly as the expression of a personal and cherished conviction; and, further, that the system taught in these symbols is the system which will be drawn out of the Scriptures in the prosecution of the teaching to which you have called me—not, indeed, because commencing with that system the Scriptures can be made to teach it, but because commencing with the Scriptures I cannot make them teach anything else.[24]

Confessing his unwavering commitment to Reformed orthodoxy, Warfield moves on in his lecture to ask the critical question, "Is the church doctrine of the plenary inspiration of the New Testament endangered by the assured results of modern biblical criticism?"[25] The answer, as we will see, is an emphatic "No!"

The way in which Warfield answers his own rhetorical question demonstrates quite clearly the beginnings of a distinct apologetic approach. Some feel it is a radical departure from previous Reformed orthodoxy—a debatable point indeed. This approach, from Warfield's own perspective, sees this critical methodology as a tool which, when used properly, will *not* destroy Christianity, but will, in fact, actually serve to vindicate it. We get a glimpse of this emphasis when Warfield defines inspiration as:

> A doctrine which claims that by a special supernatural influence of the Holy Ghost, the sacred writers have been guided in their writing in such a way, as while their humanity was not superseded, it was yet so dominated that their words became at the same time the words of God, and thus in every case and all alike, absolutely infallible.[26]

24. Warfield, "Inspiration and Criticism," 395–96.
25. Ibid., 396.
26. Ibid., 399.

Warfield, then, immediately contends that we cannot simply argue in a circle: "We do not assume inspiration in order to prove inspiration."[27] This is the seminal germ of a Warfieldian emphasis which will come to maturity a few years later (1894), when he would write:

> The supernatural origin and contents of Christianity, not only may be vindicated apart from any question of the inspiration of the record, but, in point of fact, always are vindicated prior to any question of the inspiration of the record. We cannot raise the question whether God has given us an absolutely trustworthy record of the supernatural facts and teachings of Christianity, before we are assured that there are supernatural facts and teachings to be recorded. The fact that Christianity is a supernatural religion and the nature of Christianity as a supernatural religion, *are matters of history*; and are independent of any, and of every theory of inspiration.[28]

Thus according to Warfield, the claims of Christianity (i.e., the historical events upon which it is based, such as the resurrection of Christ) must be "proven" to be true by factual evidence since this is a matter of history, before we affirm that our doctrine of inspiration is true simply because Scripture says so. This means that any discussion of inspiration must be subsequent to apologetics. Warfield viewed apologetics as a kind of theological prolegomenon: we must first vindicate the Christian truth claim on a factual basis, before we set out a doctrine of inspiration. The "proof" that Christianity is a supernatural religion is linked to history, rather than faith. Since this "proof" precedes any discussion of

27. Ibid., 399–400.

28. B. B. Warfield, "The Church Doctrine of Inspiration," repr. in *The Inspiration and Authority of the Bible* (Phillipsburg: P&R Publishing, 1948), 121. This assertion also demonstrates that Warfield faithfully followed the apologetic methodology set out by A. A. Hodge in 1881, in the famous essay "Inspiration." A. A. Hodge, who authored the first 29 pages of the article, stated, "Hence it follows that, while the inspiration of Scripture is true, and being true is a principle fundamental to the adequate interpretation of Scripture, it nevertheless is not in the first instance a principle fundamental to the truth of the Christian religion. In dealing with skeptics it is not proper to begin with the evidence which immediately establishes inspiration, but we should first establish theism, then the historical credibility of the Scriptures, and then the divine origin of Christianity. Nor should we ever allow it to be believed that the truth of Christianity depends upon any doctrine of inspiration whatever." See A. A. Hodge and B. B. Warfield, "Inspiration," in *The Presbyterian Review* (April 1881), 225–60; repr. in A. A. Hodge and B. B. Warfield, *Inspiration* (ed. Roger Nicole; Grand Rapids: Baker Book House, 1979), 8.

inspiration of the text, critical methodology must be enlisted to "prove" the case that Christianity is true.[29] Warfield's basic argument which he will continually develop over the course of his career is nascent in his inaugural address at Western Theological Seminary.

The relationship between critical methodology and Reformed orthodoxy must be carefully and precisely set out. Warfield writes, "If the New Testament writers, being sober and honest men, claim verbal inspiration, and this claim was accepted by the contemporary church, and their writings in no respect in their character or details negate it," then he observes, "it seems idle to object to the doctrine of verbal inspiration on any critical grounds."[30] In order for the Christian faith and its doctrine of verbal inspiration to be overturned, critical scholarship must be able to demonstrate "either that the New Testament writers do not claim inspiration; or that this claim was rejected by the contemporary church; or that it is palpably negatived by the fact that the books containing it are forgeries."[31] In addition, such critical methodology must demonstrate that the New Testament writings contain "errors of fact or contradictions of statement."[32]

As Warfield sees it, this is the very thing that "objective" critical scholarship cannot do, for "modern biblical criticism does not in any way weaken the evidence that the New Testament writers claim full, even verbal inspiration."[33] Far from being an enemy of faith, critical methodology can serve as its hand-maiden. "If we approach the study of the New Testament under the guidance of and in the use of the methods of modern biblical science, more clearly than ever before it is seen that its authors make such a claim [i.e., for full inspiration]."[34] Unlike most conservative scholars, Warfield took a more positive view of higher criticism. It is not critical scholarship that is the enemy of orthodoxy. Rather, he believed, it is the lack of the objective application of the methodology itself, because of an *a priori* anti-supernaturalism that prevents these tools from being used properly and obtaining proper results.

---

29. Rogers and McKim consider this approach a clear instance of Warfield's "avowed commitment to Thomistic scholasticism. ... For Warfield, therefore, philosophy preceded theology. The requirements of human reason had to be met before God could give faith." See *The Authority and Interpretation of the Bible*, 328–29.
30. Warfield, "Inspiration and Criticism," 400.
31. Ibid.
32. Ibid.
33. Ibid., 400.
34. Ibid., 401.

But do the claims of modern critical scholarship actually demonstrate that "this claim of inspiration was disavowed by the contemporaries of the New Testament writers"? Here again argues Warfield, "Our answer must again be in the negative."[35] In fact:

> It is exceedingly clear, then, that modern criticism has not proved that the contemporary church resisted the assumption of the New Testament writers or withstood their claim to inspiration: directly the contrary. Every particle of evidence in the case exhibits the apostolic church, not as disallowing, but as distinctly recognizing the absolute authority of the New Testament writers.[36]

Warfield goes on to point out, with an undaunted confidence typical of someone who has drawn deeply from the well of the Baconian and Scottish Common Sense belief in the objectivity of truth, "modern biblical criticism has not disproved the authenticity of a single book of our New Testament. It is a most assured result of biblical criticism that every one of the twenty-seven books which now constitute our New Testament is assuredly genuine and authentic."[37] But Warfield was aware that this point will not be granted by all, no matter how boldly asserted; things are not that simple:

> There is, indeed much that arrogates to itself the name of criticism and has that honorable title carelessly accorded to it, which does claim to arrive at such results as set aside the authenticity of even the major part of the New Testament. One school would save five books only from the universal ruin. To this, however, true criticism opposes itself directly, and boldly proclaims every New Testament book as authentic. But thus two claimants to the name of criticism appear, and the question arises, before what court can the rival claims be adjudicated? Before the court of simple common sense it may be quickly answered.[38]

Here Warfield makes a critical distinction between what he considers to be "true criticism," which only serves to strengthen the case for the truth of Christianity, and that which instead abrogates to itself the title of "criticism." The latter is in reality an arch-enemy of Christianity and

35. Ibid.
36. Ibid., 407.
37. Ibid., 408.
38. Ibid., 408–09.

cannot really be called criticism or "science" at all. How, then, are we to distinguish between the two? Warfield explains:

> By criticism is meant an investigation with three essential characteristics: (1) a fearless, honest mental abandonment, apart from presuppositions, to the facts of the case, (2) a most careful, complete and unprejudiced collection and examination of the facts, and (3) the most cautious care in founding inferences upon them. The absence of any one of these characteristics throws grave doubts upon the results; while the acme of the uncritical is reached when in the place of these critical graces we find guiding the investigation that the other trio,—bondage to preconceived opinion, incomplete or prejudiced collection and examination of the facts,—and rashness of inference.[39]

This leads Warfield to pointedly ask, "Is that true criticism which starts with the presupposition that the supernatural is impossible [and] proceeds by sustained effort to do violence to the facts, and ends by erecting a gigantic historical chimera—overturning all established history?"[40] Warfield describes the "negative" criticism of his day as a "series of wild dreams" established on "the basis of airy nothing." Each new critical school proceeds by "executing judgment on its predecessor. So Paulus goes down before Strauss, Strauss falls before Baur, and Baur before the resistless logic of his own negative successors"[41]—a scholarly domino effect.

Yet, even though this is the case, warns Warfield, the arguments raised by critical scholarship cannot be simply dismissed. "As false as it is, its attacks must be tested and the opposition of true criticism to its results exhibited." For "an honest Theist, thus, is open to evidence either way; an honest Pantheist or Materialist is not open to any evidence for the supernatural."[42] Consistent then, with his inductive methodology, Warfield is perfectly willing to admit that there is indeed the possibility that the factual claims made for Christianity as a supernatural religion

39. Ibid., 409. This point not only echoes Reid's concern that reason is generally reliable and can discern truth from error in a "common sense" manner, Warfield anticipates the later discussion among advocates of so-called "Reformed epistemology" about the nature of "warranted belief." See Nicolas Wolterstorff, *Thomas Reid and the Story of Epistemology* (Cambridge: Cambridge University Press, 2001), 209–12.
40. Ibid.
41. Ibid.
42. Ibid., 410.

can be overturned. This can only occur, however, if this can be "proven" to be the case by using the same methodology "objectively" and then by demonstrating that these same factual claims made about Christianity are false. This can only be the result if the evidence so warrants, something theoretically possible, but not very probable.

There are several significant issues raised by Warfield's lecture which require evaluation. First, Warfield's definition of inspiration is clearly in line with historic Reformed orthodoxy.[43] But as Mark Noll points out:

> The theologians at Princeton were among the American intellectuals who most consistently used the language and the categories of this philosophy [Scottish Common Sense Realism] even when, as later observers would contend, its tenets seemed to contradict Princeton commitments to Scripture and Reformed tradition.[44]

It is important to note that Warfield views Baconian induction and Scottish Common Sense Realism categories of truth as objective realities, accessible to all. His robust dependence on these philosophical approaches determined his entire attitude toward critical methodology. Warfield's confidence that truth was objective, and that the inevitable result of the correct application of the inductive method established both the necessity of defending the faith and clearly guided the apologetical direction.[45] He believed that Christianity, though a supernatural religion, is open to ordinary historical investigation. History, not blind faith, is the ground for the defense of the faith.

Second, Warfield saw critical tools of "modern biblical scholarship," as "neutral," ready to be used to defend the faith. If used correctly, and without anti-supernatural presuppositions, such tools could only lead the critical scholar to the truth. The critical tools of European biblical scholarship, when used "objectively," are perfectly compatible with orthodoxy, in his view. Any problems that may arise for orthodoxy because of modern biblical criticism, do so because of anti-supernatural presuppositions brought to the process. When used by the radical

43. See Richard A. Muller, *Post-Reformation Reformed Dogmatics, Volume 2, Holy Scripture: The Cognitive Foundation of Theology* (Grand Rapids: Baker Book House, 1993), especially 239–70.

44. Mark A. Noll, *The Princeton Theology, 1812–1921* (Grand Rapids: Baker Book House, 1983), 30.

45. See Darryl Hart's essay treating similar themes in the efforts of Warfield's successor, J. Gresham Machen, "The Princeton Mind in the Modern World and the Common Sense of J. Gresham Machen," in *The Westminster Journal* 46 (1984), 1–27.

critics, these methods are not used to discover truth. In his famous essay "Inspiration," written just a year later, and co-authored with A. A. Hodge, Warfield speaks of such critical methodology when approached with such biases as "overreaching itself and building on fancies."[46] Although still in their infancy, the basic arguments set out by Warfield in his inaugural address of 1880 did not change materially from this point to his death in 1921.

THE NEW SCIENCE OF TEXTUAL CRITICISM

As Theodore Letis points out, "A good deal of Warfield's early academic career ... was spent mastering the discipline of New Testament text criticism so as to tame and neutralize this threat [to the doctrine of verbal inspiration]."[47] According to Letis, this means that "contrary to most critical evaluations of Warfield, the primary influence upon him at this point was not Reformed scholasticism, but rather, the Enlightenment," because this approach "demanded that Scripture be approached 'as any other literature,' and it legitimized the use of the radical technique of conjectural emendation—the very foundation of the higher critical method."[48] If Letis is correct, then the great champion of verbal inspiration and militant defender of the inerrancy of the original biblical autographs, quite unwittingly opened the door to destructive higher criticism. The views of the German higher critics would eventually rule the day after the reorganization of Princeton Seminary in 1929.[49] Letis' first contention is certainly borne out by the fact that the new professor's first major book-length work, *An Introduction to the Textual Criticism of the New Testament* (1886), was essentially the first effort by an American scholar "to produce a primer on the German practice of New Testament text criticism."[50] It was highly regarded in its day by the likes of Joseph

46. A. A. Hodge and B. B. Warfield, *Inspiration*, 39–40.
47. Letis, "B. B. Warfield, Common-Sense Philosophy and Biblical Criticism," 175.
48. Ibid., 176. Letis argues that Archibald Alexander, Charles Hodge, and Caspar Wistar Hodge all regarded as a "fixed law" the illegitimacy of the practice of conjectural emendation because they viewed this as a destructive tool, which would allow the critic to make alterations, and this would destroy the authority of Scripture (178).
49. Ibid., 177.
50. Ibid. Although as the author points out, "While Philip Schaff did write a *Companion* three years earlier than Warfield which contained a great deal of text critical information, it had several contributors—including Warfield— and was too broadly based to be regarded strictly as a primer in the discipline" (189, see note 30).

Henry Thayer, the noted Harvard Divinity School professor and author of the Greek-English lexicon that bears his name.[51]

In this volume Warfield defines textual criticism as "the careful, critical examination of a text, with a view to discovering its condition, in order that we may test its correctness on the one hand, and, on the other emend its errors."[52] Warfield sees this as an essential discipline:

> And even when the document that lies before us is written with absolutely exact correctness, it requires the application of textual criticism, i.e., a careful examination, to discover and certify this fact. Let us repeat it, then: wherever written matter exists, textual criticism is not only legitimate, but an unavoidable task; when the writing is important, such as a deed or a will, or a charter, or the Bible, it is an indispensable duty.[53]

Warfield's underlying apologetic agenda (if indeed there is one) may come into view when he states, "It is important to certify ourselves of the correctness of our text as it is to correct it if erroneous; and the former is as much the function of criticism as the latter."[54] Warfield cautiously admits that "the current New Testament text must be adjudged, in comparison with a well-printed modern book, extremely corrupt." But this is not an insurmountable situation, for "if we compare the present state of the New Testament text with that of any other ancient writing, we must render the opposite verdict and declare it to be marvelously correct."[55] Warfield loosely connects the preservation of the text to his doctrine of providence, something he had done earlier, when he addressed the subject of inspiration with A. A. Hodge in response to issues raised by Charles Augustus Briggs of Union Seminary.[56] Warfield states:

---

51. See Joseph Thayer, "Review" of *An Introduction to the Textual Criticism of the New Testament*, by B. B. Warfield, in *The Andover Review*, vol. 8 (January 1887), 100–01. Thayer describes Warfield's primer as a "bright little book," but is concerned about "his liability to a mechanical use of the [genealogical] method."

52. B. B. Warfield, *An Introduction to the Textual Criticism of the New Testament* (New York: Thomas Whittaker, 1887), 4.

53. Ibid., 7.

54. Ibid., 10.

55. Ibid., 12.

56. See the study of the ongoing clash between Warfield and Briggs, in Gary L. W. Johnson, "Warfield and C. A. Briggs: Their Polemics and legacy," in *B. B. Warfield: Essays on His Life and Thought* (ed. Gary L. W. Johnson; Phillipsburg: P&R Publishing, 2007), 195–240. In the essay "Inspiration," Hodge and Warfield contend that inspiration, as a subset of revelation, means that "its essence was superintendence. This

> Such has been the care with which the New Testament has been copied,—a care which has doubtless grown out of true reverence for its holy words,—such has been the providence of God in preserving for His Church in each and every age a competently exact text of the Scriptures, that not only is the New Testament unrivaled among ancient writings in the purity of its text as actually transmitted and kept in use, but also in the abundance of testimony which has come down to us for castigating its comparatively infrequent blemishes. The divergence of its current text from the autograph may shock a printer of modern books; its wonderful approximation to its autograph is the undisguised envy of every modern reader of ancient books.[57]

Therefore, if "we undertake the textual criticism of the New Testament under a sense of duty," we will most certainly attain our goal, "because the autographic text of the New Testament is distinctly within the reach of criticism ... that we cannot despair of restoring to ourselves and the Church of God, His Book, word for word, as he gave it by inspiration to men."[58] Later in the volume, Warfield asserts, "When dealing absolutely with each reading, we are seeking directly the autographic text,"[59] and "we seek the original text of the New Testament in the extant

---

superintendence attended the entire process of the genesis of Scripture, and particularly, the process of the final composition of the record." See A. A. Hodge and B. B. Warfield, "Inspiration," 6. Later in the essay, the authors affirm, "It is also evident that our conception of revelation must be conditioned upon our view of God's relation to the world, and his methods of influencing the souls of men (p. 9)," i.e., providence. Thus if God's providence (and the distinctly supernatural production of Scripture as a subset of that providence) extends to the production of Scripture, it is then easy to argue that God providentially ensures that the biblical text is generally preserved, though it is the duty of textual criticism to reconstruct the autographic text from the evidence at hand. It must also be duly noted that Warfield himself took issue when his view of inspiration was described by an editorial in the *Presbyterian Review*, as one which simply affirmed "*mere providential* superintendence over the external production of Scripture." Warfield points out his problem with the use of the term "mere," which he noted was purely an editorial insertion, and did not describe his own views on the matter. He goes on to point out that he and Hodge contend that they view God's activity in inspiration to be "a controlling influence from without," which is a "special superintendence by God in the entire process of *writing*." Repr. in *Inspiration*, 73–76.

57. Warfield, *An Introduction to the Textual Criticism of the New Testament*, 12–13.

58. Ibid., 14–15.

59. Ibid., 84.

[manuscripts]."[60] That this is vital to Warfield's understanding of inerrancy, follows from an earlier assertion stated jointly with A. A. Hodge, that the "absolute infallibility of the record in which the revelation, once generated, appears in the original autograph."[61] If then, through such critical methodology we are able to reconstruct the text, we have practical access to the original autographic text.

Not surprisingly then, Warfield makes several comments regarding the need for "objective" application of critical methodology. "All trustworthy appeal to intrinsic evidence is a delicate historical process," writes Warfield, "by which the critic, having steeped himself in the times of the writer and having assimilated himself to his thought and style, thinks his thoughts and estimates the value and fitness of his words with his scales."[62] Warfield goes on to state:

> Above all other processes of criticism this method requires in its user a fine candour and an incorruptible mental honesty which are content to read from the authors with which they deal only what those authors have put into their words, and which can distinguish between what Paul, for instance, says, and what we wish he had said. ... And the business of the textual critic is not to correct their grammar, and brighten their obscurities, and perfect their logic, and chasten their style, but to restore their text exactly as they intended to write it, whatever there may be in it to offend our taste or contradict our opinions.[63]

In fact, if these methods are applied correctly, the "verdicts sometimes reach a practical certainty."[64] Here again, we see a very clear example of Warfield's Scottish Common Sense Realist inductive methodology. He claimed the resulting high probability as a "practical certainty," or as stated elsewhere, a "moral certainty."[65]

Theodore Letis, however, argues that the embrace of the new science of textual criticism at Princeton brought a significant shift at Princeton four years before Warfield published his book. Therefore, according

60. Ibid., 136. See also page 183, where Warfield asserts, "When the findings of the various methods agree the conclusion is certain, and we may feel sure that we have obtained the autographic text."

61. A. A. Hodge and B. B. Warfield, "Inspiration," 6.

62. Warfield, *An Introduction to Textual Criticism of the New Testament*, 85.

63. Ibid., 85–86.

64. Ibid., 86.

65. Ibid., 115.

to Letis, "Warfield was now prepared to go beyond what anyone at Princeton had ever been willing to do—doubt the inspiration of one of the resurrection accounts,"[66] Mark 16:9–20. Indeed, Warfield had published two important articles in 1882 that shed a great deal of light on his subsequent methodology. The first of these was a rather glowing review of B. F. Westcott and F. J. A. Hort's *The New Testament in the Original Greek* published in April,[67] and the second, published in December's *Sunday School Times*, was an article wherein Warfield rejected outright on textual-critical grounds, the genuineness of Mark 16:9–20.[68] Warfield flatly asserted that textual critical methodology clearly demonstrates that the twelve-verse ending that appears in the AV is "no part of the word of God. We are not then to ascribe to these verses the authority due to God's word."[69] Here, the "objective" use of critical methodology led Warfield to conclude that the original ending to Mark's Gospel had been lost, and that there was no textual evidence, either internal or external, that the present ending was anything other than a later addition. Five years later, when his primer on textual criticism was published, Warfield would continue to affirm that "every appearance, in a word, goes to show that the author of the Gospel did not write verses 9–20 as the conclusion of the narrative begun in verses 1–8." Indeed, "the author of the Gospel did not write these verses."[70] What about the shorter ending of Mark? Warfield dismisses this too. "No one doubts that this shorter ending is a

66. Letis, "B. B. Warfield, Common-Sense Philosophy and Biblical Criticism," 181. Letis argues that Warfield and C. W. Hodge were essentially in agreement upon the idea that since lower criticism dealt with "facts" it could be used "objectively," unlike higher criticism, which was seen as utterly speculative. C. W. Hodge also doubted Markan authorship of the passage, but not the canonicity of the passage. However, when Letis asserts that "what Warfield failed to address was the fact that large blocks of material traditionally found in those books were now, in his opinion, to be dispensed with as corruptions of the text, 'facts' produced as a result of modern criticism," he surely overstates the matter. Letis' work is repeatedly marred by such hyperbolic assertions. Warfield himself affirmed quite the opposite, namely that "a comparatively very small portion of the text is thus left in uncertainty." See B. B. Warfield, "The Greek Testament of Westcott and Hort," in *The Presbyterian Review*, vol. III, (April 1882), 325–56.

67. Warfield, "The Greek Testament of Westcott and Hort," 325–56.

68. B. B. Warfield, "The Genuineness of Mark 16:9–20," in *Sunday School Times*, vol. XXIV (December 1882), 755 ff.

69. Ibid.

70. Warfield, *An Introduction to Textual Criticism of the New Testament*, 203.

spurious invention of the scribes; but it would not have been invented, save to fill the blank."[71]

While Warfield is vilified by some of our contemporaries for his views regarding inerrancy,[72] it is quite ironic that Warfield was vilified at the time for his "liberal" position on the "spurious" ending of Mark's Gospel. One professor, N. M. Wheeler of Lawrence University, fumed in the very next issue of the *Sunday School Times*: "We must ask the critics every morning what is the latest conclusion in order to know what is that Scripture inspired of God."[73] Wheeler feared the opening of Pandora's Box, resulting in a complete loss of confidence in the historical reliability of the New Testament. Warfield saw it as the exact opposite: This was the key to the recovery of the autographic text.

Warfield's lengthy review of the Westcott-Hort volume *The New Testament in the Original Greek*, and its treatment of textual criticism, is also quite significant. Here we find the first clear statement of Warfield's understanding of the compatibility of critical methodology and the defense of the faith. "After having given thus a calm review of the new work, we feel bound ... to express our conviction of its great value very clearly." He says these authors "furnish us for the first time with a *really scientific method*; they reduce guesswork reconstruction to the narrowest limits, and substitute for it a sound inductive procedure."[74] Warfield was so impressed with the work that he was convinced that all Westcott-Hort adversaries, such as Dean Burgeon, will now "pass quietly away and leave no successors." Not given to easy praise, Warfield nonetheless extols that the "text which the new editors have given us is, in our judgement, the best and purest that has ever been passed through the press, and, for the future, must be recognized as the best basis for further work."[75]

It is unmistakably clear that Warfield saw the methodology as set out by Hort as the way to recover the autographic text. Warfield repeatedly asserts "the result is sure, and the process by which it is obtained, in

71. Ibid., 200.

72. See, for example, James D. G. Dunn, *The Living Word* (Philadelphia: Fortress, 1988), 107.

73. N. M. Wheeler, "Uncanonical Inspiration," in *Sunday School Times*, Vol. 25 (January 1883), 4. Cited in Letis, "B. B. Warfield, Common-Sense Philosophy, and Biblical Criticism," 181.

74. Warfield, "The Greek Testament of Westcott and Hort," 355. Italics mine.

75. Ibid.

either case, trustworthy."[76] Elsewhere he states, "It is plain that we have here an exceedingly clear and trustworthy scheme."[77] And, with certitude, "It seems on the face of it, to be impossible to doubt the legitimacy of the process or the surety of the results."[78] Unlike scholars who continued to argue for the superiority of the *textus receptus*, Warfield chooses the method set out by Hort because:

> [It] work[s] its way from one fact to another by a strictly inductive method; and the other to jump at once crudely to its last conclusion. The difference in a word, is ... between the Baconian and the so-called Aristotelian methods of thought—between science and guessing.[79]

Warfield moves on to discuss the "old method, once so popular, of critical conjecture. The vagaries of those who have most used this method long since brought it into not undeserved contempt."[80] But he is quite reluctant to totally abandon it. For as Warfield contends:

> *A priori* it will be difficult to see why it [critical conjecture] should be excluded from possible resort in reconstructing the text of the New Testament alone, of ancient books. The documentary evidence, mechanically applied, will take us here, too, only to the earliest transmitted text, and whether this be the autographic text as well, or a more or less corrupt descendent of it, can be learned only by an appeal to the two varieties of internal evidence. ... The very act of reconstructing the text on any other method than that of absolutely mechanically applying the documentary evidence admits the legitimacy of conjectural emendation.[81]

Warfield realizes that the method can go awry and warns, "It may be said here, again, that thus a wide door is opened for the entrance of the deceitful dealing with the Word of Life. The danger is apparent and imminent. But we cannot arbitrarily close the door lest we incur the same charge."[82] Rather than outright rejecting the practice of conjectural emendation, safeguards should be in place regarding its usage. One

76. Ibid., 335.
77. Ibid., 339.
78. Ibid., 341.
79. Ibid., 345.
80. Ibid., 347.
81. Ibid.
82. Ibid.

would not wish to end up like the Germans, where "such hands have handled it and in such a spirit as would keep it in disgrace."[83]

Safeguards include, first of all, "that clear occasion for conjecture shall be required in each case where it is offered, and, unless not only its legitimacy can be proved, but in each case also its *necessity*, we shall allow none of it."[84] Second, "it must be demanded that, even if the necessity for conjecture be proved in a particular case, no emendation offered be accepted unless it perfectly fulfills the requirements of both varieties of internal evidence."[85] In fact, Warfield asserts that Westcott and Hort concede too many times that "primitive error exists in the reconstructed text which must be removed by conjecture." Warfield says, with some alarm, "We cannot feel that the claim of necessity for it is very plausible, much less made out."[86] Nevertheless, Warfield concludes by congratulating the authors since "they have not deformed their text with conjectural emendations, but have in every case printed the best attested reading, and relegated their emendations to the Appendix."[87] Warfield was the first conservative scholar to assure that the "teacher and preacher alike may rest upon and use the text already in hand with the calm consciousness that substantially the autographic text is before him, and that probably all future criticism will not result in throwing doubt on more than one word in a thousand."[88] Time has proved that the new critical methodology has done all Christians a great service.

EVALUATING WARFIELD'S CRITICAL METHODOLOGY

Theodore Letis sees Warfield's two published articles on textual criticism as advancing a kind of paradigm shift at Princeton. He contends that Warfield completely broke with the prior Princeton position on the emerging science of textual criticism by his endorsement of conjectural emendation. Letis recognizes that in most treatments of Warfield, "there is little attention paid to the significance of his work in text criticism."[89] Evaluations of Warfield's views on inerrancy and biblical au-

83. Ibid., 348.
84. Ibid.
85. Ibid.
86. Ibid.
87. Warfield, "The Greek Text of Westcott and Hort," 348–49.
88. Ibid., 356.
89. Letis, "B. B. Warfield, Common Sense Philosophy and Biblical Criticism," 189, n. 48.

thority abound,[90] but Theodore Letis was the first scholar to set out in detail Warfield's indebtedness to critical methodology for the defense of the faith.

He, however, describes this shift in ominous terms. "No Princetonian prior to this had ever doubted the canonical authority of these verses [Mark 16:9–20]."[91] Letis argues that since C. W. Hodge had not gone as far as Warfield later would, it is Warfield who, in effect, "said that in text critical matters, the faithful follow the same method as the Germans."[92] This is borne out, according to Letis, by the fact that:

> Another aspect of the German method that Warfield adopted via Westcott and Hort was the practice of conjectural emendation. We have already established that no N. T. scholar at Princeton had, until Warfield, accepted this method of guessing, aside from manuscript evidence, at what the true reading was (based upon the assumption that all extant copies are, at this point, corrupted).[93]

This leads Letis to conclude that it is Warfield who is responsible for a "wholly new" paradigm at Princeton regarding critical methodology.

Letis also contends that A. A. Hodge's comments regarding the emerging higher-criticism, published a year after the latter's death (in 1887), further serve to demonstrate the degree to which Warfield had broken with previous Princeton convictions. Letis cites the following comments from A. A. Hodge's work *Evangelical Theology*:

> There is an arrogant phase of the "higher criticism" that is far more ambitious and attempts to correct, or even to reconstruct, the existing text by wide inductions from the history of the times, from the other writings, and from the known style, situation, or the subject of the writer. ... But it is very plain that this process of "higher criticism" is liable to be coloured, and even wholly controlled, by the subjective conditions of the critic—by his sympathies, by his historical and philosophical and religious theories,

90. Warfield's efforts in this area and recent secondary literature are effectively surveyed in Peter Maarten van Bemmelen, "Issues in Biblical Inspiration: Sanday and Warfield," (Ph.D. diss., Andrews University, 1987), especially 197–309.
91. Letis, "The Protestant Dogmaticians and the Late Princeton School on the Status of the Sacred Apographa," 34.
92. Letis, "B. B. Warfield, Common Sense Philosophy and Biblical Criticism," 182.
93. Ibid.

> and by his *a priori* judgments as to what the sacred writer ought to say.[94]

From this, Letis draws the conclusion that "Warfield had used nearly every one of these arguments to reject the long ending of Mark."[95] Thus according to Letis, the shift had ironically occurred largely through Warfield's efforts to defend the faith.

Letis' interpretation of Warfield's early career raises several important issues that merit response. First, it must be pointed out that Warfield was still teaching at Western Theological Seminary during this period, and did not arrive at Princeton until 1888, after the death of A. A. Hodge. While Warfield had very close associations with A. A. Hodge and the Princeton community, he was not actually a faculty member at Princeton during the period when Letis contends that this "paradigm shift" took place. Warfield pursued these endeavors while in the employ of another institution as professor of New Testament. It must also be noted that Warfield's subsequent appointment at Princeton was to the chair of didactic and polemical theology, not as professor of New Testament. Thus from this point on, Warfield's theological interests move in a different direction, though Warfield was never far away from these specific New Testament issues.

Warfield's championing of the Westcott-Hort methodology *does* represent a very significant movement beyond previous boundaries at Princeton. Clearly, Warfield was much more amenable to textual criticism as practiced by the Germans (as seen through the grid of Westcott and Hort) than were his predecessors, specifically Charles Hodge, A. A. Hodge, and C. W. Hodge. Yet, there are several important facts which Letis does not duly consider which mitigate against his conclusion that it is Warfield who imported higher criticism into Princeton. Warfield himself was keenly aware of the problems associated with conjectural emendation, and stated as much. Despite his glowing review of Westcott-Hort, he raises grave concerns regarding the looseness with which Westcott and Hort had used this methodology. But Warfield did not feel that this seriously detracted from the overall impact of the book because Westcott and Hort had placed their own conjectural emendations in a separate appendix, and not in the critical text itself. This

94. A. A. Hodge, *Evangelical Theology* (1890), repr. (Carlisle: Banner of Truth, 1976), 66–67.

95. Letis, "B. B. Warfield, Common Sense Philosophy, and Biblical Criticism," 183.

reinforced for Warfield that the methodology was "neutral" and perfectly capable of being used "objectively."

Third, this "paradigm shift," contrary to Letis' implication, was not strictly the result of Warfield's personal efforts to covertly import "conjectural emendation" into Princeton circles. Certainly, there is a marked paradigm shift in view with the publication of *The New Testament in the Original Greek*. But this shift encompassed all of the English speaking world, and not just Princeton Theological Seminary and the Princeton circle. Whatever shift that did occur is much more likely the product of the inevitable consequence of the ground-breaking efforts made by Westcott and Hort. Bruce Metzger calls the publication of the Westcott-Hort critical text, "the most noteworthy critical edition of the Greek Testament ever produced by British scholarship." This was hardly an insignificant event which Warfield managed to magnify out of proportion. Metzger also makes the observation that "the overwhelming consensus of scholarly opinion recognizes that their critical edition was truly epoch-making."[96]

Thus, the tidal wave that hit Princeton did not originate from within. Indeed, Letis points out that before Westcott-Hort's work was endorsed by Warfield, the Princeton faculty had, by and large, defended the *textus receptus* and generally endorsed the work of Griesbach over that of Scrivener.[97] But once Westcott and Hort had done their work, none of the prior Princeton convictions about textual criticism were tenable, whether Warfield had endorsed the new critical methodology or not. Letis' failure to make this observation tarnishes an otherwise valuable insight into the development of the Princeton apologetic. Warfield is not breaking with the past in a "wholly new" manner. Rather he is attempting to use the new method as a means of advancing the traditional Princeton apologetic in a new historical context. Given his commitment to Scottish Common Sense Realism and Baconian induction, Warfield clearly saw Westcott-Hort's work as a boon to the defense of the faith. Finally, to Warfield, was the "really scientific method" to recover the infallible and inerrant autographic text.

Despite Letis' attempt to drive a wedge between Warfield and A. A. Hodge, he actually shows strong continuities between the two men. Like Warfield, Hodge was not so much worried about the method itself,

---

96. Bruce M. Metzger, *The Text of the New Testament: Its Transmission, Corruption, and Restoration* (New York: Oxford University Press, 1968), 129–37.
97. Letis, "B. B. Warfield, Common Sense Philosophy, and Biblical Criticism," 178–80.

as the "misuse" of the method. He makes clear that his concern is with "higher criticism" not "lower criticism" per se. This becomes apparent in the comment found in Hodge's work immediately preceding the citation adduced by Letis: "Ordinary historical criticism is a perfectly legitimate and necessary process by which all light, external and internal, afforded by history, literature and the intrinsic characteristics of the books or texts in question is collected." According to A. A. Hodge then, "We judge by means of the best evidence we have, what conclusions we have to draw in reference to their integrity, or the reverse."[98] These are almost precisely the exact concerns repeatedly expressed by Warfield during the early years of his career as professor of New Testament. Like Warfield, what worried Hodge was the *a priori* anti-supernatural presuppositions of skeptical critics, who used critical methodology to prove a point, rather than to discover truth. Warfield follows in A. A. Hodge's footsteps when he contends that the truth of Christianity is a matter of history, not faith.[99]

Whether one evaluates Warfield's efforts in these areas positively or negatively depends largely upon whether one is favorably inclined toward Scottish Common Sense Realism.[100] Unquestionably Warfield is consistent to the basic tenets of Baconian induction and Scottish Common Sense Realism. Recent scholarship has fleshed out the precise ways which the Scottish epistemology colored so many aspects of the Princeton school. Theodore Letis traces the overlooked influence of critical methodology upon Warfield's efforts to defend the truth of Christianity, and its effect on the fledgling doctrine of the inerrancy of the biblical autographs. Warfield saw absolutely no incongruity between the new critical methodology that he likely learned first-hand in Germany as part of a long standing Princeton tradition, and Scottish Common Sense epistemology. In fact, Warfield, as the young professor of New Testament, saw this as a marriage made in apologetics heaven. Since truth can only be uncovered via the inductive method and through the gathering and elucidation of factual evidence, whatever tools that enabled this process to go forth were quickly enlisted to aid in the task of defending the truth of Christianity as the "absolute religion." Textual criticism was seen as a valuable and neutral science, which would enable scholars to at long last reach the autographic text

98. A. A. Hodge, *Evangelical Theology*, 66.

99. See Hodge and Warfield, *Inspiration*, 8.

100. McClanahan, "Benjamin B. Warfield: Historian in Defense of Orthodoxy," 45–46.

of Scripture. Thus he championed this new science when appropriate safeguards were maintained.

Warfield, the Scottish Common Sense Realist, was quick to point out the problems with the radical anti-supernaturalism of the skeptical Germans and the emerging Protestant liberalism in America. Criticism itself is not the enemy of faith, but the "so-called" criticism, which is a cover for the blatant attack upon the foundational historical events of Christianity. Warfield, the young professor of New Testament, also passionately defended the Westminster Standards against all comers. In defending the faith, Warfield will never be far from the pages of the New Testament. Indeed, we risk misunderstanding much of Warfield's work in the field of apologetics, if we fail to keep his lifelong interests in New Testament studies in view.

4

Apologetics

WARFIELD'S CONTINUING INFLUENCE

Even though B. B. Warfield died in 1921, over 70 years later his name still evokes a surprising amount of discussion in the ongoing debate among evangelicals over apologetic methodology. Norman Geisler, for example, contends that his own volume *Christian Apologetics* "is in essence the approach used by the old Princetonian theologians like Warfield."[1] John Gerstner and R. C. Sproul offer what some consider to be a kind of Old Princeton apologetic *redivivus* in their work *Classical Apologetics*.[2]

While there are those who appeal to Warfield as a positive example of apologetic methodology, others adamantly reject his approach to defending the faith. Alvin Plantinga, for example, contends that the

1. Norman L. Geisler, *Christian Apologetics* (Grand Rapids: Baker Book House, 1976), 7. This is a most debatable point indeed since Geisler is an Arminian and a dispensationalist and his book bears little if any resemblance to Warfield's apologetic methodology as set out in the balance of this chapter.

2. See R. C. Sproul, John Gerstner, and Arthur Lindsley, *Classical Apologetics: A Rational Defense of the Christian Faith and a Critique of Presuppositionalism* (Grand Rapids: Zondervan, 1984). It must be pointed out that Sproul *et al* make no direct connection between this work and Old Princeton's distinctive apologetic, but the authors' fondness for "Old Princeton" is clear in several related articles. See for example: John H. Gerstner, "Warfield's Case for Biblical Inerrancy," in *God's Inerrant Word* (ed. John W. Montgomery; Minneapolis: Bethany Fellowship, 1974), 115–42; and "The Contributions of Charles Hodge, B. B. Warfield, and J. Gresham Machen to the Doctrine of Inspiration," in *Challenges to Inerrancy: A Theological Response* (ed. Gordon R. Lewis and Bruce Demarest; Chicago: Moody Press, 1984), 347–81. Certain affinities between *Classical Apologetics* and the "Old-Princeton" apologetic have also been noted. See James Samuel McClanahan, "Benjamin B. Warfield: Historian of Doctrine in Defense of Orthodoxy, 1881-1921" (Ph.D. diss.: Union Theological Seminary in Virginia, 1988), 40–46. As I will argue in this chapter, however, the primary affinity between them is the rejection of the Kuyper–Van Til apologetic, since Warfield's methodology is in practice, if not in substance, quite different from that of Sproul and Gerstner.

Reformed tradition has steered clear of apologetic efforts grounded in natural theology, and singles out Warfield as an example of a Reformed thinker who endorses the classical theistic proofs.[3] Cornelius Van Til,

3. Alvin Plantinga, "The Reformed Objection to Natural Theology," in *Rationality in the Calvinian Tradition* (eds. Hendrik Hart, Johan Van Der Hoeven, and Nicholas Wolterstorff; Lanham: University Press of America, 1983), 363. Plantinga's comments about Warfield are placed within the context of certain thinkers that are described as "within and without officially Catholic philosophy." These include Anselm, Aquinas, Scotus, Occam, Descartes, Spinoza, and Leibnitz. Plantinga follows this assertion by citing Herman Bavinck's comments to the effect that a believer's knowledge of God does not depend upon the so-called "proofs," but is instead based upon faith. It is implied that Warfield cannot hold to his apologetic methodology and remain a "consistent Calvinist," as thinkers who advocate these classical proofs are "Catholic," or hold to a "Catholic philosophy," and would likely deny the Reformed understanding of the noetic effects of sin. A second and related point is that Warfield's method is derived from thinkers, such as Thomas Aquinas, who are accused of exalting human reason above special revelation. This raises several observations about Plantinga's treatment of Warfield, which as we will see, is quite typical of much of the contemporary Reformed critique of Warfield. In the first place, the source of Warfield's basic epistemological method, as has been shown, is not that of classical Thomism or "official Catholic philosophy," but is instead indebted to the intuitional realism of Scottish Common Sense Philosophy, inherited in part from Thomas Reid but especially from James McCosh. This is the same Thomas Reid who Plantinga admits has exerted a great deal of influence in his own thinking (see "The Foundations of Theism: A Reply" in *Faith and Philosophy*, vol. 3, no. 3 (July 1986), 303–06.). If Warfield cannot be a "consistent Calvinist" because he adopts Reid's variety of foundationalism, then neither can Plantinga. Unfortunately, *ad hominem* arguments cut both ways. It must also be demonstrated that Warfield is outside of the traditional Reformed understanding of the necessary and complementary relationship between general and special revelation, in which both natural and supernatural revelation are present because of God's revelatory activity in making himself known to humanity through both of these media. Warfield affirms this necessary and complementary relationship in several places. For two very clear examples of Warfield's care in making these precise points, see: "The Biblical Idea of Revelation," in *Inspiration and Authority of the Bible* (Phillipsburg: P&R Publishing, 1948), 71–102, and "God," *A Dictionary of the Bible* (ed. John D. Davis; Philadelphia: Westminster Press, 1898), repr. in *Studies in Theology* (Grand Rapids: Baker Book House, 1981), 109–14. In response to the second implication, it has been shown that according to Common Sense epistemology, reason is merely a tool which by virtue of the *imago Dei* enables humanity to apprehend and use the *prior* revelation of God. This in no way means that Warfield treats reason as the *principium* of Christian theology, since reason only apprehends revelation and does not supplant it. It is unfortunate that the method of critique used by many contemporary Reformed apologists in their treatment of "Old-Princeton," whatever Princeton's virtues or liabilities may be, amounts to accusations of "Thomism." This *ad hominem* approach has been effectively critiqued in Arvin Vos' work, *Aquinas, Calvin, & Contemporary Protestant Thought* (Grand Rapids: Eerdmans, 1985).

late professor of apologetics at Westminster Theological Seminary and, ironically, in many ways the heir to the Old Princeton apologetic, overtly rejects Warfield's methodology. He categorically states "I have chosen the position of Abraham Kuyper."[4] Van Til even goes so far as to call Warfield's methodology inherently "Arminian."[5] This is quite surprising since virtually all interpreters of Warfield would agree with John J. Markarian's assessment that Warfield is above all things the "very Calvinist professor."[6]

This disparity, both from within the Reformed tradition, and without, is based upon several factors. First, as James S. McClanahan has pointed out, opinions are often "determined by whether one is positively or negatively inclined toward Scottish Realism. If one is opposed to it, one's criticism of the Princetonians will be more sharp than if one is, even with critical sympathy, disposed to certain tenets of it."[7] Second, Warfield never produced a single book or major journal-length treatment on apologetic methodology. Warfield's efforts in the field of apologetics are scattered throughout numerous articles, book introductions

4. See Cornelius Van Til, *The Defense of the Faith* (Grand Rapids: Baker Book House, 1967), 264–65. It must be noted that Van Til himself expresses reservations about certain aspects of Kuyper's apologetic—or lack thereof. See *Defense of the Faith*, 286 ff. Nevertheless, I am of the opinion that Van Til's method is much closer to Kuyper than Warfield and is in essence a modified version of Kuyper rather than a kind of *via media* between Princeton and Amsterdam.

5. See Cornelius Van Til, *The Protestant Doctrine of Scripture* (n.p.: den Dulk Foundation, 1967), 57.

6. John Jacob Markarian, "The Calvinistic Concept of the Biblical Revelation in the Theology of B. B. Warfield," (Ph.D. diss., Drew University, 1963), 40. Markarian concludes that "Warfield is clearly in the stream of Calvin's thought. ... [He] is like Calvin in his thinking on all the following points: regeneration is the beginning of the spiritual life; it is important to distinguish between infused and imputed righteousness in justification; and there is necessary an inviolable union of what Christ does for man and what Christ does in man (pp. 73–74)."

7. McClanahan, "Benjamin B. Warfield: Historian of Doctrine in Defense of Orthodoxy, 1881–1921," 45–46. As we have seen in chapter 2, champions of Reformed epistemology finds much of value in Thomas Reid (except in the area of natural theology), while Cornelius Van Til and Reformed presuppositionalists find the relationship between Reid and the Princeton theologians problematic (a theme discussed in chapter 7). Paul Helseth ably defends Warfield against the charge of rationalism, because of the stress in Warfield's thought on the subjective elements of knowing mitigate the negative influence of "Enlightment Rationalism." Nevertheless, the apologetic arguments which Warfield actually uses clearly reflect those tests for truth typical of SCSR (the point will be discussed further here and in chapter 7). See Paul Kjoss Helseth, *"Right Reason" and the Princeton Mind: An Unorthodox Proposal* (Phillipsburg: P&R Publishing, 2010), xxiv, 66–72.

and reviews written over a period of many years.[8] In addition, Warfield produced several other major articles that contain important collateral materials that have a direct bearing on his overall apologetic efforts.[9]

---

8. See, for example, in chronological order: "The Resurrection of Christ a Historical Fact, Evinced by Eye-witnesses," in *Journal of Christian Philosophy* III (April 1884), 305–18, and reprinted in *Selected Shorter Writings*, vol. 1 (ed. John H. Meeter; Nutley: P&R Publishing, 1970), 178–92; "Christian Evidences: How Affected by Recent Criticisms," in *Homiletic Review* XVI (August 1888), 107–12, and reprinted in *Selected Shorter Writings*, vol. 2 (ed. John H. Meeter; Nutley: P&R Publishing, 1973), 124–31; "Darwin's Arguments against Christianity and Against Religion," in *Homiletic Review* XVII (January 1889), and reprinted in *Selected Shorter Writings*, vol. 2, 132–41; "How to Get Rid of Christianity," in *The Bible Student* I (March 1900), 121–27, and reprinted in *Selected Shorter Writings*, vol. 1, 51–60; "Christianity the Truth," in *The Bible Student* III (January 1901), 1–5, and reprinted in *Selected Shorter Writings*, vol. 2, 332–38; "Introductory Note," to Francis Beattie's *Apologetics*, vol. 1 (Richmond: Presbyterian Committee on Publications, 1903), 19–32, and reprinted in *Selected Shorter Writings*, vol. 2, 93–105; "The Question of Miracles," in *The Bible Student*, VII (March, April, May, June 1903), 121–26, 193–97, 243–50, 314–20, and reprinted in *Selected Shorter Writings*, Vol. 2, pp. 167–204; "Review of Herman Bavinck's *De Zekerheid des Geloofs*," in *Princeton Theological Review* I (Jan 1903), 138–48, and reprinted in *Selected Shorter Writings*, vol. 2, 106–123; and "Apologetics," *New Schaff-Herzog Encyclopedia of Religious Knowledge* (ed. S. M. Jackson; New York: Funk & Wagnalls, 1908), I, 232–38, and reprinted in *Studies in Theology* (Grand Rapids: Baker Book House, 1981), 3–21.

9. These include the two major articles Warfield produced on faith: "Faith," in *Dictionary of the Bible* (ed. James Hastings; Edinburgh: Clark, 1898), I, 827–38 and reprinted in *Biblical Doctrines*, as "The Biblical Doctrine of Faith," pp. 467–508; and "On Faith in its Psychological Aspects," in *Princeton Theological Review* IX (October 1911), 537–66, and reprinted in *Studies in Theology* (Grand Rapids: Baker Book House, 1981), 313–42. In addition, Warfield produced major articles on Calvin's and Augustine's doctrine of the knowledge of God. Both of these have bearing on his own apologetic thought. See "Calvin's Doctrine of the Knowledge of God," in *Princeton Theological Review* VII (April 1909), 219–325, and reprinted in *Calvin and Augustine* (Grand Rapids: Baker Book House, 1956), 29–130; "Augustine's Doctrine of Knowledge and Authority," in *Princeton Theological Review* (July, October 1907), 353–97, 529–78, and reprinted in *Calvin and Augustine*, 387–477. There are other articles related to Warfield's historical-evidential apologetic. These include: "The Real Problem of Inspiration," in *Presbyterian and Reformed Review* IV (April 1893), 171–221, and reprinted in *The Inspiration and Authority of the Bible*, 169–226; "Revelation," in *The International Standard Bible Encyclopedia*, Vol. 4 (ed. James Orr; Chicago: Howard-Severance, 1915), 2573–82, and reprinted as "The Biblical Idea of Revelation," in *Inspiration and Authority of the Bible*, 71–102; "The Inspiration of the Bible," in *Bibliotheca Sacra* LI (October 1894), 614–40, and reprinted as "The Church Doctrine of Inspiration," in *The Inspiration and Authority of the Bible*, 105–28; and "Inspiration," in *The International Standard Bible Encyclopedia*, vol. 3, 1473–83, and reprinted as "The Biblical Idea of Inspiration," in *The Inspiration and Authority of the Bible*, 131–66.

Third, there is a marked absence of secondary source treatment of Warfield's apologetic methodology.[10]

There are several possible ways to assess Warfield's approach toward defending the faith. One may opt for a chronological approach but this is not fruitful, since Warfield's apologetic efforts do not change substantially over the course of his career. The various subjects with which he interacts follow a rather broad and evolving pattern, however. Wilber Wallis has argued that various theological challenges bring "stages of emphasis," which develop throughout Warfield's career. These begin in the 1880's with "apologetic foundations in revelation and inspiration."

---

10. The notable exception is Helseth's *"Right Reason" and the Princeton Mind: An Unorthodox Proposal.* Remarkably, there is only one doctoral dissertation that deals directly with Warfield's apologetic methodology and it is, in my opinion, quite deficient. See William D. Livingstone, "The Princeton Apologetic as Exemplified by the Work of Benjamin B. Warfield and J. Gresham Machen: A Study in American Theology 1880–1930," (Ph.D. diss., Yale University, 1948). In addition, there are several doctoral dissertations that treat Warfield's apologetic methodology indirectly. These include: John Markarian, "The Calvinistic Concept of the Biblical Revelation in the Theology of B. B. Warfield"; Clyde Norman Krause, "The Principle of Authority in the Theology of B. B. Warfield, William Adams Brown, and Gerald Birney Smith," (Ph.D. diss., Duke University, 1961); Peter Maarten van Bemmelen, "Issues in Biblical Inspiration: Sanday and Warfield," (Th.D. diss., Andrews University, 1987); and James McClanahan, "Benjamin B. Warfield: Historian of Doctrine in Defense of Orthodoxy, 1881–1921." It must also be pointed out that while there are no book-length or monograph treatments of Warfield's apologetic method and thought, there are several substantial discussions of Warfield in volumes not devoted specifically to him. These include: Mark A. Noll, *The Princeton Theology, 1812–1921* (Grand Rapids: Baker Book House, 1983), which contains a treatment of Warfield's apologetic method, see especially pages 241–316; Jack Rogers and Donald McKim, *The Authority and Interpretation of the Bible: An Historical Approach* (San Francisco: Harper & Row, 1979), 323–61; Cornelius Van Til, *A Christian Theory of Knowledge* (Nutley; P&R Publishing, 1977), especially pages 235–55; and *Defense of the Faith*, 260–99. There are no treatments of Warfield's methodology in the standard evangelical apologetic surveys such as Bernard Ramm's *Varieties of Apologetic Systems* (Grand Rapids: Baker Book House, 1979), or Gordon Lewis' *Testing Christianity's Truth Claims* (Chicago: Moody Press, 1976). In addition, there are few journal-length articles devoted exclusively to Warfield's apologetic, although several include peripheral treatments which are helpful. These include: Darryl G. Hart, "The Princeton Mind in the Modern World and the Common Sense of J. Gresham Machen," *The Westminster Theological Journal* 46 (1984), 1–25; Paul Kjoss Helseth, "B. B. Warfield's Apologetical Appeal to 'Right Reason': Evidence of a Rather Bald Rationalism?" *The Scottish Bulletin of Evangelical Theology*, 16, 2 (Autumn 1998), 156–77; John H. Gerstner, "Warfield's Case for Biblical Inerrancy," 115–142, and "The Contributions of Charles Hodge, B. B. Warfield, and J. Gresham Machen to the Doctrine of Inspiration," 347–81; and Wilber B. Wallis, "Benjamin B. Warfield: Didactic and Polemical Theologian, Part II" *Presbyterion: Covenant Seminary Review*, 3 (April 1977), 73–94.

The pattern continues in the 1890's with apologetic development of the "historical origins of Christianity," in response to the rise of German rationalism and mysticism. By the turn of the century, Warfield was devoting his energies to Christology. During the last 10 years of his life, he focused on responding to errors regarding the application of redemption, primarily in his response to "perfectionism."[11] Nevertheless, the inductive and evidentialist methodology Warfield uses remains remarkably consistent.

Another approach is to evaluate each of Warfield's major articles and reviews that specifically discuss apologetics, and then summarize Warfield's overall thought. The problem with approaching the materials in this manner is that Warfield never intended any of these articles to be part of a larger systematic treatment. A topical approach is the third and best option. By examining one-by-one the various apologetic themes, beginning with his most thorough article addressing the subject, in which Warfield defines terms and spells out in outline form his overall approach to defending the faith, one can see his apologetical framework. This approach provides a context from which to treat Warfield's infrequent statements regarding the classical proofs, his highly developed evidential-historical arguments for the resurrection, and the arguments he adduces for the inspiration and authority of the Bible. It also provides a format in which the collateral materials may be related to each individual topic.

THE NATURE AND SCOPE OF APOLOGETICS

B. B. Warfield's most complete discussion of apologetic methodology is found in the article "Apologetics," originally written in 1908, for *The New Schaff-Herzog Encyclopedia of Religious Knowledge*. Warfield begins by making an important distinction between "apologies," which are specific individual defenses of Christianity and that of "apologetics," which is a positive science devoted "not [to] the defense, not even the vindication, but the establishment ... of that knowledge of God which Christianity professes to embody."[12] Apologetics is not merely a defense of the Christian truth claim, but is, in fact, the basis for that claim of which

11. Wallis, "Benjamin B. Warfield: Didactic and Polemical Theologian," 73.
12. Warfield, "Apologetics," 3. Warfield elsewhere expresses his belief that Calvin's *Institutes* has such an "apologetical construction" with its stress upon the knowledge of God, and which Warfield argues actually constitutes "for the first time in the history of Christian theology ... in outline that plan of a complete structure of

"it is the business of theology scientifically to explicate."[13] Accordingly, though vindicating the Christian truth claim in response to opponents is a necessary activity, it is incidental to the positive task of apologetics. On this scheme, individual "apologies" are contained within the broader discipline of apologetics.

For Warfield, apologetics is an offensive, rather than defensive, science. "So little is defense or vindication of the essence of apologetics that there would be the same reason for its existence and the same necessity for its work, were there no opposition in the world to be encountered and no contradiction to be overcome."[14] Apologetics therefore is an essential element of theological prolegomena. Since apologetics is assigned a positive and constructive role, the defensive posture can be avoided. The problem with a defensive approach is that individual "apologies" may be left to develop in isolation in both form and content "from the prevailing opposition."[15] In other words, individual "apologies" are shaped by the external forces opposing Christianity and do not reflect the discipline's true agenda, which is to establish the knowledge of God. Apologetics must be understood as a "constructive science" with any necessary refutation of opposing views seen as incidental. Warfield likely would approve the saying, "the best defense is a good offense." In his review of Herman Bavinck's *De Zekerheid des Geloofs* (1903), Warfield clearly expresses this point:

> But we are arguing that Apologetics has its part to play in the Christianizing of the world: and that this part is not a small part: nor is it merely a subsidiary or defensive part—as if its one end were to protect an isolated body of Christians from annoyance from the surrounding world. It has a primary part to play and a conquering part. ... In the face of the world, with its opposing points of view and its tremendous energy of thought and incredible fertility in attack and defense, Christianity must think through and organize its, not defense merely, but assault. It has been placed in the world to reason its way to the dominion of the world. And it is by reasoning its way that it has come to its

Christian Apologetics." See also Warfield, "Calvin's Doctrine of the Knowledge of God," 30.

13. Ibid., 3.
14. Ibid., 4.
15. Ibid.

> kingship. By reasoning it will gather to itself all its own. And by reasoning it will put its enemies under its feet.[16]

Positive and constructive apologetics "finds its deepest ground ... not in the accidents which accompany the efforts of true religion to plant, sustain, and propagate itself in this world; not even in the most pervasive and portentous of all these accidents, the accident of sin." Its deepest ground is simply "the fundamental needs of the human spirit."[17] This emphasis can be directly traced to the epistemology of Scottish Common Sense Realism. Thomas Reid's view of human nature and epistemology posits that necessary and contingent first principles are foundational for all subsequent human knowledge.

Warfield's comments echo these beliefs regarding necessary and contingent truths. By virtue of the *imago Dei*, man has the capacity for knowledge. The content of that knowledge is the general and special revelation given by God, embodied in the truths of Christianity, which apologetics seeks to establish. Because Christianity is based upon an objective revelation, both in the natural order and in the supernatural revelation embodied in Holy Scripture, knowledge can be established. "If it is incumbent on the believer to be able to give a reason for the faith that is in him," (see 1 Peter 3:15) then "it is impossible for him to be a believer without a reason for the faith that is in him; and it is the task of apologetics to bring this reason clearly out in his conscience, and make its validity plain."[18] This same point is found in Warfield's article "The Biblical Doctrine of Faith," (1905) where Warfield writes that:

> It is, accordingly, solely from its object that faith derives its value. ... Jesus Christ, God the Redeemer, is accordingly the one object of saving faith, presented to its embrace at first implicitly and in promise, and ever more and more openly until at last it is entirely explicit and we read that "a man is not justified save through faith in Jesus Christ."[19]

Faith, then, is complete trust in Jesus Christ, about whom one must possess objective knowledge. Warfield's introduction to Francis Beattie's *Apologetics* (1903), discusses the key role of evidences:

16. Warfield, "A Review of *De Zekerheid des Geloofs*," 120–21.
17. Warfield, "Apologetics," 4.
18. Ibid.
19. Warfield, "The Biblical Doctrine of Faith," 502–03.

> We are arguing that faith is, in all its exercises alike, a form of conviction, and is, therefore necessarily grounded in evidence. And we are arguing that evidence accordingly has its part to play in the conversion of the soul; and that systematically organized evidence which we call Apologetics similarly has its part to play in the Christianizing of the world.[20]

There can be no proper exercise of faith until a ground for faith has been established. "In other words," writes Warfield, "it is the function of apologetics to investigate, explicate, and establish the grounds on which a theology—a science, or systematic knowledge of God is possible."[21] Apologetics assumes a vital role in theological prolegomena and "necessarily takes its place at the head of the departments of theological science and finds its task in the establishment of the validity of that knowledge of God which forms the subject-matter of these other departments."[22]

One of the chronic problems that must be corrected, Warfield believes, is the confusion that has existed about the function and place of apologetics. "Nearly every writer has a definition"—including Warfield—"of the discipline in a fashion more or less peculiar to himself. ... There is scarcely a corner in the theological encyclopedia into which it has not been thrust."[23] Often there is no clear distinction made between apologetics as a comprehensive theological discipline, and individual apologies themselves. If no careful distinction is made, "apologies" can be assigned to virtually any place in the theological encyclopedia from homiletics to practical theology.[24] He singles out Dutch theologian

---

20. Warfield, "Introductory Note to Francis Beattie's *Apologetics*," 99. When Warfield boldly asserts that faith (in the biblical sense) is a conviction necessarily grounded in evidence, he is reflecting SCSR's antipathy toward epistemological skepticism, and/or those theories of "ideas" which would argue that faith is to be conceived of as something purely subjective (or irrational). Reid argues this point in many places, and his understanding of evidence as the basis for knowing (not "perception") is effectively summarized in: John Greco, "Reid's Reply to the Skeptic" in Terrance Cuneo and René Van Woudenberg, *The Cambridge Companion to Thomas Reid* (Cambridge: Cambridge University Press, 2004), 134–55.

21. Ibid.

22. Ibid. This role of apologetics as the basis for other theological disciplines is also spelled out in Warfield's treatment of systematic theology, in "The Idea of Systematic Theology," (1896) in *Studies in Theology* (Grand Rapids: Baker Book House, 1981), 41–87.

23. Ibid., 5.

24. Ibid.

Abraham Kuyper and fellow Princeton Theological Seminary faculty member Francis L. Patton as examples of those who fail to make such distinctions.[25] According to Warfield, Kuyper errs by "distinguishing between polemics, elenctics, and apologetics, opposing respectively heterodoxy, paganism and false philosophy."[26] This results in a confusing relationship, allowing each discipline to be set out as a distinct entity, only to be rejoined "to form a larger whole to which is given the same encyclopedic position. ... [The] 'antithetic dogmatological' group of disciplines."[27] Five years earlier, in the "Introduction" to Beattie's *Apologetics*, Warfield lamented that Kuyper was "one of the really great theologians of our day, [who] is a very striking instance" of those who disparage the use of Christian evidences in apologetics. He pointedly wrote:

> It is not to be supposed that Dr. Kuyper would abolish Apologetics altogether. He has written an *Encyclopedia of Sacred Theology*, and in it he gives a place to Apologetics among the other disciplines. But how subordinate a place! And in what a curtailed form! Hidden away in a subdivision of a subdivision of what Dr. Kuyper calls the "Dogmatological Group" of disciplines (which corresponds roughly to what most encyclopaedists call "systematic theology"), one has to search for it before he finds it, and when he finds it, he discovers that its function is confined closely, we might almost say jealously, to the narrow task of defending developed Christianity against philosophy, falsely so called. ... The least of these [disciplines] is Apologetics, which concerns itself only with the distinctively philosophical assault on Christianity. Meanwhile, as for Christianity itself, it has remained up to this point—let us say it frankly—the great assumption.[28]

Another factor which drives the diversity of views is the problem of identifying the actual object that apologetics should establish. "Whether it be, for example, the truth of Christian religion, or the validity of that knowledge of God which theology presents in a systematized form,"[29] the object in view will ultimately determine the way in which

25. See the illuminating discussion of Patton's apologetic methodology in Bradley J. Gundlach, "The Evolution Question at Princeton, 1845–1929" (Ph.D. diss., University of Rochester, 1995), 227–39.
26. Warfield, "Apologetics," 6.
27. Ibid.
28. Warfield, "Introductory Note to Francis Beattie's *Apologetics*," 95–96.
29. Warfield, "Apologetics," 6.

apologetics itself is defined and how it is related to theology. Warfield is very straightforward: "If we think of apologetics as undertaking the defense or the vindication or even the justification of the 'Christian religion,' that is one thing." But "if we think of it as undertaking the establishment of the validity of that knowledge of God, which 'theology' systematizes," our understanding will differ.[30] If theology is understood in a subjective sense as the science of faith, then the practical effect is that "its subject-matter is the subjective experience in the human heart; and the function of apologetics is to inquire whether these subjective experiences have any objective validity."[31] If we define theology as the science of religion, wherein theology is merely descriptive, "investigat[ing] the purely historical question of what those who are called Christians believe," apologetics will be defined along the lines of an investigatory process through which it is determined whether Christians are "justified in believing these things." Warfield will not accept either definition of theology or the resulting apologetic approach.

> But if theology is the science of God, it deals not with a mass of subjective experiences, nor with a section of the history of thought, but with a body of objective facts; and it is absurd to say that these facts must be assumed and developed unto their utmost implications before we stop and ask whether they are facts. So soon is it agreed that theology is a scientific discipline and has as its subject-matter the knowledge of God, we must recognize that it must begin by establishing the reality as objective facts of the data upon which it is based.[32]

Warfield's allegiance to Common Sense Realism is readily apparent in such comments. He maintains a great stress upon the historical

30. Ibid.

31. Ibid., 7.

32. Ibid. This approach also surfaces in Warfield's treatment of inspiration. In the essay, cited earlier, "The Church Doctrine of Inspiration," originally published in 1894, Warfield writes that "the supernatural origin and contents of Christianity, not only may be vindicated apart from any question of the inspiration of the record, but, in point of fact, always are vindicated prior to any question of the inspiration of the record. We cannot raise the question whether God has given us an absolutely trustworthy record of the supernatural facts and teachings of Christianity, before we are assured that there are supernatural facts and teaching to be recorded. The fact that Christianity is a supernatural religion and the nature of Christianity as a supernatural religion, are matters of history; and are independent of any, and of every, theory of inspiration (p. 121)."

objectivity of the redemptive events described in Scripture. This underlying epistemological structure can be seen throughout Warfield's efforts to develop an effective historical-evidential apologetic.

As far as the appropriate nomenclature for the discipline, Warfield admits that "natural theology," "rational theology," or "philosophical theology" are each technically acceptable, but "Apologetics is the name which most naturally suggests itself ... and has been consecrated to this purpose."[33] Accordingly, "apologetics offers itself with equal readiness to designate the discipline by which the validity of the knowledge of God set forth is established," whether that be the general revelation of God given through the natural order, or through "the full revelation of God as documented in Scripture."[34] Warfield adds that the designation "apologetics" is in fact superior because "it need imply no more than natural theology requires for its basis." But "when the theology which [apologetics] serves is ... the complete theology of the Christian revelation, it guards its unity and protects from the fatally dualistic conception which sets natural and revealed theology over against each other as separable entities." If a dualistic understanding of general and special revelation is allowed, each category would require separate treatment since each would have separate presuppositions. This allows apologetics to be "split into two quite diverse disciplines, [and] given very different places in the theological encyclopedia."[35]

Since apologetics is defined as the theological science devoted to establishing the knowledge of God, then the truth claim presented becomes an exclusive one. "Apologetics certainly does establish the truth of Christianity as the absolute religion."[36] "How does apologetics do this?" Warfield asks. He answers this question by arguing, "It is certainly not the business of apologetics to take up each tenet of Christianity in turn and seek to establish its truth by a direct appeal to reason."[37] Rejecting the "old vulgar rationalism," Warfield follows a sophisticated form of the inductive method inherited from McCosh's variety of Scottish Common Sense Realism throughout his discussion of apologetics.[38] "We are not

33. Ibid., 7–8.
34. Ibid. 8
35. Ibid.
36. Ibid.
37. Ibid.
38. This point can be clearly demonstrated in response to some of Warfield's critics. William D. Livingstone, for example, concludes that Warfield's apologetic methodology was so utterly rationalistic that it equated theological truth with mathematical

truth. This contention is completely unjustified. See, for example, Livingstone, "The Princeton Apologetic as Exemplified by the Work of B. B. Warfield and J. Gresham Machen," 342; and Mark A. Massa, *Charles Augustus Briggs and the Crisis of Historical Criticism* (Minneapolis: Fortress, 1990), 59 ff. There is also a helpful discussion of this question of methodology in Peter M. van Bemmelen, "Issues in Biblical Inspiration: Sanday and Warfield," (313–27). While correctly defending Warfield against charges that he was a "deductivist," van Bemmelen engages in a lengthy discourse on the issue of the compatibility of induction and deduction, concluding that Warfield was "inductive" in method, even though he used deduction at times. The discussion is clouded by the failure to acknowledge that use of the "inductive" method refers primarily to the direction of methodology applied—in induction, the process of evaluation moves from particulars to universals, in which deduction must be used at virtually every step of the way in the actual comparison of individual "particulars" to be evaluated in forming a "universal." The "inductive method" should not be seen to preclude any use of "deductive" logical conclusions in the process of the broader move from particulars to universals—the use of inductive method (in this broad sense) involves deduction. We should not be surprised that such a consistent inductivist as Warfield does in fact use deductive logic in formulating conclusions. Warfield's adherence to the inductive method in apologetics is clearly demonstrated in the essay "The Real Problem of Inspiration" (1893). Warfield moves from the data (specific biblical assertions) to a formulation which he feels best explains the data in question (the doctrine of "plenary" inspiration). He then spells out the degree of certitude attached to the underlying foundation of the data itself (the truth of the original assertion that Christianity does possess a revelation of God—apologetics). "Let it not be said that in speaking thus we are refusing the inductive method of establishing doctrine. We follow the inductive method. When we approach the Scriptures to ascertain their doctrine of inspiration, we proceed by collecting the whole body of relevant facts. ... The evidence for the truth of the doctrine of the plenary inspiration of Scripture is just the whole body of evidence which goes to show that the apostles are trustworthy teachers of doctrine. ... All these doctrines stand as supported by the same weight and amount of evidence—the evidence of the trustworthiness of the biblical writers as teachers of doctrine. ... Inspiration is not the most fundamental of Christian doctrines, nor even the first thing we prove about the Scriptures. It is the last and crowning fact as to the Scriptures. These we first prove authentic, historically credible, generally trustworthy, before we prove them inspired (pp. 205–210)." Whether one agrees with Warfield's interpretation of what the apostolic doctrine of the character of Scripture actually reveals, is another question entirely. Clearly, Warfield is not operating in a deductive and rationalistic manner, but in a carefully formulated inductive fashion. As for the degree of certitude that Warfield applied to such apologetical-historical foundations upon which he based theological doctrines such as inspiration, Warfield wrote, "Of course, this evidence is not in the strict logical sense 'demonstrable'; it is 'probable' evidence. It therefore leaves open the metaphysical possibility of its being mistaken. But it may be contended that it is about as great in amount and weight as 'probable' evidence can be made, and that the strength of conviction which is adapted to produce may and should be practically equal to that produced by demonstration itself (pp. 218–219)." There are several additional treatments of this. See: William J. Abraham, *Divine Inspiration* (New York: Oxford University Press), 1981; and D. A. Carson's to begin by developing Christianity into all its details, and only after this task has been performed, tardily ask whether there is any truth in all this."[39] On the contrary, "we are to begin by establishing the truth of Christianity as a whole, and only then proceed to explicate it into its details, each of which if soundly explicated, has its truth guaranteed by its place as a detail in an entity already established in its entirety."[40]

Warfield argues that if this point is clearly understood, one of the nagging questions raised about apologetics as a theological discipline can be eliminated. Do we deal with the details of Christianity or merely its essence? The answer is neither. "Apologetics does not presuppose either the development of Christianity into its details, or the extraction from it of its essence. The details of Christianity are all contained in Christianity: The minimum of Christianity is Christianity itself."[41] If Christianity is the "absolute" religion, its details and its essence are contained within its "absoluteness." Apologetics, therefore, "has for its object the laying of the foundations upon which the temple of theology is built, and by which the structure of theology is determined."

Apologetics is, therefore, virtually synonymous with theological prolegomena:

> It is the department of theology which establishes the constitutive and regulative principles of theology as a science; and in establishing these it establishes all the details which are derived from them by the succeeding departments in their sound explication and systematization. Thus it establishes the whole, though it establishes the whole in the mass, so to speak, and not in its details, but yet in its entirety and not in some single element deemed by us its core, its essence, or its minimum expression.[42]

Thus, once apologetics has established that Christianity possesses a knowledge of God, one has established Christianity as the "absolute" religion in its whole and all of its constituent parts. The theologian can now proceed to do the work of explication and systematization.

"Review" of Abraham's book in *The Journal of the Evangelical Theological Society*, vol. 26, no. 3 (Sept 1983), 337; and Kern Robert Trembath, *Evangelical Theories of Biblical Inspiration: A Review and Proposal* (New York: Oxford University Press, 1983), 20–27.

39. Warfield, "Apologetics," 8.
40. Ibid., 9.
41. Ibid.
42. Ibid.

Once the subject matter of apologetics has been defined, Warfield moves to detail the actual individual elements that compose the discipline. Since apologetics has been defined as "the proof of the Christian religion," it has been commonplace to treat apologetics merely as "the evidences of Christianity." However, since apologetics takes on a foundational character, it may also be called "fundamental theology." Some have, Warfield believes, "more justly combined the two conceptions."[43] Yet, because theology is understood as a science, there are three necessary elements that must be considered "as in the case of all sciences." The first element is "the reality of the subject-matter," the second is "the capacity of the human mind to receive into itself and rationally reflect this subject-matter," and the third, "the existence of media of communication between the subject-matter and the percipient and understanding mind."[44]

These correspond to God, religion, and revelation in theology and are clearly derived directly from Scottish epistemology with its distinction between necessary and contingent truths. Since there:

> ... can be no theology, conceived according to its very name as the science of God, unless there is a God to form its subject-matter, a capacity of the human mind to apprehend and so far to comprehend God, and some media by which God is made known to man. That a theology, as the science of God, may exist, therefore, it must begin by establishing the existence of God, the capacity of the human mind to know Him, and the accessibility of knowledge concerning Him. In other words, the very idea of theology as the science of God gives these three great topics which must be dealt

43. Ibid. Warfield is critical of Henry B. Smith's attempt to do this because, according to Warfield, Smith does not have a "firm hold upon the idea of the discipline" as some of his contemporaries. See Henry B. Smith, *Apologetics: A Course of Lectures* (New York: A. C. Armstrong & Son, 1882). Smith conceives of apologetics as: "(1) Vindication against assault; (2) Vindication which establishes the truth of Christianity and shows the falsity and error of the opponents; *i.e.*, which not only defends Christianity but attacks its foes. (3) It is scientific vindication. It vindicates in a scientific way, so as to include the apologies, so as to bring out the ultimate general principles in the case. (4) It gets from the whole course of conflict a brighter light in which to exhibit Christianity as the absolute religion (p. 3)."

44. Ibid., 11.

> with in its fundamental department, by which the foundations for the whole structure are laid—God, religion, revelation.[45]

Only after these three facts are established by apologetics can theology, as a science of God, even become possible. But while these three elements are necessary categories, they are not sufficient in themselves. Again following the inductive route, Warfield writes, "No science can arbitrarily limit the data lying within its sphere to which it will attend." A scientific discipline "must exhaust the means of information open to it, and reduce to a unitary system the entire body of knowledge within its sphere."[46] A science cannot truly represent itself as a science and then arbitrarily ignore important and relevant data. Using astronomy as an example, Warfield argues that it would be completely illegitimate for astronomy to be defined as a science if the data upon which it was based was limited to observation by the naked eye, particularly when information was also available from the spectroscope, and other more precise and effective methods of gathering data. This leads Warfield to conclude:

> In the presence of Christianity in the world making claim to present a revelation of God adapted to the condition and needs of sinners, and documented in the Scriptures, theology cannot proceed a step until it has examined this claim; and if this claim be substantiated, this substantiation must form a part of the fundamental department of theology in which are laid the foundations for the systematization of the knowledge of God. In that case, two new topics are added to the subject-matter with which apologetics must constructively deal, Christianity—and the Bible. It thus lies in the very nature of apologetics as the fundamental department of theology, conceived as the science of God, that it should find its task in establishing the existence of a God who is capable

45. Ibid. When discussing the same methodology in the "Introduction, to Beattie's *Apologetics*," Warfield clearly relates the problem of the knowledge of God to Reidian categories in the use of first principles. He writes, "We must assure ourselves that there is a knowledge of God in the Scriptures. And, before we do that, we must assure ourselves that there is a knowledge of God in the world. And, before we do that, we must assure ourselves that a knowledge of God is possible for man. And, before we do that, we must assure ourselves that there is a God to know. Thus we inevitably work back to first principles. And thus working back to first principles, we exhibit the indispensability of an 'Apologetical Theology,' which of necessity holds the place of the first among the five essential theological disciplines (p. 98)."
46. Ibid., 12.

> of being known by man and who has made himself known, not only in nature but in revelations of his grace to lost sinners, documented in the Christian Scriptures. When apologetics has placed these great facts in our hands—God, religion, revelation, Christianity, the Bible—and not till then are we prepared to go on and explicate the knowledge of God thus brought to us, trace the history of its workings in the world, systematize it, and propagate it in the world.[47]

Warfield proceeds by developing five distinct categories with which apologetics must deal. Warfield sets these out as "subdivisions," and qualifies the categories by noting that the third and fourth subdivisions are closely related, enough so that they may in fact be combined. The five "subdivisions" correspond directly to Warfield's assertion that there are three necessary, and two contingent categories, which establish apologetics as a science which is able to deal with all of the relevant data belonging to its proper jurisdiction.

The first subdivision is *"philosophical apologetics,"* which "undertakes the establishment of the being of God" and his divine attributes. This division deals with theism and, incidentally, with discussion of anti-theistic theories.[48] The second subdivision is *"psychological apologetics,"* which is devoted to establishing the "religious nature of man and the validity of his religious sense." Under this division would be subsumed "the psychology, the philosophy, and the phenomenology of religion, and therefore includes what is loosely called 'comparative religion' or the 'history of religions.' "[49] The third subdivision is the *"establishment of the reality of the supernatural factor in history."* This category deals primarily with the way in which God chooses to make himself known to men. The goal here "is the establishment of the fact of revelation as the condition of all knowledge of God, who as a personal spirit can be known only so far as He expresses Himself." This results in the uniqueness of theology as a science, wherein "the object is not at the disposal of the subject, but vice versa."[50] The fourth subdivision is *"historical apologetics."* Here the aim is the establishment of Christianity as a historical religion with a divine origin. Under this division naturally falls what

47. Ibid.
48. Ibid., 13.
49. Ibid.
50. Ibid.

is usually known as the department of Christian evidences.[51] The fifth subdivision is what Warfield calls "*bibliological apologetics*," which seeks to demonstrate "the trustworthiness of the Christian Scriptures as the documentation of the revelation of God for the redemption of sinners." The scope of bibliological apologetics includes "the divine origin of the Scriptures; the methods of divine operation in their origin ... and in the process of revelation; the nature, mode, and effect of inspiration."[52]

This structure reflects the inherited epistemology of Scottish Common Sense Realism, and is perfectly consistent with Common Sense formulations of truth claims. There is no evidence here of a latent Thomism, though the epistemologies of Reid and Thomas do intersect at points and may bear a familial resemblance to one another.[53] It is very important to note that Warfield's own apologetic interests do not lie in the area of philosophical apologetics. In fact, virtually all of his apologetic energies are spent in the establishment of the validity of special revelation. This point is particularly noticable when one observes that Warfield makes virtually no use of formal proofs for the existence of God in his own apologetic arguments.

THE "CLASSICAL" PROOFS FOR GOD'S EXISTENCE

In an article entitled "God," originally written for the *Davis Bible Dictionary* (1898), Warfield sets forth his most complete discussion of the so-called "classical proofs" associated with what is now commonly called "classical apologetics."[54] The context of that discussion is very important. Relating the knowledge of God derived from nature to the knowledge of God derived from special revelation, Warfield concludes that the primary human "idea of God" is summed up in the term "theism." The idea of God "is the product of that general revelation which God makes of Himself to all men, on the plane of nature." This is necessarily complemented by the Scriptures in which "the truths involved in it [general revelation in nature] are continually reiterated, enriched, and deepened." These truths "are not so much revealed by them as

51. Ibid.
52. Ibid., 13–14.
53. On the contrast between Reid's method and that of Aquinas, see Nicolas Wolterstorff, *Thomas Reid and the Story of Epistemology* (Cambridge: Cambridge University Press, 2001), 250–53. Wolterstorff speaks of Reid's "epistemological piety" as one of humility and active gratitude in contrast to that of Thomas.
54. See Sproul, *Classical Apologetics.*

presupposed at the foundation of special revelation with which the Scriptures busy themselves—the great revelation of the grace of God to sinners."[55] Warfield carefully asserts that natural revelation is limited to the fact that "men can only learn what God necessarily is, and what, by virtue of his essential attributes."[56] Natural revelation is also limited by the fact that "there is no hint of the Trinity," and "nature has nothing to say of redemption."[57] Thus, if humanity is to have true, though limited, knowledge of God as the Triune God of redemption, there must be a complementary role for general and special revelation. Warfield concludes:

> ... The nature of God has been made known to men, therefore, in three stages, corresponding to the three planes of revelation, and we will naturally come to know Him, first, as the infinite Spirit or the God of nature; then, as the Redeemer of sinners, or the God of grace; and lastly as the Father, Son, and Holy Ghost, or the Triune God.[58]

Thus, the carefully defined relationship between natural and special revelation becomes the basis for the historical/logical order of revelation. First, there is nature, which gives us the existence of God, and the determination of his invisible power and divine perfections—echoing Romans 1. Second, there is the history of redemption, beginning with the mysteries of the Old Testament economy, culminating in the manifestation of God in human flesh. And finally, there is the completed revelation of God, as found in the whole of Scripture itself, which reveals the Triune God. This constitutes Warfield's very brief discussion of the "proofs" themselves, and gives us a clue to the reason that they are so quickly set aside in apologetic debate for arguments supporting the resurrection.

In a section of the article titled, "God, The Infinite Spirit," Warfield contends that "the conviction of the existence of God bears the marks of an intuitive truth in so far as it is the universal and unavoidable belief of men, and is given in the very same act with the idea of self."[59] In words which could have been penned by Thomas Reid,[60] Warfield writes that

55. Warfield, "God," 109.
56. Ibid.
57. Ibid., 110.
58. Ibid.
59. Ibid.
60. Compare Thomas Reid, *Inquiry and Essays* (ed. Ronald E. Beanblossom and Keith Lehrer; Indianapolis: Hackett, 1983), 116–18. This whole section betrays

the existence of God is "at once dependent and responsible and thus implies one on whom it depends and to whom it is responsible." This is an "immediate perception," which is "confirmed and the contents of the ideas developed by a series of arguments known as the 'theistic proofs.' "[61]

> These [proofs] are derived from the necessity we are under of believing in the real existence of the infinitely perfect Being, of a sufficient cause for the contingent universe, of an intelligent author of order and of the manifold contrivances observable in nature, and of a lawgiver and judge for dependent moral beings, endowed with the sense of duty and an ineradicable feeling of responsibility, conscious of the moral contradictions of the world and craving a solution for them, and living under an intuitive perception of right which they do not see realized.[62]

Here, Warfield merely affirms the validity of the cosmological, teleological, and moral arguments for the existence of God, all presented in terminology echoing Scottish Common Sense defenses of the faith. Surprisingly, Warfield only mentions them in passing in his other apologetic writings, though he does endorse them when employed by others.[63]

He sees embodied in the special revelation of Scripture, "The cogency of these proofs is currently recognized in the Scriptures, while they add to them the supernatural manifestations of God in a redemptive process, accompanied at every stage by miraculous attestation."[64] Here we are given a hint of the primary apologetical interest of the

---

Warfield's epistemological dependence upon Reid and McCosh. To accuse Warfield of "Thomism" for making these kinds of statements is both irrelevant to whether Warfield's assertions are true or false, and completely ignores the genealogy of Scottish Common Sense Realism in Warfield's own intellectual development.

61. Warfield, "God," 110.

62. Ibid., 110–11.

63. One specific instance in which Warfield does use the argument from causality is found in his essay, "On the Antiquity and the Unity of the Human Race." Warfield does make appeal to causality in an effort to respond to naturalistic Darwinianism. See B. B. Warfield, "On the Antiquity and the Unity of the Human Race," in *The Princeton Theological Review*, vol. IX (1911), 1–25, and reprinted in *Studies in Theology* (Grand Rapids: Baker Book House, 1981), 246–48. More importantly, however, Warfield does very clearly endorse the attempts of others to do this. See for example Warfield's "Introduction" to Beattie's *Apologetics*, which is a very stout and robust effort to present and defend the classical proofs from contemporary philosophical objections. Warfield states, "We accord it our heartiest welcome (p. 105)."

64. Warfield, "God," 111.

Princetonian–the supernatural character of Christianity as both a redemptive-historical and absolute religion. Warfield's summary remarks relate the natural knowledge of God back to special revelation. "From the theistic proofs ... we learn not only that a God exists, but also necessarily, on the principle of a sufficient cause, very much the nature of the God which they prove to exist." He goes on to state that "the idea" of God "is still further developed, on the principle of interpreting by the highest category within our reach, by our instinctive attribution to Him, in an eminent degree, of all that is the source of dignity and excellence within ourselves." Again, this reflects the concerns of Scottish Common Sense Realism, in which our knowledge of God is in some senses intuitive, and in some senses acquired. "We come to know God as a personal Spirit," and in his divine attributes. These "are not only recognized," in nature, "but richly illustrated in Scripture, which puts the seal of its special revelation upon all of the details of the natural idea of God."[65]

His purpose for validating the classical proofs, and then for all practical purposes ignoring them, is likely due to several factors. First, as Warfield asserts, the knowledge of God derived from nature is not sufficient in itself. God's eternal power and divine attributes can be known through nature, but not his triune character, nor his redemptive love for lost humanity. If Scripture is required to "put the divine seal" upon natural revelation, the use of the proofs, pragmatically speaking, becomes secondary to arguments for the validity of special revelation.

Second, following Common Sense reasoning, natural knowledge of God can be presupposed. Those who deny the existence of God do so on self-consciously irrational grounds since truth is objective and clear to all rational folk (even if denied by some in unbelief). Thus arguments for special revelation take on new importance since this is where the "objective" truth is most easily proven.

Third, for Warfield, the situation was more complicated than it was for Reid and others, for since the days of Kant, "faith ... can be no longer looked upon as a matter of reasoning and does not rest on rational grounds, but is an affair of the heart."[66] The two enemies Warfield saw pressing in upon the citadel of faith were mysticism and rationalism. These opponents were best fought by stressing the objective and

---

65. Ibid.
66. Warfield, "Apologetics," 14.

historical nature of the "facts" of Christianity as the basis for its claim to be a supernatural and absolute religion.[67]

Fourth, this endeavor involved new tactics. These were buttressed by a historical approach to establishing the knowledge of God, which enabled the apologist to place the five necessary and sufficient facts in the hands of the theologian: (1) that there is a God, (2) that man has a religious nature, (3) that God has revealed himself in nature and history, (4) that Christianity possesses such a knowledge of God, and (5) that the Bible is God's redemptive revelation of himself to sinners.

THE RESURRECTION AS THE ESSENTIAL "FACT" OF CHRISTIANITY

Warfield's most significant presentation of this "evidential" or historical approach to defending the faith is found in an early article (1884), written for *The Journal of Christian Philosophy*: "The Resurrection of Christ: A Historical Fact." This article sets forth, perhaps more clearly than any other, Warfield's own distinctive evidential apologetic. It is the foundational statement of an apologetic methodology that he maintained throughout the course of his career. The focus of Warfield's defense of the absolute religion is the "objective" nature of the great fact of Jesus Christ's resurrection. This in turn becomes the basis for the truth of the claims of Christ. Once it has been established that Christ is God in human flesh, who rose again from the dead in time and space, one can find in that same Christ the vindication of both his claims to possess a supernatural revelation from God and absolute truth. Those who have called Warfield a "rationalist," such as Livingstone, ignore the fact that the claim to "absolute truth" comes after Warfield first uses the inductive

67. This emphasis assumes importance in Warfield's essay, "How to Get Rid of Christianity." Warfield is responding to those who raise the question of reducing Christianity from a "historical" to an "ideal" religion. "That [question] depends on what Christianity is. If it is a religion that is founded on the actual—if it is a religion of fact—if it has any historical content—it is evaporated with its history. If it is a religion of 'ideas,' it is of course unaffected by the destruction of any history that may have become accidentally associated with it. ... The issue is just Christianity itself. Christianity is a historical religion, all of whose doctrines are facts. He who assaults the trustworthiness of the record of the intervention of God for the redemption of the world, is simply assaulting the heart of Christianity. ... If there is to be no historical content in our religion, in a word, Christianity is but another form of that religious aspiration common to all men, clothed in forms which are a product of the chance conditions of the men who have created it (pp. 59–60)."

approach to establish the fact of the resurrection. Once this is established by strictly "probable" evidence (though of such weight as to be practically or morally certain), he then simply applies the law of contradiction to Jesus' own claim to be the way, the truth, and the life (John 14:6). If Jesus is who he says he is, then he is "absolutely" right when he makes such categorical assertions about the way of salvation. In short, God, religion, revelation, Christianity, and the Bible, can all be established from the objective and historical character of the resurrection.

The factual basis for Christianity underlies any doctrinal assertions stemming from explication of Scripture. "It is somewhat difficult to distinguish between doctrines and facts. The doctrines of Christianity are doctrines only because they are facts." The relationship between the two is such that "the facts of Christianity become its most indispensable doctrines."[68] Warfield implicitly acknowledges that this relationship presents a problem, for no one actually witnesses the mysterious acts of God in rescuing sinful man, such as the union of God and man in the incarnate birth of Christ. The same could be said of the resurrection—no one saw what transpired within the tomb. And yet, these things simply cannot be dismissed as myth, because these events are reported as "objective" events, which occurred in ordinary history despite their very mysterious character. The resurrection is "the cardinal doctrine of our system: on it *all other doctrines hang*."[69] If Christ rose from the dead, he is God in human flesh, and if he did not, Christianity collapses as an absolute and supernatural religion. Thus, the offspring of "the modern skepticism"—rationalism and mysticism— "must be rid of the resurrection of Christ. It has recognized the necessity and has bent all its energies to the endeavor."[70] Here the line of demarcation must be drawn. If the resurrection of Christ is a historical fact, Christianity possesses a knowledge of God, and clearly shows it is a supernatural religion capable of defending its absolute claim. God in human flesh reveals the meaning of these great historical and redemptive events, and preserves them in Scripture as an inspired and living record.

"The early followers of the Savior ... recognized the paramount importance of this fact; and the records of Christianity contain a mass of proof for it; of such cogent variety and convincing power that Hume's

68. Warfield, "The Resurrection of Christ a Historical Fact," 178.
69. Ibid. The Italics are mine.
70. Ibid.

famous dilemma recoils on its own head."[71] Warfield dealt with Hume and others at great length regarding miracles in a series of articles originally written for *The Bible Student* in 1903. In "The Question of Miracles," Warfield's critique of Humean forms of skepticism uses the inductive method to defend the faith. Framed with the inherent Common Sense anathema to epistemological skepticism, Warfield writes:

> If we begin with assuming that miracles are impossible, we shall find little in concluding that no conceivable evidence will accredit the occurrence of a miracle to us. The validity of this reasoning clearly depends, however, on the validity of our assumption of the irre formability of our non-miraculous world-view. And the question presses, Have we a right to assume that no event can possibly have occurred, which, if it occurred, would compel a revision of the conception we have formed of the universe? The real dilemma, then, is clearly between the world-view we have formed for ourselves and the facts that come to us, accredited by testimony sufficient in itself to prove their reality—apart that is, from the presumption cherished against them in our minds on the credit of our world-view. In other words, are the facts that are permitted to occur in the universe to be determined by our precedently conceived world-view? Or is our world-view to be determined by a due consideration of all the facts that occur in the universe? And it is just clearly the dilemma between an *a priori* determination of facts and an *a posteriori* determination of theory.[72]

Warfield isolates the source of the problem to presuppositions regarding the universe, either theistic or atheistic. Here is where he feels that allies in all other regards, such as Abraham Kuyper, have left the faith without defense. Christianity remains the "great assumption" for Kuyper, the same methodological leap which enemies of the faith, such as Hume, use to deny the possibility of miracles. The *a priori* theory cannot be allowed to triumph over the *a posteriori* evaluation of facts, wherever they may lead. To do otherwise is to betray the scientific method as Warfield understood it. The weight and type of the evidence in the

71. Ibid., 178–79.
72. Warfield, "The Question of Miracles," 181. Compare Colin Brown's treatment of the possible tension in Warfield's apologetic between the objectivity of evidences and the anti-supernatural presuppositions of atheists, materialists, and pantheists in *Miracles and the Critical Mind* (Grand Rapids: Eerdmans, 1984), 198 ff.

New Testament is such that the witnesses cannot be dismissed. More important, those who had means, motive, and opportunity to overturn such claims were silenced.

"The opponents of revelation themselves being witnesses, the testimony of the historical books of the New Testament if the testimony of eye-witnesses is amply sufficient to establish this, to them, absolutely crushing fact."[73] Therefore, since the Gospels contain "testimony for the resurrection of Christ, which if it stand, *proves that fact*; and that if Christ rose from the dead all motive for, and all possibility of, denial of any supernatural fact of Christianity is forever removed."[74] Thus, inductive, historical arguments for the resurrection of Christ are the primary arsenal of Warfield's apologetic methodology.

The testimony of the witnesses is the major point of contention "for the deniers of a supernatural origin of Christianity." The skeptics must "impeach the credibility of these witnesses."[75] Such critics often argue that the Gospels are not eye-witness materials at all, but were composed well into the second century. They claim that the narratives are not factual in any common sense understanding of term, "but the dreams of a mythological fancy or the wilder inventions of unscrupulous forgery; and that, therefore, they are untrustworthy of credit and valueless as witness to fact."[76]

Warfield provides two primary methods to combat these views. First, if the authenticity of the Gospels are denied, "we may either prove their authenticity and hence the autoptic character of the testimony they contain," or second, "we may waive all question of the books attacked, and, using only those which are by the sceptics themselves acknowledged to be genuine, prove from them that the resurrection of Christ actually occurred."[77] Since the first approach, proving the authenticity of the Gospel events, is the most direct, Warfield indicates that it is usually the course adopted. "Here the battle is intense; but the issue is not doubtful." By using the standard apologetic approach of examining internal and external evidence to determine if the Gospels contain actual

73. Warfield, "The Resurrection of Christ a Historical Fact," 179.

74. Ibid. This seems to mitigate Richard Lints' assertion that in "the Princeton apologetic ... historical evidences are neither the beginning nor the end of apologetics." See Richard Lints, "Two Theologies or One? Warfield and Vos on the Nature of Theology," in *The Westminster Theological Journal*, vol. 54, no. 2 (Fall 1992), 248.

75. Ibid.

76. Ibid.

77. Ibid., 179–80.

eye-witness testimony, Warfield is breaking no new ground. "Internally, those books evince themselves as genuine," as they contain truths about human nature and psychology, an account of the incarnation and the revelation of the "divine-human Personality." The Gospels are also presented in a historical context that, both individually and cumulatively, defies the possibility of human invention. Coupled with the striking coincidences between Paul's Epistles and Luke's account of the early church in Acts, the only possible explanation is "on the hypothesis" that the biblical writers "were simply detailing actual facts."[78]

When the external evidence is examined, "the authenticity of the New Testament historical books is irrefragable." The early church very likely possessed them before the end of the first century. Matthew and Acts are placed among the "Holy Books" and cited as Scripture along with the Old Testament by several of the Fathers. "All quote these historical books with respect and reverence. There is on external, historical grounds no room left for denying the genuineness of the Gospels and Acts; and hence, no room left for denying the resurrection."[79] The centrality of the resurrection, as the supreme "fact" of Christianity, underlies all of these apologetic efforts.

The second approach in dealing with skepticism about the historical character of the New Testament, is to begin by acknowledging from the beginning those writings which are universally accepted by critics. "The most extreme schools of s[k]cepticism admit that the Book of Revelation is by St. John; and that Romans, 1 and 2 Corinthians, and Galatians are genuine letters of St. Paul." Even though "most leaders of anti-Christian thought admit other epistles also ... we wish to confine ourselves to the narrowest ground." The reason is, of course, "to show that the testimony of these confessedly genuine writings of the apostles is enough to establish the fact of the resurrection."[80] Warfield concludes that Paul's letters, which are accepted by all as genuine, "have a great deal to say about the resurrection."[81]

---

78. Ibid., 180.
79. Ibid., 180–81.
80. Ibid., 181.
81. Ibid. In another place, Warfield advocates the same tactics in dealing with the radical Tübingen school. This is to simply accept the epistles that are acknowledged to be genuinely Pauline, and then proving from them the fact of the resurrection. Instead of seeing the critics as a threat, Warfield sees them almost as a boon to orthodoxy. "Every criticism creates against itself a new apologetic. ... For example, the attack of the Tübingen school on the New Testament has developed a direct

Thus, the Pauline doctrine of the resurrection takes on extreme apologetic import. First, "Paul claims to be himself an eye-witness of a risen Christ." Indeed, it is upon this fact that Paul bases his very apostolic office. Warfield concludes, "It will not do to say that Paul claims only to have had a 'theophany' ... which would not imply the resurrection of his body."[82] Second, Paul's letters are "bristling with marks of his intense conviction of the fact of the resurrection. ... Paul was thoroughly convinced that he had seen the risen Jesus; and the sceptics themselves feel forced to admit this fact."[83] But what are we to make of Paul's testimony to Christ's resurrection? Did he experience a "deceiving vision" perhaps? "Paul certainly thought it a body and a sight."[84] But may not have Paul been given to an "enthusiastic spiritual temperament ... which fails to distinguish between vivid subjective ideas and external facts"? Warfield's response is important to note—"This visionary hypothesis is shattered on the simple fact that Paul knew the difference between this 'sight' of Jesus and his visions, and draws the distinction sharply between them."[85] Paul's reference to a vision in 2 Corinthians 12 is described in terms which express his "uncertainty as to what had happened to him then." Paul himself never refers to the Damascus Road experience as anything other than "sight."[86] Skeptics such as Strauss

historical apologetic, which has well nigh made a separate science of the history of the second century, and at the same time called out a body of reasoning, based on Paul's four chief epistles, which has almost itself grown to the stature of a complete and satisfying 'system of Christian evidences.' " Compare Warfield, "Christian Evidences and Recent Criticism," 126–27.

82. Ibid., 181–82.

83. Ibid., 182.

84. Ibid.

85. Ibid., 183.

86. Ibid. It is also important to note that Warfield's philosophical sophistication is apparent in this distinction as well. He plainly moves away from a naive, primitive realism, for a more critical, reflexive position in which the knowing subject can make important distinctions about an object of knowledge, even though these may not be directly evident to the senses. Paul is seen as capable of distinguishing between a "vision," and the encounter with the Risen Christ, which while Christophanic, was nevertheless an occurrence in time and space. This distinction is also spelled out in Warfield's review of *The Spirit of Man*, by Arthur Chandler, in *The Presbyterian and Reformed Review* 3 (1896), 586. Warfield writes that "knowledge is no doubt produced by the interaction of sensation and reason; and sensation itself is no doubt as little a copy of outside reality as the spectrum of a star is a copy of its constitution or its motion. Sensation needs interpreting to give knowledge, and reason is the interpreter. But our confidence in the truth of interpreted sensation, i.e., in its conformity to outside reality, is ineradicable; and accordingly the common-sense view that

and Baur are forced to present an elaborate "vision" hypothesis, but this "fails to account for the facts,"[87] and which does not take into account Paul's dramatic change in character "from the most blood-thirsty of fanatics to the tenderest of saints." This leads Warfield to conclude:

> We find ourselves, then, in this dilemma: If Acts is not true history, then these facts cannot be so used; if Acts is true history, then Paul's conversion occurred quite otherwise; and again, if Acts is true, then so is Luke's Gospel; and Acts and Luke are enough to authenticate the resurrection of Christ.[88]

Another factor that must be considered when looking at the Pauline doctrine of the resurrection is that "Paul believed in the resurrection of Christ not only because he had seen the Lord, but also on the testimony of others." In fact, "Peter, James, and John, then, believed with the same intensity that Christ rose from the dead. ... In 1 Cor. xv. 3 ff., Paul brings before us a cloud of witnesses."[89] Not only were the apostles mentioned by Paul, but over 500 also saw the risen Christ. "They were not an unknown mob. ... Most of them were still living when Paul wrote." The effect of Paul's testimony is that this "is equivalent to their individual testimony. Paul is admitted to be a sober and trustworthy writer: this Epistle is admitted to be genuinely his; and here he in a contemporary document challenges an appeal to eye-witnesses."[90]

Warfield's arguments here bear strong resemblance to legal approaches to truth claims, which themselves have a strong affinity with Scottish Common Sense Realism. The Princetonians had in several cases heartily endorsed such legal approaches to apologetics, in part because these approaches were perfectly consistent with the general reliability of human testimony in even the most controversial matters.

---

knowledge is a copy of the world ... will always rule." Reason has the ability to make critical adjustments/interpretations of sensation so as to ensure true knowledge, i.e., a distinction between a "vision," and a miraculous, though real, Christophanic appearance of Christ. The ability is innate and is dependent upon the *imago Dei*. The formulation is typical of SCSR.

87. Ibid. This is as clear a declaration of Warfield's adherence to the "correspondence test for truth," as can be found anywhere in his writings. Elsewhere, in the same article, Warfield stresses critical tests in judging evidence. The resurrection was accepted so readily, because "men able and more than willing to apply critical tests to evidence were firm believers in it (p. 186)."

88. Ibid., 184.

89. Ibid.

90. Ibid., 184–85.

A. A. Hodge, Warfield's friend, and in some respects a mentor, offered a rather glowing assessment of those who used the legal model as a way of framing an evidential apologetic:

> The foundations of the Christian faith rest upon documentary evidence. ... It is a great point gained, therefore, when lawyers, who can be charged with no professional bias, and who are, of all men most skilled in dealing with evidence and in determining its competency, step forward to vindicate the conclusive character of the documentary evidence establishing the great facts of Christianity.[91]

Among those Hodge singles out for praise include Chief Justice Gibson, Simon Greenleaf (noted expert on legal evidence at Harvard), and the author of the work under review by Hodge, Charles R. Morrison.

Very closely related to the previous point is the fact that this "sight" not only convinced Paul and the apostles, "but it was also so with the whole body of Christians. Not only did Paul base the truth of all Christianity on the truth of his testimony, and found his conversion on it; but so did all Christians," simply on the strength of the eye-witness testimony of those who had seen the risen Lord.[92] The cumulative evidence for the Pauline doctrine of the resurrection is such that "it was felt by Paul that he could count on it above all other facts as the starting-point of Christianity. ... It is plain, then, that the resurrection of Christ was in Paul's day deemed a primordial, universal, and essential doctrine of Christianity."[93] Summing up the evidence gleaned from the four undisputed Epistles of Paul, Warfield makes the following conclusions:

> First, that the resurrection of Christ was universally believed in the Christian Church when the Epistles were written: whatever party lines there were, however near they came, yet did not cut

91. See A. A. Hodge, "Review of 'Proofs of Christ's Resurrection: From a Lawyer's Standpoint,' " in *The Presbyterian Review*, vol. 4, no. 13 (January 1883), 197. Hodge's review was written just over one year before Warfield's defense of the historicity of the resurrection.

92. Warfield, "The Resurrection of Christ A Historical Fact," 185.

93. Ibid., 185–86. For an interesting parallel, see Warfield's apologetically oriented sermon on Romans 1:3–4, "The Christ that Paul Preached," in *The Expositor*, 8th ser., v. vx, 1918, 90–110, and reprinted in *Biblical Doctrines*, 235–52. The entire sermon is an apologetic for a fully developed Pauline doctrine of the two natures of Christ in a very primitive Pauline letter. The resurrection, of course, as a primordial doctrine, figures very prominently in this whole effort.

> through this dogma. Second, that the original followers of Christ, including his apostles claimed to be eye-witnesses of the fact of his resurrection; and, therefore, from the beginning (third day) the whole Church had been convinced of its truth. Over two hundred and fifty of these eye-witnesses were living when Paul wrote. Third, that the Church believed universally that it owed its life, as it certainly owed its continued existence and growth, to its firm belief in this dogma.[94]

While the Pauline doctrine of the resurrection is one important line of evidence supporting the historicity of the resurrection, another, and perhaps equally significant line of "factual support," is to be found in the empty tomb. Warfield begins this ancillary line of argument with the famous "trilemma" (Jesus is either Lord, liar, or lunatic), later popularized by C. S. Lewis, and further publicized by the efforts of campus lay-apologist Josh McDowell. "There are only three theories which can possibly be stated to account for these facts [the universal belief in a resurrection by the early church]." These are as follows, "either, the original disciples of Christ were deceivers and deliberately concocted the story of the Resurrection; or, they were woefully deluded; or the resurrection was a fact."[95]

The first of these theories, that the disciples were deceivers, collapses under the weight of the empty tomb. This theory "is now admitted on all sides to be ridiculous. ... The dead body of Christ lying in his grave ready to be produced by the Jews at any moment, of itself destroys this theory."[96] If the body was not to be found in the tomb after three days, where was it? Neither the Romans nor the Jewish leaders had anything to gain by this, for if they had stolen Christ's body "it would have been produced in disproof of the Resurrection." The only other alternative is that the body was stolen by the disciples, but as Warfield asks, "Was this stolen, mangled lifeless corpse the rallying point of Christians? Was it the sight of this that ... fortified, and filled [them] with the most daring courage, the most deathless hopes?"[97] Even Strauss and Volkmar, "our opponents," have "declared this supposition absurd."[98]

94. Ibid., 187.
95. Ibid.
96. Ibid., 188.
97. Ibid., 188–89.
98. Ibid. His review of David Strauss' *Das Leben Jesu*, Warfield expressed some rather surprising sentiments about the value of Strauss' work: "The republication of

What about the second objection, that the disciples were themselves deceived?[99] "How could the whole body of men be so deceived in so momentous a matter with the means of testing its truth readily at their hand?" And how could these, being deceived, remain so adamant in their testimony as to the appearances of the resurrected Christ? "There is the unimpeachable testimony of eye-witnesses that the appearances began on the third day; and the equally assured fact ... that the body was not thrown on a dunghill but that there was a veritable grave."[100] This leads Warfield to conclude:

> So that the empty grave stares us still in the face. If Christ did not rise, how came the grave empty? Here is the crowning difficulty which all the ingenuity of the whole modern critical school has not been able to lay aside. Was it emptied by Christ's own followers? That would have been imposture, and the sceptics scorn such a resort: moreover, the hypothesis that the apostles were impostors has been laid aside already. ... Was it then, emptied by his enemies? How soon would the body have been produced, then, to confront and confound the so rapidly growing heresy![101]

If the disciples were deceived, what happened to the body? This theory cannot explain the fact of the empty tomb.

'George Elliot's translation of Strauss' *Leben Jesu*' places that book once again in the hands of students of the history of destructive criticism, and is, in point of view, a thing to be welcomed. There can be no safety obtained by evangelical Christianity through ignorance of the work of those who have sapped and mined its foundations." Warfield lamented the fact that too many Christians allowed their distaste for the subject to leave them unawares as to the continuing battle over the general trustworthiness of the New Testament. "We must have our Neanders, and Ebrards, and Lechlers, and Lightfoots always with us, that the Strausses and Baurs may be recognized as interesting curiosities of bygone days." See B. B. Warfield, "Review of *The Life of Jesus Critically Examined*, by Dr. David Friedrich Strauss," in *The Presbyterian and Reformed Review*, vol. V (July 1894), 512–13.

99. That this question has not gone away, even some 100 years later, was made painfully evident in the recent debate about Christ's resurrection between Anthony Flew and Gary Habermas. Flew dismissed the resurrection as a historical event on the grounds that he preferred to believe a psychological miracle had taken place (that the disciples were all deceived) rather than a biological one (that Jesus had in fact, been raised). See Gary Habermas and Anthony Flew, *Did Jesus Rise From the Dead?* (ed. Terry L. Miethe; San Francisco: Harper & Row, 1987), especially pages 3–13. Warfield's apologetic is surprisingly relevant.

100. Warfield, "The Resurrection of Christ a Historical Fact," 189.

101. Ibid.

What about the "swoon theory"? Did a merely wounded Jesus himself "creep from the tomb" as suggested by Schleiermacher?[102] Again, appealing to evidential testimony, Warfield points out that this is "in direct contradiction with the eye-witness testimony ... which is explicit that Christ died; but it has been felt by all the leaders of sceptical thought to be inadequate as an explanation."[103] Since the testimony is so overwhelming that Jesus actually expired, how do we explain the empty tomb? This leads Warfield to state in the most certain of terms, "the empty grave is alone enough to found all Christianity upon."[104] In a sermon titled "The Risen Christ," Warfield writes:

> It is natural to think, first of all, of the place of this great fact in Christian apologetics. Opinions may conceivably differ whether it would have been possible to believe in Christianity as a supernaturally given religion if Christ has remained holden of the grave. But it is scarcely disputable that the fact that He did rise again, being once established, supplies an irrefragable demonstration of the supernatural origin of Christianity, of the validity of Christ's claim to be the Son of God, and of the trustworthiness of His teaching as a Messenger from God to man. ... Christ has risen from the dead! After two thousand years of the most determined assault upon the evidence which establishes it, the fact stands. And so long as it stands, Christianity too must stand as the one supernatural religion. The resurrection of Christ is the fundamental apologetic fact of Christianity.[105]

What about Renan's vision hypothesis? "That grave stares us in the face again: if the body was still in it, there was no place left for visions of it as living and out of it; if not in it, how came it out?"[106] Warfield also offers several additional comments designed to refute this particular objection regarding deception. The first is that there was no expectation for visions, "hence no ground for visions. ... How could Mary Magdalene's own mind have created the vision of Jesus when she did not recognize

102. Ibid.
103. Ibid., 190.
104. Ibid. Italics mine.
105. See B. B. Warfield, "The Risen Christ," in *Saviour of the World* (New York: Hodder & Stoughton, 1914), 191–213. Repr. in *The Person and Work of Christ* (Philadelphia: P&R Publishing, 1950), 535–46.
106. Warfield, "The Resurrection of Christ a Historical Fact," 190.

him as Jesus when he appears?"[107] Second, there was no time for a mythological belief in a resurrection to develop. The development of myth takes many generations to successfully evolve. And third, 500 witnesses, most of whom were still living, were far and away too many people to deceive, or as Warfield puts it, "These five hundred are too many visionaries to create."[108] What does all of this lead Warfield to conclude about the resurrection?

> And thus we cannot but conclude that all attempts to explain the belief of the early followers of Christ in his resurrection as a delusion, utterly fail. If it was not founded on fraud or delusion, then, was it not on fact? There seems no other alternative: eye-witnesses in abundance witness to the fact; if they were neither deceivers nor deceived, then Christ did rise from the dead.[109]

None of these three theories can withstand the tried and true evidential test of Scottish Common Sense Realism—"the test of facts." This means that by "taking all lines of proof together, it is by no means extravagant to assert that no fact in the history of the world is so well authenticated as the fact of Christ's resurrection."[110] Thus, B. B. Warfield is perfectly satisfied to base the whole of the Christian truth claim upon the historicity of the resurrection. Of course, one immediately thinks of the criticisms of someone like Lessing at this point. Warfield had considered objections such as Lessing's in a journal article, "Christless Christianity."

> But the general line of argument remains the same. History can only give us probabilities. Religion, therefore, which requires certainties, cannot be dependent upon historical facts. ... As Lessing reminds us, we cannot base certainties on uncertainties.[111]

The way out of this dilemma, as Warfield argues, is to consider two factors. One, is to examine the nature of "proof" and probability, and the second, is to clearly distinguish between the two types of probability. As far as the first point:

> It can scarcely be expected that at this time of the day the ancient debate with Rationalism should be taken up afresh and threshed

107. Ibid., 190–91.
108. Ibid., 191.
109. Ibid.
110. Ibid.
111. B. B. Warfield, "Christless Christianity," in *The Harvard Theological Review*, v. (1912), 423–73. Repr. in Warfield, *Christology and Criticism*, 313–67.

> out over again. Butler's "Analogy" is still extant, with its initial insistence upon probability as the guide of life, and its solid proof of the reasonableness of an historical revelation. It might not even be amiss to invite those to whom matters of fact appear to be intrinsically doubtful, or at least to become at once on occurrence incapable of establishment beyond "reasonable doubt," to bring their philosophy down to earth by a course of reading in such primary text-books such as Greenleaf on "Evidence" and Ram "On Facts."[112]

Here Warfield shows the propensity to favor forensic tests on evidence which establish "probability" as an effective test for truth, placing it "beyond all reasonable doubt." As for the second point, Warfield writes:

> "Every science," observes Eberhard Vischer, "builds its conclusions on particular experiences which men have had. Every observation in the natural sciences, every experiment, gives us in the first instance not knowledge of what is, but of what the moment of the observation, of the experiment, the observer experiences. ... As experience had by the scientific observer, therefore an historical fact, is the foundation-stone on which is grounded, as in general the entire conduct of man, so also all scientific attainment." If, then, historical facts are by their very nature uncertain,—"if nothing that befalls man can be certainly known, then all scientific certainty whatever passes into the realm of the impossible."[113]

Thus, epistemological skepticism is raised again as the enemy of the historical apologetic. The solution to this is to distinguish between types of probability.

> As the opposite of "demonstrative," "probable" refers to the nature of the ground on which the judgement of truth or reality rests; as the opposite of "certain" it refers to the measure of assurance which the grounds on which this judgement rests are adapted to produce. Historical facts may be "only probable" in the one usage and yet not less than "certain" in the other.[114]

---

112. Warfield, "Christless Christianity," 338.
113. Ibid., 341–42.
114. Ibid.

Therefore, even though the evidence for the resurrection is in the strictest sense "probable," it may be seen as "certain" in a moral, legal, and even scientific sense, if this last sense is limited to the "science" of historical investigation. We are talking about historical events after all, not Euclid's geometry.

Written very early in his academic career, this article on the resurrection first articulates a theme that will surface throughout Warfield's apologetic writings. Once the resurrection is established as a fact, then "all Christianity is established too. Its supernatural element is vindicated: its supernatural origin evinced."[115] In this scheme, there is no need to develop a sophisticated natural theology. Inductive historical arguments bring us to the historical incarnate God-man, who died and rose again from the dead. By virtue of this, Warfield believes that he has established God, religion, and Christianity. Once the resurrection establishes the deity of Christ, the foundation is laid for apologetic arguments for special revelation. This then serves to establish his two other apologetic concerns: the knowledge of God, and the Bible.

THE DOCTRINE OF INSPIRATION

In an important article written in 1894, "The Inspiration of the Bible," Warfield spells out the relationship between the historical events underlying the doctrine of inspiration and apologetics, specifically how the testimony of the resurrected Christ relates to the doctrine of inspiration. This amounts to accepting the "doctrine of inspiration which was held by the writers of the New Testament and by Jesus as reported in the Gospels. It is this simple fact that has commended it to the church of all ages as true doctrine."[116] Jesus held a particular view of the Bible and taught it to the disciples, and now we find it in the New Testament. "It is the doctrine of the Biblical writers themselves, and has therefore the whole mass of evidence for it which goes on to show that the Biblical writers are trustworthy as doctrinal guides."[117] In other words, we believe the doctrine of inspiration, because Jesus, the incarnate God believed and taught it.

> We believe this doctrine of the plenary inspiration of Scriptures primarily because it is the doctrine which Christ and the apostles

115. Warfield, "The Resurrection of Christ a Historical Fact," 191.
116. Warfield, "The Church Doctrine of Inspiration," 114.
117. Warfield, "The Real Problem of Inspiration," 173.

> believed, and which they have taught us. It may seem difficult to take our stand frankly by the side of Christ and his apostles. It will always be found safe.[118]

Inspiration as a doctrine, therefore, rests upon the fact of revelation. Accordingly, on Warfield's evidentialist apologetic, "the supernatural origin and contents of Christianity ... always are vindicated prior to any question of the inspiration of the record." In fact, Christianity must be demonstrated to be a historical religion before one can even talk about inspiration.[119] Thus, the fact that revelation has been given by God must be vindicated before the testimony of that revelation about itself can be adduced as evidence for the inspiration of Scripture. Warfield's willingness to put that claim to the test is revealed in a remarkable openness to critical testing. "The doctrine of inspiration which has become open to all legitimate criticism, and is to continue to be held only as, and so far as, it is ever anew critically tested and approved."[120] In other words, he who lives by the inductive method must be open to die by it, if he be consistent.

Warfield's defense of the doctrine of inspiration amounts to establishing the resurrection of Christ on a factual, historical footing. Then one can go to the Gospel record to discover what Jesus and the apostles believed about the Bible. Belief in the resurrected Christ leads Warfield to ask the following question: "Stated plainly it is just this: Are the New Testament writers trustworthy guides in doctrine? Or are we at liberty to reject their authority, and frame for ourselves contrary doctrines?"[121] This is dangerous business, for as Warfield points out, it is the incarnate and resurrected Christ who instructs us. "The weight of the testimony to the Biblical doctrine of inspiration, in a word, is no less than the weight attached to the testimony of God—God the Son and God the Spirit."[122] Thus, the evidential, historical arguments become the foundation for the doctrine of inspiration as well.

118. Warfield, "The Church Doctrine of Inspiration," 128.
119. Ibid., 121.
120. Warfield, "The Real Problem of Inspiration," 172.
121. Ibid.
122. Ibid., 213–14.

EPISTEMOLOGICAL CONCERNS

Warfield's efforts to ground the Christian faith in historical evidences raises a number of epistemological issues. There can be little doubt that the Princetonian had obviously thought about the relationship between objective and subjective aspects of knowledge and faith in some detail.

He developed his distinction between the subjective and objective aspects of knowing in a number of interrelated settings, never in a single comprehensive essay. We find Warfield's subjective-objective distinction set forth most fully in his treatment of Calvin's doctrine of the knowledge of God, though this distinction also appears throughout his writings in the field of systematic theology. Warfield addresses the relationship between faith and evidence in a number of contexts, though he devotes special attention in an essay, "On Faith in its Psychological Aspects," published in 1911. In addition, Warfield has a carefully framed doctrine of the witness of the Holy Spirit which appears in a number of related contexts.

Perhaps Warfield first learned of the subjective-objective distinction at his grandfather's knee,[123] but he also found it throughout Calvin's *Institutes*. Calvin's doctrine posits an innate knowledge of God in nature and providence, but because of human sinfulness it "fails of its proper effect." An "objective revelation of God, embodied in the Scriptures was rendered necessary, and as well, a subjective operation of the Spirit of God on the heart, enabling sinful man to receive this revelation."[124] Needed is a kind of "repairing action," whereby the Holy Spirit testifies to the truth of objective revelation, and on the subjective side "prepares the heart to respond to and embrace it. But the objective revelation can take no effect on the unprepared heart."[125] The objective side of knowledge is the content of God's redemptive word and acts as recorded in Holy Scripture, while the subjective aspect is a new ability granted by the Holy Spirit to embrace the Christ revealed in that same Scripture.

> Calvin does not present special revelation, or the Scriptures as special revelation documented, as the entire cure [needed because of human blindness due to sin], but places by the side of

123. Warfield's grandfather, Robert Breckinridge, had organized his own theological system around the knowledge of God subjectively and objectively considered. See Robert J. Breckinridge, *The Knowledge of God Objectively and Subjectively Considered*, 2 vols. (New York: Robert Carter & Brothers, 1858).
124. Warfield, "Calvin's Doctrine of the Knowledge of God," 31.
125. Ibid., 32.

> it the *testimonium Spiritus Sancti*. Special revelation, or Scripture as its documented form, provides in point of fact, in the view of Calvin, only the objective side of the cure he finds has been provided by God. The subjective side is provided by the *testimonium Spiritus Sancti*. The spectacles are provided by the Scriptures: the eyes are opened that they may see even through these spectacles, only by the witness of the Spirit in the heart.[126]

Warfield endorses Calvin's use of the image of spectacles and contends that Calvin's stress on the objective aspect of knowledge demonstrates the Reformer's special interest in theistic argument.[127] Whether Warfield is accurately describing Calvin's view of theistic evidences or not, he points out that such proofs, "whether the conclusive testimony of witnesses, or the overwhelming evidence of rational considerations," are not capable of "producing true faith."[128] The fault lies not in the proofs themselves, but because human sinfulness renders them ineffective. For these proofs and evidences to be effective is a "union of the objective and subjective factors." The objective need is supplied by the Word, while the subjective is supplied by the Spirit.[129] Warfield later notes that "the testimony of the Spirit is the subjective preparation of the heart to receive the objective evidence in a synthetic embrace."[130]

For Warfield this explains why human sinfulness cannot be overcome by mere reason and apologetic argumentation. Yet it underscores why such arguments and evidences should not be rejected outright, but have, in fact, an important role in serving as the ground for faith.[131] Warfield notes:

---

126. Ibid., 69–70.
127. See, for example, Edward A. Dowey's criticism of Warfield for elevating the objective (*indicia*) to the status of rational arguments. Compare Edward A. Dewey, *The Knowledge of God in Calvin's Theology* (New York: Columbia University Press, 1952), 116. T. H. L. Parker offers much the same criticism in *Calvin's Doctrine of the Knowledge of God* (Grand Rapids: Eerdmans, 1952), 9. Thus it is possible, if not likely, that Warfield is reading his own subjective-objective distinction anachronistically back into Calvin.
128. Warfield, "Calvin's Doctrine of the Knowledge of God," 76.
129. Ibid., 82–83.
130. Ibid., 85, n. 60.
131. George Marsden contends that "Warfield saw the effects of the Fall on human consciousness as pervasive but quite limited." This, supposedly, is a problem endemic to Scottish Common Sense Realism and supposedly places Warfield outside the tradition of Augustine, Calvin, Jonathan Edwards, Abraham Kuyper, and Herman Bavinck. See George M. Marsden, *Fundamentalism and American Culture*, (New York:

> Sin may harden the heart so that it will not admit, weigh, or yield to evidence: but sin, which affects only the heart subjectively, and not the process of reasoning objectively, cannot alter the relations of evidence to conclusions. Sin does not in the least degree affect the cogency of any rightly constructed syllogism. No man, no doubt, was ever reasoned into the kingdom of heaven: it is the Holy Spirit alone who can translate us into the kingdom of God's dear Son. But there are excellent reasons why every man should enter the kingdom of heaven; and these reasons are valid in the form of every rational mind, and their validity can and should be made manifest to all.[132]

These arguments would still be valid even if no one believed them. The Spirit works through the means of these evidences, not in spite of them.

This, then, leads to the question about the relation of faith to evidences, a matter which Warfield treats in some detail in his essay "On Faith in Its Psychological Aspects." Defining his terms carefully, Warfield begins by noting that " *'belief,' 'faith'* is the consent of the mind to the reality of the thing in question; and when the mind withholds consent to the reality, *'belief,' 'faith'* is not present; they designate the response of the mind to evidence in a consent to the adequacy of the evidence."[133] Rejecting Kant's definition of faith as "conviction founded on evidence which is subjectively adequate,"[134] Warfield places himself squarely within Augustinian tradition, going so far as to say of Augustine's view

---

Oxford University Press, 1980), 115. While Warfield very likely overstates the degree to which Calvin endorsed theistic argumentation, he does not, conversely, depreciate Calvin's doctrine of the blinding effects of sin. Warfield endorses it.

132. Warfield, "Calvin's Doctrine of the Knowledge of God," 124, n. 99.

133. Warfield, "On Faith in Its Psychological Aspects," 318. Warfield is careful to point out that this evidence need not be infallible, "for objective adequacy and subjective effect are not exactly correlated." Indeed, an individual's presuppositions and mental capacity also factor in. "The amount, degree, and quality of the evidence which will secure consent varies from mind to mind and in the same mind from state to state. Some minds, or all minds in some states, will respond to very weak evidence. There is no 'faith,' 'belief' possible without evidence or what the mind takes for evidence; 'fath,' 'belief' is a state of mind grounded in evidence and impossible without it. But the fullest 'faith,' 'belief' may ground itself in very weak evidence — if the mind mistakes it for strong evidence. 'Faith,' 'belief' does not follow the evidence itself, in other words, but the judgement of the intellect upon the evidence. And in the judgement of the intellect naturally will vary endlessly, as intellect differs from intellect or as the states of the same intellect differ from one another (pp. 318–319)."

134. Ibid., 319.

on this matter that "no Scotchman of our day could express it better."[135] Endorsing Scottish philosopher Sir William Hamilton's assessment of Augustine,[136] Warfield contends that "knowledge" is conviction based upon reason and perception, while faith or belief rests upon testimony. According to Warfield:

> When the proximate ground of our conviction is reason, we call it "knowledge"; when it is authority we call it "faith, " "belief." Or to put it in other but equivalent terms, we know what we are convinced of on the ground of perception: we believe what we are convinced of on the ground of testimony. ... We cannot believe, any more than we can know, without adequate grounds: it is not faith but "credulity" to accord credit to insufficient evidence; and an unreasonable faith is no faith at all. But we are moved to this act of conviction by the evidence of testimony, by the force of authority—rationally determined to be trustworthy—and not by the immediate perception of our own rational understandings. In a word, while both knowing and believing are states of conviction, sureness—and the surety may be equally strong—they rest proximately on different grounds. Knowing is seeing, faith is crediting.[137]

This is important for several reasons. First, it means that the distinction often drawn between "knowledge" and "faith" is certainly overdrawn.

> Matters of faith, matters of belief are different from matters of knowledge—not as convictions less clear, firm or well grounded, not as convictions resting on grounds less objectively valid, not as convictions determined rather by desire, will, than by evidence—but as convictions resting on grounds less direct and immediate to the soul, and therefore involving a more prominent element of trust, in a word, as convictions grounded in authority, testimony as distinguished from convictions grounded in rational proof.[138]

135. B. B. Warfield, "Augustine's Doctrine of Knowledge and Authority," 393.
136. Warfield cites Hamilton's treatment of this from his critical notes found in *The Works of Thomas Reid*, which Hamilton edited. See "On Faith in Its Psychological Aspects," 325.
137. Ibid., 326.
138. Ibid., 330.

Any attempt to base knowledge upon direct perception and facts, while at the same time contending that faith is a kind of irrational leap (based upon purely subjective factors), completely misses the point. Instead, Warfield contends that "religious belief may differ from other belief only in the nature of its objects; religious beliefs are beliefs which have religious conceptions as their contents."[139] Therefore, faith cannot be seen as irrational or subjective, but must be based upon sufficient objective grounds, in this case the evidence for the truthfulness of Christianity.

Second, following the Scottish dogma that "an element of trust underlies all our knowledge," we must presume our rationality and trust that our senses do not deceive us.[140] Warfield can conclude that " 'faith' then emerges as the appropriate name of those acts of mental assent in which the element of trust is predominant. Knowledge is seeing; faith, belief, is trusting."[141] This is not problematic because we are said to "know" when we trust that our senses are not deceiving us, and we "believe" when we trust the testimony of another in exactly the same sense.

In this context, Warfield returns again to the subjective-objective distinction. In his understanding, then, there must be two elements present to the mind, in order for there to be faith: "(1) the object on which it is to repose in confidence; (2) adequate grounds for the exercise of this confidence."[142] The object is the Word of God, and the grounds for the exercise of the confidence is the activity of God the Holy Spirit. Restating the matter, Warfield notes, "There are two factors in the production of faith. On the one hand, there is the evidence on the ground of which the faith is yielded. On the other hand, there is the subjective condition by virtue of which the evidence can take effect in the appropriate act of faith."[143] Warfield expands his concept:

> There can be no belief, faith without evidence; it is on evidence that the mental exercise which we call belief, faith rests; and this exercise or state of mind cannot exist apart from its ground in evidence. But evidence cannot produce belief, faith, except in a mind open to this evidence, and capable of receiving, weighing, and responding to it. A mathematical demonstration is demonstrative proof of the proposition demonstrated. But even such a

139. Ibid., 331.
140. Ibid., 329.
141. Ibid., 331.
142. Ibid., 334–35.
143. Ibid., 335.

> demonstration cannot produce conviction in a mind incapable of following the demonstration. ... No conviction, whether of the order of what we call knowledge or of faith, can be produced by considerations to which the mind to be convinced is inhabile. Something more, then, is needed to produce belief, faith, besides the evidence which constitutes its ground. The evidence may be objectively sufficient, adequate, overwhelming. The subjective effect of belief, faith is not produced unless this evidence is adapted to the mind, which is to be convinced.[144]

There is "no faith without evidence; but not no evidence without faith." Taking the doctrine of sin seriously, Warfield states without qualification, "If the evidence which is objectively adequate is not subjectively adequate the fault is in us."[145] Required where faith in the things of God is the object is "the creation by God the Holy Spirit of a capacity for faith under the evidence submitted."[146] This "capacity," to use Warfield's term is "called by the significant name of regeneration." Warfield notes:

> The reestablishment of *this* faith in the sinner must be not the act of the sinner himself but of God. This is because the sinner has no power to render God gracious, which is the objective root, or to look to God for favor, which is the subjective root of faith in the fiducial sense. Before he can thus believe there must intervene the atoning work of Christ canceling the guilt by which the sinner is kept under the wrath of God, and the recreative work of the Holy Spirit by which the sinner's heart is renewed in the love of God.[147]

Unless God the Holy Spirit creates a capacity to believe, "the sinful heart—which is enmity towards God—is incapable of that supreme act of trust in God—or rather entrusting itself to God, its Saviour."[148]

Warfield has a well-developed doctrine of the witness of the Holy Spirit, perhaps framed under the influence of McCosh's own epistemological formulations. It is quite similar to that of the Scottish Presbyterian evidentialist tradition, upon which Warfield may have been partly indebted. As Warfield understands the witness of the Spirit, the Holy Spirit does indeed bear witness to the truth of the evidence

144. Ibid., 335–36.
145. Ibid., 336.
146. Ibid.
147. Ibid., 339.
148. Ibid., 337.

and supplies what Warfield calls the "new ability" of the fallen heart to accept as divine truth what the mind already has grasped, but sinfully tries to reject and suppress.

> Though faith is the gift of God, it does not in the least follow that the faith which God gives is an irrational faith, that is, a faith without cognizable ground in right reason. We believe because it is rational to believe in Him, not even though it be irrational. Of course mere reasoning cannot make a Christian; but that is not because faith is not the result of evidence, but because a dead soul cannot respond to evidence. The action of the Holy Spirit in giving faith is not apart from the evidence, but along with the evidence; and in the first stage consists in preparing the soul for the reception of the evidence[149]

Elsewhere Warfield writes:

> It is easy, of course, to say that a Christian man must take his stand point not above the Scriptures, but in the Scriptures. He very certainly must. But surely he must first have the Scriptures, authenticated to him as such, before he can take his standpoint in them. It is equally easy to say that Christianity is attained, not by demonstrations, but by a new birth. Nothing could be more true. But neither could anything be more unjustified than the inferences that are drawn from this truth for the discrediting of apologetics. ... It is beyond all question only the prepared heart can fitly respond to the "reasons"; but how can even the prepared heat respond when there are no "reasons" to draw out its action? The Holy Spirit does not work a blind, an ungrounded faith in the heart. What is supplied by his creative energy in working faith is not a ready-made faith, rooted in nothing and clinging without reason to its object; nor yet new grounds of belief in the object presented; but just a new ability of the heart to respond to the grounds of faith, sufficient in themselves, already present to the understanding.[150]

149. Warfield, "Apologetics," 15.
150. Warfield, "Introductory Note," to Beattie's *Apologetics*, 98–99; this same statement appears almost word for word in Warfield's "Review of Bavinck's *De Zekerheid des Geloofs*," 115.

Warfield's evidential apologetic is therefore consistent with his Calvinistic monergism (redemptive acts emanating from God alone), his doctrine of the "witness of the Holy Spirit," and the intellectual priority intrinsic in his doctrine of faith. He does this through the means of the subjective-objective distinction, which enables him to combine the Scottish epistemology, with its stress upon the objective aspects of knowing, with the Reformed understanding of total inability.

ASSESSMENT OF WARFIELD'S APOLOGETICS

B. B. Warfield's apologetic efforts, despite the lack of a single comprehensive treatment of the subject, show a remarkable breadth and unity of thought. There is no evidence of a "mature" Warfield, whose thought evolves significantly over the course of time. Warfield was presenting the same types of apologetic arguments in 1884 that he did at the end of his career, 37 years later. This is due to his methodological dependence upon Scottish Common Sense Realism, a system of thought which enabled Warfield to use the same types of arguments and tests for truth in new apologetic situations. Indeed, while others were already abandoning the tried and time-tested Scottish epistemology, Warfield tenaciously held on to its major principles.[151] Whatever one may think of B. B. Warfield's evidential apologetic, it is difficult to criticize him for any lack of consistency or vigor in defending the absolute truth of the Christian faith. It is surprising that Warfield's methodology has been variously criticized, both for its supposed rationalist tendencies by equating faith with mathematical certitude, and for advocating an approach, which can never attain the certainty of faith.

Those who accuse Warfield of supposed "Arminian" tendencies construe his stress on an intellectual priority in faith as an implicit denial of monergism. This despite his express references to monergism, and the consistency with which he works this out in his doctrine of the witness of the Holy Spirit. There is nothing in Warfield's apologetic which is inherently "Arminian," for the Princetonian placed no confidence in the abilities of the fallen will. His confidence was in the sufficiency of the objective evidence that God had given, as well as in the power of the

151. The same thing held true for Warfield's successor of sorts, J. Gresham Machen. See Hart, "The Princeton Mind in the Modern World and the Common Sense of J. Gresham Machen," 1–25.

Holy Spirit to create the subjective conditions for belief. Warfield will forever remain "the Calvinist Professor."

There is also no justification for the suspicion that Warfield is a latent "Thomist." While Scottish Common Sense Realism and "Thomism," as species of classical foundationalism, bear some resemblance to each other, there is no historical convergence between the two. All branches in Warfield's intellectual genealogy lead to his Princeton forebears, Thomas Reid, Francis Turretin, and the Scottish Free Church theologians and not to Paris and Saint Thomas Aquinas. It is simply inaccurate to describe Warfield's apologetic as an attempt to establish a natural theology because of his endorsement of the classical proofs. Warfield's use of Common Sense Realism enabled him to affirm the validity of the proofs, and then, exclusively use the evidential and historical arguments for the resurrection as his primary apologetic undertaking. Those, such as Livingstone, who accuse Warfield of being a "Rationalist," are simply in error. Warfield's apologetic is consistently inductive; at times it borders on an almost forensic methodology.

Warfield's familiarity with the advances of contemporary scholarship greatly enhanced his effectiveness as an apologist. He was stimulated by current objections to orthodoxy, viewing critical thought not as an enemy, but as a tool to strengthen the case for orthodoxy. The anti-supernatural bias that accompanies so much of critical thought was the problem. The questions raised by the radical theologians only served, for Warfield, to show the weight and strength of the historical evidence for the facts of Christianity. The new theories, however "reasonable" at first glance, were far less plausible than the orthodox position when subjected to the same critical canons that the critics themselves applied to the New Testament.

Despite the ill-deserved confusion that surrounds his methodology, B. B. Warfield must be placed among the most significant American apologists of the period. He stood on the "fact" of the resurrection as the apologetic basis for Christianity, proving that it alone possesses the redemptive knowledge of God in Jesus Christ.

5

Systematic Theology

PREDECESSORS AND MENTORS

Benjamin Breckinridge Warfield never produced his own complete systematic theology during his 34-year tenure as Professor of Polemical and Didactic Theology at Princeton Theological Seminary. The reason for this may be simply that Charles Hodge (1797–1878), who was Warfield's esteemed mentor at Princeton, had published a three-volume systematic theology during the years of 1871–1872. In addition, Warfield's immediate predecessor and Charles Hodge's own son, Archibald Alexander Hodge, had also published his own work, *Outlines of Theology*, in a revised edition in 1878.[1] It is very likely that Warfield simply did not believe that another attempt to produce an entire theological system was justified. Given Warfield's immense respect for Dr. Hodge and his son, it is reasonable to assume that he saw no need for an additional theological system of his own. Warfield often expressed nothing but deep affection and strong admiration for Dr. Hodge:

> I have sat under many noted teachers, and am yet free to say that as an educator I consider Dr. Hodge superior to them all. He was in fact my ideal of a teacher. ... I can only say that in that room of Systematic Theology, I think that I had daily before me examples of perfect teaching.[2]

1. See Charles Hodge, *Systematic Theology*, 3 vols. (New York: Charles Scribner's Sons, 1872–73), also in a reprint edition: *Systematic Theology*, 3 vols. (Grand Rapids: Eerdmans, 1979); A. A. Hodge, *Outlines of Theology* (New York: Robert Carter & Brothers, 1860; rev. ed. 1878), also in a reprint edition: *Outlines of Theology* (Grand Rapids: Zondervan, 1972).

2. B. B. Warfield, "Dr. Charles Hodge as a Teacher of Exegesis," repr. in *Selected Shorter Writings of Benjamin B. Warfield*, vol. 1 (ed. John E. Meeter; Phillipsburg: P&R Publishing, 1980), 439–40. While aware that exegesis was not Dr. Hodge's specialty, Warfield nevertheless had only glowing words for Dr. Hodge as a professor of systematic theology, and used Hodge's *Systematic Theology* as a textbook in his own

There are other reasons to be considered in this regard as well. Warfield's longtime friend and Princeton colleague Francis Patton notes that two other factors contributed to Warfield's hesitancy to complete his own system. "In the first place, he was largely occupied with the business of teaching, which left him little time for the constructive work of building a system."[3] Second, according to Patton, Warfield:

> ... was by temperament a controversial rather than a systematic theologian. His habit of writing elaborate articles for the Princeton Review led him perhaps to put more emphasis on certain phases of religious thought than would be proper in a treatise on systematic theology. ... It is quite safe to say that he was a dogmatic rather than a systematic theologian, and was less interested in the system of doctrine than in the doctrines of the system.[4]

When one looks for fundamental structures in B. B. Warfield's theology, one immediately encounters several real difficulties. First, Warfield did not write systematically but occasionally. Therefore, one must examine in detail Warfield's writings which address specific subjects under review. Only then can one attempt to see if there are any basic structures or modes of thinking which underlie them. Another difficulty is that Warfield had little desire to construct an entire theological system. Francis Patton, Warfield's friend and colleague, states:

> I do not think that Dr. Warfield cared much about how the materials that enter into a theological system are organized. He cared more about the separate blocks of doctrine than the shape of the building constructed out of them. If we may care to use a geometrical symbol, a system of theology may take the form of an ellipse, the two foci being the Disease and the Remedy, as was the case in Chalmers' *Institutes*, or God objectively and subjectively revealed as in the theology of Dr. Breckinridge. Again we may very properly symbolize by the triangle: the main divisions being based on the three Persons of the Trinity, as in Calvin's *Institutio Christianae religionis*. Or, yet again, we may have a Christocentric system of theology, the separate doctrines radiating from the central truth

courses. See Richard Lints, "Two Theologies or One? Warfield and Vos on the Nature of Theology," *Westminster Theological Journal* 54 (1992), 235, n. 1.

3. Francis L. Patton, "Benjamin Breckinridge Warfield, D.D., L.L.D., Litt.D. A Memorial Address," *The Princeton Theological Review* Volume XIX (1921), 386.

4. Ibid.

> of the Incarnation as was the case in Dr. Henry B. Smith's system. But Dr. Warfield seems not to have been much interested in the mode of organizing the units that constitute the Body of Divinity. Dr. Hodge's quadrilateral consisting of Theology, Anthropology, Soteriology, and Eschatology suited his purpose very well, and he had no desire to modify it. That there is in it a logical fault of division there can be no doubt; but what of it?[5]

Since B. B. Warfield was apparently not directly concerned with organizing an entire theological system, he did not elaborate much about what he would consider to be fundamental to such a system.

But we are not totally in the dark here. Warfield, the Princetonian and the Presbyterian, inherited two conceptual structures that color virtually all his theological reflection. As a Princetonian and protégé of James McCosh, Warfield clearly stands in the long tradition of Scottish Common Sense Realism. As a Presbyterian, Warfield stands in the lineage of Scottish Presbyterianism and the Westminster Confession of Faith. Both these streams converged in the person of Robert J. Breckinridge, his maternal grandfather, who was in his own right an influential Presbyterian theologian.[6] As Patton notes, it was Breckinridge who organized his theological system around the categories of knowledge of God objectively and subjectively considered, with a corresponding emphasis upon the inductive and deductive method.[7] This same conceptual grid will reappear through Warfield's occasional writings treating the right and nature of systematic theology. Although Warfield chose not to produce a complete theological system of his own, he did write very extensively on the idea, nature, methodology, and right of systematic theology. This chapter will investigate Warfield's conception of the "idea" and nature of systematic theology as a science and the "right" of systematic theology to establish the necessary doctrinal foundations for the Christian faith.

5. Patton, "Benjamin Breckinridge Warfield, A Memorial Address," 387.
6. See Wilber B. Wallis, "Benjamin B. Warfield: Didactic and Polemical Theologian," Two Parts, *Presbyterion: Covenant Seminary Review*, vol. III, no. 1 (Spring 1977), 4.
7. See Robert J. Breckinridge, *The Knowledge of God Objectively and Subjectively Considered*, 2 vols. (New York: Robert Carter & Brothers, 1858).

TWO MAJOR ESSAYS ON SYSTEMATIC THEOLOGY

Throughout his career, B. B. Warfield completed two major essays on the subject of systematic theology. These are "The Idea of Systematic Theology,"[8] first published in April of 1896, and the more polemical "The Right of Systematic Theology" published in July of that same year.[9] In addition, Warfield completed an important summary article, "The Task and Method of Systematic Theology," in April of 1910.[10] Warfield also produced several other minor articles,[11] as well as a host of book reviews and review articles all devoted to the subject of systematic theology. During this same period Warfield wrote a series of more polemical articles, applying his own methodology in specific situations. He was quite concerned about "progressive" or "mediating" thought making its way from Germany across the Atlantic. One important article was "Recent Reconstructions of Theology from the Point of View of Systematic Theology" written in 1898.[12] So even though he did not

---

8. B. B. Warfield, "The Idea of Systematic Theology," *The Presbyterian and Reformed Review* vii (April 1896) 243–71, and reprinted in *Studies in Theology* (Grand Rapids: Baker Book House, 1981), 49–87. According to Warfield bibliographers John E. Meeter and Roger Nicole, this essay was actually an expanded edition of Warfield's inaugural address given at Princeton in 1888 entitled "The Idea of Systematic Theology Considered as a Science" and later published under the same name by Princeton Theological Seminary in May of 1888. See John E. Meeter and Roger Nicole, *A Bibliography of Benjamin Breckinridge Warfield: 1851–1921* (P&R Publishing, 1974), 1, 14–15, 23.

9. B. B. Warfield, "The Right of Systematic Theology" was originally published in *The Presbyterian and Reformed Review* (July 1896), 412–58, and then later as a book with a forward by Scottish theologian James Orr: *The Right of Systematic Theology* (Edinburgh: Clark, 1897). This has been reprinted in its entirety in B. B. Warfield, *Selected Shorter Writings* vol. 2 (ed. John E. Meeter; Phillipsburg: P&R Publishing, 1980), 219–79.

10. B. B. Warfield, "The Task and Method of Systematic Theology" in *The American Journal of Theology* xiv. (April 1910), 192–205. Repr. in *Studies in Theology* (Grand Rapids: Baker Book House, 1981), 91–105.

11. B. B. Warfield, "The Indispensableness of Systematic Theology to the Preacher," from the *Homiletic Review* XXXIII (February 1897), 99–105, and reprinted in *Selected Shorter Writings*, vol. 2, 280–88; and B. B. Warfield, "Theology as a Science" in *The Bible Student* (January 1900), 1–4, and reprinted in *Selected Shorter Writings*, vol. 2, 207–12.

12. B. B. Warfield, "Recent Reconstructions of Theology from the Point of View of Systematic Theology," in *Homiletic Review* XXXV (March 1898), 201–08. Repr. in *Selected Shorter Writings*, vol. II, 289–99.

produce his own systematic theology, B. B. Warfield left us with a great deal of material reflecting upon the "queen of the sciences."[13]

"THE IDEA OF SYSTEMATIC THEOLOGY"

Warfield's first major treatise on the subject, "The Idea of Systematic Theology,"[14] was published in 1896. It was an expansion and reworking of his inaugural address, given in May of 1888 when he joined the faculty at Princeton. This treatise is the most comprehensive of Warfield's theological writings. Warfield begins with a series of definitions, noting at the outset that the very term "systematic theology" had come under increasing criticism in recent years.[15] The key objection advanced by critics claimed that the term "systematic theology" was nothing more than a tautology. Warfield challenges this "hypercritical" assumption by arguing that what distinguishes systematic theology as a discipline is the very fact that it presents material "in the form of a system." He explains, "Other disciplines may use a chronological, a historical, or some other method: This discipline must needs employ a systematic, that is to say, a philosophical or scientific method."[16]

---

13. Fred G. Zaspel's *The Theology of B. B. Warfield: A Systematic Summary* (Wheaton, Ill.: Crossway, 2010), offers a comprehensive survey of Warfield's theology, doctrine by doctrine. For a survey of Warfield's work in soteriology, see R. W. Cousar, "Benjamin Warfield: His Christology and Soteriology," (Th.D. diss., University of Edinburgh, 1954). For references which deal with specific aspects of Warfield's theological method, see Lints, "Two Theologies or One?" 235–53, and Wilber B. Wallis, "Benjamin B. Warfield: Didactic and Polemical Theologian," *Presbyterion: Covenant Seminary Review* (Spring 1977), vol. 3, no. 1–2, 3–20; 73–94.

14. J. I. Packer has recently noted that Warfield's essay is "almost a benchmark account of the discipline" of systematic theology. Packer says, "What Warfield affirmed overall was a masterful mainstream statement of the Reformational idea of proper theological procedure as it presented itself to a fine mind toward the close of the Christian era, when it was still possible to think of the Christian faith and philosophy as a community commitment, of Christian theology as the growing point to Western culture, and of the Christian theological enterprise as the supreme human endeavor." Packer goes on to "augment Warfield" in light of new questions and emphases. See J. I. Packer, "Is Systematic Theology a Mirage? An Introductory Discussion," in *Doing Theology in Today's World* (ed. John D. Woodbridge and Thomas Edward McComiskey; Grand Rapids: Zondervan, 1991), 24–25.

15. Warfield, "The Idea of Systematic Theology," 49.

16. Ibid. Elsewhere, Warfield had stressed the importance of the "systematic" nature of the discipline. "By 'Systematic Theology' is meant that department or section of theological science which is concerned with setting forth systematically, that is to say, as a concatenated whole, what is known concerning God." See Warfield, "The Task and Method of Systematic Theology," 91.

Therefore, "systematic theology" can just as easily be designated "philosophical or scientific theology," though to do so really does not eliminate any ambiguities. Plus, any advantages gained by the use of alternative terms are quickly lost by the fact that the use of the term "philosophical" may give the idea that theology is somehow subordinate to a particular school of philosophical thought. The term "scientific" may convey the idea that theology can be reduced "to an empirical science, or dependent upon the 'experimental method.' "[17]

Despite these caveats, Warfield unequivocally asserts that systematic theology is indeed a science in the true sense of the term. Systematic theology is "in its essential nature a science. ... When we have made the simple assertion of 'Systematic Theology' that it is in its essential nature a science, we have already determined most of the vexing questions which arise concerning it in a formal point of view."[18] Accordingly, Warfield addresses these vexing questions by setting out eight specific points.

The first point is Warfield's insistence that the discipline of systematic theology be understood in purely an "ideal" sense, *not* in a historical sense.

> Let us observe that to say that Systematic Theology is a science is to deny that it is a historical discipline, and to affirm that it seeks to discover, not what has been or is held to be true, but what is ideally true; in other words, it is to declare that it deals with absolute truth and aims at organizing into a concatenated system all the truth in its sphere.[19]

Since this is the case, systematic theology can be compared to other "scientific" disciplines such as geology, which Warfield argues "is a science, and on that account there cannot be two geologies; its matter is all the well-authenticated facts in its sphere, and its aim is to digest all these facts into one all-comprehending system."[20] This leads Warfield to the

17. Ibid., 50.
18. Ibid., 51. See Warfield's short essay, "Theology a Science," (January 1900), where Warfield argued that "Theology, we say, is that science which treats of God in himself and in his relations (p. 207)."
19. Ibid.
20. Ibid. This point stands in sharp relief over against Abraham Kuyper's notion that there are indeed two kinds of science, a palingenetic science and an unregenerate science. See Abraham Kuyper, *Principles of Sacred Theology* (trans. J. Hendrik DeVries; Grand Rapids: Baker Book House, 1980), 155–82.

obvious conclusion that "just because theology is a science, there can be but one theology. This all-embracing system will brook no rival in its sphere, and there can be two theologies only at the cost of one or both of them being imperfect, incomplete, false."[21] Here, as well as at subsequent points, Warfield is clearly indebted to certain elements of the Common Sense Realism of his Scottish fathers, especially Princeton President James McCosh.[22]

Warfield's key point is that systematic theology must seek for an ideal system of theology, not merely the historical expression of a particular system of Christian theology.

> It is because theology, in accordance with a somewhat prevalent point of view, is often looked upon as a historical rather than a scientific discipline, that it is so frequently spoken of and defined as if it were but one of many similar schemes of thought. There is no doubt such a thing as Christian theology, as distinguished from Buddhist theology or Mohammedan theology; and men may study it as the theological implication of Christianity considered as one of the world's religions.[23]

When theology is studied from this historical perspective, "it forms a section of a historical discipline and furnishes its share of facts for a history of religions." In fact, on these terms, theology can also supply the basis for a science or philosophy of religion as well.[24] If systematic theology is historically understood, there are distinct Pelagius and Augustinian theologies, and distinct Calvinistic and Arminian theologies, but Warfield notes "we are speaking as historians and from a historical point of view."[25] He is careful to point out that the "Pelagius and Augustinian theologies are not two coordinate sciences of theology; *they are rival theologies*. If one is true, just so far the other is false, and there is but one theology."[26] The true-false dichotomy is characteristic of the

21. Ibid., 52.
22. I have attempted to establish the historical connection for this in chapter 2, "The Wisdom of the Vulgar."
23. Warfield, "The Idea of Systematic Theology," 52.
24. Ibid.
25. Ibid.
26. Ibid. The italics are mine. It is interesting to note that Warfield would echo these same sentiments much later in his career. What upset Warfield was the lack of understanding that some evangelicals displayed regarding the importance of a theological system. In reviewing *He That is Spiritual*, which was Dallas Theological Seminary founder Louis Sperry Chafer's treatise on the Christian life, Warfield was

older orthodoxy as well.[27] This leads Warfield to conclude, "This we may identify with empirical fact, with either or neither; but it is at all events one, inclusive of all theological truth and exclusive of all else as false and not germane to the subject."[28] To assert that systematic theology is a science is to assert that "in its subject-matter it includes all the facts belonging to that sphere of truth which we call theological; and we deny that it needs or will admit of limitation by a discriminating adjectival definition."[29] For Warfield then, it is just as correct to speak of it "as Christian theology just as we may speak of it as true theology."[30]

Warfield's prescribed methodology is unashamedly that of the inductive method moderated and received from his own Scottish epistemological forebears.

> We may describe our method of procedure in attempting to ascertain and organize the truths that come before us for building into the system, and so speak of logical or inductive, of speculative or organic theology; or we may separate the one body of theology into its members, and, just as we speak of surface and organic geology or of physiological and direct psychology, so speak of the theology of grace and sin, or of natural and revealed theology. But all these are but designations of methods of procedure in dealing with the one whole, or of the various sections that together constitute the one whole, which in its completeness is the science of theology, and which, as a science, is inclusive of all the truth in its sphere, however ascertained, however presented, however defended.[31]

Warfield also stands upon the shoulders of Charles Hodge in this regard, at whose feet he himself had learned systematic theology.[32]

---

quite concerned about the eclectic tendency of those such as Chafer, who attempt to synthesize that which Warfield believed to be diametrically opposed systems of thought. We will take up Warfield's criticism of Chafer in depth in Chapter Six. See B. B. Warfield, "Review of Louis Sperry Chafer's *He That is Spiritual*" in *The Princeton Theological Review*, Vol. XVII, No. 2 (April, 1919), 322–27.

27. Richard A. Muller, *Post-Reformation Reformed Dogmatics: Vol. 1 Prolegomena to Theology* (Grand Rapids: Baker Book House, 1987), 106–12.

28. Warfield, "The Idea of Systematic Theology," 52.

29. Ibid.

30. Ibid.

31. Ibid., 53.

32. See Charles Hodge, *Systematic Theology*, vol. 1, 1–12; A. A. Hodge, *Outlines of Theology*, 16.

Thus the goal of systematic theology is not to develop the history of rival systems, but to develop the "ideal" and "true" system using the inductive method from the relevant data. This data is the raw material that ultimately composes the theological system itself that Warfield will frequently describe as "facts." Warfield's second point is to elaborate upon the epistemological basis of systematic theology—if it is to be a science in the true sense of the term. In the Princetonian conception of "science" during the Warfield era, there are three necessary, though not sufficient conditions that must be presupposed:

> For the very existence of any science, three things are presupposed: (1) the reality of its subject-matter; (2) the capacity of the human mind to apprehend, receive into itself, and rationalize this subject-matter; and (3) some medium of communication by which the subject-matter is brought before the mind and presented to it for apprehension.[33]

Warfield views this to be the case with all sciences as for example, astronomy. As a Scottish Common Sense Realist he believed that all such sciences operate upon the same basic epistemological presuppositions. However, the mere presence of any of these three presuppositions (which are necessary conditions) do not by themselves constitute sufficient conditions for such a science to exist. "Facts do not make a science; even facts as apprehended do not make a science; they must be not only apprehended, but also so far comprehended as to be rationalized and thus combined into a correlated system."[34] In other words, the availability of suitable subject-matter, the ability of men and women to observe, understand and organize the subject-matter into a coherent system, as well as the presence of proper modes of communication by which the subject-matter may be transmitted, requires a certain organizing principle, a conceptual "gestalt," or a "system."

> The mind brings to every science somewhat which, though included in the facts, is not derived from the facts considered in themselves alone, as isolated data, or even as data perceived

33. Warfield, "The Idea of Systematic Theology," 52. Warfield's three presuppositions come directly from Scottish Common Sense Realism and fit under McCosh's heading of "necessary truths" (in contrast to the "contingent truths") which are the basis for all human knowledge as set out in James McCosh, *The Scottish Philosophy* (New York: Robert Carter & Brothers, 1875), 217–18.
34. Ibid., 53.

in some sort of relation to one another. Though they be thus known, science is not yet; and is not born save through efforts of the mind in subsuming the facts under its own intuitions and forms of thought. No mind is satisfied with a bare cognition of facts: its very constitution forces it on to a restless energy until it succeeds in working these facts not only into a network of correlated relations among themselves, but also of a rational body of thought correlated to itself and its necessary modes of thinking. The condition of science, then, is that the facts which fall within its scope shall be such as stand in relation not only to our faculties, so that they may be apprehended; but also to our mental constitution so that they may be understood as to be rationalized and wrought into a system relative to our thinking.[35]

The philosophical fingerprints of James McCosh and Charles Hodge are once again evident here.[36] In other words, a "true" science does not exist until the three necessary epistemological conditions are themselves organized into a system so that the mind can use the data that it receives or that it intuits. Warfield cites several contemporary examples of natural sciences that he understands in this sense, as for example, the science of aesthetics which requires an aesthetic ability, as well as moral science which requires a moral nature. Likewise the science of logic requires the ability to understand and use its propositions, as does the science of mathematics require the ability to reason mathematically.

Here once again, Warfield returns to a major epistemological theme—the subjective/objective distinction—that runs throughout his systematic,[37] apologetical, and historical writings.[38] "Subjectively speak-

35. Ibid., 53–54.

36. McCosh, *The Scottish Philosophy*, 217–18; Charles Hodge, *Systematic Theology*, 1–22.

37. See Warfield's discussion of the "Witness of the Holy Spirit" where he clearly develops a fundamental distinction between the "objective" aspects of epistemology and the more "subjective" aspects of knowledge. See B. B. Warfield, "Introduction to Francis R. Beattie's *Apologetics: or the Rational Vindication of Christianity*"; Reprinted in *Selected Shorter Writings* vol. 2, 93–105.

38. See Warfield's comments on this distinction in his treatment of Calvin's doctrine of the *testimonium Spiritus Sancti*. See B. B. Warfield, "Calvin's Doctrine of the Knowledge of God," in *The Princeton Theological Review* vii. (April 1909), 219-325, and reprinted in B. B. Warfield, *Calvin and Augustine* (Philadelphia: P&R Publishing, 1956), see especially pages 31, 47, and 69. Warfield stresses the same distinction in his treatment of Augustine. See B. B. Warfield, "Augustine's Doctrine of Knowledge and Authority" in *The Princeton Theological Review* V. (October 1907), 353–97, and reprinted in *Calvin and Augustine*, especially page 393.

ing, sense perception is the essential basis of all science and external things; self-consciousness, of internal things."[39] But Warfield goes on to say that "objective media are also necessary. For example, there could be no astronomy, were there no trembling ether through whose delicate telegraphy the facts of light and heat are transmitted to us."[40] This means that "subjective and objective conditions of communication must unite, before the facts that constitute the material of a science can be placed before the mind that gives it its form."[41] Therefore, like other sciences, systematic theology:

> for its very existence as a science, presupposes the objective reality of the subject-matter with which it deals; the subjective capacity of the human mind so far to understand this subject-matter as able to subsume it under the forms of its thinking and to rationalize it into not only a comprehensive, but also a comprehensible whole; and the existence of trustworthy media of communication by which the subject-matter is brought to the mind and is presented before it for perception and understanding.[42]

Warfield now relates the subjective/objective distinction to each of the three presuppositions that must underlie any true science. The first presupposition is related to "the affirmation that theology is a science [and] presupposes the affirmation that God is, and that He has relation to His creatures." The subjective aspect of knowledge, epistemologically speaking, and which corresponds to Warfield's second presupposition, is "the affirmation that theology is a science," and therefore, "presupposes the affirmation that man has a religious nature, that is, a nature capable of understanding not only that God is, but also to some extent, what He is."[43]

Warfield now adds a third element, which corresponds to the third presupposition regarding an appropriate and objective medium to communicate this information: "The affirmation that theology is a science presupposes the affirmation that there are media of communication by which God and divine things are brought before the minds of men."[44] In other words, the existence of God, the religious nature

39. Warfield, "The Idea of Systematic Theology," 54.
40. Ibid.
41. Ibid.
42. Ibid., 55.
43. Ibid.
44. Ibid., 55–56.

of man, and the existence of an objective revelation in the Scriptures, compose these three epistemological presuppositions which are necessary for systematic theology to exist as a science, properly conceived. In Warfield's words:

> When we affirm that theology is a science, we affirm not only the reality of God's existence and our capacity so far to understand Him, but we affirm that He has made Himself known to us—we affirm the objective reality of a revelation. Were there no revelation of God to man, our capacity to understand Him would lie dormant and unawakened; and though He really existed it would be to us as if He were not. There would be a God to be known and a mind to know Him; but theology would be as impossible as if there were neither the one nor the other.[45]

Here we can see the essential and foundational role that Warfield assigns to apologetics, which Warfield argues serves to make it possible for the subsequent construction of a systematic theology. "Not only, then, philosophical, but also the whole mass of historical apologetics by which the reality of revelation and its embodiment in the Scriptures are vindicated."[46] The accomplishment of this task, in effect, is the presupposition and foundation for all subsequent systematic theology altogether.

Warfield's third point regarding the "idea" of systematic theology is to consider the problems associated with the subject matter of the "science" of systematic theology. "A science is defined from its subject-matter; and the subject-matter of theology is God in His nature and in His relations with His creatures. Theology is therefore that science which treats of God and of the relations between God and the universe."[47] Such common definitions of theology as the "science of God" or as "the science of God and of divine things" or even the science of the

45. Ibid., 56.

46. Ibid. See chapter 3, "Apologetics," where I attempt to point out the close relationship that Warfield establishes between apologetics and theological prolegomena.

47. Ibid. This definition certainly echoes Charles Hodge. Hodge notes, "We have, therefore, to restrict theology to its true sphere, as the science of the facts of divine revelation so far as those facts concern the nature of God, and our relation to him, as his creatures, as sinners, and as the subjects of redemption." See Charles Hodge, *Systematic Theology*, vol. 1 (Grand Rapids: Eerdmans, 1979), 21. Wilber B. Wallis, one of the few who has undertaken even a brief evaluation of Warfield's writings in the field of systematic theology, remarks that this definition strikes him for its simplicity. See Wallis, "Benjamin B. Warfield: Didactic and Polemic Theologian," 73.

"supernatural" fail not so much by erroneous conception, but in "precision of language."[48]

Warfield now argues that those such as Schleiermacher err by deriving a definition of theology from the sources of theology, rather than from the subject-matter of theology. These theologies allow the subjective aspects of epistemology to completely swallow up all of the objective aspects of knowledge. Once this happens:

> The definition of theology as the "science of religion" thus confounds the product of the facts concerning God and His relations with His creatures working through the hearts and lives of men, with those facts themselves; and consequently, whenever strictly understood bases theology not on the facts of the divine revelation but on the facts of the religious life.[49]

According to Warfield, this leads to tremendous confusion since the objective and subjective aspects of knowledge become inverted, making impossible both proper science *and* proper systematic theology. The subject matter of theology, which Warfield understands to be the objective revelation found in Holy Scripture, is exchanged for a subjective "science" of religion. Such theology is lowered simply to the "aspirations and imagining of man's own heart,"[50] derailing the quest for objectively "true" theology. When this happens, "It is natural to take a step further and permit the methodology of the science, as well as its idea, to be determined by its distinguishing element: Thus theology, in contradiction to its very name becomes Christocentric."[51]

48. Warfield, "The Idea of Systematic Theology," 56. With Warfield's concerns so clearly set forth here, it strikes me as somewhat ironic that Warfield's fellow *Princeton Theological Review* editor, Caspar Wistar Hodge, would himself define theology simply "as the science of God." See C. W. Hodge, "The Idea of Dogmatic Theology" *The Princeton Theological Review* VI (1908), 61.

49. Ibid., 57.

50. Ibid.

51. Ibid. Warfield laments that his contemporary, Emanuel V. Gerhart, Professor of Systematic and Practical Theology at the Theological Seminary of the Reformed Church (Lancaster, Pennsylvania), had fallen into what Warfield believed to be the same error. After stating that an entire review of Gerhart's work was to eventually be undertaken, Warfield remarks "meanwhile we cannot refrain from expressing the sorrow it brings to us to note how entirely, as it begins to seem, one of the chief schools of our sister Church has drifted from the old Reformed theology into the arms of the modern *Vermittelungstheologie*, called here, euphemistically, 'Christological.' Dr. Gerhart speaks of Calvinism from without. ... It seems to be true, therefore, that the replacement of the old Reformed theology by Schleiermachianism at the oldest

Warfield readily acknowledges that from a historical perspective Christianity is christological—"It is by its doctrine of redemption that it is differentiated from all other theologies that the world has known." But the problem here is that theology is not the science of redemption, for:

> ... as a science, theology must be theocentric. So soon as we firmly grasp it from the scientific point of view, we see that there can be but one science of God and of His relations to His universe, and we no longer seek a point of discrimination but rather a center of development; and we quickly see that there can be but one center about which so comprehensive a subject-matter can be organized—the conception of God. He that hath seen Christ, has beyond all doubt seen the Father; but it is one thing to make Christ the center of theology so far as He is one with God, and another thing to organize all theology around Him as the theanthropos and in His specifically theanthropic work.[52]

Constructing a theological system from a purely christological perspective builds an entire system upon a *particular* aspect of the entire system, rather than on a *universal* aspect upon which the system itself must be properly grounded. Warfield does not stand for this.

Warfield's fourth point in his consideration of systematic theology as a science centers on the "sources of theology." Here the role of revelation in theology must be carefully set out. Revelation is defined as "the medium by which the facts concerning God and His relations to His creatures are brought before men's minds, and so made the subject matter of a possible science. The word accurately describes the condition of all knowledge of God."[53] There can be no knowledge of God, therefore, unless God first reveals himself to men and women through the appropriate media.

---

school of the (German) Reformed Church is complete." See B. B. Warfield, "Review of Emanuel Gerhart, *Institutes of the Christian Religion*" in *The Presbyterian and Reformed Review* (October 1891), 716–17. Gerhart is also singled out for criticism in Warfield's article, "Recent Reconstructions of Theology" (March 1898). Repr. in *Selected Shorter Writings*, vol. 2, as a prime example of an attempt by an American theologian to import the "mediating" theology of Dorner, Ebrard, and Martensen into America (289).

52. Ibid., 57–58.

53. Ibid., 58. Warfield develops his conception of "The Biblical Idea of Revelation," in great detail in an article originally written for *The International Standard Bible Encyclopedia*, vol. 4 (ed. James Orr; Chicago: The Howard-Severance, 1915), 2573–82. This article has been reprinted in its entirety in B. B. Warfield, *The Inspiration and Authority of the Bible* (Phillipsburg: P&R Publishing, 1948), 71–102.

> Our reaching up to Him in thought and inference is possible only because He condescends to make Himself intelligible to us, to speak to us through word or work, to reveal Himself. We hazard nothing therefore, in saying that, as the condition of all theology is a revealed God so, without limitation, the sole source of theology is revelation.[54]

Yet in making this point, Warfield also asserts that God can and does reveal himself to his creatures in many "divers" ways, including nature, providence, and Christian experience. Therefore, we are to "accept [these divers means] with no reserve ... as true and valid sources" of theology. In addition, we are to see them as including "the well-authenticated data yielded by these are to be received by us as revelations of God, and as such to be placed alongside of the revelations in the written Word and wrought with them into one system."[55]

Warfield is careful to assert that not all of these diverse sources are of equal clarity or importance. "The mere fact that He has included in these 'divers manners' a copious revelation in a written Word, delivered with an authenticating accompaniment of signs and miracles," in addition to the added consideration of fulfilled prophecy, quickly pushes us to the conclusion that the written Word is "incomparably superior to all other manifestations of Him in the fullness, richness, and clearness of its communications."[56] This does not invalidate nature, providence, and Christian experience as sources of theology. On the contrary, they have legitimate roles to play in the construction of a complete systematic theology. Warfield's point is that the Scriptures exponentially surpass these other sources in clarity and content. He stresses that "the revelation of God in His written Word—in which are included the only authenticated records of the revelation of Him through the Incarnate Word" also contains that which men must know about eternal things. This written

54. Ibid.
55. Ibid., 59. In his essay "The Biblical Idea of Revelation," Warfield mentions three distinct modes of revelation. These include "theophany" which he believed was characteristic of the Patriarchal age, prophecy as characteristic of the age of the prophets, and "inspiration," as characteristic of the New Testament age, which Warfield describes as the age of the Spirit (p. 82). Warfield is careful to qualify his remarks by asserting that all three of these modes occur in all ages, but they are, however, characteristic of the ages as Warfield describes them. Warfield notes that nature and providence as particular aspects of revelation are "divinely directed and assisted second causes (p. 77)."
56. Ibid., 60.

revelation alone serves as "the norm of interpretation for what is revealed so much more darkly through other methods of manifestation. The glorious character of the discoveries made in it throws all other manifestations into comparative shadow."[57] Warfield concludes:

> With the fullest recognition of the validity of all the knowledge of God and His ways with men, which can be obtained through the manifestations of His power and divinity in nature and history and grace; and the frankest allowance that the written Word is given, not to destroy the manifestations of God, but to fulfill them; the theologian must yet refuse to give these sources of knowledge a place alongside of the written Word in any other sense than that he gladly admits that they, alike with it, but in unspeakable lower measure, do tell us of God. And nothing can be a clearer indication of a decadent theology or of a decaying faith, than a tendency to neglect the Word in favor of some one or all of the lessor sources of theological truth, as fountains from which to draw our knowledge of divine things. This were to prefer the flickering rays of a taper to the blazing light of the sun; to elect to drink water from a muddy run rather than dip it from the broad bosom of the fountain itself.[58]

Despite the fact that such a superior, authenticated revelation[59] has been in the possession of the Church throughout its existence, "men have often sought to still the carvings of their souls with a purely natural theology." Even worse, there are those who "to-day prefer to derive their knowledge of what God is and what He will do from an analysis of the implications of their own religious feelings."[60] In either case, we do

57. Ibid., 60–61.
58. Ibid., 61.
59. Warfield elsewhere had argued that the authentication of Scripture was *prior* to every theory of inspiration. Warfield had written that "The supernatural origin and contents of Christianity, not only may be vindicated apart from any question of the inspiration of the record, but, in point of fact, always are vindicated prior to any question of the inspiration of the record." See B. B. Warfield, "The Inspiration of the Bible," from *Bibliotheca Sacra* Vol. 51 (October 1894), 614–40. Repr. in Warfield, *Inspiration and Authority of the Bible*, 105–28, under the title "The Church Doctrine of Inspiration," 121.
60. Warfield, "The Idea of Systematic Theology," 61. Here the two enemies identified by Warfield—rationalism and mysticism—rear their heads again. This is a common theme in Warfield's writings. It is treated for instance in his writings on the inspiration of Scripture, see the "Church Doctrine of Inspiration," 112–13; and in

not find God as he reveals himself, but instead we find the God "who we would fain should be." In words reminiscent of Calvin's opening chapters of the *Institutes*, Warfield concludes that "the natural result of resting on the revelations of nature is despair; while the inevitable end of making our appeal even to the Christian heart is to make for ourselves refuges of lies in which there is neither truth nor safety."[61] While we may certainly draw inferences from religious experience, nature, and providence, Warfield cautions that it is very important that we do not step beyond the limits of such inferences. The only way to do this is to evaluate all such modes of revelation in light of the clearest mode—Holy Scripture. "There may be a theology without the Scriptures—theology of nature, gathered by painful, and slow, and sometimes doubtful processes from what man sees round him in external nature and in the course of history."[62] Warfield equates such an attempt with the science of astronomy, and these "divers manners" with the tools of astronomy. But the comparison soon breaks down, for "the Word of God is to theology as, but vastly more than, these instruments are to astronomy. It is the instrument which so far increase the possibilities of the science as to revolutionize it and to place it upon a height from which it can never descend."[63] Thus Warfield concludes, "The Scriptures form the only sufficing source of theology."[64]

Warfield's fifth aspect of the idea of systematic theology as a science relates to the relationship that systematic theology must maintain with the other closely related theological disciplines. Here Warfield generally follows conventional wisdom, with the possible exception of the role that he assigns to apologetics. "We may adopt here the usual fourfold distribution of the theological disciplines into the Exegetical, the Historical, the Systematic, and the Practical, with only the correction of prefixing to them a fifth department of Apologetical theology."[65] Thus systematic theology alone stands out as the "crown and the head."

---

his polemical writings, see "Christless Christianity," from *The Harvard Review*, vol. V (October 1912), 423–73, and reprinted in B. B. Warfield, *Christology and Criticism* (Grand Rapids: Baker Book House, 1981), 313–67, especially pages 338 ff.

61. Ibid., 62.
62. Ibid., 63.
63. Ibid., 62.
64. Ibid.
65. Ibid., 64. In the "Task and Nature of Systematic Theology" (p. 92), Warfield had written, "It is clear at once that 'systematic theology' forms the central, or perhaps

Apologetical theology "prepares the way for all theology by establishing its necessary presuppositions without which no theology is possible."[66] This means that apologetics is virtually synonymous with theological prolegomena and serves the purpose of establishing the foundation for all theology—"the existence and essential nature of God, the religious nature of man which enable him to receive a revelation from God, the possibility of a revelation and its actualization in the Scriptures."[67] The perceived role of the apologist is to place within the hands of the exegete the Scriptures themselves, authenticated as a revelation from God and now ready for "investigation and study." Exegetical theology "investigates their meaning; presenting us with a body of detailed and substantiated results, culminating in organized systems of Biblical History, Biblical Ethics, Biblical Theology, and the like, which provide material for further use in the more advanced disciplines."[68] The role of historical theology is one which:

> ... investigates the progressive realization of Christianity in the lives, hearts, worship, and thought of men, issuing not only in a full account of the history of Christianity, but also in a body of facts which come into use in the more advanced disciplines, especially in the way of manifold experiments that have been made during the ages in Christian organization, worship, living and creed-building, as well as the sifted results of the reasoned thinking and deep experience of Christian truth during the past.[69]

As a distinct theological and scientific discipline, systematic theology must certainly draw from the vast resources supplied by this history of doctrinal development. Systematic theology "gladly utilizes all the material that Historical Theology brings it, accounting it, indeed, the very precipate of the Christian consciousness of the past."[70] Yet, systematic theology cannot draw uncritically from historical theology and the

---

we may better say the culminating, department of theological science. It is the goal to which apologetical, exegetical, and historical theology lead up."

66. Ibid.

67. Ibid.

68. Ibid., 62.

69. Ibid., 64. Warfield's work in the field of historical theology is the subject of a very substantial doctoral dissertation. See James Samuel McClanahan, "Benjamin B. Warfield: Historian of Doctrine in Defense of Orthodoxy, 1881–1921," (Ph.D. diss.: Union Theological Seminary in Virginia, 1988).

70. Ibid.

systematician must constantly remember systematic theology's primary relationship is to "Exegetical Theology which is its true and especial handmaiden."[71]

It is also important to consider in this connection the role assigned to biblical theology, which was at the time a rather new, but booming, field at Princeton under the guidance of its new Professor of Biblical Theology, Geerhardus Vos. Vos had arrived at Princeton in 1894, just two years before Warfield's article now under review was published. Warfield defines biblical theology as:

> not a section of Historical Theology, although it must be studied in a historical spirit, and has a historical face; it is rather the ripest fruit of Exegetics, and Exegetics has not performed its full task until its scattered results in the way of theological data are gathered up into a full and articulated system of Biblical Theology. ... The task of Biblical Theology in a word, is the task of coordinating the scattered results of continuous exegesis into a concatenated whole, whether with reference to a single book of Scripture or to a body of related books or to the whole Scriptural fabric. ... It is to reproduce the theological thought of each writer or group of writers in the form in which it lay in their own minds, so that we may be enabled to look at all of their theological statements at their angle, and to understand all their deliverances as modified and conditioned by their own point of view.[72]

It is important to note that Warfield was very critical of biblical theology when the discipline was used by critics to emphasize discontinuities between the biblical writers, rather than emphasize what Warfield saw as obvious continuities between them.[73]

Warfield believed that "the relation of Biblical Theology to Systematic Theology is based on a true view of its function." This means that

71. Ibid., 65.

72. Ibid., 65–66.

73. In this regard, Warfield had written several years later, "this new discipline of 'Biblical Theology' came to us indeed wrapped in the swaddling clothes of rationalism, and it was rocked in the cradle of the Hegelian recasting of Christianity; it did not present, at first, therefore, a very engaging countenance, and seemed to find for a time its chief pleasure in setting the prophets and apostles by the ears. But already in the hands of men like Schmid and Oehler it began to show that it was born to better things." B. B. Warfield, "The Century's Progress in Biblical Knowledge," in *The Homiletic Review* (March 1900), 195–202 and reprinted in *Selected Shorter Writings*, vol. 2, 3–13.

systematic theology does not derive its materials from exegetical theology, since exegetical theology is not complete unless the raw data it produces is organized by biblical theology, properly conceived. Since biblical theology is the primary source of material for systematic theology, it must be clear in our minds that "Biblical theology is not a rival of Systematics; it is not even a parallel product of the same body of facts, provided by exegesis; it is the basis and source of Systematics."[74] It is interesting to contrast Geerhardus Vos' perspective on this point with that of Warfield, when Vos comments, "Biblical Theology draws a *line* of development. Systematic Theology draws a *circle*."[75]

Warfield notes that a word of qualification is in order here. "Systematic Theology is not a concatenation of the scattered theological data furnished by the exegetic process; it is the combination of the already concatenated data given to it by Biblical Theology."[76] This enables the theologian to view the whole, the parts, the end, the beginning, and other such aspects of the biblical revelation as they are seen individually, in their relation to each other, and then in turn, their differing relations with each other. "And thus we do not make our theology, according to our own pattern, as a mosaic, out of the fragments of the Biblical teaching; but rather," writes Warfield, "look out from ourselves upon it as a great prospect framed out of the mountains and plains of the theologies

74. Warfield, "The Idea of Systematic Theology," 66.

75. Geerhardus Vos, *Biblical Theology: Old and New Testaments* (Grand Rapids: Eerdmans, 1977), 16.

76. Warfield, "The Idea of Systematic Theology," 66–67. Richard Lints points out that Warfield seems to take little notice of the problem that the recent development of the discipline presents to Warfield's overall schema. "The irony here is that the discipline which was to provide the basis for systematic theology was nonexistent for most of the historical life of systematic theology. The child [systematic theology] was apparently much older than the parent [biblical theology] (though roughly the same age as the grandparent). Systematic theology (on Warfield's own reckoning) was as old as the Christian church and yet biblical theology, being relatively new, was somehow to have furnished the data out of which systematic theology was to rise. How was it possible for there to be such a thing as systematic theology without a prior biblical theology? Without noticing this problem, Warfield suggested that there was a clear and straightforward relationship between these two theological methodologies. In point of historical fact, the relationship seemed far more complicated than Warfield at least formally recognized it to be." See Richard Lints, "Two Theologies or One?," 238. Perhaps it is better to see Warfield's scheme as setting out the ideal situation, rather than the historical situation.

of the Scriptures, and strive to attain a point of view from which we can bring the whole landscape into our field of sight."[77]

Once the theologian has done this, "we find no difficulty in understanding the relation in which several disciplines stand to one another, with respect to their contents." Using a very clever analogy, Warfield compares the role of exegesis to that of a military recruiting officer, who, in effect, draws out from among the mass of mankind, those individuals who will eventually compose the entire army itself. Biblical theology is compared to basic military organization, where chosen individuals are placed into particular companies and regiments, each with specific purposes and duties. Systematic theology, in this analogy then, organizes all of these individual companies and regiments into an entire army—"a single and unitary whole, determined by its own all-pervasive principle."[78] Systematic theology is the crowning jewel of these related disciplines since it alone performs the most comprehensive and most inclusive of tasks, and as such, systematic theology still reigns supreme as the "queen of the sciences."

Warfield's sixth area of discussion concerns the role that systematic theology, when conceived as a science, must occupy in relationship to other sciences. Warfield asserts that the role of systematic theology must be seen as "far out of all comparison above all other sciences as the eternal health and destiny of the soul are of more value than fleeting life in this world."[79] Since the queen of the sciences deals with the most fundamental questions of life, "Theology, thus, enters into the structure of every other science. Its closest relations are, no doubt, with the highest of the other sciences, ethics."[80] But if the science of ethics were to be pursued on purely natural grounds, ethics as a scientific enterprise would unfortunately be "a meager thing indeed, while the theology of the Scriptural revelation for the first time affords a basis for ethical investigation at once broad enough and sure enough to raise that science to its true dignity."[81] When seen in this light, systematic theology has a paramount role to play in relationship to the other sciences. In fact, Warfield states, "Something like it in kind and approaching it in degree

77. Ibid., 67.
78. Ibid., 68.
79. Ibid.
80. Ibid., 69.
81. Ibid.

exists between theology and every other science, no one of which is so independent of it as not to touch and be touched by it." Warfield adds:

> Something of theology is implicated in all metaphysics and physics alike. It alone can determine the origin of either matter or mind, or of the mystic powers that have been granted to them. It alone can explain the nature of second causes and set the boundaries to their efficiency. It alone is competent to declare the meaning of the ineradicable persuasion of the human mind that its reason is right, its processes trustworthy, its intuitions true. All science without God is mutilated science, and no account of a single branch of knowledge can ever be complete until it is pushed back to find its completion and ground in him. ... The science of Him and His relations is the necessary ground of all science. All speculation takes us back to Him; all inquiry presupposes Him; and every phase of science consciously or unconsciously rests at every step on the science that makes Him known.[82]

With this in mind, Warfield concludes, "Theology, thus, as the science which treats of God, lies at the root of all science. It is true enough that each could exist without it, in a sense and to some degree; but through it alone can any of them reach its true dignity."[83] Systematic theology is the most important of all sciences, then, since "it is only in theology, therefore, that the other sciences find their completion. Theology,

---

82. Ibid., 70. I am struck how much this sounds like Cornelius Van Til, or better yet, how much Van Til sounds like Warfield! In actuality, this is again drawn from Scottish Common Sense Realism as set out in McCosh, *The Scottish Philosophy*, 217–18.

83. Ibid., 71. Louis Berkhof, himself a student of Warfield, follows Warfield to a degree here, but there is clearly a moderation of some of Warfield's statements, especially as to how theology as a science "compares" with natural sciences. "Theology has its own distinctive method, but there is after all a great deal which it has in common with the other sciences. If the matter with which theology deals is given by revelation, so is, strictly speaking, also the matter which the other sciences build into a system. ... Theology, then, does not move into the sphere of the natural sciences, and therefore does not and cannot apply its methods. It would succeed only in destroying itself by the application of the experimental method. ... It should be borne in mind that theology is not merely a descriptive science, which yields only historical knowledge, but very decidedly a normative science which deals with absolute truth, given by revelation and binding on the conscience." See Louis Berkhof, *Introduction to Systematic Theology* (Grand Rapids: Baker Book House, 1979), 47–48. For a brief discussion of Berkhof's time at Princeton, see Henry Zwaanstra, "Louis Berkhof," in *Reformed Theology in America* (ed. David F. Wells; Grand Rapids: Eerdmans, 1985), 154–57.

formally speaking, is accordingly the apex of the pyramid of the sciences by which the structure is perfected."[84] The obvious implication of this statement is that all other sciences are "subsidiary to it, and it builds its fabric out of the material supplied by them" since systematic theology "is the science which deals with the facts concerning God and His relations with the universe."[85] The comprehensive nature of systematic theology as a science can be also be seen in the case in view because "such facts include all the facts of nature and history: and it is the very function of the several sciences to supply these facts in scientific, that is, thoroughly comprehended form."[86] Warfield concludes then, "Scientific theology thus stands at the head of the sciences as well as at the head of the theological disciplines."[87]

Warfield is, of course, aware that such comments demand some immediate qualification:

> It would seem to be a mistake, for example, to conceive of scientific theology as the immediate and direct synthesis of three sources—Natural Theology, Biblical Theology, and Comparative Theology—so that it would be considered the product in like degree or even in similar manner of the three. All three furnish data for the completed structure; but if what has been said in an earlier connection has any validity, Natural and Comparative Theology should stand in a different relation to Scientific Theology from that which Biblical Theology occupies—a relation not less organic indeed, but certainly less direct. The true representation seems to be that Scientific Theology is related to the natural and historical sciences, not immediately and independently for itself, but only indirectly, that is, through the mediation of the preliminary theological discipline of Apologetics.[88]

Again, for Warfield, apologetics assumes an extremely important role, since in his conception, it falls to the apologist to establish the foundation upon which the theologian must build by drawing upon the materials provided by the natural sciences. Additionally, it falls to the apologist to supply the raw materials to the subsidiary disciplines

84. Ibid.
85. Ibid., 71–72.
86. Ibid., 72.
87. Ibid.
88. Ibid., 73.

of exegesis and biblical theology. These disciplines then turn these raw materials into the finished material for inclusion into the theological system. According to Warfield, "The work of Apologetics in its three branches, Philosophical, Psychological, and Historical, results not only in presenting the Bible to the theological student, but also in presenting to him God, Religion and Christianity."[89] In doing this, the apologist has supplied the materials usually subsumed under the headings of comparative and natural theology. Therefore, exegetics and biblical theology provide the materials for the systematician who is assigned the task of assembling these materials into a complete system. Systematic theology also uses "the results of the age-long life of men under Christianity through historical theology."[90] It is clear that "scientific theology rests, therefore, most directly on the results of Biblical exegesis as provided in Biblical Theology; but avails itself likewise of all the material furnished by all the preceding disciplines."[91] Warfield details this relationship in a chart, which sets out these relationships in their proper detail and is reproduced on the following page.[92]

89. Ibid. See chapter 3, "Apologetics," where I attempt to develop this relationship in some detail.
90. Ibid., 73.
91. Ibid., 73–74.
92. I have reproduced the chart in its entirety found on the bottom of page 74 in "The Idea of Systematic Theology."

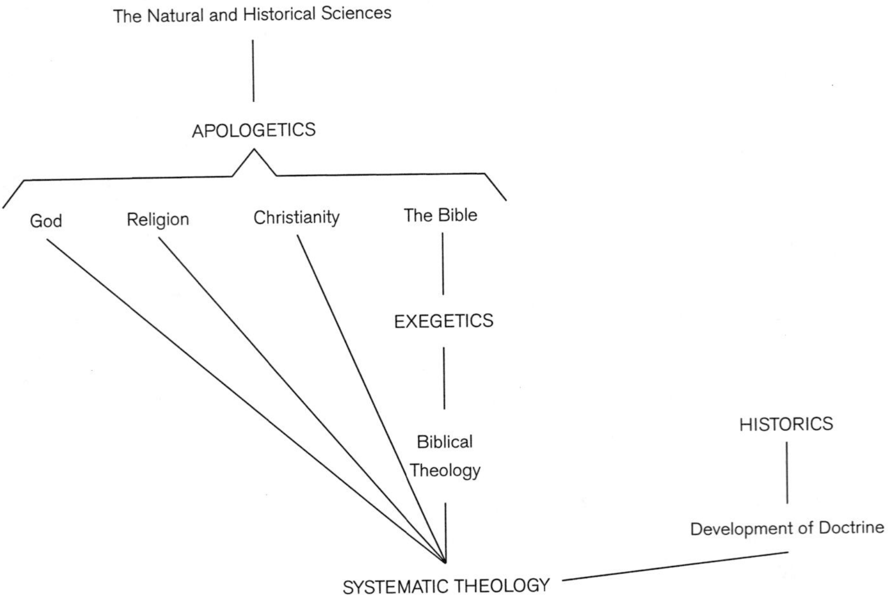

Warfield's seventh area of discussion addresses his conception that theology is a "progressive science," thus possessing innumerable advantages over other sciences. Warfield believes that systematic theology alone possess its facts in a written document "intended to convey a plain message," instead of being forced to interpret the facts as raw data, without the benefit of such a revelation. "Theology has, therefore, an immense advantage over other sciences, inasmuch as it is more an inductive study of facts contained in a written revelation, than an inductive study of facts conveyed in life."[93] Warfield argues that this is why theology was "the first-born" of all of the sciences, since the science of theology developed in its fullness far earlier in the history of Western Civilization than did other sciences. And yet, Warfield does not wish to deny the progressive nature of theology as a developing science either. "In exactly the same sense in which any other science is progressive, this is progressive."[94] The Princetonian cautions, "There is a vast difference between the progress of a science and increase in its material."[95]

93. Warfield, "The Idea of Systematic Theology," 74.
94. Ibid., 75.
95. Ibid.

The material possessed may be more fully explicated and systematized, but this does not constitute "new data."

Warfield describes this progressive development of Christian theology in terms of his objective/subjective distinction:

> The affirmation that theology has been a progressive science is no more, than, to assert that it is a science that has had a history—and a history which can and should be genetically traced and presented. First, the objective side of Christian truth was developed: pressed on the one side by the crass monotheism of the Jews and on the other by the coarse polytheism of the heathen, and urged on by its own internal need of comprehending the sources of its life, Christian theology first searched the Scriptures that it might understand the nature and modes of existence of its God and the person of its divine Redeemer. Then, more and more conscious of itself, it more fully brought out from those same Scriptures a guarded expression of the subjective side of its faith; until through throes and conflicts it has built up the system which we all inherit. Thus the body of Christian truth has come down to us in the form of an organic growth; and when we conceive of the completed structure as the ripened fruit of the ages, as truly as we can think of it as the perfected result of the exegetical discipline. As it has come into our possession by this historic process, there is no reason that we can assign why it should not continue to make for itself a history. We do not expect the history of theology to close in our own day.[96]

Given the progressive nature of the theological enterprise then, it should come as no surprise that Warfield expressed a great deal of optimism about the future of theology as a science—indicating his postmillennial eschatological optimism perhaps[97]—when he asserted that

96. Ibid., 75–76.

97. Warfield's eschatological optimism can be clearly seen in several essays. In his book, *The Plan of Salvation*, for example, Warfield asserts: "If you wish, as you lift up your eyes to the far horizon of the future, to see looming on the edge of time the glory of a saved world ... and that in His own good time and way [God] will bring the world in its entirety to the feet of Him whom He has not hesitated to present to our adoring love not merely as the Saviour of our own souls but as the Saviour of the world. ... The Scriptures teach an eschatological universalism, not an each and every universalism. When the Scriptures say that Christ came to save the world, that He does save the world, and that the world shall be saved by Him ... they mean that He came to save and does save the human race; and that the human race is being led by

"the finished texture is ever and will ever continue to be before us until we dare affirm that there is no truth in the Word which we have not perfectly apprehended."[98] Warfield describes several examples of this ongoing process:

> The conditions of progress in theology are clearly discernable from its nature as a science. The progressive men in any science are the men who stand firmly on the basis of the already ascertained truth. The condition of progress in building the structures of those great cathedrals whose splendid piles glorify the history of art in the Middle Ages, was that each succeeding generation should build upon the foundations laid by its predecessor. If each architect had begun by destroying what had been accomplished by his forerunners, no cathedral would ever have been raised. The railroad is pushed across the continent by the simple process of laying each rail at the end of the line already laid. The prerequisite of all progress is a clear discrimination which as frankly accepts the limitations set by the truth already discovered, as it rejects the false and bad. Construction is not destruction: neither is it the outcome of destruction. There are abuses no doubt to be reformed; errors to correct; and falsehoods to cut away. But the history of progress in every science and no less in theology, is a story of impulses given, corrected and assimilated.[99]

God into a racial salvation; that in the age-long development of the race of men, it will attain at last unto a complete salvation, and our eyes will be greeted with the glorious spectacle of a saved world." (See B. B. Warfield, *The Plan of Salvation* (Grand Rapids: Eerdmans , 1980), 99–103. Such sentiments are also evident in Warfield's polemical defense of the Reformed notion of particular redemption in an essay on the meaning of 1 John 2:2. Warfield again speaks of a "saved world." According to the Princetonian, "John means only, he says, that Christ is the Saviour with abiding power for the whole human era; through all ages He is mighty to save, though He saves only his own. It is much more common silently to assume that 'by the whole world' John has in mind the whole race of mankind throughout the entire range of its existence in time. ... Where the expositors have gone astray is in not perceiving that this salvation of the world was conceived by John—any more than the salvation of the individual—as accomplishing itself all at once. Jesus came to save the world, and the world will through Him be saved: at the end of the day, He will have a saved world to present to His father." See B. B. Warfield, "Jesus Christ the Propitiation for the Whole World," from *The Expositor*, XXI (1921), 241–53.

98. Warfield, "The Idea of Systematic Theology," 76.

99. Ibid., 76–77.

Thus Warfield concludes, "It is utter folly to suppose that progress can be made otherwise than by placing ourselves in the line of progress."[100]

This gives Warfield the opportunity to respond to what was labeled as "progressive orthodoxy"[101] and which was a term used, according to Warfield, "in [a] somewhat strange connection. ... Let us assert that the history of theology has ever been and ever must be a progressive orthodoxy." Since Warfield affirms this point, he must also affirm that "progressive orthodoxy and retrogressive heterodoxy can scarcely be controvertible terms."[102] The orthodox must remain at the same time both progressive and orthodox, as they collectively strive to move the theological enterprise toward the greater establishment of the truth—laying new ties and rails on the end of the line, and yet at the same time they must remain orthodox in that they cannot regard as progress the willful destruction or repudiation of what has gone before. In a sense, then, "progress brings increasing limitation, just because it brings increasing knowledge."[103] Warfield is concerned that in order for systematic theology to exist as a true science, progress must exist as an essential element. However, progress that undermines the existing system is not progress at all. The theologian's job is to add and to build upon the system that he inherits. Destruction of that system is not progress; for Warfield, it is unbelief.

Warfield's eighth and final area of concern as expressed in "The Idea of Systematic Theology" relates to the fact that "when we speak of progress our eyes are set upon a goal." Because systematic theology is a progressive science with a unique subject matter and "when we consider the surpassing glory of the subject-matter with which theology deals, it would appear that if ever science existed for its own sake, this might surely be true of this science."[104] The subject matter of systematic the-

100. Ibid., 77.

101. Warfield's response to "progressive orthodoxy" in the areas of nature and grace, revelation and inspiration, Christology and soteriology, was the subject of a brief descriptive article by Robert Swanton, "Warfield and Progressive Orthodoxy," in *The Reformed Theological Review* Vol. XXIII (October, 1964), 74–87.

102. Warfield, "The Idea of Systematic Theology," 77.

103. Ibid., 78–79. In his fine article detailing the relationship between Warfield's and Vos' conception of theology, Richard Lints makes an important point in this regard. "As biblical theology grows, so ought systematic theology, and as historical theology makes us more aware of the development of doctrine, so systematic theology should develop and locate itself in its own historical niche. In this sense, systematic theology is a progressive theology for Warfield." See Lints, "Two Theologies or One?," 245.

104. Ibid., 79.

ology is "the most worthy of all truths of study and examination." The theologian quickly learns that facts given to us by God are also given for a specific purpose "to save and sanctify the soul."[105] Thus:

> [The study of theology is] well worth our most laborious study, then, as it is, for its own sake as mere truth, it becomes absorbingly interesting, but inexpressibly precious to us when we bear in mind that the truth with which we thus deal constitutes, as a whole, the engrafted Word that is able to save our souls. The task of thoroughly exploring the pages of revelation, soundly gathering from them their treasures of theological teaching, and carefully fitting these in their due places in system whereby may be preserved from misunderstanding, perversion, and misuse, and given a new power to convince the understanding, move the heart, and quicken the will, becomes thus a holy duty to our own and our brothers' souls as well as an eager pleasure of intellectual nature.[106]

There is in Warfield's conception, the sense that the more we know about the revelation of God, the greater the effect of the Word of God will be upon us. The greater our ability to systematize the great truths contained in that revelation, the greater will be our ability to communicate them to others. Conversely, those areas where we err only serve to cause a stunting of true and proper growth. Thus, "the character of our religion is, in a word, determined by the character of our theology." Warfield adds, "Thus the task of the systematic theologian is to see that the relations in which the separate truths actually stand are rightly conceived, in order that they might exert their rightful influence on the development of the religious life."[107] Although Warfield is often portrayed as a cold-hearted rationalist, he passionately claims, "No truth is so insignificant as to have no place in the development of our religious life, so no truth is so unimportant that we can dare neglect it or deal deceitfully with it in adjusting it into our system."[108]

Warfield also points out that theological progress is often driven by the purely practical demands of the Church.

105. Ibid., 75.
106. Ibid., 79–80.
107. Ibid., 80.
108. Ibid. This question of the supposed "cold-heartedness" of the Princetonians has been effectively addressed in W. Andrew Hoffecker's book, *Piety and the Princeton Theologians* (Phillipsburg: P&R Publishing, 1981).

> We wholly misconceive the facts if we imagine that the development of systematic theology has been the work of cold scholastic, recluses, intent only upon intellectual subtleties. It has been the work of the best heart of the whole Church, driving on and utilizing in its practical interests, the best brain.[109]

Thus "theology as a science of God and in His relations with the world" flourishes whenever the practical needs of the Church are greatest. "We do not possess the separate truths of religion in the abstract: we possess them only in their relations, and we do not properly know any of them—nor can it have its full effect on our life—except as we know it in its relations to other truths, that is systematized."[110] This clearly means that if we do not have proper knowledge of our doctrines systematically, we will misunderstand both the nature of the doctrine and the proper effect of that doctrine upon the religious life. Without a proper systematic theology, the Church is incapable of fulfilling its divinely ordained mission.

Echoing the older orthodoxy on this point,[111] Warfield concludes that systematic theology is the most practical of all of the theological disciplines because "the systematic theologian is preeminently a preacher of the Gospel; and the end of his work is obviously not merely the logical arrangement of the truths that come under his hand, but the moving of men to love God with all their hearts and their neighbors as themselves; to choose their portion with the Saviour of their souls."[112] Thus the theologian cannot escape the tremendous importance of the divine task given to him. "He needs to be not merely a student, not merely a thinker, not merely a systematizer, not merely a teacher—he needs to be like

109. Ibid., 81.

110. Ibid., 83.

111. See for example, Francis Turretin, *Institutio Theologiae Elencticae* (New York: Robert Carter, 1847), I.vii.I–XV.

112. Warfield, "The Idea of Systematic Theology," 86. In his essay, "The Indispensableness of Systematic Theology to the Preacher," (1897) Warfield wrote, "It is summed up in the propositions that it is through the truth that souls are saved, that it is accordingly the prime business of the preacher to present this truth to men, and that it is consequently his fundamental duty to become himself possessed of this truth, that he may present it to men and so save their souls. ... And Systematic Theology is nothing other than the saving truth of God presented in systematic form (pp. 280–281)."

the beloved disciple himself in the highest, truest and holiest sense, a divine."[113]

"The Idea of Systematic Theology" stands as one of Warfield's most important contributions, not only to the field of systematic theology specifically, but also in terms of his insight into the task of a theologian and the nature of theology proper.

"THE RIGHT OF SYSTEMATIC THEOLOGY"—THE PROBLEM WITH "INDIFFERENT LATITUDINARIANS"

B. B. Warfield's second significant endeavor in the field of systematic theology came with the publication of "The Right of Systematic Theology," in July of 1896. This substantial article (some 45 pages in its original form, and later published as a book with a forward by James Orr) was completed on the heels of the previous essay, "The Idea of Systematic Theology," which had been published in April of the same year. In "The Idea of Systematic Theology," Warfield had primarily concerned himself with defining the nature, scope, and parameters of the science of systematic theology. "The Right of Systematic Theology" has a markedly cynical, if not sarcastic tone. In this essay, Warfield sets out to vindicate the right, and defend the very necessity, of systematic theology as a distinct theological science. Warfield will also attempt to connect the "facts" of Christianity to doctrine, and in doing so demonstrate the futility of attempting to ground the Christian faith in the life of the believing subject rather than in the objective historical events recorded in the New Testament.

In "The Right of Systematic Theology" Warfield exhibits little patience for those he describes as "indifferentists" and "latitudinarians"—those who disparage the role of precise theological formulations. Warfield laments, "The right of Systematic Theology to reign is not only the thing that is brought into question these days: its very right to exist is widely challenged."[114] The reason for this, declares Warfield, is because of the impatience of so many "with the effort to define truth and to state with precision the doctrinal presuppositions and the contents of Christianity."[115] Given Warfield's allegiance to Common Sense Realism, his own frustration with romantic and subjective definitions

113. Ibid., 87.
114. Warfield, "The Right of Systematic Theology," 220–21.
115. Ibid., 221.

of Christianity quickly becomes evident, making his writing more caustic than usual. As Warfield sees it, the basic problem needing to be addressed is indifference to doctrine, which is indifference to Christianity itself. Warfield pointedly contends:

> The basis of this impatience is often a mere latitudinarian indifferentism, which finds its expression in neglect of formulated truth and is never weary of girding at what it represents as the hair-splitting ingenuity of theologians and the unprofitableness of theological discussion. But this indifference is at root dislike; and the easy affirmation that doctrines are useless passes very readily into the heated assertion that they are noxious. Now the contemptuous smile gives way to the flush of anger, and instead of an unconcerned expression of the opinion that theology is a more or less amiable weakness, we have the passionate assertion that theology is killing religion.[116]

This unfortunate situation is not seen as altogether disastrous however, because "a certain relief often comes with the outbreak of open war."[117] The essay "The Right of Systematic Theology" is therefore Warfield's response to this state of war and indicates a concerted effort to cross swords with the "indifferent" and "latitudinarian" foes of the science of systematic theology. But this whole enterprise can be quite frustrating because "it is not hard to show the folly of theological indifferentism: but just because it is indifferent, indifferentism is apt to pay little attention to our exhibition of its folly. If only we could get it to care!"[118]

Theological indifference does not usually fall under Warfield's apologetic gaze, because the matter is "to be discussed between men professing to be Christians, instead of one in debate between Christian and non-Christian worlds."[119] According to Warfield, "The question, then, that we propose to consider lies within the limits of the theological disciplines. It assumes the right of theology at large, and inquires concerning the right of Systematic Theology in particular."[120] Since systematic theology, as a distinctive theological discipline, was under an intense attack, Warfield states the present dilemma as clearly as he can. "We

116. Ibid.
117. Ibid.
118. Ibid.
119. Ibid., 219
120. Ibid., 219–20.

are accustomed to regard theology as the queen of the sciences, and Systematic Theology as queen among the theological disciplines. But these are the days when lofty claims are not readily allowed."[121]

In Warfield's estimation, things have reached such a low level that it is all too commonplace to hear that "theology is killing religion."[122] The basis for this situation, it is often asserted, is that those who are described as the "latitudinarian indifferentists," have grown weary of theological hair-splitting and simply attempt to avoid discussion of doctrine because of its supposed unprofitable nature. On the contrary, there is much more at stake than mere indifference to doctrine. For under the guise of such "indifference," there exists a marked hostility toward the discipline of systematic theology that is in reality a serious challenge to Christianity itself. This hostility is not only seen in the academy, but according to Warfield:

> The whole mass of popular religious literature of the period seems surcharged with attacks on "Intellectualism" and "Dogmatism," and glowing with highly colored portraitures of "good Christians" of every name and no name, of every faith and no faith, under each of which stands the legend written that since good Christians arise under every form of faith or no faith alike, it cannot be of much importance what men believe.[123]

The real problem, then, was more than just mere indifference concerning the legitimacy of the discipline of systematic theology. The underlying issue was a fundamental crisis of truth, which ultimately called all of dogmatic science into question. Objective truth and doctrinal propositions, which characterized the Princeton theology, were being replaced by subjective experience and personal morality, which destroyed the uniqueness of Christianity. The epistemological foundation of Reid and McCosh was giving way to the intellectual children of Kant and Hegel. Christianity was no longer perceived as a matter of propositions and truth claims, for in this new intellectual climate, Christianity was increasingly equated with sentimentality and subjectivism. The basic problem, as defined by Warfield, is that the "whole latitudinarian position is built upon the fancy that the product of the

121. Ibid., 220.
122. Ibid., 220–21.
123. Ibid., 223–24.

religious sentiment is Christianity."[124] In this post-Kantian world, doctrine was not only seen to be of little if any value, but was actually declared a hindrance to true religion.

If the exercise of religious sentiment is equated with Christianity, and is merely the result of the exercise of the natural religious nature of mankind, we are forced to ask, "What remains of Christianity itself?" At this point Warfield adduces a kind of *reductio ad absurdum* into his argument. Pity the poor man who ends up like the man described in the essay—who attempted to teach an anonymous Muslim carpenter to embrace the "true religion," only to find to his embarrassment that the Muslim a man possessed a much deeper religious nature than he himself. How could the poor man teach the Muslim about "true religion" on these grounds? Why should the man not do what he eventually ended up doing—giving "distinctive Christianity up" altogether?[125] If Christianity is equated with mere sentiment or morality, why even be a Christian at all? Indeed, any ethical or moral system such as Islam can easily be substituted for Christianity.

Warfield concludes, "To be indifferent to doctrine is thus but another way of saying that we are indifferent to Christianity."[126] "If then, we take the ground that nothing is needed but a deep religious sentiment and its fruits, we have cut up Christianity, in any intelligible sense, by the roots."[127] This is anathema because in the Princeton conception, religious sentiment is not, and cannot be, the basis for the Christian faith. In an oft-repeated theme in Warfield's writings,[128] he points out that "what after all, is peculiar to Christianity is not the religious sentiment and its working, but its message of salvation—in a word, its doctrine."[129]

---

124. Ibid., 226.
125. Ibid.
126. Ibid., 227.
127. Ibid., 226.
128. See for example, Warfield's essay, "Christless Christianity," 313–67. In this essay, Warfield sets out a similar line of argument: "Unquestionably, Christianity is a redemptive religion, having as its fundamental presupposition the fact of sin, felt both as guilt and as pollution, and offering as its central good, from which all other goods proceed, salvation from sin through an historical expiation wrought by the God-man Jesus Christ (p. 355)." Warfield regards Christianity as a religion entirely based upon God's entrance into human history in the person of Jesus Christ, and not as a product of the outworking of mankind's religious nature or sentiment.
129. Warfield, "The Right of Systematic Theology," 226–27. Elsewhere, Warfield had stated, "We cannot preach at all without preaching doctrine; and the type of religious life which grows up under our preaching will be determined by the doctrines

If doctrine, not sentiment or morality, is the basis of Christianity, then doctrine cannot be a matter of indifference. Warfield sets this argument out in some detail:

> If there be some doctrines to which as Christian men, we cannot be indifferent, then it is no longer true that doctrines as such are matters of indifference. There may be some doctrines which we esteem as less important than others, or even as of no importance in the framing of a specifically Christian life; but so long as there remain others, the maintenance of which we esteem essential to the very existence of Christianity, our attitude toward doctrine as such cannot be that of amused contempt. The very center of the debate is now shifted. And so little can doctrine be neglected on this new ground, that a serious attempt becomes at once imperative to distinguish between essential and unessential doctrines. Men may conceivably differ as to the exact point at which the line of discrimination between these classes should be drawn. But the very attempt to draw it implies that there are doctrines which are useful, important, necessary. And the admission of this yields the whole point in the debate. If there be any doctrines, however few, which justly deserve the name of essential doctrines and stand at the root of the Christian life as its conditions, foundations, or presuppositions, it surely becomes the duty as well as the right of the Christian man to study them, to seek to understand them in themselves and in their relations, to attempt to state them with accuracy and to adjust their statement to the whole body of known truth—in a word, the right and function of Systematic Theology is vindicated.[130]

Thus if Christianity has any essential doctrinal core whatsoever, the right, indeed the necessity, of systematic theology is thereby established as the means by which this doctrinal core is to be set out. In Warfield's mind, "the right of and function of Systematic theology is vindicated."

But given the increasingly romantic, sentimental religious climate in which Warfield found himself, "the widely diffused dislike of doctrine takes the more directly polemical form of declaring [doctrines] not merely useless but actively noxious," and so it is here "that the real

---

that we preach." See Warfield, "The Indispensableness of Systematic Theology to the Preacher," 286.

130. Ibid., 227.

controversy begins."[131] The "indifferentists" were not really indifferent to doctrine at all. While they may contend that "Christ ... did not come to teach a doctrine or to institute a hierarchy; he came to found a religion,"[132] by doing so, the "indifferentists" were actually engaged in a full frontal assault upon the Christian faith. As Warfield describes the matter, "theology is killing religion, we are told; and the hope of the future rests on our killing theology first that religion may live."[133] Thus, "doctrine" or "dogma," must be excised from Christianity so that the religion of sentiment, to which the "indifferentists" unashamedly reduce Christianity, may live on in peace and tranquility.

Warfield will have none of this, for this is "only the expression of an innate antipathy to clear thinking and not of a rare incapacity for truth—a sort of color-blindness to truth."[134] What provokes this sarcastic response from the usually gentlemanly Kentuckian, is that this frontal assault does not come from outside the faith, but tragically comes from within. "There are many theologians to whom truth in propositional form is in like manner distasteful, and half, or all, its life seems dissipated, for the same reason—because they too are afflicted with a 'lamentable and constitutional inaccuracy.' "[135] In a rare flash of cynicism, if not temper, Warfield writes:

> Men like these must be classified as deficient; and we can no more yield the right of theology in obedience to their outcries than the physicist can consent to refuse all discussion of color to please the color-blind, or the musician all study of harmony lest he should bore those who have no ear for music. Men who have no faculty for the truth will always consider an appeal to truth an evil. But the assault upon doctrinal Christianity is far from being confined to those whom we must believe to possess reason, indeed, for they too are men, but who seem very chary of using it. On the contrary, it is being carried on today by the very leaders of Christian thought—by men whose shining intellectual gifts are equalled only by their trained dialectical skill and the profundity of their theological training. "Theology is killing religion" is not merely the wail of those who are incapable of theology and would

131. Ibid., 228.
132. Ibid., 229.
133. Ibid.
134. Ibid.
135. Ibid., 230.

> nevertheless fain preserve their religion. It is the reasoned assertion of masters of theological science whose professed object is to preserve Christianity in its purity and save it from the dangers which encompass it in this weak and erring world. It is a position, therefore, which deserves our respectful consideration, and if we still feel bound to refuse it, we owe it to ourselves to give a reason for the faith that is in us.[136]

Drawing deeply from the well of Scottish Common Sense, Warfield cannot allow what he sees to be a false dichotomy between religious sentiment (supposedly associated with true piety), and Christian doctrine. He can readily and easily compare the truth claim of Christianity with that of the natural sciences and humanities. But he simply cannot allow "masters of theological science" to despair over the use of reason and dogmatics because it supposedly "kills religion."

Warfield does not let his temper get the best of him for long, however, because after briefly expressing his exasperation, he quickly returns to his methodical analysis. Next, Warfield isolates two specific issues associated with this assault on doctrinal Christianity and systematic theology. Warfield understands the two critical issues as follows:

> There are two chief points of view from which the right of doctrinal Christianity is denied by leading theologians of our day. The watchword of one of these schools of thought is that Christianity consists of facts, not dogmas: that of the other is that Christianity consists of life, not doctrine.[137]

The first school of thought, characterized as a "denial of doctrinal Christianity," is based upon the assertion that:

> Christianity, then, we are told, consists of facts, not of dogmas. What we rest upon for our salvation is not a body of theories, intellectual constructions, speculative ideas, but a series of mighty acts of God, by which He has entered into the course of human history and wrought powerfully for the salvation of our lost race.[138]

In this conception then, we are not saved by subscribing to any particular "theory" of the atonement, but instead we are saved by the act of atonement itself. Why not then reject all "theories" of the atonement?

136. Ibid.
137. Ibid.
138. Ibid.

Since such "theories" are not necessary to maintain Christianity, and since such theories can only become divisive, then perhaps it is best to reject these theories outright, so as to maintain the fact of Christ's death, without the unnecessary theological and doctrinal explanations.

For Warfield, the consequences of such formulations are grave. There is no real indifference to doctrine, only open hostility to doctrine masquerading as "indifference." Warfield quite pointedly writes, "This—this mighty series of divine acts—this is Christianity: by the side of these facts all human theories are only so many impertinences."[139] Therefore, "theories," dogmas, or doctrines can only obscure the real essence of Christianity, which is the act of redemption itself, not the man-made dogmas which bury true piety under a barren dogmatism and intellectualism. Thus the proponents of this viewpoint must argue that "Christianity consists of these facts, not of dogmas: and it is the sole business of the theologian to establish these facts, not to invent dogmas."[140] In many cases, those who hold this view exhort Christians "to lay aside their 'theological' creeds and adopt 'religious' ones—that is, creeds which consist in the mere enumeration of the great facts which lie at the basis of Christianity," with "something like the Apostles' Creed in mind."[141] Therefore, a non-dogmatic, "generic" Christianity of the lowest common denominator is to be preferred by the "indifferentists."

Warfield singles out Mr. Robert F. Horton of London, who is characterized as "a brilliant preacher, who, however, must not be taken too seriously as a theologian."[142] It is Horton who declares in his book *Faith and*

---

139. Ibid.
140. Ibid.
141. Ibid., 232.
142. Warfield, "The Right of Systematic Theology," 232. Warfield makes unusually negative remarks in reference to Mr. Horton's various works in several critical review articles. In a review of the same book under discussion here, Warfield describes Horton's "Essay on the Atonement" as characterized by an odd " 'half-wayness' which readers of Mr. Horton have learned to expect of him. ... He gives us much for which we are grateful. ... But he stops unreasonably short. How can he fail to see that if he should interpret the New Testament with the same directness with which he interprets the Fathers, he would not miss finding 'a theory' of the Atonement in the New Testament; that, in fact, its writers teach the 'satisfaction theory' a hundredfold more clearly than any Father teaches either of the theories which Mr. Horton attributes confidently to them." See B. B. Warfield, review of *Faith and Criticism*, in *The Presbyterian and Reformed Review*, vol. V (1894), 355–56. In an earlier review of another work, Warfield describes Horton's volume, *The Inspiration of the Bible*, as "one which we can call neither useful or admirable. Mr. Horton's methods are hopelessly vicious, his scholarship crude, and his results unacceptable." See

Criticism that "the New Testament has no theory of the atonement ... nor is the case fully stated when we deny that the New Testament contains a theory."[143] Warfield also suspects that Horton is the object of some of James Denny's stinging criticisms in his work *Studies in Theology*, which is based upon a series of lectures given at Chicago Theological Seminary in 1894.[144] It is this "fact-without-dogma" based religion, such as is advocated by Horton, that provokes Warfield's cynical question: "Is it, then, indeed true that Christianity loves darkness more than light, and thrives best where it is least understood?"[145]

Warfield responds to this by attempting to establish a direct connection between "doctrines" and "facts." He does so by developing a direct correlation between these "facts" and their interpretation as "doctrines." Warfield states in this regard, "We may cherish doubts as to the value of facts without their interpreting doctrines, but we cannot but be sure that doctrines to which no facts correspond can be nothing other than myths—let us say it frankly, lies."[146] In other words, there may be scriptural facts that have no doctrinal connection or have no doctrinal importance, but there can be no true doctrines apart from corresponding facts. Warfield is quite clear on this point. A supposed "doctrine" not having a factual basis, is a either a myth, or worse, a lie. Here again, Warfield is heavily dependent upon the correspondence theory of truth, characteristic of Scottish Common Sense Realism, which states that a "fact" is that which corresponds to reality.[147]

With this in mind, Warfield returns to his well-established line of defense. "What Christianity consists in is facts that are doctrines, and doctrines that are facts." This is the case, "because it is a true religion, which offers to man a real redemption that was really wrought out in history, its facts and doctrines entirely coalesce. All its facts are doctrines and

B. B. Warfield, "Review of *Inspiration of the Bible*," in *The Presbyterian and Reformed Review*, vol. II (1891), 162.

143. Cited in Warfield, "The Right of Systematic Theology," 232, n. 11. See Robert F. Horton, "The Atonement" in *Faith and Critcism: Essays by Congregationalists*, vol. V (New York: E. P. Hutton, 1893), 188, 222, 237.

144. James Denny, *Studies in Theology* (Grand Rapids: Baker Book House, 1976), 106.

145. Warfield, "The Right of Systematic Theology," 233–34.

146. Ibid., 234.

147. See James McCosh, *Realistic Philosophy Defended in a Philosophic Series*, vol. 1, Expository (New York: Charles Scribner's Sons, 1887), 50–77. In this section describing his basic epistemological method, McCosh discusses facts, the inductive method, and the complexity of knowledge.

all its doctrines are facts."[148] Here we can clearly see the direct correspondence in Warfield's conception of Christianity as a factually based historical religion essentially linked to the doctrines that constitute the body of Christian doctrine. Warfield argues, "If doctrines which stand entirely out of relation to facts are myths [and] lies, [then] facts which have no connection with what we call doctrine have no meaning to us whatsoever. It is what we call a doctrine which gives significance to facts. A fact without doctrine is simply a fact not understood."[149] A fact then, must have doctrinal significance to be meaningful, for a fact without such meaning is unintelligible. The supposed chasm developed by Horton and others between the "facts" of the New Testament and the barren intellectualist dogmas of the theologians is, therefore, quite untenable. The fact of Christ's death necessitates an interpretation, and the doctrine connected to it gives the cross of our Lord the only meaning that it can have for us as Christians.

It is important to follow Warfield's line of reasoning carefully at this point, since several of Warfield's recent critics have made the assertion that Warfield vastly underestimated the role of presuppositions on the part of each individual interpreter, as well as depreciating the noetic effects of sin in evaluating such "facts." George Marsden, as but one example, contends that for both the Old Princeton school in general, and for Warfield in particular, "the ideal for truth was an objective statement of fact in which the subjective element was eliminated almost completely. ... True to the demands of Common Sense, Warfield saw the effects of the Fall on human consciousness as pervasive but quite limited."[150] Actually, in this essay, Warfield offers what is perhaps his most extensive treatment of the relationship between facts and their interpretation, and he sets out what he believes to be the role of the Holy Spirit in the interpretive process.

Warfield's basic epistemological structure leads quite naturally to his next assertion: "That intellectual element brought by the mind to the contemplation of facts, which we call 'doctrine,' 'theory,' is the condition of any proper comprehension of facts."[151] Warfield, ever faithful to

148. Warfield, "The Right of Systematic Theology," 234.
149. Ibid., 235.
150. George M. Marsden, *Fundamentalism and American Culture: The Shaping of Twentieth Century Evangelicalism 1870–1925* (New York: Oxford University Press, 1980), 114–15.
151. Warfield, "The Right of Systematic Theology," 235.

Common Sense Realism, eschews the *tabula rasa* empiricism of Locke, while nevertheless retaining the inductive method and the notion that the facts contain within themselves the criteria for correct interpretation. Since in the Scottish epistemology, knowledge is a complex act requiring both objective data and a rational knowing subject, Warfield can contend therefore that "so closely welded are those intellectual elements—those elements of previous knowledge, or of knowledge derived from other sources—to facts as taken up into our minds in the complex act of apperception" that we cannot separate these elements from one another as the "indifferentists" would have us to believe.[152] Thus Warfield can ask, "If, then, we are to affirm that Christianity consists of facts, wholly separated from those ideas by which these facts obtain their significance and meaning which it pleases to call 'dogmas'—what shall we do but destroy all that we know as Christianity altogether?"[153] Facts torn asunder from interpretation are nothing, and Christianity itself is destroyed. It is important to mention that Warfield was not alone among the Princetonians on this point. As Richard Lints notes, "there is common also to [Geerhardus] Vos and Warfield, a conviction of the relative perspicuity of the text. ... The facts of theology strike the interpreter with a certain kind of irresistibility in this Princeton tradition."[154] Thus the facts that constitute Christianity are necessarily and essentially connected to doctrine.

> The great facts that constitute Christianity are just as "naked" as any other facts, and are just as meaningless to us as any other facts, until they are not only perceived but understood, that is, until not only they themselves but their doctrinal significance is made

152. Ibid., 236.

153. Ibid., 237.

154. Richard Lints, "Two Theologies or One?," 246–47. Lints goes on to state, "The theological facts which Warfield discovered in the text may seem submerged in the text to some modern eyes, but it is important to notice the strong conviction in Warfield that these doctrines arise in the first instance because the text demands them (p. 247)." David Wells, on the other hand, contends, "It is almost startling to read a book like B. B. Warfield's *Right of Systematic Theology*. It is true that he was not addressing the question of theological method directly, but what is so striking is the innocence of his conception. What he seems to assume is that if the Bible is treated as divinely inspired, as it should be, it will naturally and without difficulty deliver its doctrinal cargo. ... Warfield, of course, was writing in a context in which it was still widely accepted that the natural world would yield its meaning to those who would simply apply their powers of observation and deduction to it." See David Wells, "The Theologians Craft," in *Doing Theology in Today's World*, 184.

> known to us. The whole Christianity of these facts resides in their meaning, in the ideas which are involved in them, but which are not independently gathered from them by each observer, but are attributed to them by those who interpret them to us—in a word, in the doctrines accompanying them.[155]

Notice that Warfield locates the meaning of the facts, not in "each observer," but in the doctrines themselves which interpret the facts for us. This leads Warfield to ask the critical question:

> What are the facts which constitute Christianity? Strip them free from "dogma," from that interpretation which has transformed them into doctrine, and what we have left at the most is this: that once upon a time a man was born, who lived in great poverty and charity, died on the cross and rose again. An interesting series of facts, no doubt with elements of mystery in them, of the marvelous, of the touching: but hardly in their naked form constituting what we call Christianity. For that they require their interpretation.[156]

Here then, Warfield makes the logical connection between the facts that constitute Christianity and the doctrines which interpret them for us. Apart from the doctrines, the facts are left uninterpreted and are therefore meaningless. But if we connect the facts with the doctrines, the situation is altogether different. "This man was the Son of God, we are told; he came in the flesh to save sinners; he gave himself to death as a propitiation for their sins; and he rose again for their justification. Now, indeed, we have Christianity."[157] The fact without the doctrine is nonsensical, but the interpreted facts are the essential doctrine of the Christian faith. Warfield therefore concludes:

> But it is not constituted by the "bare facts," but by the facts as interpreted, and indeed by the facts as thus interpreted and not otherwise. Give the facts no interpretation and we cannot find in them what we can call Christianity; give them another interpretation and we shall have something other than Christianity.[158]

155. Warfield, "The Right of Systematic Theology," 237.
156. Ibid.
157. Ibid., 238.
158. Ibid. It is interesting to note that presuppositionalists often charge evidentialists such as Warfield, with allowing for "brute facts," that is, facts which are supposedly uninterpreted. Notice that Warfield expressly denies that facts have meaning

This means that "Christianity is constituted, therefore, not by the facts, but by the 'dogmas'—that is, by the facts as understood in one specific manner. Surely it is of importance therefore to the Christian man to investigate this one Christian interpretation of the great facts that constitute Christianity: and this is the task of systematic theology."[159] Once the connection is made between fact and doctrine, the right of systematic theology is established.

There are several important loose ends that Warfield must now tie up before moving on. Since facts and their interpretations are supplied to us in Scripture as doctrines, the focus inevitably shifts to the nature of the authority that these doctrines possess. "We must not fail to emphasize that the conclusion at which we have thus arrived implies that there lies at the basis of Christianity not only a series of great redemptive facts, but also an authoritative interpretation of those facts."[160] Here

---

apart from interpretation specifically given them by the Scriptures themselves in the form of doctrines. According to John Frame, in his volume *The Doctrine of the Knowledge of God* (Phillipsburg: P&R Publishing, 1987), "Some apologists have dreamed that the whole edifice of Christianity could be established by a reference to something called 'the facts' which could be understood apart from any Christian commitment. ... The basis of Christianity and of all thought is God's revelation. The 'facts' are the facts of that revelation interpreted by God, known and therefore already interpreted to man. There are no facts devoid of such interpretation, and if there were, they could not be known, let alone used as the basis of anything (72–73)." Frame's comments are aimed primarily at John Warwick Montgomery, whose apologetic methodology is surprisingly similar to that of Warfield. See, for example, John Warwick Montgomery, "Biblical Inerrancy," in *God's Inerrant Word* (ed. John Warwick Montgomery (Minneapolis: Bethany Fellowship, 1974), 15–42; and "Biblical Authority," in *The Suicide of Christian Theology* (ed. John Warwick Montgomery; Minneapolis: Bethany Fellowship, 1975), 314–79. Frame also goes on the criticize Charles Hodge (and certainly by implication the entire Princeton School, including Warfield) for allowing the existence of "brute facts" and because Hodge supposedly has a "too intellectualist concept of theology" since Hodge sees theology as "an exercise in theory construction, in description of facts, in the accurate statement of 'principles' or 'general truths' (p. 78)." Warfield emphatically denies the existence of "brute facts," what he describes as "bare" or "naked" facts, though he would disagree with Frame that the primary aspect of knowledge was the presuppositional grid of the knower, rather than the objective character of the evidence. Warfield certainly agrees with Hodge as to the methodology of the theologian in this process. While Frame emphatically rejects the assertion that fact can be separated from doctrine, and arguing that since Scripture is not essentially "facts in their proper relations," but language designed to meet human needs, he ironically comes quite close to the "latitudinarian indifference" that Warfield so militantly opposes.

159. Ibid.

160. Ibid.

Warfield's stress is clearly upon the authority of the doctrinal assertions in Scripture. "It is evident that we are face to face here with an anxious question. And it means nothing less than this, that the existence of a doctrinal authority is fundamental to the very existence of Christianity." In Warfield's conception, if the facts are inexorably connected to doctrines, the matter of authority ultimately reduces to Christology:

> We find that doctrinal authority ultimately, of course, in Christ. In him we discern one in whose knowledge of the meaning of the great series of Christian facts in which he was chief actor, we can have supreme confidence; and to whom, with the apostles whom he appointed to teach all nations, we may safely go for the interpretation of the Christian facts. In the teachings of Christ and his apostles therefore we find authoritative Christian doctrine—"dogma" in the strictest sense of the word: and this "dogma" enters into the very essence of Christianity.[161]

So we are not left in the darkness, as Warfield had alluded to earlier. "Obviously the Bible does not give us a bare list of 'naked facts': but a rich account and development of significant facts held in a special meaning—of facts, understood and interpreted."[162] Thus the position of those such as Robert Horton that we cling to the facts of the New Testament as though those facts have no connection to doctrine is untenable.

Before moving on to evaluate those who reject doctrinal Christianity for a Christianity based upon life, Warfield next levels his sights at the "curious religious positivism which has gained such vogue of late through the vigor of the followers of Albrecht Ritschl ... which occupies a sort of transitional position between the type of thought which declares that Christianity consists in facts, not dogmas, and that which represents it as consisting in life, not doctrine."[163] Here again, we see an attempt to strip from Christianity any doctrinal content, and under moralistic guise, to portray our Lord as the founder of a religion, not as one who introduced us to speculative metaphysics. "We are told," notes Warfield, "that Christianity is in essence religion, while dogmas are metaphysical products ... therefore, so far from being essential to Christianity, are corruptions of Christianity." And so, "If we would have Christianity in its purity, we must strip off from it every remnant of

161. Ibid., 238–39.
162. Ibid., 239–40.
163. Ibid., 245.

'Greek dogma.' "[164] In other words, we are to reduce Christianity to its lowest common denominator, "the fact of Christ." While Warfield admires the attempt to insulate Christianity "from the metaphysics of the schools,"[165] and notes that Ritschlism "has often wrought a good work in theological circles in Germany, and earned for itself a good degree,"[166] nevertheless, the Princeton professor finds such an argument weak. "It is hard to take seriously the sharp discrimination that is proposed between religious and metaphysical knowledge."[167] In the words of Henri Bois as set forth in *Le Dogme Grec*, a volume devoted to responding to the notion that Christianity has been unduly influenced by Hellenism,[168] and quoted approvingly by Warfield, "If you wish to be rid of metaphysics at any cost, abstain from speaking of God. Whoever says, 'I believe in God,' deals with metaphysics."[169] The same argument, developed at great length to link fact and doctrine, is now applied by Warfield to Ritschlism:

> The apostolic interpretation is an inseparable element in the fundamental fact-basis of Christianity: and it cannot be rejected because a part of the providentially formed peculiarity of the apostolic mode of thought is distasteful to us. Call it metaphysical, call it Greek, if you will. But remember that it is of the essence of Christianity.[170]

Ultimately, however, the most trenchant critique is simply that if we wish to reduce Christianity to the "fact of Christ," then it must be pointed out that "Christianity consists not merely of 'Jesus Christ,' but of that Jesus Christ which the apostles give us—in a word, of the Jesus of apostolical 'dogma,' and not of any Jesus we may choose to fancy in this nineteenth century of ours."[171] Thus facts and doctrine are necessarily

164. Ibid.
165. Ibid.
166. Ibid., 247.
167. Ibid.
168. In Warfield's review of this work he refers to the author "as a brilliant young professor," who shows with "admirable acumen that the whole outcry against 'Greek dogma' is only another form of the modern attack upon the doctrinal content of historical Christianity." See B. B. Warfield, "Review of Henri Bois' *Le Dogme Grec*, in *The Presbyterian and Reformed Review* Vol. VI (1895), 782.
169. Cited in Warfield, "The Right of Systematic Theology, p. 248, note 24. The translation is apparently Warfield's.
170. Ibid., 256.
171. Warfield, "The Right of Systematic Theology," 255.

connected, and doctrines are authoritative interpretations of the facts, given to us by Jesus and the apostles as infallible teachers of doctrine.[172]

Warfield next focuses on a second area of concern, the attempt to ground Christianity in life rather than in doctrine. He proceeds, however, a bit more cautiously then he has previously, by expressing:

> With the heartiest recognition, however, of the precious elements of truth which are embraced in this mode of thought, and of the service it has rendered in emphasizing them, we may still be unable to allow that it is able to do justice to Christianity, or even to those special elements of Christianity which it thus has taken up, when, in its preoccupation with the sharp separation which it institutes between life and doctrine, it declares that Christianity consists wholly in life and not at all in doctrine.[173]

Warfield sees this attempt to ground Christianity in life rather than in doctrine as a serious problem because the epistemological structure is primarily subjective and experiential, rather than objective and grounded in facts. The result is that once again doctrine is divorced from fact.

Warfield criticizes, "The learned professor of Reformed theology at Paris, Prof. Auguste Sabatier," along with his followers who had recently produced "certain documents apparently designed precisely to serve as a manifesto of his [Sabatier's] school."[174] Auguste Sabatier (1839–1901) had argued that theological method was largely historical and psychological in nature, meaning that the focus of theological method should be placed upon observing religious phenomena in its historical outworking. According to Warfield, this approach carried with it the inevitable and problematic result: the relativizing of dogma. It has been argued by some that Sabatier's approach is reminiscent of Schleiermacher, though

172. See Warfield's essay, " 'It Says:' 'Scripture Says:' 'God Says'" in *The Presbyterian and Reformed Review*, Vol. X (1899), 472–510. Repr. in B. B. Warfield, *The Inspiration and Authority of the Bible* (Phillipsburg: P&R Publishing, 1948), 299–348.

173. Warfield, "The Right of Systematic Theology," 259.

174. Ibid. See Warfield's remarks about Sabatier in his review of the Frenchman's work on the atonement. "No one who has ever read ten lines of the writings of the late Prof. Auguste Sabatier but will have been impressed with the grace of his style and the truly Gallic attractiveness of his method of opening and presenting a subject. ... Whatever else he was he was always eminently readable." See B. B. Warfield, "Review of August Sabatier, *The Doctrine of the Atonement and Its Historical Evolution*," in *Critical Reviews* (Grand Rapids: Baker Book House, 1981), 106.

Warfield does not make this connection himself.[175] As Warfield sets out the issues, he notes that, initially at least, it was noted commentator Frederic Godet who took up the defense against Sabatier and his followers. But Warfield favorably singles out Henri Bois, a young French theologian, for his subsequent efforts to respond to Sabatier.

Warfield's list of criticisms of Sabatier begin with the epistemological starting point. "At the bottom of all M. Sabatier's religious thinking there proves to lie a crass philosophical empiricism,"[176] which Warfield associates with Englishman Herbert Spencer, a noted philosopher and early advocate of evolutionary theory. "Modern agnosticism," Warfield declares, "takes its start in the philosophy of Kant and runs its course through Hamilton and Mansel to culminate in the teaching of Herbert Spencer."[177] Therefore, the problem with Sabatier's adoption of this method is that "sensation lies behind and is the source of all knowledge."[178] This methodological dictum of pure empiricism "now being anew pressed upon our acceptance by certain of our physiological psychologists," allows Sabatier to set up his own religious dualism, which

175. See Haddon Willmer, "Sabatier, Louis Auguste," in *The New International Dictionary of the Christian Church* (ed. J. D. Douglas; Grand Rapids: Zondervan, 1981), 867. Warfield notes that Sabatier is "conscious that [his system] is the outcome of Socinian and Rationalistic criticism, and in point of fact it merely reproduces the characteristic view of these schools of destructive criticism." See Warfield, "Review of Auguste Sabatier," 109.

176. Warfield, "The Right of Systematic Theology," 259–60.

177. B. B. Warfield, "Agnosticism (1908)." Repr. in *Selected Shorter Writings*, vol. 2, 34.

178. Warfield, "The Right of Systematic Theology," 260. Warfield was not the only Princeton theologian who gave negative reviews to Sabatier's work. W. Brenton Greene, in reviewing Sabatier's *Outlines of a Philosophy of Religion Based on Psychology and History* (1897), offers an equally pointed critique. "The religion whose supposed evolution has been so carefully traced is not Christianity. ... The religion, therefore, which can be explained without these [creeds], which can be accounted for merely as the result of 'cosmic evolution,' cannot be Christianity. Admit if you will, that such a religion would be more wonderful and more excellent than Christianity, but do not identify it with it. Courtesy, not to say fairness, requires that things be called by their right names." Greene concludes that Sabatier's book is a "cup of poison; and we fear that it will prove the destruction of many just because the first taste of it is delicious. Any system that makes feeling the ultimate test of truth is bound to be as attractive to the natural heart of man as it cannot fail to be hostile to the truth of God." See W. Brenton Greene, "Review of *Outlines of a Philosophy of Religion Based On Psychology and History*, by Auguste Sabatier," in *The Presbyterian and Reformed Review* Vol. X (January 1899), 144–49.

Warfield labels his "fundamental theological postulate."[179] In Warfield's understanding, Sabatier's conception works itself out as follows:

> As sensation is the mother of ideas, so the Christian life is the mother of Christian doctrine. Life, then, is before doctrine, not merely in importance but in time: and doctrine is only a product of the Christian life. It follows, of course, at once that God does not reveal himself except through and by means of the Christian life: there is not and cannot be any such thing as an "objective revelation."[180]

Thus, since there can be no objective revelation on these terms, this means that on the contrary, "God reveals himself only in and by piety," because "it is faith that produces dogma."[181] Sabatier's conception, if true, necessitates a complete and fundamental inversion of the conception of fact and dogma that Warfield had labored so vigorously to establish. In the words of one writer of the Sabatier school, quoted by Henri Bois and cited by Warfield, this inversion is not an afterthought nor is it accidental:

> We need a dogmatic; there is a Christian verity in Christianity; there is a Christian philosophy; it is the most extensive of all philosophies. Only, *instead of placing it at the beginning, I place it at the end*; instead of making it precede the Christian life, we make it proceed from the Christian life. This is the difference between us and our opponents, but it is great enough to make us say, Here are two opposed theologies.[182]

Unlike more simplistic "indifferentists," such as Robert Horton, who attempt to dismiss doctrine by merely professing disinterest in it, the followers of Sabatier clearly understood the philosophical implications of their mentor's scheme. There can be no doubt that in Sabatier's conception, in marked contrast to those such as Warfield with the opposite epistemological construct, they are "opposed theologies." This is a point with which Warfield, of course, would not take issue. He certainly agrees that these are contradictory epistemologies.

179. Ibid.
180. Ibid.
181. Ibid.
182. Ibid., 260–61. The writer mentioned in passing by Warfield is M. Dandiran. The italics are in the original.

The result of this inverted order is that "all Christian doctrine being thus but the manifestation of precedent Christian life, doctrine will of course, vary as the Christian life varies."[183] Theological method concerns itself primarily with evaluating these varied lives and the resulting varied doctrines. Theological method is primarily historical and psychological. And it is here, then, as Warfield sees it, that Sabatier's method is fatally flawed.[184] This is the case because of its inherent subjectivity, and because of its unfortunate dependence upon the evolutionary model, which leads to "the evolution of religion and with it the evolution of religious thought, and finally of Christian dogmas."[185] Warfield writes elsewhere in this regard, "what Prof. Sabatier calls the 'historical method' ... is dominated by the assumption that when you have worked out the historical development of a doctrine you have 'explained' that doctrine—which in the view of the writers of this class is the same as to say you have explained it away."[186] There is no objectively true doctrine, only experientially meaningful doctrine, which is itself in the ongoing process of historical development. Warfield describes Sabatier's conception of this evolutionary development as follows:

> The religion of law succeeded the nature religions, the religion of love has succeeded the religion of law. But the stream still flows on; and as the stream of religious ideas dependent on the spiritual life flows on, and our doctrines vary, age by age, in spite of themselves. ... The river of the underlying spiritual life, and the river of intellectual concepts and doctrinal ideas dependent on the fluctuations of the spiritual life, inevitably flow on forever.[187]

Warfield concludes: "This is, then, what M. Sabatier means when he says that Christianity is a life, not a doctrine."[188]

The major problem with this is that this reduces the truth claim of Christianity to a kind of relativism, because "the theory amounts to

183. Ibid., 261.

184. Another Frenchman, Auguste Lecerf, comments about Warfield in this regard, "Benjamin Breckinridge Warfield, one of the highest authorities in all that concerns Calvinistic thought, has underlined the characteristic trait of the Calvinistic turn of mind which may be described as antipsychologism in dogmatics." Auguste Lecerf, *An Introduction to Reformed Dogmatics* (trans. Andre Schlemmer; Grand Rapids: Baker Book House, 1981), 390.

185. Warfield, "The Right of Systematic Theology," 261.

186. Warfield, "Review of Auguste Sabatier," 108.

187. Warfield, "The Right of Systematic Theology," 261.

188. Ibid.

the formal renunciation of Christianity as anything else than one stage in the religious development of humanity."[189] Therefore, doctrine in Sabatier's scheme is always dynamic and never static. Sabatier rejects the "traditional religion," which clings "in one way or another to 'external authority,' [and] profoundly distrusts the efforts of the human spirit."[190] According to Sabatier and his followers, since Christianity must be understood relative to its own age and time, "it is therefore folly for orthodoxy to wish to 'elevate to the absolute what was born in time and must necessarily be subject to modification if it is to live in time.' "[191] Therefore, Warfield can conclude that "in M. Sabatier's conception, everything is in a flux: and the doctrines which Christianity proclaims, and even the form of life which underlies them and of which they are the expression, are only one evanescent moment in the ceaseless advance of mankind."[192] Here, perhaps, more clearly than anywhere else, do we see the evolutionary spirit underlying Sabatier's scheme.

Warfield's initial response to Sabatier's formulation is to point out that the Frenchman cannot make good on his own claims: "M. Sabatier cannot refrain from speaking of the religion of love, with which he identifies Christianity, as the perfect and definitive religion, and of Christ as having perfectly realized this perfect religion in his own life."[193] However, "if ever an illogical thinker was fairly scourged out of this inconsistency, we may believe that M. Sabatier's incoherences of his kind have been cured by M. Bois' lash."[194] As Henri Bois delightfully points out, the problem is that whenever Sabatier "speaks of Christ and Christianity in the traditional manner,"[195] his own evolutionary scheme completely ignores that fact that the traditional understanding of Christ and Christianity are merely first-century religious conceptions and are, therefore, hardly worthy of men and women who have the benefit of nearly 1,900 years of evolutionary religious progress. Why has Jesus, a first-century figure, become the religious ideal for sophisticated 19th-century Frenchmen, who have had nearly two millennia to move beyond the primitive conceptions of New Testament Christianity? This ideal held out by Sabatier

189. Ibid., 261–62.
190. Warfield, "Review of Auguste Sabatier," 106.
191. Warfield, "The Right of Systematic Theology," 262.
192. Ibid.
193. Ibid., 264.
194. Ibid.
195. Ibid., 266.

is—as Warfield points out in his subsequent review of Sabatier's work on the atonement—Jesus' own religious self-consciousness. "When Prof. Sabatier commends to us the religion of Jesus, he means rather the religion which Jesus had than the religion that has Jesus."[196] At this point, Sabatier's inconsistencies reach their highest level. Not only is there no reason under the terms of his own scheme for 19th century Frenchmen to seek for the primitive religion that Jesus practiced, once Jesus' own religious consciousness is drawn from the historical record of the New Testament, what ground remains to reject Jesus as an authoritative teacher of doctrine? In either case, Sabatier's self-contradictions cannot be allowed to stand.

The next point raised by Warfield in response to Sabatier is drawn from a lengthy citation from Sabatier's *Discourse on the Evolution of Dogmas*,[197] in which Sabatier describes a hypothetical congregation worshiping in a great church. As he eloquently describes the scene, there are poor women present, and many are ignorant and superstitious. There are moderately educated middle-class men and merchants also present in significant numbers. There are several well-educated scholars and philosophers also on hand, men who are quite conversant with Kant and Hegel and contemporary philosophical literature. There may even be a theologian or two in the congregation. But each person present, despite their different cultural backgrounds and intellectual ability, repeat the Creed together, and each one of them feels a similar rush of emotion when they are reminded of our Lord's words in his high priestly prayer that "they may all be one." Each worshiper has a markedly different conception of God. The simple women, for instance, picture God as a wise old man, recalling the depiction of God they had seen in the religious art of their youth. The middle class men and merchants have deistic conceptions of God retained from their college days. The philosophically sophisticated think of God as "The Unknowable" in unmistakably Kantian terms. After describing the imaginary scene, Sabatier reaches the conclusion that "for all, however, the doctrine of God subsists and it is because it is still living that it lends itself to so many different interpretations."[198] Sabatier asks, "Why is this a 'living' conception of God? It is living ... only because it serves to express a piety felt in common by

196. Warfield, "Review of Auguste Sabatier," 108.
197. Warfield, "The Right of Systematic Theology," 267–68.
198. Ibid., 267.

all these believers."[199] Thus doctrine flows from the life of the worshiper, and piety from the common feeling shared by all.

The problem with this, according to Warfield, is that these people are not in the great church to collectively "elevate and purify their partial or wrong impressions of God" and where they can learn about "who and what really is the God and Father of our Lord and Savior Jesus Christ."[200] Instead of Warfield's conception wherein correct doctrine corrects the false religious conceptions of those in the congregation, Sabatier leaves us with only "another picturesque plea for the extremest religious indifferentism."[201] For each individual worshiping in Sabatier's imaginary church has a different conception of God, which in Sabatier's scheme, is equally valid. Each of these individuals, with such vast and divergent backgrounds, are nevertheless "one" through their common sentiment and experience, not because they have one confession of faith and one conception of God. When all is said and done, Sabatier has left us with nothing new:

> The goal to which M. Sabatier's theories have conducted him, is just the popular latitudinarianism of the day. ... And we may best look upon his work as an attempt to justify this indifferentism by placing beneath it a philosophical foundation, in a theory of religious knowledge and a theory of religious evolution.[202]

The system collapses under the weight of its own inconsistencies because:

> Indifferentism cannot remain Christian except at the cost of admitting the claims of Christian doctrine and providing for the essential work of that doctrine in forming a distinctively Christian life, then, for the Christian man, this rational basis for indifferentism must fall with it.[203]

For Sabatier to admit to any "distinctly Christian doctrines" would be utterly self-contradictory. Therefore, the "arguments against M. Sabatier's theories, in other words, are the arguments against indifferentism in religion"[204] in general, and many of the points that Warfield

199. Ibid., 267–68.
200. Ibid., 268.
201. Ibid.
202. Ibid., 269.
203. Ibid.
204. Ibid.

had previously argued will certainly apply not only to the likes of Robert Horton, but to Auguste Sabatier as well.

The real point of contention can now be exposed. "Indifferentism, we will remember, does not precisely condemn Christian doctrine; it only neglects it. And true to his indifferent results, M. Sabatier does not deny the possibility of even the necessity of Christian doctrines, or even of Christian dogmatics."[205] In Sabatier's conception of religion, "he confesses that a living religion must needs express itself in appropriate religious thinking and in those doctrines which embody his thinking. ... No faith is a living faith which does not produce doctrine."[206] This is misleading, however, because "it is not then exactly against the possibility or right of Christian doctrine that he protests: it is only its usefulness that he denies."[207] It is not as though the question is whether there can be distinctively "Christian" doctrine or not, but more or less a question of whether we need distinctively Christian doctrine at all. As Warfield is quick to point out, this means that "doctrine fluctuates according to the life-movements of which it is only a reflection."[208] Even worse, when this conception is carried to its logical conclusion, "the more unstable a doctrine is, the more living it is: a really living Christianity we are told, renders its doctrinal product peculiarly supple and malleable. In this, it seems, we reach the very apotheosis of religious indifferentism."[209] This inevitably leads to a kind of nebulous universalism, which Warfield characterizes as follows:

> For if we are to define religion in this exclusive sense as a feeling, and to define Christianity as a religion in terms of the religious feeling alone, we have certainly identified Christianity with the religious sentiment, and have failed to institute any essential distinction between it and other religions, the products like it of the religious sentiment. The most that could be said on this ground would be that in what we call Christianity the religious feeling first comes to its rights, and for the first time expresses itself fully and freely in accordance with its truth. But even so, Christianity is represented as essentially one with all other religions, differing from them only as the perfect differs from the imperfect. All

205. Ibid., 270.
206. Ibid.
207. Ibid.
208. Ibid.
209. Ibid.

> religions at once take their places as relatively true: They stand no longer in opposition to Christianity, as the false to the true, but in a hierarchy of relatively partial or complete.[210]

We are left to ask the telling question, "What remains that is unique about Christianity?" Indeed, while emotions and religious experience are certainly produced by a Christian's union with Christ through faith, Warfield is compelled to ask, "Why is it that the Christian man feels, religiously speaking, specifically different from the Buddhist, the Shamanist, the fetish-worshiper?"[211] Warfield answers his own question by affirming that "the old answer was that the difference in the form which the religious sentiment takes in the diverse religions arises from the difference in the religious conceptions characteristic of these religions: and we do not see that any better answer has been or can be offered."[212] Ultimately, the difference between diverse religions is doctrinal. If it is not, then all that we are left with is collective religious experience.

> If this be so, a religion independent of conceptions, "dogmas," would be confined to a religion of nature and possess nothing not common to all religions: and to proclaim Christianity independent of doctrine would be simply to cast off distinctive Christianity and revert to the fundamental natural religion.[213]

It is doctrine and doctrine alone that distinguishes Christianity from mere natural religion, and "which forms for it a specific type of religious experience and religious life."[214] This means that life does not, and indeed cannot, logically precede doctrine, despite sentimental, indifferent, and latitudinarian arguments to the contrary. Doctrine necessarily precedes life. "To be indifferent to this doctrine as if it were only an index of the life flowing on steadily beneath it and independently of it, is therefore to be indifferent to distinctive Christianity itself."[215] "Christianity" based on life is nothing more than natural religion. Such "Christianity" is not Christianity at all.

210. Ibid., 271.
211. Ibid., 272.
212. Ibid.
213. Ibid., 273.
214. Ibid.
215. Ibid., 274.

Warfield is very careful at this point to qualify what he means by his assertion that doctrine precedes life. For in an important sense, the converse is true.

> We not only have no desire to deny, we rather wish to proclaim, the great truth involved in the watchword of the greatest of the fathers and schoolmen, *Credo ut intelligam*, and adopted by the Reformers in the maxim of *Fides praecedit rationem*, and before the Reformers or schoolmen or fathers, proclaimed by Paul in the immortal words that "the natural man receiveth not the things of the Spirit of God, for they are foolishness unto him; and he cannot know them because they are spiritually judged" (1 Cor. ii.14). None but the Christian man can understand Christian truth; none but the Christian man is competent to state Christian doctrine.[216]

While Aristotle gives us an epistemological "low ground" on which to establish this same principle, "Paul has taught the Christian a much higher doctrine" notes Warfield. "It is only through the guidance of the Holy Ghost dwelling within us, that we can reach to the apprehension of the deep things of God. Were this all that were meant by the assertion that life must precede doctrine, we would give it our heartiest assent."[217] But as Warfield has pointed out, Sabatier is not arguing for the orthodox formulation *Credo ut intelligam*. The Princeton theologian is, however, very likely arguing that reason has an essential, though ministerial function, rather than a magisterial function.[218]

Although, as we will see, this is disputed by several of Warfield's interpreters, Warfield never asserts that human reason can somehow apprehend God apart from both an objective revelation and a subjective acceptance of that objective evidence which occurs only through a direct

216. Ibid.

217. Ibid.

218. See Richard A. Muller's discussion of this in *Post Reformation Reformed Dogmatics: Volume 1 Prolegomena to Theology*, 243 ff. Warfield commented two years later, "Apart from the revelation of God deposited for us in the Scriptures, there is no Christianity. Obliterate this revelation—theology may remain, but it is no longer a Christian theology; religion may remain, but it is no longer the Christian religion. In proportion, therefore, as faith in the Biblical revelation is abolished, and the outlines of doctrines dependent on trust in that revelation are washed out, in that proportion Christianity will be effaced. ... We inevitably drift toward a purely natural religion." See B. B. Warfield, "Recent Reconstructions of Theology (1898)," reprinted in *Selected Shorter Writings*, 294–95.

operation of the Holy Spirit upon the heart of the sinner.[219] Therefore, reason is the necessary tool by which we apprehend and understand the verbal revelation that God gives to us in the Holy Scriptures. This means that Warfield does not reject, deny, or soften the role of the Holy Spirit in regeneration and illumination as essential to the act of faith. Warfield emphatically states, "And so far as this assertion may be thought to mean that doctrine alone cannot produce life, we would welcome it, as it has already been said, with acclamations."[220] Thus it is not a case where one accepts the ministerial use of reason *or* emphasizes the role of the Holy Spirit in giving sight where there has been blindness. Rather, it is more a case where both reason and the Holy Spirit are in view, rather than an either/or dichotomy between reason *or* the Holy Spirit.

Warfield makes this point as clearly as he can:

> There is no creative power in doctrines, however true; and they will pass over dead souls leaving them as inert as they found them: it is the *Creator Spiritus* alone who is competent to quicken dead souls into life; and without him there has never been and never will be one spark of life produced by all the doctrines in the world.[221]

Sabatier's conception, though, is markedly different at this point. In the words of Warfield, "This is not what is intended by the watchword that life precedes doctrine. What is meant by it," in Sabatier's scheme "is that the Christian life blooms and flourishes wholly independently of Christian conceptions, and that it is indifferent to the Christian life whether these conceptions—however fundamental—are known or not."[222] In response to this assertion, Warfield writes, "We protest with all the energy possible, and pronounce its proclamation a blow at distinctive Christianity itself."[223] Sabatier's conception denies al-

219. As noted in chapter 3, this subjective-objective distinction is an important theme throughout much of the Warfield corpus. As but one example where this distinction is spelled out in great detail, specifically in setting forth the relationship between faith and evidence, Warfield states quite clearly, "The mode of the divine giving of faith is represented … as involving the creation by God the Holy Spirit of a capacity for faith under the evidence submitted." See B. B. Warfield, "On Faith in its Psychological Aspects," in *Biblical and Theological Studies* (Philadelphia: P&R Publishing, 1968), 398.
220. Warfield, "The Right of Systematic Theology," 274.
221. Ibid.
222. Ibid.
223. Ibid.

together any role for special revelation, since religion in general, and Christianity in particular, are subjectively grounded in the human consciousness and feeling, rather than in an objective revelation given in and through history.

Here, the contrast reaches its zenith. Once you conclude that life flows from doctrine, then "the right conception of these ideas it is the task of Systematic Theology to investigate and secure: and thus the right and function of Systematic Theology is already vindicated."[224] If what makes Christianity distinctive is its doctrine, then the right of systematic theology is secured as the means by which the doctrine is explicated. It would help in this regard, says Warfield, "to remind ourselves that such was evidently the conception of the founders of the Christian religion concerning the relations of doctrine and life."[225] Taking as but one example, Warfield points to the letters of Paul, wherein we consistently find that "it is ever first the doctrine and then the life."[226] In fact, if we examine the relationship of Jesus to his apostles, we find that "knowledge of God's will with them was ever the condition of doing God's will."[227] This can only mean that doctrine precedes life, and not vice-versa.

In concluding the essay, Warfield returns to now familiar ground. "Other religions have sought to propagate themselves in various ways, but this is what is characteristic and peculiar to Christianity: it made its appeal from the first to man's reason."[228] Here again, Warfield is setting out the conception that it is reason which apprehends revelation. Warfield enlists the support of two Scots to support this contention. Citing Dr. James MacGregor's *The Apology of the Christian Religion*, Warfield returns to the notion that Christianity is preeminently the apologetical religion. " 'No other religion,' says Dr. MacGregor, 'has ever seriously set itself ... to reason the sinful world out of worldliness into Godliness ... in addressing itself to the reason in order to reach the man in the conscience

224. Ibid., 276.
225. Ibid.
226. Ibid.
227. Ibid., 277.
228. Ibid. Warfield makes very similar comments in his article "Christianity the Truth," in which he states, "The primary claim of Christianity [is] that it is 'the truth.' ... The task it has set for itself is no less than to *reason* the world into acceptance of the 'truth.' ... Christianity is in its very nature an aggressive religion; it is in the world in order to convince men; when it ceases to *reason*, it ceases to exist." See B. B. Warfield, "Christianity the Truth (1901)," repr. in *Selected Shorter Writings*, vol. 2, 213–16. The italics are in the original.

and the heart.' "[229] Warfield concludes, "Other religions have sought to propagate themselves in various ways, but this is what is characteristic and peculiar to Christianity: it made its appeal from the first to men's reason."[230] Christianity as a missionary religion is a religion based upon the proclamation of the saving work of Jesus Christ, and that means that Christianity is doctrine. Warfield also enlists the support of James Orr, who remarked in his apologetic *The Christian View of God and the World*, "If there is a religion in the world which exalts the office of teaching it is safe to say it is the religion of Jesus Christ. ... It comes to men with definite, positive teaching; it claims to be the truth; it bases religion on knowledge, though a knowledge which is attainable under moral conditions."[231] Since Christianity is, in Warfield's conception, the pre-eminent rational religion, and therefore an apologetical religion, it is also "pre-eminently the doctrinal religion. Above all other religions, it consists

---

229. Ibid. James MacGregor (1830–94), was a devoted disciple of William Cunningham, and replaced James Buchanan as professor of systematic theology in 1868 at New College. He was vigorously involved in defending the Westminster Confession and spent much of his energy opposing Amyraldianism, then arising in the Free Church of Scotland. He also produced a trilogy on apologetics, *The Apology of the Christian Religion* (1891), *The Revelation and The Record* (1893), and *The History of Christian Apologetics* (1894). See Sherman Isbell, "MacGregor, James," in *Dictionary of Scottish Church History and Theology* (ed. Nigel Cameron; Downers Grove: InterVarsity Press, 1993), 515–16. B. B. Warfield describes MacGregor's work as being characterized by "ability and grasp, with wide knowledge and above all with marked independence. ... They embody a substantial contribution to the apologetical literature of our time." See B. B. Warfield, "Review of *Revelation and the Record* and *Studies in the History of Christian Apologetics*, in *The Presbyterian and Reformed Review*, vol. VIII (1897), 772–73.

230. Warfield, "The Right of Systematic Theology," 277. Donald Bloesch indicates that such statements indicate Warfield's "rationalist bent." See Donald Bloesch, *Holy Scripture: Revelation, Inspiration & Interpretation* (Downers Grove: InterVarsity Press, 1994), 81.

231. Ibid. This citation is taken from James Orr, *The Christian View of God and the World*, 1st ed. (1893), 23. Orr's comments from a later edition of the same work virtually echo those of Warfield. "A religion based on mere feeling is the vaguest, most unreliable, most unstable of all things. A strong, stable, religious life can be built up on no other ground than that of intelligent conviction. Christianity therefore, addresses itself to the intelligence as well as to the heart." See James Orr, *The Christian View of God and the World* (New York: Charles Scribner's Sons, 1897), 20–21. For a discussion of the similarity and dissimilarity between Warfield and Orr on Scripture, see Robert J. Hoefel, "B. B. Warfield and James Orr: A Study in Contrasting Approaches to Scripture," in *Christian Scholar's Review*, XVI:1 (September 1986), 40–52; and Robert J. Hoefel, "The Doctrine of Inspiration in the Writings of James Orr and B. B. Warfield: A Study in Contrasting Approaches to Scripture," (Ph.D. diss., Fuller Theological Seminary, 1983).

in doctrines: it has truth to offer to men's acceptance, and by their acceptance of this truth it seeks to rule their lives and save their souls."[232] Since Christianity is based on its doctrine, rather than in a particular expression of the common religious nature of men and women, it is a religion which will also therefore stand or fall on the truth of its doctrine as facts. It is the duty of apologetics to establish the truth of these facts. For this point, Warfield seeks biblical support:

> It is probably then, not mere accident that in Rom. vii.23, it is from the νούς—the "mind"— that the conquest of Christianity over life proceed outwardly to the members. Christianity makes its appeal to the "mind" and secures the affection of the "inward man" first, and thence advances to victory over the "flesh" and "members." Accordingly it is by the renewing of their mind (τού νοός) that sinners are to be metamorphosed as to be no longer fashioned according to the world, but to prove the will of God (Rom. xii.2). Compare the rich expressions of Eph. iv.18–24. The noetic root of salvation is continually insisted on in the Scriptures.[233]

This is further borne out by the fact that the very propagation of Christianity, while certainly a "hidden work of the Spirit of God in the heart," is also based upon the great commission, which is "*Go, preach:* and the promise is to him that *heareth and obeyeth.*"[234] Warfield sees no dichotomy between the work of the Spirit in regeneration and conversion, and the role of reason as the means by which the proclamation of the gospel is apprehended. It is important to note that the work of the Spirit cannot be separated from the objective preaching of the gospel, which is addressed to the intellect:

> It is very evident that the founders of Christianity earnestly believed, not that the so-called word of God is the product of faith and its only use is to witness to the faith that lies behind it and gives it birth, but that the Veritable Word of God is the seed of faith, that faith cometh by hearing and hearing by the Word of God, or, in other words, that behind the Christian life stands the doctrine of Christ, intelligently believed.[235]

232. Ibid., 277–78.
233. Ibid., 278, n. 57.
234. Ibid., 278.
235. Ibid., 278–79.

Therefore, Warfield connects the work of the Spirit directly to the objective preaching of the gospel, a theme that surfaces throughout Warfield's writings. The apostles can preach the gospel, addressed objectively to the mind of the hearing, knowing full well that the gospel, not human reason, is the power of God unto salvation. "In insisting, therefore, on the primacy of Christian doctrine, and on the consequent right and duty to ascertain and accurately to state this doctrine—which is the task of Systematic Theology—we have consciousness of being imitators of Paul even as he was of Christ."[236] This is, according to Warfield, why Paul can "preach the whole counsel of God," why he can insist that he is not one who "corrupts the truth." This is why Paul insists on "preaching Christ and him crucified" (see Gal 6:14). And this is why Paul pronounces the harshest of curses upon those who preach a false gospel (see Gal 1:6-8). This is why "Paul impresses upon us the duty and the supreme importance of preserving that purity of doctrine which is the aim of Systematic Theology in its investigation into Christian truth to secure."[237] Warfield is quite convinced on these terms that the right of the science of systematic theology is, therefore, clearly established.

THE TASK OF THE THEOLOGIAN: ADDING TIES AND RAIL TO THE TRACK

B. B. Warfield was certainly a man of his times, something that several of his critics have tended to see as a character flaw. However, that Warfield was a man of his times should not surprise nor dismay us. As Warfield developed his conception of systematic theology as a science, he is clearly indebted to the prior work of his own theological mentors, Charles and A. A. Hodge, as well as to his Scottish philosophical fathers, Thomas Reid and James McCosh. We must also add the Reformed scholastics to the list of influences upon Warfield. There is no doubt that Warfield conceived of his own task as a theologian as adding ties and rail to the track that Charles Hodge had previously laid, and that in turn Warfield apparently felt that Hodge's work in the field had been to add to that which Francis Turretin had passed down. Warfield seemingly saw himself as standing in that great intellectual line descending from Calvin down through the Reformed scholastics to Princeton itself.

236. Ibid., 279.
237. Ibid.

Warfield, accordingly, appears to set out little that is original to him, though his stress on apologetics as the foundation for theology is not found as militantly in Charles Hodge's *Systematic Theology*.[238] A. A. Hodge, however, does set forth basically the same conception of the role of apologetics and its relationship to systematic theology in his *Outlines of Theology*[239] (1860) as Warfield does in "The Idea of Systematic Theology." Warfield, though, expands this relationship beyond that set out by A. A. Hodge. In fact, as Warfield works out this relation in detail, the discipline of systematic theology is virtually impossible in his conception without the prior epistemological foundation established by apologetics. As we have seen, Warfield equates the role of apologetics with that of theological prolegomena. Warfield also assigns to the apologist the task of gleaning from the natural sciences that which is both useful and necessary in developing a suitable foundation upon which the theologian must build. For Warfield, then, there can be no systematic theology without apologetics paving the way.

What is a bit more innovative in Warfield's essay "The Idea of Systematic Theology," however, appears to be his willingness to relate the science of systematic theology to the natural sciences of his day, something which one of his more famous students, Louis Berkhof, was not quite as eager to do. Yet Warfield's understanding of the definition and meaning of science is not only compatible with the basic epistemology of Scottish Common Sense Realism, which saw the foundation of all science in such a fashion, it is actually an easy and quite natural connection for him to make. But even with this connection between systematic theology and the natural sciences in view, Warfield repeatedly points to the superiority of theology in relationship to these other sciences, since theology's subject matter (God) and its goal (the glory of God) far transcends that associated with the natural sciences. Therefore, according to Warfield, theology must be seen in comparison to the secular sciences by way of analogy only, since systematic theology is the queen before whom all other sciences should willingly bow. In this view, theology is the highest and noblest of all sciences since no other science can exist

238. Lints notes that Warfield understood—more clearly than Charles Hodge did—that the relationship between exegesis and systematic theology "is far more complex than Hodge had realized (in large measure because of the birth of the new discipline of biblical theology)." See Richard Lints, "Two Theologies or One?," 239.
239. A. A. Hodge, *Outlines of Theology*, 17–20.

in purity and exercise its proper domain apart from theology's normative influence.

Warfield's primary concern throughout both essays is with the objective nature of truth. This is why the theologian must seek for the "ideal" expression of truth rather than content himself with identifying the mere historical expressions of various competing systems of truth. This is the natural outworking of Warfield's reliance upon Common Sense. Individual pieces of data, what Warfield calls "the facts contained in revelation," must be combined and organized into a coherent system if a true science is to exist at all. Therefore, the objective side of epistemology (God, Christ, and the Bible) as well as the subjective aspects of knowledge (man's capacity to receive revelation from God and the science of religion), must come together in a "synthetic embrace," for a science to exist at all. There is no proper knowledge of God apart from the existence such an interpretive and organizing system. Here, Warfield clearly echoes the epistemological foundationalism of James McCosh and Thomas Reid. The consequences of Warfield's views are such that all aspects of theology are impacted. Even the parish preacher is dependent upon systematic theology, if he is to be faithful to Warfield's conception of the minister's calling. The preacher is primarily a divinely ordained preacher of the truth and he cannot present the truth properly unless it is in the form of a system. The implications of this for the religious life are beyond estimation. One cannot grow in the grace and knowledge of God unless one properly understands the truth, and one cannot properly understand truth unless the various facts of revelation are seen in relationship to one another. One cannot love God with all his mind, soul, heart, and strength, nor his neighbor as himself, unless he first has some grasp of these doctrines in relation to each other. This is the business of systematic theology; no mere natural science can make such a claim.

In marked contrast, however, to his earlier descriptive essay, "The Idea of Systematic Theology," in "The Right of Systematic Theology," Warfield's patience clearly wears thin with the likes of indifferentists such as Robert Horton and latitudinarians such as Auguste Sabatier. "The Right of Systematic Theology" is a distinctly polemical effort designed to topple the arguments of those advocating a kind of naive denial of the connection between fact and doctrine, and of those mounting a more sophisticated attempt to draw doctrine from life instead of from Holy Scripture. Both cases, whether indifferentism or latitudinarianism, amount to a direct attack upon the historic Christian faith. If allowed to stand unchallenged, both of these ideologies, in the name of Christianity, destroy Christianity itself. Warfield passionately argues, all doctrines are facts, and all facts are doctrines; to try and drive a wedge between fact and doctrine is an impossibility. In addition, to attempt to derive doctrine from life is equally untenable for there is nothing left of distinctive Christianity. Once Warfield establishes the necessary connection between fact and doctrine and shows the futility of attempting to draw doctrine from life, he then makes the case that Christianity is the supreme doctrinal religion. Therefore, the right and the necessity of systematic theology as the still reigning queen of the sciences is established.

"The Right of Systematic Theology" is an important essay in other aspects as well. In this essay, Warfield makes some of his most important statements concerning his conception of the nature of facts and their interpretation. Some in the Reformed tradition, such as George Marsden, contend that Warfield's dependence upon Scottish Common Sense Realism minimized the role of the presuppositions of the individual interpreters of those facts. Marsden also implies that because of Warfield's insistence upon the objectivity and inviolability of truth, he somehow has a less than orthodox conception of the noetic effects of sin. Warfield, however, insists upon both the ministerial use of reason to apprehend revelation, and the necessity of the immediate operation of the Holy Spirit in opening a person's mind and the heart. While there is certainly an open question as to how and to what degree the process of knowing is influenced by subjective factors, the Scottish Epistemology definitely comes down on the side of objectivity in these matters. Contrary to the position of many in the contemporary Reformed tradition, Warfield considers both subjective and objective aspects of knowledge as essential factors. Thus to attempt to understand Warfield's views on the objectivity of facts, the noetic effects of sin, and the role of the Holy Spirit in a person's coming to faith, the investigator must see these distinct elements in light of Warfield's carefully defined objective-subjective distinction. To treat Warfield's rather confident statements about the objectivity of facts, apart from Warfield's equally thorough discussion of the subjective aspects of knowing, is to miss half of the picture. Sadly, this is often the case in many discussions of Warfield's views about the priority of reason. Warfield's treatment of these issues throughout "The

Right of Systematic Theology," is quite typical of the way in which he handles these matters elsewhere.

Even though B. B. Warfield did not produce a theological system of his own, there is no doubt that he stands as one of the most important theologians of his age. His most lasting contribution, in his own humble terms, is the addition of new theological track to that already laid down by Charles Hodge.

6

Didactics and Polemics

STINGING REBUKES

Even though he wrote quite extensively in the fields of systematic theology and apologetics, Benjamin Breckinridge Warfield did not serve at Princeton Theological Seminary as professor of systematic theology or apologetics. He took the chair of professor of didactic and polemical theology upon A. A. Hodge's death in 1887 and there is no doubt that he approached this task with all his energies. George M. Marsden has pointed out that the Princetonian distrusted theological intervention and pounced upon any threat to Reformed orthodoxy as defined by the Westminster Standards.[1] Bibliographers John E. Meeter and Roger Nicole cite well over 750 critical book reviews and hundreds of published articles coming from his pen covering virtually every aspect of theological discussion. Therefore, when one sets out to evaluate Warfield's career as a polemicist, the daunting question that must be asked is, "Where to begin?" This difficulty is further exacerbated by the fact that much of what Warfield wrote, specifically in the fields of apologetic and systematic theology, also has a definite polemical bent. James S. McClanahan points out in his important evaluation of Warfield's work in historical theology, that Warfield "may be studying Tertullian, but he has an eye on Harnack. He may be describing the Westminster Assembly, but he's watching Briggs and McGiffert, too."[2] B. B. Warfield believed the Westminster Standards *ex corde*, and any departures from those standards started his ink flowing. He was no doubt a capable

1. George M. Marsden, *Fundamentalism and American Culture* (New York: Oxford University Pres, 1980), 98.
2. James Samuel McClanahan, "Benjamin B. Warfield: Historian of Doctrine in Defense of Orthodoxy, 1881–1921," (Ph.D. diss.: Union Theological Seminary, 1988), 630.

theologian and a capable apologist, but he may have been most formidable as a polemicist.[3]

First and foremost, Warfield's aversion to all things Arminian can be seen in his stinging rebuke of several of the noted progenitors of American fundamentalism. He challenged all things Arminian as well as all those who enthusiastically endorsed Revivalism. Warfield's aversion to mysticism can be seen in his published response to the work of Evelyn Underhill. Many of his polemical articles focus on the dire influence of German rationalism upon the American theological scene, such as his critique of "Ritschlism." Throughout these many endeavors, we find Warfield at his best, and clearly demonstrating that "he mastered the whole field of theological learning as few others."[4]

QUALMS ABOUT THE EMERGING FUNDAMENTALISM

Theological controversy has a way of making strange bedfellows. As Mark Noll has pointed out, "The rise of fundamentalism placed the Princeton Theology in an ambiguous situation." Although the Princetonians "certainly applauded the fundamentalists adherence to scriptural infallibility, and they heartily approved the fundamentalistic insistence upon a supernatural faith,"[5] they were apparently quite alarmed by several critical theological distinctives of the emerging fundamentalist movement. As the Princeton theologians saw such matters (especially B. B. Warfield), the degree to which fundamentalists managed to remain faithful to the increasingly fading memory of their Protestant and Reformational heritage, was the degree to which common cause could be formed with them. Only the most theologically grounded could be effective co-belligerents against the increasingly vociferous attacks upon the historicity of the Bible by German rationalists.

Yet, while the Princetonians lauded the fundamentalists' thoroughgoing supernaturalism and high regard for biblical infallibility, in many

3. A number of Warfield's polemical efforts have been effectively surveyed by McClanahan. William Livingstone also treated a number of these issues in his doctoral dissertation of 1948, "The Princeton Apologetic as Exemplified by the Work of Benjamin B. Warfield and J. Gresham Machen: A Study in American Theology 1880–1930," (Ph.D. diss.: Yale, 1948), though Livingstone's failure to distinguish between apologetics and polemics is quite problematic in this regard.

4. McClanahan, "Benjamin B. Warfield: Historian of Doctrine in Defense of Orthodoxy," 28.

5. Mark Noll, *The Princeton Theology: 1812–1921* (Grand Rapids: Baker Book House, 1983), 299.

ways the alliance between the two parties became quite tenuous. The fissure grew as fundamentalists increasingly identified themselves with a non-confessional, Arminian, revivalistic, and dispensational theology, all of which Princeton had historically opposed.[6] While the emerging fundamentalist movement and Princeton Theological Seminary may have become co-belligerents in the effort to turn back the tide of theological liberalism, they could never be considered true allies. At best there was an uneasy truce. As Mark Noll points out, the Princetonians generally, and Warfield in particular, were quite "squeamish about the anti-intellectual tendencies and the snap theological judgements that often characterized the movement."[7] Indeed, some of Warfield's polemical writings display open disdain for the work of several notable figures of the fundamentalist movement.

While some church historians, most notably Ernest Sandeen, have tended to minimize the theological divide between Princeton and the fundamentalists because of their common views regarding biblical inspiration and authority,[8] there were substantial theological divisions. Although many of the fundamentalist leaders eagerly looked to Princeton's scholarship for help in controversies surrounding questions of biblical authority, they somehow managed to ignore Princeton's

6. As John W. Stewart has argued, "The newer strains of nineteenth-century Protestantism did not mix well with the antebellum Princeton Theology." See John W. Stewart, "The Tethered Theology: Biblical Criticism, Common Sense Philosophy, and the Princeton Theologians, 1812–1860" (Ph.D. diss., The University of Michigan, 1990), 299. Charles Hodge's antagonism toward revivalism is documented in: Charles Andrew Jones, "Charles Hodge, The Keeper of Orthodoxy: The Method, Purpose and Meaning of His Apologetic" (Ph.D. diss., Drew University, 1989), 80–117; and David B. Calhoun, *Princeton Seminary: Faith and Learning 1812–1868* (Carlisle: Banner of Truth, 1994), 291–319.

7. Noll, *The Princeton Theology*, 299.

8. See Ernest R. Sandeen, *The Roots of Fundamentalism: British and American Millenarianism 1800–1930* (Grand Rapids: Baker Book House, 1979), 130–31. Sandeen contends that "it ought to be noticed that the effort of the Princeton doctrine of the Scriptures and the millenarian literalistic method of interpreting the Scriptures was very much the same. Both Princeton and the millenarians had staked their entire conception of Christianity upon a particular view of the Bible based ultimately upon eighteenth-century standards of rationality. Both of these schools of thought had vowed to defend the Bible or die in the attempt." It is important to notice that Warfield specifically opposed the fundamentalist method of proof-texting, and he was especially concerned about fundamentalists misusing the inductive method, presumably the 18th-century standard of rationality, to which Sandeen is referring. Notice too, that Sandeen himself speaks of the Princetonians and the fundamentalists as "two movements."

pointed critique of much of American fundamentalism.[9] In a useful biographical essay on Warfield, Mark Noll contends that there are three important factors that consistently emerge in Warfield's rather terse criticism of fundamentalists.

The first factor, according to Noll, is that Warfield "held that fundamentalist proof-texting represented a retrograde step in studying the Bible."[10] Warfield was quite critical, for example, of Moody Bible Institute's Reuben Archer Torrey and his popular and influential book *What the Bible Teaches*.[11] Noll identifies dispensationalism as a second source of Warfield's theological ire toward fundamentalism, and as Noll correctly puts it, Warfield "was thoroughly unimpressed by the dispensationalism that became so important in American fundamentalism."[12] As significant as these first two factors were, these were not the only tensions that existed between Princeton and the fundamentalists, Noll points out.

9. As but one example of this tendency, see the work by Dallas Theological Seminary founder Lewis Sperry Chafer, *Systematic Theology*, where Chafer repeatedly appeals to Warfield's work regarding the inspiration and authority of the Scriptures and yet ignores Warfield's stinging criticism of his own understanding of the Christian life as one characterized by the distinction between "spiritual" and "carnal" Christians. See Lewis Sperry Chafer, *Systematic Theology*, vol. 1 (Dallas: Dallas Seminary Press, 1980), 53, 80; and B. B. Warfield, "Review of *He That Is Spiritual*, by Lewis Sperry Chafer," *The Princeton Theological Review*, vol. XVII, no. 2 (April 1919), 322–27.

10. Mark A. Noll, "B. B. Warfield," in *Handbook of Evangelical Theologians* (ed. Walter A. Elwell; Grand Rapids: Baker Book House, 1993), 32.

11. B. B. Warfield, "Review of R. A. Torrey's *What the Bible Teaches*," in *The Presbyterian and Reformed Review* Vol. X (July 1899), 562–64. Ernest Sandeen correctly notices that Warfield was critical of this work, but mistakenly ascribes the criticism to Warfield's "attacks upon the dispensationalists." See Ernest R. Sandeen, "Towards a Historical Interpretation of the Origins of Fundamentalism," in *Church History*, vol. XXXVI, no. 1 (March, 1967), 74–75. Contra Sandeen, Warfield never mentions Torrey's dispensationalism, but he does clearly attack Torrey's methodology in handling and interpreting the Scriptures, something that Sandeen had argued that the two held largely in common. Also see Timothy P. Weber, "The Two-Edged Sword: The Fundamentalist Use of the Bible," in *The Bible in America: Essays in Cultural History* (eds. Nathan O. Hatch and Mark A. Noll; New York: Oxford University Press, 1982), 110 ff.

12. Mark Noll, "B. B. Warfield," 32. Sandeen correctly notes that while Warfield was critical of dispensationalism, he often favorably reviewed various dispensationalists' works dealing with biblical authority. Ernest Sandeen, "Origins of Fundamentalism," 75, n. 34.

The greatest point of tension between Warfield and the fundamentalists is Warfield's openness to the possibility of theistic evolution.[13] Following his philosophical mentor, James McCosh, and his theological predecessor, A. A. Hodge, "Warfield thought it was possible to affirm evolution within the boundaries of historic Christian doctrines."[14] Warfield had no trouble declaring that "the antiquity of man has of itself no theological significance," while at the same time affirming that "the whole doctrinal structure of the Bible account of redemption is founded on its assumption that the race of man is one organic whole."[15] Warfield was perfectly willing to allow for the full evolutionary development of humanity until the time of Adam. At the same time he unashamedly affirmed the existence—indeed the necessity—of a historical individual named Adam and the historicity of the creation account.[16] In allowing for the possibility of theistic evolution, Warfield enlisted the support of

13. The degree of Warfield's openness to evolution is the subject of two important volumes. In the first, Mark Noll and David Livingstone contend that while Warfield "consistently rejected naturalistic, reductonistic, or ateleological explanations for natural phenomena (explanations that he usually associated with Darwinism), Warfield just as consistently entertained the possibility that other kinds of evolutionary theses, which avoided Darwin's rejection of design, could satisfactorily explain the physical world." See Mark A. Noll and David N. Livingstone, *B. B. Warfield: Evolution, Science, and Scripture* (Grand Rapids: Baker Books, 2000), 42. Fred Zaspel, on the other hand, contends "The fact is that Warfield never overtly acknowledges evolution as true. The picture we have of him on this subject is continuously one of noncommittal. What he allows as a possibility both theologically and theoretically-that the Christian as such has 'no quarrel with evolution when confined to its own sphere as a suggested account of the method of divine providence'-he never explicitly endorses." See Fred G Zaspel's *The Theology of B. B. Warfield: A Systematic Summary* (Wheaton Illinois: Crossway, 2010), 387.

14. Mark A. Noll, *The Scandal of the American Mind* (Grand Rapids: Eerdmans, 1994), 180. Also see David N. Livingstone, "B. B. Warfield, the Theory of Evolution and Early Fundamentalism," in *The Evangelical Quarterly* Volume LVIII (1986), 69–83; "The Idea of Design: The Vicissitudes of a Key Concept in the Princeton Response to Darwin," in *Scottish Journal of Theology*, vol. 37 (1984), 329–57; and *Darwin's Forgotten Defenders: The Encounter Between Evangelical Theology and Evolutionary Thought* (Grand Rapids: Eerdmans, 1987), 115–22. Also see Bradley J. Gundlach, "The Evolution Question at Princeton, 1845–1929," (Ph.D. diss.: University of Rochester, 1995); and Deryl Freeman Johnson, "The Attitude of the Princeton Theologians Toward Darwinianism and Evolution from 1859–1929," (Ph.D. diss.: University of Iowa, 1968). It is interesting to note the recent re-printing of Charles Hodge's *What is Darwinianism?* (eds. Mark A. Noll and David N. Livingstone; Grand Rapids: Baker Book House, 1994).

15. B. B. Warfield, "On the Antiquity and Unity of the Human Race," in *Studies in Theology* (Grand Rapids: Baker Book House, 1980), 235–58.

16. Ibid.

none other than John Calvin, who Warfield declared "doubtless had no theory whatever of evolution; but he teaches a doctrine of evolution."[17] On this issue, there can be no doubt that Warfield, a lifelong naturalist and devoted member of the Audubon Society,[18] held an opposing view from the vast majority of fundamentalists. According to Bradley Gundlach, "Warfield was a theist, but more than a theist," and therefore, opposed Darwinian naturalism with great vigor. Yet Warfield was "an evolutionist, but more than an evolutionist. Theism and evolution were to him only partial, natural visions of the work of the living, redeeming, supernatural God."[19]

B. B. Warfield will be forever associated with a fundamentalism essay on "The Deity of Christ," published in *The Fundamentals* in 1909. But the "aging lion of strict Presbyterian orthodoxy"—as George Marsden has described him[20]—clearly stands apart from much of the emerging fundamentalist movement at a number of critical points.[21] Despite his awareness of Warfield's disdain for perfectionist notions of sanctification,[22] historian Mark Noll has nevertheless overlooked one of the most important sources of tension: Warfield's animosity to all things Arminian, especially revivalism and "holiness teaching." George Marsden points out:

> Unlike most of his contemporaries, Warfield was not in the least distracted by the popularity, success, or practical results of a doctrine. True to the Princeton tradition, he spotted a major doctrinal

17. B. B. Warfield, "Calvin's Doctrine of Creation," in *Calvin and Calvinism* (Grand Rapids: Baker Book House, 1981), 305.
18. Ethelbert D. Warfield, "A Biographical Sketch of Benjamin Breckinridge Warfield," in B. B. Warfield, *Revelation and Inspiration* (Grand Rapids: Baker Book House, 1980), vi.
19. Gundlach, "The Evolution Question at Princeton, 1845–1929," 324.
20. Marsden, *Fundamentalism and American Culture*, 98.
21. As George Marsden notes, while *The Fundamentals* included essays which display "an overwhelming emphasis on soul-saving, personal experience, and individual prayer," themes which would not be altogether foreign to Princeton, especially since *The Fundamentals* "showed remarkable restraint in promoting the more controversial aspect of their views," namely premillennialism and dispensationalism. Keswick notions regarding the Christian life were present, however. See George Marsden, *Fundamentalism and American Culture*, 119–120. The personal piety of the Princetonians has been capably discussed by Andrew Hoffecker, *The Piety of the Princeton Theologians* (Phillipsburg: P&R Publishing, 1981); and David B. Calhoun, *Princeton Seminary: Faith & Learning*.
22. Noll, "B. B. Warfield," 37–38.

> innovation and pounced. During the next several years [after the Keswick conferences came to Princeton in 1916–1918], in a series of sharp and condescending criticisms, Warfield attempted to tear apart once and for all innovative holiness teachings of every sort.[23]

Warfield's outright hostility toward the Keswick movement and other manifestations of holiness teaching led to Warfield's increasingly harsh criticisms of many fundamentalist leaders. It is also probably no accident that he wrote against the movement immediately after the Keswick conferences had invaded his home turf.

Warfield's aversion to revivalism and perfectionism, (which he clearly associated with Wesleyan Arminianism, and he viewed as the pure Pelagianism of Charles Grandison Finney),[24] was a major factor in Warfield's negative views toward many of the fundamentalist leaders. Warfield was part of a longstanding Princeton criticism of Finney, as well as the New Haven Theology, from which it was believed that Finney developed his own theological system.[25] Closely related is the equally long-standing Princetonian aversion to Arminianism, which Warfield had described as a "defection" from the theology of historic Protestantism.[26]

To best understand B. B. Warfield's increasing uneasiness with the fundamentalist movement, one should begin with Warfield's critique of Arminianism as a theological system.[27] While Warfield was perfectly willing to grant that Arminianism was historically associated with evangelical Christianity because of the system's commitment to a

---

23. Marsden, *Fundamentalism and American Culture*, 98.
24. Warfield's criticisms of Finney are quite extensive and merit a monograph length treatment in their own right. Warfield was equally critical of Finney and his Oberlin compatriot, Asa Mahan. See the critical essays all published in *The Princeton Theological Review* Vol. XIX (1921) "Oberlin Perfectionism: I. The Men and the Beginnings," (1–63); "II. Mahan's Type of Teaching," (225–88); "III. The Development of the Oberlin Teaching," (451–93); and "IV. The Theology of Charles Finney," (568–619). These have all been reprinted in their entirety in B. B. Warfield, *Perfectionism*, vol. II (Grand Rapids: Baker Book House, 1980), 3–215.
25. Warfield, "The Men and the Beginnings," 18.
26. B. B. Warfield, "Calvinism" in *Calvin and Calvinism* (Grand Rapids: Baker Book House, 1980), 361.
27. In his essay, "John Calvin the Theologian," Warfield argues that Arminianism is "the rebellious daughter" of the Reformed tradition. See B. B. Warfield, "John Calvin the Theologian," in *Calvin and Augustine* (Phillipsburg: P&R Publishing, 1974), 490.

thoroughly supernatural soteriology,[28] Warfield asks whether or not the "cherished evangelicalism of the Wesleyan ... constructions is not more theoretical than practical."[29] Warfield saw Arminianism as erroneous and necessary of refutation whenever it reared its head.

Those who worked closely with Warfield at Princeton identified his personal commitment to the Reformed faith and his animosity to any departures from it as perhaps *the* most memorable thing about him. O. T. Allis, a former student and later faculty colleague of Warfield at Princeton, recalls:

> Dr. Warfield was *orthodox*; he was a Calvinist by conviction. He believed the Westminster Standards to be the "final crystallization of the very essence of evangelical religion." He did not find this system of doctrine which he was pledged by his ordination and inaugural oaths to teach and defend a hair shirt or strait-jacket which he must wear, however much it might irk or cramp his freedom. On the contrary he wore it as a coat of mail, clad in which he was prepared to enter the lists to meet all comers; and he was approved himself as a valiant defender of the faith in his knightly combat. He did not compromise, he did not water down the truth. He was not a minimalist but a maximalist. He would not settle for the shortest possible creed in order to win the multitudes. He wanted a full-orbed Christianity and not one which was tailored to meet the demands of the latitudinarian and ecumenist. He valued truth above conformity and conciliation. He was not a bigot, but he aimed to be no broader than the Bible, to speak the truth in love, but the truth at all costs.[30]

B. B. Warfield felt compelled to take up his pen against the Pelagius and Arminian tendencies of the fundamentalist movement as a matter of principle. He saw this as his fundamental duty as professor of polemical theology serving at an institution unequivocally committed to the Westminster Standards.

---

28. B. B. Warfield, *The Plan of Salvation* (Grand Rapids: Eerdmans, 1980), 31.
29. Ibid., 78.
30. O. T. Allis, "Personal Impressions of Dr. Warfield," in *The Banner of Truth*, 89 (Fall 1971), 13. No doubt that Allis' remarks may be hagiographic to a degree, but nevertheless, this is the characteristic way in which Warfield was remembered.

A CALVINISTICALLY WARPED MIND—WARFIELD ON JOHN MILEY'S ARMINIANISM

Warfield's later strong criticism of the noted fundamentalist leaders Andrew Murray, R. A. Torrey, and Lewis Sperry Chafer were based on his deep dispute with Arminianism. His arguments against Arminianism can perhaps best be seen in his "Review" of Methodist theologian John Miley's *Systematic Theology*. Although Miley was not associated with the fundamentalist movement, this review represents Warfield's criticism of Arminianism as a distinct theological system. Warfield, though critical of Miley's contentions, still respects him as a scholar. His appreciation for Miley stands in sharp contrast to the tone of subsequent reviews of books from major fundamentalist leaders.

B. B. Warfield's "Review of *Systematic Theology*, by John Miley," is a two-part review article originally published from 1893 to 1895. It corresponds directly to the sequential publication of Miley's two-volume work (1892–1894). Warfield describes the volume as an "altogether good book, which the Arminian should find satisfying, and with which the Calvinist should count it a privilege to join issue."[31] He praised the work as "clear, direct, and strongly written; ... characterized by candor, restraint, and modesty; it is orderly in arrangement and lucid in discussion."[32] But Warfield's respect for Miley, a noted Methodist theologian and professor of systematic theology at Drew Theological Seminary, did not deter the Princetonian from offering direct criticisms. After all, one of Miley's express goals was to refute two of Warfield's own beloved mentors, Charles and Archibald Alexander Hodge.[33]

Warfield begins his review with an evaluation of the way in which Miley has organized his system. "The first volume included the topics which fall under the heads of Theology proper and Anthropology."[34] The second volume completed the system discussing "Christology, Soteriology and Eschatology. Three appendices ... discuss, respectively,

31. B. B. Warfield, "Review of *Systematic Theology*, by John Miley," originally published in two parts—*The Thinker: A Magazine of Christian Literature* (April 1893), and *The Magazine of Christian Literature* (Feb. 1895)—and reprinted on their entirety in *Selected Shorter Writings*, vol. 2 (ed. John E. Meeter; Phillipsburg: P&R Publishing, 1980), 308.
32. Ibid.
33. See, for example, John Miley, *Systematic Theology*, vol. 2 (New York: Eaton & Mains, 1894), 143 ff.
34. Warfield, "Review of *Systematic Theology*, by John Miley," 314.

the inspiration of the Scriptures, the angels, and the Arminian treatment of original sin."[35] As Warfield sees it, the supreme value of Miley's work lies in its clarity. All essential differences between the Calvinistic system, as defined in the Westminster Standards, and the distinctly Arminian theological system of which John Miley is a capable advocate, are clearly set forth. In Warfield's estimation:

> The material is handled in a masterly manner, and the volume as a whole sets forth the Arminian scheme of salvation in as powerful and logical a form as that scheme admits of. For Dr. Miley presents himself here as above all things an Arminian, and as above most Arminians ready to follow his Arminianism to its logical conclusions. Here, indeed, we find the highest significance of the book. It is the Arminian "Yea" to the Calvinistic declaration of what Arminianism is in its essential nature, where its center of gravity lies, and what it means with reference to that complex of doctrines which constitute the sum of evangelical truth.[36]

The importance of Miley's work, in Warfield's estimation, lies in its consistency and in the willingness of the author to follow the logic of the Arminian system to its ultimate end. This is extremely valuable because Miley himself confirms the litany of charges that Calvinists have historically raised against Arminianism.

Miley's treatment of theological prolegomena dominates the opening pages of the first volume. There are over 50 pages devoted to "the nature, sources, scope, and method of systematic theology."[37] Other than expressing his oft-stated concern that apologetics is not treated under the heading of "Theism," Warfield notes that the introductory material in volume one is "very illuminating" in its treatment of the nature of systematic theology. In addition, Miley offers what Warfield considers to be a "very sensible criticism of the so-called 'Christocentric' method. Dr. Miley despairs of attaining a single 'unifying principle' in theology and holds that systematizing must proceed 'in a synthetic mode.' "[38] In apparent agreement with Dr. Miley, Warfield notes that he "follows the customary order of topics."[39] He also makes note of the fact that Dr.

35. Ibid.
36. Ibid., 314.
37. Ibid., 309.
38. Ibid.
39. Ibid.

Miley has done a very effective job—with "skill and success" as Warfield describes it—in his treatment of the relationship between reason and feeling.[40]

Warfield subsequently launches into a critical evaluation of the Arminian system itself, as represented by John Miley. The first specific criticism is the tension inherent within the Arminian system between the "modes of knowledge" (which Miley divides into "natural" and "revealed"), and in the "mode of acquisition" of that knowledge, which in the case of natural knowledge is "purely human" and in the case of revealed knowledge, "is immediately given by the supernatural agency of God."[41] The tension stems from the fact that Miley, "at a later point (p. 11), [is] apparently deserting this ground,"[42] when he speaks of the knowledge of God derived by "the heathen" from purely natural revelation.

> He there seems to posit a reception by heathen men of a divine revelation, which comes to them through their human faculties, and is not verified to the recipient as from God. Here he seems to step beyond the wall of his own definition, with the effect of throwing himself into the hands of the mystic rationalists. We must hasten to add, however, that when he comes to treat formally of mysticism (p. 16), he rejects the mythical path for attaining religious truth altogether, and deals very stringently with the modern doctrine of the Christian consciousness. We must confess that we do not know how the views expressed at p. 11, as to a not uncommon revelation to heathen seekers, can be accorded with the criticism here; unless we are to suppose that God is nearer to the heathen than to Christians, and deals more intimately with them than with Christians.[43]

Not only is Warfield eager to point out the internal tension within the Arminian system on this point, but he also rejects what he perceives as the erroneous notion that the "reception of a divine revelation, which comes to them through their human faculties ... is not verified to the recipient as from God." It is interesting to note at this point that those such as Cornelius Van Til, who have accused Warfield of advocating an inherently Arminian apologetic and who criticize Warfield for "attributing

40. Ibid., 310.
41. Ibid., 309.
42. Ibid.
43. Ibid., 309–10.

to 'right reason' the ability to interpret natural revelation correctly,"[44] have failed to notice that Warfield overtly rejects the Arminian conception of such natural knowledge of God. He disputes the claim that "the heathen" autonomously derive true knowledge from divine revelation, when nothing in that revelation supposedly bears exclusive witness of the God who gave it to them.

Warfield next critiques Dr. Miley's treatment of omniscience, which Warfield contends also suffers from an internal tension common to the Arminian system, and unresolved "perplexities which emerge from it for Arminian thought [and which] are not disguised."[45] This tension results from Miley's apparent unwillingness, as a consistent Arminian, to deny "the foreknowledge of free actions," and yet at the same time, be equally unwilling to follow through on the logic of this conclusion and embrace the orthodox Reformed conception of God's decree as encompassing his foreknowledge of future events. It is this perceived inconsistency on Miley's part which Warfield attempts to exploit:

> We cannot think, however, that he has followed out his own arguments to their legitimate conclusions. They not only involve the admission of the certainty (as distinguished from the necessity) of free actions (p. 183), which is all any Calvinist believes; but they distinctly imply the Calvinistic doctrine of predestination. For example, he acutely reduces the difficulties which are asserted to stand in the way of God's foreknowledge of the free acts of men to absurdity, by pointing out that the same difficulties would press equally against God's foreknowledge of his own free acts. This is unanswerable. But it will require an immeasurably more acute logic still to distinguish God's foreknowledge of his future choices, from a fore-intention to make these choices; and this is just the Calvinistic doctrine of predestination.[46]

How is it, then, that Miley can still contend that God can certainly foreknow whatever comes to pass, and at the same time reject the connection made in Scripture and demanded by logic between that knowledge and God's eternal decree?

---

44. Cornelius Van Til, *The Defense of the Faith* (Phillipsburg: P&R Publishing, 1955), 264–65.
45. Warfield, "Review of *Systematic Theology* by John Miley," 310.
46. Ibid., 310–11.

The reason Miley rejects the Reformed doctrine of predestination as a possible solution to this problem is because Miley finds it inconsistent with our notions of divine goodness that God would create souls who are predestined to be damned.[47] Such a doctrine of predestination is inconsistent with the Arminian *fundamentum*, which is the freedom of the human will.[48] Here, Warfield attempts to point out the difficulties that Miley's formulation raises:

> The objection that it would be inconsistent with the divine goodness to create souls whose rejection of salvation is certainly foreknown, is justly set aside with the remark that nescience will not obviate the objection; inasmuch as it presses almost equally against the creation of souls with the known possibility of their loss, and quite equally against the continuance of the race after the fact of such numerous losses has emerged in experience. But surely the bottom of the matter is not yet reached; for if God creates souls which he certainly foreknows will be lost, he must create them with the intention, in this sense, of their being lost; and this is the whole content of the Calvinistic doctrine of predestination in this case—of that *decretum horrible* to which men seem so unceasingly to object, but which is as surely a truth of reason as it is of Scripture.[49]

Thus, asks Warfield, when Miley subsequently attempts to deal with the origin of evil, "how is it permissible to create these moral beings and put them in this probationary economy, with the knowledge, not that they *might possibly* fall, but that they *certainly would* fall?"[50] While Miley may shrink back from what Warfield sees as the obvious conclusion, Warfield does not: "The only tenable ground here is the Calvinistic ground that such action on God's part involves the divine intention, in this sense, of the fall—that is, its predestination."[51]

Next, following Miley's ordering of topics, the Princetonian moves on to discuss "anthropology." It is here, Warfield states, "The Calvinistic reader will find most which will seem to him open to question; and this the more that Dr. Miley occupies in this sphere the extremest Arminian

47. Miley, *Systematic Theology*, vol. 2, 263–66.
48. Ibid., 276.
49. Warfield, "Review of *Systematic Theology*, by John Miley," 311.
50. Ibid., 312.
51. Ibid., 313.

ground."[52] Warfield gladly acknowledges that Miley has effectively and honestly described the Augustinian position, though Miley himself will only allow for a native and not a penal depravity. In addition, Miley "teaches that all men are naturally depraved, and out of that depravity will commit sin; but that this depravity does not come to them in any true sense by way of penalty." In Miley's scheme, the "law of nature" works as a kind of substitute for the category of penal depravity, "because they are born with it and do not produce it, they cannot be held responsible for it."[53] The primary target, then, of Warfield's remarks is Miley's use of the phrase "law of nature." According to Warfield, the phrase functions as a kind of synthetic *a priori*, which in Warfield's estimation gives us "no explanation at all: it is the deification of a phrase."[54] Warfield remarks somewhat sarcastically:

> It passes the comprehension of our Calvinistically warped mind to understand how so close a thinker can, on the one hand, hang the whole weight of depravity on a "law of nature," or, on the other, deny the condemnability of a state of depravity which inevitably produces sin in every action into which it issues.[55]

Apparently, it "passes the comprehension" of the Princetonian's "Calvinistically warped mind" when Miley lays forth a scheme in which a "subjective depravity" is described as inevitably producing actual sins, yet is not itself subject to divine judgment. According to Warfield, such a formulation confounds "all our ideas of God as a moral agent."[56]

In his review of Miley's second volume (published in 1894 and reviewed by Warfield the following year), the discussion subsequently moves to soteriology, and it is here, that the differences between Princeton and the classical Arminianism of Methodism are most evident. This is particularly important to Warfield, because "in the great evangelical revival of the last century, the Wesleyan leaders offered to the world an Evangelicalized Arminianism."[57] But for Warfield, the pressing question is, "whether the Evangelical elements thus taken up

---

52. Ibid., 312.
53. Ibid., 312–13.
54. Ibid., 313.
55. Ibid.
56. Ibid.
57. Ibid., 314.

could consist with the Arminian principle."[58] From Warfield's perspective, the answer was clearly no.

> Calvinists earnestly urged that the union was an unnatural one, and could not be stable: that either the Evangelical elements ought to rule to the exclusion of the unharmonized Arminian principle, in which case we should have consistent Calvinism; or else the Arminian principle would inevitably rule to the exclusion of the Evangelical doctrines forced into artificial conjunction with it, and we should have consistent Arminianism.[59]

It is precisely at this point, Warfield argues, that Miley has performed his greatest service in the publication of such a clear and consistent Arminian system. "After a century of conflict, Dr. Miley's admirably reasoned volumes come to tell us frankly that the Calvinists have been right in these contentions,"[60] namely, that evangelicalism and Arminianism—each when logically conceived—are mutually exclusive on several critical points:

> Arminianism, he says, has no logical place in its system for a doctrine of race sin, either in the sense of the participation of the race in the guilt of Adam's first sin, or in the sense of the infection of the race with a guilty corruption. Arminianism, he says, has no logical place in its system for a doctrine of penal substitution of Christ for sinners and of an atonement by satisfaction. If the Arminian principle is to rule, he says, the doctrine of race sin must go, and the doctrine of vicarious punishment must go. And,

58. Ibid., 315.
59. Ibid. Later, Warfield was to write, "[In] Calvinism, then, objectively speaking, theism comes to its rights; subjectively speaking, the religious relation attains its purity; soteriologically speaking, evangelical religion finds at length its full expression and its secure stability. Theism comes to its rights only in a teleological conception of the universe, which perceives in the entire course of events the orderly outworking of the plan of God, who is the author, preserver, and governor of all things, whose will is consequently the ultimate cause of all. The religious relation attains its purity only when an attitude of absolute dependence upon God is not merely temporarily assumed in an act, say of prayer, but is sustained through all the activities of life, intellectual, emotional, executive. And evangelical religion reaches stability only when the sinful soul rests in humble self-emptying trust purely upon the God of grace as the immediate and sole source of all the efficiency which enters into its salvation. And these things are the formative principles of Calvinism." See Warfield, "Calvinism," 365.
60. Warfield, "Review of *Systematic Theology*, by John Miley," 315.

> as he thinks that the Arminian principle ought to rule, he teaches that men are not by nature under the condemning wrath of God, and that Christ did not vicariously bear the penalty of sin. Thus, in his hands, Arminianism is seeking to purify itself by cleansing itself from the Evangelical elements with which it has long been conjoined.[61]

This is an important point, and why Warfield views Miley's work as so valuable. "Dr. Miley ... clears away the Evangelical accretions from the Arminian core," and in doing so he "commands our complete admiration. It is quiet logic, working its way to an irrefutable end."[62] But it is an end to which Warfield himself cannot go. In his estimation, "It is better far to be inconsistently Evangelical than consistently Arminian."[63] It is because of Dr. Miley's clarity and consistency that the attempt to combine evangelicalism and Arminianism ultimately fails in Warfield's estimation. As Miley's efforts so clearly demonstrate, "the world should come to know with the utmost clearness that these Evangelical doctrines are uncomfortable with Arminianism. It is just as well that the world should realize ... that Evangelicalism stands or falls with Calvinism."[64] In Warfield's mind, "Every proof of Evangelicalism is a proof of Calvinism."[65]

After briefly touching upon Miley's treatment of Christology and eschatology, Warfield moves on to investigate in some detail Miley's doctrine of the atonement. Here again, Miley's clarity is commended, because in this case, "the Governmental theory of the Atonement is

61. Ibid.
62. Ibid., 316.
63. Ibid.
64. Ibid. Elsewhere, Warfield defines "evangelical truths" as "salvation by faith only, dependence for salvation on the blood of Christ alone, the necessity for salvation by the regeneration of the Holy Spirit," elements which "evangelical Arminians," such as Wesley, tried to combine (as Warfield believed inconsistently—but blessedly so) with distinctly Arminian elements. Warfield clearly felt that Miley had demonstrated the impossibility of this, *if* one attempted to remain faithful to the Arminian principle of human freedom as the foundation for a Christian theology. See B. B. Warfield: "In Behalf of Evangelical Religion," *The Presbyterian*, (September 23, 1920), 20 ff; and reprinted in B. B. Warfield, *Selected Shorter Writings*, vol. 1 (ed. John E. Meeter; Phillipsburg: P&R Publishing, 1980), 387.
65. Ibid. This is because Warfield understood Calvinism as "just religion in its purity. We have only, therefore, to conceive of religion in its purity, and that is Calvinism." B. B. Warfield, "What is Calvinism?" in *The Presbyterian* (March 2, 1904), 6–7. Repr. in Warfield, *Selected Shorter Writings*, vol. 2, 389.

expounded and advocated with freshness and force."[66] Since, as Miley himself freely admits, "freedom is fundamental in Arminianism," therefore, "the [Arminian] system holds accordingly the universality of the atonement and provisory nature of the atonement, and the conditionality of salvation."[67] The problem which Miley faces, according to Warfield, is "to find a doctrine of atonement comfortable to the Arminian *fundamentum*, which Dr. Miley does not hesitate to locate in its psychology of the will."[68] Dr. Miley, being the very capable theologian that he is, again follows this Arminian *fundamentum* through to its logical conclusion. To demonstrate this, Warfield cites Miley's views that " 'the cardinal doctrines of the Wesleyan Soteriology' are—'that the atonement is only provisory in its character, rendering men savable, but not necessarily saving them'; and that salvation is conditional in the sense of a real Synergism (p. 169)."[69] The critical point in all of this is, according to Warfield, that once again "we go thoroughly with Dr. Miley in his clear proof (p. 122) of the untenableness of those schemes which seek to unite an atonement of penal substitution and conditional universalism."[70]

It is important to note that this is not simply another round in the ongoing debate between the Calvinists and the Arminians over the extent of the atonement, because in Warfield's estimation, there is far more at stake here. Ultimately, the historic Protestant conception of the character of God as "the infinitely holy and just One, [who] must react upon sin with a moral indignation which is exactly proportionate to its guilt, and which burns inextinguishably until it is satisfied by adequate punishment" is the real point of contention in this debate.[71] The problem in Miley's conception is that God does not need to react to sin as a holy and righteous avenger:

> "If justice," he says, "must punish sin simply for the reason of its demerit, penal substitution is the only possible atonement" (p. 169). That the rectoral theory of the atonement may be held, and with it the Arminian system, therefore, we must deny to God that moral indignation in view of evil, which we cannot help recognizing as one of the highest endowments of moral beings, and must

66. Ibid., 317.
67. Miley, *Systematic Theology*, vol. 2, 275.
68. Warfield, "Review of *Systematic Theology*, by John Miley," 317.
69. Ibid. Warfield is citing from Miley's *Systematic Theology*, vol. 2, 169.
70. Ibid.
71. Ibid., 318.

> transmute his "justice" into merely public justice of a wise ruler; we must revise in a word, all our natural notions of the relations of an infinitely holy being to sin. Dr. Miley attacks this problem at an early point (pp. 93 ff.), the result of his discussion being that he concludes that while punishment may not be inflicted where there is no sin, and may never go beyond the intrinsic demerit of sin—"and God has the exact measure of its desert"—yet sin need not be "punished according to its desert" (p. 97) —provided that the requirements of God's moral government are not endangered by the failure to punish it. In other words, while sin may not be punished beyond its desert, it may be punished below its desert, if it can be rendered safe to do so.[72]

This conception of God's holiness and justice leads Warfield to conclude that this issue is "certainly one of the watersheds between Calvinism and Arminianism." It becomes clear that "those who believe that God must, by virtue of his all-perfect nature, visit sin with a punishment fitted to the exact measure of its desert—no more certainly, but just as certainly, no less—must, so far as logic can compel them, become Calvinists."[73] When the logic of Miley's conception of the atonement is set forth, there can only be one conclusion in Warfield's mind. "If it be 'safe' to forgive sin on the ground of a 'substitute for penalty,' it would seem just as 'safe' to make a sincere personal repentance that substitute as to make the suffering of an alien such substitute."[74] Warfield concludes: "Dr. Miley's argument seems to us to issue in setting aside all real necessity for atonement."[75] Almost lamentably, Warfield notes that in Dr. Miley's system, "forgiveness itself remains an act of pure grace,"[76] therefore, there is no need for atonement in the first place, and the question is raised as to why Christ suffered at all. Why did the Son of God have to die if some other possible means of dealing with sin, such as personal repentance, could serve as a legitimate method of remitting the penalty due us as sinners?

72. Ibid.
73. Ibid.
74. Ibid., 318–19.
75. Ibid., 319.
76. Ibid.

NAYSAYING THE "COTERIE OF BIBLE TEACHERS"

Although Warfield did not in any way mitigate his criticisms of John Miley's Arminianism, he was respectful toward his important and articulate work. However, Warfield's patience seemed quite strained when he reviewed popular works by highly visible fundamentalist leaders with Arminian and revivalist leanings. Two revealing illustrations of this can be found in Warfield's sour reviews of books by fundamentalist luminaries Andrew Murray and R. A. Torrey.

In his short but curt review of Andrew Murray's *The Spirit of Christ* (1888), Warfield concludes that the "author treats this greatest of all Christian subjects with adequate reverence and tender devoutness but scarcely with sufficient judiciousness."[77] Murray, a prominent minister in the Dutch Reformed Church of South Africa, had become an important, though controversial figure in both England and America. Considered by some to be a kind of proto-Pentecostal, Murray's orthodoxy had been the subject of question.[78] He had recently spoken at D. L. Moody's Northfield Convention in Northfield, Massachusetts (1895), though he was most closely associated with the Keswick Holiness conferences in England.[79] One of Murray's previous books, *Be Perfect*, had become quite influential among one group of late 19th-century evangelicals, who were on what Douglas Frank describes as a quest for "perfection."[80] Not surprisingly, Andrew Murray was the kind of figure that B. B. Warfield would grant little quarter.

As Warfield explains, the major problem with Murray's *The Spirit of Christ* is to be found in Murray's mystical tendencies. "The mystical spirit has been always of the greatest value to the Church," especially when it is "sometimes the sole preservative of true Christianity in a materialistic or legalistic age. But no tendency requires a stricter watchfulness to preserve it from extravagance."[81] But this lack of watchfulness is precisely where Warfield felt that Murray had gone astray. "Mr. Murray's

---

77. B. B. Warfield, "Review of *The Spirit of Christ: Thoughts on the Indwelling of the Holy Spirit in the Believer and in the Church*, by Rev. Andrew Murray," in *The Presbyterian Review*, vol. X (April 1889), 334–35.
78. Eddie Brown, "Murray, Andrew," in *Dictionary of Scottish Church History & Theology* (ed. Nigel Cameron; Downers Grove: InterVarsity Press, 1993), 611–12.
79. Douglas W. Frank, *Less Than Conquerors: How Evangelicals Entered the Twentieth Century* (Grand Rapids: Eerdmans, 1986), 109–13.
80. Ibid.
81. Warfield, "Review of *The Spirit of Christ*, by Andrew Murray," 334.

mystical tendency shows itself especially in laying too great stress on the duty of being conscious of the Spirit's working within us, and in an odd insistence on the duty of exercising 'faith in the indwelling' as the source of life."[82] The difficulty with such a formulation is that Murray asks us to place our faith in the indwelling Spirit "as if the Scriptures proclaimed the necessity of any other faith than that in Christ. Here, he introduces an intolerable dualism into the Christian life, finding two moments of development in it corresponding to the two objects of this two-fold exercise of faith."[83] This point was, in fact, Warfield's primary criticism of revivalist-holiness theology, since justification and sanctification can no longer be seen as two distinct but necessarily related aspects of salvation. Reformed theology sees the single exercise of saving faith resulting in the justification of the sinner, and beginning the lifelong process of sanctification. In the revivalist-holiness conception, the one act of faith only provided justification. Sanctification was seen to require a separate exercise of faith.

As Warfield saw things, a major part of the problem was that Murray had uncritically accepted the scheme formulated by Asa Mahan, with whom Warfield would later take issue in his extensive critique of perfectionism (1918).[84] Warfield argues, "It is a great pity that he adopts the confusion of the charismatic and gracious work of the Spirit upon which Mr. Mahan bases his separation of regeneration and sanctification."[85] According to Warfield:

> We must not separate the two works of the Spirit: it is no more true that whom God foreknew, them He also predestined to be conformed to the image of His Son, and whom He predestined, them He also called, and whom He called, them He also justified, than it is that whom He justified, them also He glorified, which surely includes more than external acceptance into the heavenly glory. The essence of the passage is to teach that God selects His children, chooses the goal to which He shall bring them, and brings them safely to that goal; and it justifies us in saying that without exception "whom He regenerates, them also He sanctifies." The

82. Ibid.
83. Ibid. Later in his career, Warfield would label this a distinctly Arminian tendency. See Warfield's "Review of *He That Is Spiritual* by Lewis Sperry Chafer," 322.
84. See Warfield, "Mahan's Type of Teaching," 64 ff.
85. Warfield, "Review of *The Spirit of Christ*, by Andrew Murray," 334–35.

> separation of these two begets the very evil which Murray deprecates, of the failure to live up to our privileges.[86]

Whatever remained of Warfield's patience ended. "Enthusiastic minds like Mr. Murray's need to exercise special care in adopting forms of statement from other writers."[87] Because of the author's lack of such care, "we meet every now and then in the book with a phrase or doctrine the implications of which have scarcely been thought through by him."[88] As a prime example of this, Warfield selects "the crude trichotomistic anthropology," which is adopted by Murray in one place, "only to be laid aside" elsewhere. In another place, Warfield points out, Murray sounds like a "fully developed Schleiermacherite,"[89] uncharacteristically engaging in a bit of *ad hominem* argumentation. In yet a third example, Warfield contends, "Every now and then we strike against a sentence delivered as if it contained the very kernel of the Gospel, which quite puzzles us."[90] Warfield later adds:

> For example, what idea of "Holiness" underlies the assertion that "it is as the Indwelling One that God is Holy," offered in defense of the statement that the Spirit is "the Holy Spirit" only as sent forth by the incarnate Christ? And what shall we do with the statement made in the same connection, "It is not the Spirit of Christ as such, but the Spirit of Jesus that could be sent to dwell in us," in the face of the biblical *usus loquendi*?[91]

The Princeton theologian, by now obviously exasperated, concludes that Murray's "book is marred everywhere by such straining after novel and striking forms of statement, a vice, we may add, very common with books of this class."[92] One thing is clear. B. B. Warfield was not very impressed with the work of Andrew Murray.

Some 10 years later, when Warfield reviewed Reuben Archer Torrey's book *What the Bible Teaches* (1899), the Princetonian's caustic voice in treating "books of this class" was again quite evident. Torrey (1856–1928) was a congregational minister who became superintendent of the

86. Ibid., 335.
87. Ibid.
88. Ibid.
89. Ibid.
90. Ibid.
91. Ibid.
92. Ibid.

Moody Bible Institute in 1889. Although yet to rise to his full prominence, as he would do in the first decade of the 20th century, Torrey was in many ways the closest successor to Dwight L. Moody, and was, as George Marsden notes, already "a world-touring evangelist," and "one of the principle architects of fundamentalist thought."[93] As the Princetonian sized him up, he chides, "there are many things that Mr. Torrey has yet to learn concerning the great doctrines that the Bible teaches."[94]

While Torrey's book promises to "give us a thorough and complete study of all that the Bible has to say concerning the great doctrines of which it treats," it does not deliver on its promise. "Needless to say, Mr. Torrey's useful volume hardly fulfills to the letter this great promise."[95] What Torrey has done is to give us a book that is a "serviceable but somewhat desultory collection of Bible readings on doctrinal topics."[96] The major problem with the structure of Torrey's book is that "there are many of the great doctrines of the Bible which are not treated at all here—such as all those that cluster around the fact of election of grace and all those that belong under the locus of the Church and the means of grace."[97] What is even more telling about Torrey's book is the fact that "the treatment accorded to the doctrines selected for study moves far too much on the surface to have plumbed the depths of any of them."[98] In Warfield's estimation, the breadth of Torrey's work does not compensate for its inherent shallowness.

Warfield moves on to evaluate the manner in which Torrey gathers his biblical evidence—a method Warfield simply describes as "Bible-readings."[99] Torrey's book makes "the emphatic claim ... for the method of the work as being in an especial sense 'inductive.' "[100] As Warfield sees it, Torrey and his publishers utterly fail to offer an inductive study

93. Marsden, *Fundamentalism and American Culture*, 47.

94. B. B. Warfield, "Review of *What the Bible Teaches: A Thorough and Comprehensive Study of all the Bible Has to Say Concerning the Great Doctrines of which It Treats*, by R. A. Torrey," in *The Presbyterian and Reformed Review*, Vol. X (July 1899), 564. Mark Noll thought this review significant enough—as representative of the uneasiness between Princeton and the emerging fundamentalist movement—to place this essay in his fine anthology, *The Princeton Theology*, 299–301.

95. Ibid., 562.

96. Ibid., 562–63.

97. Ibid., 563.

98. Ibid.

99. Ibid.

100. Ibid.

of the Scriptures. It is here then, with methodological concerns, that Warfield locates one of the book's most significant weaknesses:

> The chief gain that has been made by doctrinal study of late years is its acquisition of a more inductive method. That is the significance of the birth of the new discipline of "Biblical Theology."... It is becoming more usual now to rise from the thorough understanding of the teaching of complete sections of Scripture to larger and larger groups until an insight into the doctrinal whole is attained—in the unity of its historical development and the harmony of expression.[101]

The problem lies in "that Mr. Torrey's method is altogether alien to this truly inductive process."[102] Mark Noll is indeed correct when he notes the high degree of concern repeatedly expressed by the Princetonians in regard to the inductive method, which "they had greatly refined ... over the years."[103] Thus "Warfield's pain is evident when Torrey takes that carefully honed theological principle and turns it into an excuse for random proof-texting."[104] Although Torrey claims to do so, he fails to present us with a truly inductive effort. According to Warfield, Torrey's method breaks down because:

> He begins with isolated passages, collected under a purely formal *schema* already present explicitly or implicitly in his mind: and this is not made induction merely by arranging the texts first and the propositions they support second, on the printed page. We have not the remotest intention of suggesting that Mr. Torrey is not striving to give the pure teaching of the Bible in these propositions; neither do we doubt that he succeeds in giving the pure teaching of the Bible in the large majority of them. We are merely animadverting on the claim put in that the method pursued in this volume has some distinguishing right to the name of "inductive." That it certainly has not.[105]

---

101. Ibid. This is a point that is overlooked by Ernest Sandeen throughout his essay "Towards a Historical Interpretation of Fundamentalism." Sandeen does not seem to notice that Warfield and the Princetonians were, in many ways, as critical of the emerging fundamentalism as they were to "modernist foes."
102. Warfield, "Review of *What the Bible Teaches*, by R. A. Torrey," 563.
103. Noll, *The Princeton Theology*, 299.
104. Ibid.
105. Warfield, "Review of *What the Bible Teaches*, by R. A. Torrey," 563.

Torrey's "proof-texting" (as Noll describes it) is understood by Warfield as nothing more than "the exercise known as 'Bible-readings.' What he has given us is just a series of sublimated 'Bible-readings' on doctrinal topics. Any appreciative estimate of the book must proceed on the clear recognition of this fact."[106] This point must be clearly understood, because if we do not grant Torrey the benefit of the doubt and "regard it as a contribution to dogmatics, we must need look upon it as moving over the surface of the subject—an incomplete, insufficient and occasionally erroneous."[107] If, however, we are careful to note the book's true genre, "we may gladly recognize it as an admirable example of an admirable method of teaching, from which we may all learn much."[108] The problem is that Torrey's book is characterized more by its weaknesses than its strengths.

B. B. Warfield identified two primary factors that lead to his overall negative assessment of *What the Bible Teaches*; the theological perspective of the author and his technical weaknesses. "The limitations inherent in the author's equipment and [his] doctrinal views condition it."[109] But the author's "Arminianizing theory of redemption, and his Keswick doctrine of the Baptism of the Spirit, as well as his burning, evangelical blood-theory," drew Warfield's greatest ire. Warfield agrees, however, that Torrey "does know ... the most fundamental secret of all—that the Holy God hates sin and punishes it because it is sin—and how to set forth God's holy hatred of sin in language as moving to the conscience as faithful to the Word of God."[110] But again, Warfield's "Calvinistically warped mind" finds Torrey's Arminianism quite deficient. Although the "author's plumbet does not reach the bottom," in such critical discussions as "the Trinity, the Person of Christ, the idea of Eternity, Predestination and Freedom," and, despite the fact that "his exposition runs much on the surface of things and is rather external and at points even shallow," nevertheless, Warfield applauds Torrey by saying, "We see also gladly that there are many things taught by the Bible that he has learned and knows how to teach the Christian world, and we gladly put ourselves in these at his feet."[111]

106. Ibid.
107. Ibid.
108. Ibid.
109. Ibid.
110. Ibid., 563–64.
111. Ibid.

While Warfield was less than favorably disposed to the work of Andrew Murray and R. A. Torrey, it was another key figure of the fundamentalist movement whom he singled out for his sternest theological rebuke, Lewis Sperry Chafer (1871–1952), founder and president of Dallas Theological Seminary.[112] Warfield's review of one of Chafer's early works (1918), *He That Is Spiritual*,[113] is important on several accounts. The review was published in April of 1919, just short of two years before Warfield's death in February of 1921. During this latter period of his career Warfield turned his gaze almost entirely upon the subject of perfectionism, of both the German and American varieties, then taking over much of the fundamentalist movement.[114] Chafer's *He That Is Spiritual* has been described as "Chafer's version of the Victorious Life Movement."[115] Warfield was critical of this movement probably as a response to the then recent Keswick conferences held at Princeton in 1916–1918.[116] As a virtual protégé of C. I. Scofield, Chafer had been in close contact with Dwight L. Moody and virtually all of the Victorious Christian Life advocates associated with the Keswick and Northfield Conferences who promoted what Warfield believed to be an Arminianizing notion of the Christian life. Warfield's attitude toward Chafer, one of the more important and capable teachers of the Victorious Christian Life scheme, indicates Warfield's overall attitude toward much of the fundamentalism of that period.[117]

---

112. This debate is the subject of an essay by Randall Gleason, "B. B. Warfield and Lewis Sperry Chafer on Sanctification," in *The Journal of the Evangelical Theological Society*, vol. 40, no. 2 (June 1997), 241–56.

113. The absence of this review from Noll's fine anthology *The Princeton Theology* is somewhat surprising, given its importance.

114. This point is effectively argued by Frank, *Less Than Conquerors*, 109 ff. The progression of Warfield's polemical writings over time moves from Scripture to Christology to soteriology. See Wilber B. Wallis, "Benjamin B. Warfield: Didactic and Polemical Theologian," in *The Presbyterion: Covenant Seminary Review*, Part II (Spring 1977), 73.

115. Craig A. Blaising, "Lewis Sperry Chafer," in *Handbook of Evangelical Theologians* (ed. Walter A. Elwell; Grand Rapids: Baker Book House, 1993), 85.

116. Marsden, *Fundamentalism and American Culture*, 98. For Warfield's estimation of the Keswick theology, see B. B. Warfield, "The Victorious Life," in *The Princeton Theological Review*, vol. XVI (1918), 321–73. This has been reprinted in both *Perfectionism*, vol. II (Grand Rapids: Baker Book House, 1980), 561–611, and in *Studies in Perfectionism* (Phillipsburg: P&R Publishing, 1958), 349–99.

117. Noll, "B. B. Warfield," 32. It is important to consider Mark Noll's observation that "Warfield ... was thoroughly unimpressed by the dispensationalism that became so important in American fundamentalism," and of which Lewis Sperry

His condescending attitude toward Chafer brought one of Warfield's more capable contemporary opponents, W. H. Griffith-Thomas, to Chafer's defense.[118] Warfield's use of sarcasm may be attributable to his advancing age (he was approaching 70) and his overall pessimism regarding the future of Princeton Seminary.[119] In any case, Griffith-Thomas thought it beneath the great Princetonian to respond in such fashion and said as much.[120]

Warfield's critique of Chafer begins with a now familiar theme: his concerns about methodological inconsistencies and an explicit capitulation to the fundamental Arminian theological principle. This Warfield defines as a willingness to subject "all gracious workings of God to human determining."[121] From Warfield's perspective, Chafer's attempted theological synthesis between two conflicting systems—evangelicalism and Arminianism—fails miserably when Chafer applies it to the

---

Chafer was a prime example. Although Warfield does not address dispensationalism directly, there is no doubt of his long-standing postmillennial convictions—see B. B. Warfield, "The Millennium and the Apocalypse," in *The Princeton Theological Review*, vol. 2 (1904), which was reprinted in *Biblical Doctrines* (Grand Rapids: Baker Book House, 1980), 643–64—and his contemporaneous exegetical work in John's Epistle, reflecting his convictions about Christ's second advent marking a return to "saved world," which would lead Warfield to be quite critical of such a novel system as dispensationalism. See B. B. Warfield, "Jesus Christ the Propitiation for the Whole World," in *The Expositor*, vol. XXI (April 1921), 241–53, and reprinted in *Selected Shorter Writings*, vol. 1 (ed. John E. Meeter; Phillipsburg: P&R Publishing, 1980), 167–77, especially 174–76.

118. Marsden notes that W. H. Griffith-Thomas was "one of the few of the 'coterie' of evangelists and Bible teachers for whom Warfield indicated any respect." See *Fundamentalism and American Culture*, 99.

119. Ned B. Stonehouse, *J. Gresham Machen: A Biographical Memoir* (Philadelphia: Westminster Theological Seminary, 1977), 219.

120. In response to Warfield's essay, "The Victorious Christian Life," Thomas writes, "As a personal matter, I cannot refrain from expressing my sincere regret that Dr. Warfield has allowed himself to use certain phrases which do not help but rather hinder the cause which we have at heart. He writes more than once of 'Mr. Trumbull and his coterie' (pp. 352, 371); of 'Mrs. H. W. Smith and her coterie' (p. 358); of Mr. Trumbull inserting an adverb as a 'sop to Cerberus' (p. 328); of his always having something 'up his sleeve' (p. 355); of an assertion which is said to be a 'bathos of inconsequence'; and of Mr. Boardman's Higher Christian Life as 'a rag-time book' (p. 582). Even though Dr. Warfield feels very strongly about the errors of the movement, I think the matter too serious, the issues too profound, and, I will venture to add, the men and women too sincere and too much in earnest, for remarks of this kind to be made. " See W. H. Griffith-Thomas, "The Victorious Life," in *Bibliotheca Sacra*, vol. LXXVI (1919), 463. Warfield uses several of these same terms in reference to Mr. Chafer.

121. Warfield, "Review of *He That Is Spiritual*, by Lewis Sperry Chafer," 322.

Christian life and sanctification. Warfield begins his review by clearly setting out this tension:

> Mr. Chafer is in the unfortunate and, one would think, very uncomfortable, condition of having two inconsistent systems of religion struggling together in his mind. He was bred an Evangelical, and as a minister of the Presbyterian Church, South, stands committed to Evangelicalism of the purest water. But he has been long associated in his work with a coterie of "Evangelists" and "Bible teachers," among whom there flourishes that curious religious system (at once curiously pretentious and curiously shallow) which the Higher Life leaders of the middle of the last century brought into vogue; and he has not been immune to its infection. These two religious systems are quite incompatible. The one is the product of the Protestant Reformation and knows no determining power in the religious life but the grace of God; the other comes straight from the laboratory of John Wesley, and in all its forms—modifications and mitigations alike—remains incurably Arminian, subjecting all gracious workings of God to human determining. The two can unite as little as fire and water.[122]

Here again, Warfield returns to his fundamental concern that Chafer's conception of the Christian life is clearly built upon overtly Arminian presuppositions, which are, therefore, quite at odds with his Presbyterian convictions.

Another factor which disturbed Warfield is that Chafer had also uncritically accepted several unfounded notions such as trichotomy. According to Warfield, Chafer badly misreads 1 Corinthians 2:9-3:4, and as a result makes an unfortunate and unbiblical trichotomic distinction between three classes of men: "the 'natural' or unregenerated man, and the 'carnal' and 'spiritual' man, both of whom are regenerated, but the latter of whom lives on a higher plane."[123] It is the trichotomist conception of human nature that opens the door to Chafer's erroneous view of sanctification.

Chafer argues that there are two great moments in a Christian's life. The first involves the change from the "natural man" to the "saved man," and the second "is accomplished when there is a real adjustment to the Spirit," with the result being a distinct and noticeable change from a

---

122. Ibid.
123. Ibid., 323.

"carnal" to a "spiritual" life. Warfield viewed these changes as "rung on the double salvation, on the one hand from the *penalty* of sin, on the other from the *power* of sin."[124] Warfield applauds Chafer for rejecting the Pentecostal distinctives of a second blessing and the resulting Pentecostal manifestations, and he is equally pleased that Chafer rejects the terminology of "entire sanctification" and "sinless perfection." Nevertheless Warfield chides Chafer for not seeing the obvious, namely that a distinction between so-called "spiritual" and "carnal" Christians is tantamount to the same thing as "sinless perfection," especially when Chafer teaches that "it is quite unnecessary for spiritual men to sin and that the way is fully open to them to live a life of unbroken victory if they choose to do so."[125]

Again, Warfield does not have to look far to discover the source of Chafer's bifurcated Christian life. If the natural man can become a Christian by appropriating what God has provided for us in Christ, and if the "carnal" man can become a "spiritual" man merely by trusting in the power of God to do so, Arminianism must be at the root. Warfield cites Chafer, who puts it this way, "They only have to enter by faith into the saving grace from the power and dominion of sin. ... Sinners are not saved until they trust the Saviour, and saints are not victorious until they trust the Deliverer (p. 146)."[126] Thus salvation from the penalty of sin (the instantaneous transition from the condition of "natural man" to "carnal man"), and deliverance from the power of sin (the instantaneous transition from "carnal man" to "spiritual man") are both made possible for us, suspended only upon an act of faith to appropriate either blessing. One may be a Christian by faith, and yet remain "carnal" until such time as they choose to be delivered from the power of sin, this time by another act of faith. Warfield will have none of this bifurcated notion of the Christian life:

> No doubt what we are first led to say of this is that here is the quintessence of Arminianism. God saves no one—He only makes salvation *possible* for men. Whether it becomes *actual* or not depends absolutely on their own act. It is only by their act that it is made *possible* for God to save them. But it is equally true that here is the quintessence of the Higher Life teaching, which merely

124. Ibid.
125. Ibid.
126. Ibid., 324.

emphasizes that part of this Arminian scheme which refers to the specific matter of sanctification.[127]

This conception of the Christian life enables Chafer to use standard "Victorious Christian Life" and "Higher Christian Life" jargon—phrases such as "claim[ing] the higher degree 'by faith,' " "claiming it," "letting God," and "engaging the Spirit," which all provoke a very terse response from Warfield:

> We hear here too, of "letting" God (p. 84), and indeed, we almost hear of "engaging" the Spirit (as we engage say a carpenter) to do work for us (p. 94); and we do explicitly hear of "making it possible for God to do things" (p. 148)—a quite terrible expression. Of course, we hear repeatedly of the duty and efficacy of "yielding"—and the act of "yielding ourselves" is quite in the customary manner discriminated from "consecrating" ourselves (p. 84), and we are told, as usual, that by it the gate is opened into the divinely appointed path (pp. 91, 49). The quietistic phrase, "not by trying but by a right adjustment," meets us (p. 39), and naturally such current terms as "known sin" (p. 62), "moment by moment triumph" (pp. 34, 60), "the life that is in Christ" (p. 31), "unbroken walk in the Spirit" (pp. 53, 113), "unbroken victory" (p. 96), even Pearsall Smith's famous "at once": "the Christian may realize *at once* the heavenly virtues of Christ" (p. 39, the italics his). It is a matter of course after this that we are told that it is not *necessary* for Christians to sin (p. 125)—the emphasis repeatedly thrown on the word "necessary" leading us to wonder whether Mr. Chafer remembers that, according to the Confession of Faith to which, as a Presbyterian minister, he gives his adhesion, it is in the strictest sense of the term *not necessary* for anybody to sin, even for the "natural man" (XI.1).[128]

From Warfield's perspective, not only has Chafer adopted the unbiblical terminology of the "Higher Life" movement, which has its origin not in the Scriptures, but ultimately in the "laboratory" of John Wesley. His use of this jargon places him in direct opposition to the Westminster Standards, to which Chafer, as a Presbyterian minister, has supposedly

127. Ibid.
128. Ibid., 322–23.

subscribed. Either Chafer is unaware of the Confession's position in this regard, or else he has ignored it.

The degree to which Chafer has capitulated to perfectionism is seen in his treatment of the eradication versus the control of the sinful nature. "When Mr. Chafer repels the doctrine of 'sinless perfection,' he means first of all, that our sinful natures are not eradicated."[129] Thus Chafer, despite his declaration to the contrary, has entered into a long-standing debate among the perfectionists, between the " 'Eradicationists' and 'Supressionists,' " and Chafer thus allies himself "with the latter,—only preferring to use the word 'control.' "[130] In Chafer's "scheme," as Warfield calls it, the sinful nature is dealt with because the indwelling Spirit is said to "control it." But Warfield points out that "one would think that this would yield at least a sinlessness of conduct; but that is to forget that, after all, in this scheme the divine action waits on man's."[131] And so Arminianism raises its head again, for "God's provisions only make it *possible* for us to live without sinning. The result is therefore only that we are under no *necessity* of sinning. But whether we actually sin or not is our own affair."[132] The practical result of Chafer's construction is that "we can be both 'the child of God and citizen of heaven' " and we may indeed " 'live a superhuman life, in harmony with his heavenly calling by an unbroken walk in the Spirit'—that 'the Christian may realize at *once* the heavenly virtues of Christ.' "[133] The methodological problem that this raises is that Chafer has left us with "a mere postulate extorted by a theory. It is without practical significance. A universal effect is not accounted for by its possibility."[134]

A further and quite telling weakness in Chafer's discussion is his "irreducible 'either-or' " in regards to the "two general theories as to the divine method of dealing with the sin nature of believers."[135] Chafer notes, "We are either to be delivered by the abrupt removal of all tendency to sin, and so no longer need the enabling power of God to combat the power of sin, or we are to be delivered by the immediate and constant power of the indwelling Spirit."[136] But, as Warfield notes, "In point

129. Ibid., 324.
130. Ibid.
131. Ibid.
132. Ibid.
133. Ibid., 324–25.
134. Ibid., 325.
135. Ibid. Cited from Chafer, *He That is Spiritual*, 135.
136. Ibid.

of fact, both 'eradication' and 'control' are true. God delivers us from our sinful nature, not indeed by 'abruptly' but by progressively eradicating it, and meanwhile by controlling it."[137] Chafer is "quite wrong" therefore, because "the new nature which God gives us is not an absolutely new somewhat, alien to our personality, inserted into us, but our old nature itself remade—a veritable recreation, or making of all things new."[138] Warfield is quite perplexed when Chafer writes, "Salvation is not a so-called 'change of heart.' It is not a transformation of the old; it is a regeneration, or creation, of something wholly new, which when possessed in conjunction with the old so long as we are in the body."[139] Warfield is simply astonished that Chafer is "not appalled" by the fact that this "furnishes out each Christian with two conflicting natures." In fact, when Chafer goes so far as to assert, "the unregenerate have but one nature, while the regenerate have two,"[140] Warfield cannot help but point out what he sees as the obvious weakness with Chafer's assertion:

> He does not seem to see that thus the man is not saved at all; a different newly created man is substituted for him. When the old man is got rid of—and that the old man has to be ultimately got rid of he does not doubt—the saved man that is left is not at all the old man that was to be saved, but a new man that has never needed any saving.[141]

Warfield's frustration with Chafer now reaches its zenith. "It is a temptation to a *virtuoso* in the interpretation of Scripture to show his mettle on hard places and in startling results. Mr. Chafer has not been superior to this temptation."[142] Singling out Chafer's discussion of Christian love—which Chafer argues is "distinctly a manifestation of divine love *through* the human heart"—Warfield concludes that not only does Chafer make an "unjustified assertion," he adds that "this bizarre doctrine of the transference of God's love, in the sense of His active power of loving to us, so that it works out from us again as new centres, is extracted from Paul's simple statement that by the Holy Spirit which God has given us his love is made richly real to our apprehension!"[143] It is

137. Ibid.
138. Ibid.
139. Ibid.
140. Ibid.
141. Ibid.
142. Ibid.
143. Ibid., 325–26.

a pity, concludes Warfield, that Chafer did not notice that Paul does not use the term εἰσχέω, but instead uses the term ἐκχέω, and "that Paul no doubt would have used," the former term "had he meant to convey that idea."[144]

Warfield closes his "Review" by returning to his original theme. "A haunting ambiguity is thrust upon Mr. Chafer's whole teaching by his hospitable entertainment of contradictory systems of thought," i.e., evangelicalism and Arminianism. If Chafer had otherwise remained consistent to the quite evangelical assertions offered in the opening pages of his book (though Warfield cannot let it go by that such assertions were "not well expressed"), it would have "preserved Mr. Chafer from his regrettable dalliance with the Higher Life formulas."[145] If Chafer had been consistent with these assertions, he would have seen that "salvation is a unit, and that he who is united to Jesus Christ by faith receives in Him, not only justification—salvation from the *penalty* of sin—but also sanctification—salvation from the *power* of sin."[146] As Warfield scolds Chafer:

> These two things cannot be separated, and it is a grievous error to teach that a true believer in Christ can stop short in "carnality," and, though having the Spirit with him and in him, not have Him upon him—to use a not very lucid play upon prepositions in which Mr. Chafer indulges.[147]

Although Warfield believes Chafer has correctly interpreted Romans 7 as referring to the Christian believer, Warfield adds a rejoinder, namely that "the reminders of the flesh in the Christian do not constitute his characteristic. He is in the Spirit and is walking with however halting steps, by the Spirit; and it is to all Christians, not to some, that the great promise is given, 'Sin shall not have dominion over you.' "[148] Warfield concludes by reminding Chafer of what he as a fellow Presbyterian should have asserted:

> He who believes in Jesus Christ is under grace, and his whole course, in its process and in its issues alike, is determined by grace, and therefore, having been predestined to be conformed to

144. Ibid., 326.
145. Ibid.
146. Ibid.
147. Ibid.
148. Ibid., 327.

> the image of God's Son, he is surely being conformed to that image, God Himself seeing to it that he is not only called and justified but also glorified. You may find Christians at every stage of this process, for it is a process through which all must pass; but you will find none who will not in God's own good time and way pass through every stage of it. There are not two kinds of Christians, although there are Christians at every conceivable stage of advancement towards the one goal to which all are bound and at which all shall arrive.[149]

Mark Noll is absolutely correct when he notes Warfield's concerns about the fundamentalist use of Scripture, the rising popularity of dispensationalism, and the Princetonian's openness to the possibility of theistic evolution as three serious obstacles lying in the way of any possible Princeton-fundamentalist alliance. However, no assessment of Warfield's estimation of the emerging fundamentalism can be entirely accurate without noting the "Lion of Princeton's" stern critique of the Arminian, revivalist, and perfectionist elements found in much of the developing fundamentalist theology. Warfield was a Calvinist who believed with all of his heart that anything less than a full-orbed commitment to the historic Reformed faith produced an impoverished religion. Although he could cross swords with John Miley in a gentlemanly fashion typical of academic book reviewing, the Princetonian had no time for the "coterie of Bible teachers," who in his eyes offered a most impoverished variety of the Christian religion indeed.

EVELYN UNDERHILL'S MUDDLED MYSTICISM

In his *Systematic Theology*, Charles Hodge had set forth the conception that theological inquiry should follow the inductive course as set out by his Scottish forebears, and codified by the Reformed scholastics. In doing so, Hodge identified the natural enemies of the inductive method as "rationalism and mysticism."[150] Closely following his mentor in this regard, B. B. Warfield also took aim at these two perceived foes of Princeton orthodoxy, which Warfield described as "two movements of

149. B. B. Warfield, "Review of *He That Is Spiritual*, by Lewis Sperry Chafer," 327.
150. Charles Hodge, *Systematic Theology*, 3 vols (Grand Rapids: Eerdmans, 1979), vol. 1, 4–103.

thought" that inevitably lead "to a lower conception of the inspiration and authority of Scripture."[151]

In an important essay dealing with the relationship between Christianity and mysticism, Warfield contends, "There is an element in revealed religion, therefore, which is not found in any unrevealed religion. This is the element of authority."[152] Since revealed religion comes to us externally, it is, according to Warfield, "imposed upon him from a source superior to its own spirit."[153] Such revelation is made by a gracious God to rescue sinners in their need. As such it is a gift of God, "not a creation of man's." Thus natural religion, on the other hand, is a "religion of the spirit," and therefore, without any external authority to which appeal can be made. All forms of such religion are by definition "man-made." Christianity, however, is a revealed religion and, therefore, necessarily a religion of authority. As Warfield sees the matter: "Authority is the correlate of revelation, and wherever revelation is—and only where revelation is—there is authority."[154] All other forms of religion are humanly devised and can rest upon nothing more than the religious impulses of the "human spirit."[155] To put the matter

---

151. B. B. Warfield, "The Church Doctrine of Inspiration," *Bibliotheca Sacra*, vol. 51 (1894), 614–40. Repr. in B. B. Warfield, *The Inspiration and Authority of the Bible* (Phillipsburg: P&R Publishing, 1948), 113. In an essay lamenting the decline of theological education in Presbyterian circles, Warfield turned his ire toward the same enemies. "Extremes meet. Pietist and Rationalist have ever hunted in couples and dragged down their quarry together. They may differ as to why they deem theology mere lumber, and would not have the prospective minister waste his time in acquiring it. The one loves God so much, the other loves him so little, that he does not care to know him. But they agree that is it not worthwhile to learn to know him." See B. B. Warfield, "Our Seminary Curriculum," in *The Presbyterian* (Sept 15, 1909), 7–8. Repr. in B. B. Warfield, *Selected Shorter Writings*, vol. I (ed. John E. Meeter; Phillipsburg: P&R Publishing, 1980), 371.

152. B. B. Warfield, "Mysticism and Christianity," *The Biblical Review*, ii (1917). Repr. in B. B. Warfield, *Biblical and Theological Studies* (Phillipsburg: P&R Publishing, 1968), 446.

153. Ibid., 446.

154. Warfield, "Mysticism and Christianity," 446.

155. Ibid. In an important essay written years earlier in 1895, "The Latest Phase of Historical Rationalism," Warfield made the point that when "every shred of 'external authority' in religion is discarded, and appeal is made to what is frankly recognized as purely human reason: we call it Rationalism. It is only another form of the Rationalism, however, when it would fain believe that what it appeals to within the human breast is not the unaided spirit of man, but the Holy Ghost in the heart, the Logos, the strong voice of God. In this form it asks, 'Were the Quakers right?' and differs from technical Rationalism only in the matter of temperature, the feelings

bluntly, such religions have no authority, and can only express mere religious experience.

If the human spirit is seen as the source of religion, mysticism is an inevitable consequence. As Warfield says, "It is characteristic of mysticism that it makes its appeal to the feelings as the sole, or at least the normative, source of knowledge of divine things."[156] While there are certainly varieties of mysticism, what is common to them all "and what makes them mystics, is that they all rest on the religious sentiment as the source of knowledge of divine things."[157] Since this is the case, mystics differ in their accounts of their religious feelings and expressions, and the mystic finds that "his is an emotional, not a conceptual, religion; and feelings, emotions, though not inaudible, are not articulate." The mystic has "no conceptual language in which to express what he feels." If he appeals to theological or philosophical terminology to define his experiences, he is forced to make a "concession to the necessity of communicating with the external world or with his more external self,"[158] which runs counter to the mystical impulse itself. As we will see, it is the reality of this external world which serves as one of Warfield's chief objections to the mystical impulse. In this regard, Warfield argues:

> What he finds within him is just to his apprehension an "unutterable abyss." ... On the brink of this abyss the mystic may stand, and standing in awe on its brink, he may deify. Then he calls it indifferently Brahm or Zeus, Allah or the Holy Spirit, according as men about him speak of God. *He explains his meaning, in other words, in terms of the conception of the universe which he has brought with him, or, as it is more favorable now to phrase it, each in accordance with his own world-view*.[159]

---

and not the cold reason alone being involved: we call it then Mysticism." See B. B. Warfield, "The Latest Phase of Historical Rationalism," in *The Presbyterian Quarterly*, ix (1895), 36–67; and reprinted in B. B. Warfield, *Christology and Criticism* (Grand Rapids: Baker Book House, 1981), 589–90.

156. Ibid.

157. Ibid., 447.

158. Ibid., 447–48.

159. Ibid., 448. The italics are mine. Warfield had raised this same criticism some years earlier in regard to the work of Abraham Kuyper, who Warfield accused of implicitly adopting a "mystical conception" of the Witness of the Spirit by locating the ultimate source of religious authority within the self and presuppositions of the subject, rather than in the objective revelation of God as found in Holy Scripture. This certainly anticipates the contemporary debate over apologetic methodology between evidentialists and presuppositionalists. See B. B. Warfield, "Introduction to

In other words, the epistemological foundation of mysticism is the religious consciousness of the individual subject, as determined by his own unique set of presuppositions, and not the objective facts of revelation.

In the case of so-called "Christian mysticism," that is, in those cases where the mystic happens to be a theist, we are told that the religious feelings "are the effects in his soul wrought by the voluntary actions of God whom he acknowledges; and if he should happen to be a Christian, he may interpret these movements, in accordance with the teaching of the Scriptures, as the leading of the Holy Spirit or as the manifestations within him of Christ within us."[160] While this is the claim, Christian mysticism is not in any way essentially different from "the parallel phenomena which are observable in other religions. ... It is mysticism which has learned to speak in Christian language," not, as is argued, a true knowledge of God, based upon human religious feelings.[161] Rejecting pantheistic and naturalistic conceptions of the world, Christian mysticism is thoroughly supernaturalistic and "at its best," passes from true mysticism into evangelical Christianity, and "rejoices in such spiritual experiences as are summed up in the old categories of regeneration and sanctification."[162]

A tension arises, however, when evangelical Christians, who insist upon interpreting "all religious experience by the normative revelation of God recorded for us in the Holy Scriptures, and guides, directs and corrects it from these Scriptures," confront any form of consistent mysticism. Such mysticism substitutes "religious experience for the objective revelation of God recorded in the written Word as the source from which he derives his knowledge of God, or at least to subordinate the expressly revealed Word as the less direct and convincing source of knowledge of God to his own religious experience."[163] In Warfield's estimation, either the evangelical element must dominate and external authority is located in the Word of God, or else the mystical element

Francis R. Beattie's *Apologetics*: or the Rational Vindication of Christianity (1903),"; and reprinted in B. B. Warfield, *Selected Shorter Writings*, vol. 2 (ed. John E. Meeter; Phillipsburg: P&R Publishing, 1980), 94.

160. Ibid., 448.
161. Ibid., 449–50.
162. Ibid., 450.
163. Ibid., 450–51.

dominates and we are left with nothing more than natural religion as the fruit of the *semen religionis*.[164]

Acknowledging the long and diverse history of the mysticism within Christian thought, Warfield contends that the characteristic expression of so-called Christian mysticism is its "appeal to the 'inner light,' or 'internal word,' either to the exclusion of the external or written Word, or as superior to it."[165] The inevitable result of this substitution of the objective Word of God for the subjective "Christian consciousness," is that our "religious knowledge ends therefore either in betraying us into purely rationalistic mysticism, or is rescued from that by the postulation of a relation of the soul to God which strongly tends toward pantheizing mysticism."[166] This is the case because "they appeal for knowledge of God only to what is internal to man." When religious fervor is high, the tendency is toward mysticism, and when there are periods of religious decline, the mystical tendency in turn moves in the direction of rationalism.[167] As Warfield notes, the paradox in this is "the same person, indeed, sometimes vibrates between the two points of view with the utmost facility."[168]

According to Warfield, the same tendency can be seen in the history of the Christian church in the Neoplatonic trajectory that began with Neoplatonic philosophy, extended through John Scotus Erigena and continued down to Friedrich Schleiermacher. What is characteristic of this impulse is the consistent rejection of "external authority," for "the

---

164. Compare B. B. Warfield, "Review of Evelyn Underhill's *Mysticism, The Mystic Way, Immanence*, and *The Miracles of our Lord*," from the *Princeton Theological Review*, xii (1914), 105–23; and reprinted in B. B. Warfield, *Critical Reviews* (Grand Rapids: Baker Book House, 1980), 338.

165. Warfield, "Mysticism and Christianity," 451.

166. Ibid.

167. As Warfield put it elsewhere, "Once turn away from revelation and little choice remains to you but the choice between Mysticism and Rationalism. There is not so much choice between these things, it is true, as enthusiasts on either side are apt to imagine. The difference between them is very much a matter of temperament, or perhaps we may even say of temperature. The Mystic blows hot, the Rationalist cold. Warm up a Rationalist and you inevitably get a Mystic; chill down a Mystic and you find yourselves with a Rationalist on your hands. The history of thought illustrates repeatedly the easy passage from one to the other." See B. B. Warfield, "Review of *Mysticism in Christianity* by W. K. Fleming and *Mysticism and Modern Life* by John Wright Buckman, in The *Princeton Theological Review*, xiv (1916), 343–48; and reprinted in B. B. Warfield, *Critical Reviews* (Grand Rapids: Baker Book House, 1981), 366–67.

168. Warfield, "Mysticism and Christianity," 452.

Christian consciousness," "religious experience," the "inner light," or "the immanent Divine." To adopt this course, says Warfield, is "to ask us to discard Christianity and revert to natural religion."[169] Warfield next turns his attention to a catalogue of contemporary mysticism, and one of those singled out is English author and mystic, Evelyn Underhill,[170] who had been the subject of Warfield's intense scrutiny in 1914, three years earlier.

That B. B. Warfield was not favorably disposed to the mysticism of "Miss Underhill," as he calls her, should not come as a surprise. After making some introductory remarks about several volumes of fiction that Miss Underhill had previously published and her "brilliantly written" *magnum opus*—"an elaborate volume" published in 1911 under the title *Mysticism*—Warfield concludes that Miss Underhill's effort "reduces Christianity to simple mysticism."[171]

There are a number of places where Warfield takes issue with Underhill, but he begins with a familiar complaint, namely the lack of a clear and unequivocal definition of critical terms. Warfield repeatedly, and at times with great exasperation, attempts to deal with Underhill's vague definitions of "mysticism." First, she defines the term too broadly as "the innate tendency of the human spirit towards complete harmony with the transcendental order; whatever the theological formula under which that order is understood." Then Underhill attempts to separate mysticism from all " 'positive religions' whatever."[172] This provokes Warfield's comment that regardless of whatever religious connection it does or does not have, if mysticism is defined as the "innate tendency" of the human spirit toward union with the transcendental order, it is "natural religion" plain and simple. "It is therefore ... quite independent of all possible conceptions of that 'only Reality' which is here called 'the transcendental order.' "[173]

169. Ibid., 455.

170. Evelyn Underhill (1875–1941) was an Anglican with strong interests in Franciscan piety, and is variously characterized as a "mystic," a "religious poet," and "spiritual counsellor," and was a highly regarded author of religious verse. See C. G. Thorne, Jr, "Underhill, Evelyn," in *The New International Dictionary of the Christian Church* (ed. J. D. Douglas; Grand Rapids: Zondervan, 1981), 994.

171. Warfield, "Review of Evelyn Underhill's *Mysticism*, *The Mystic Way*, *Immanence*, and *The Miracles of our Lord*," 337.

172. Ibid., 337–38.

173. Ibid., 338.

Warfield is further exasperated when Underhill variously classes mysticism among the sciences (she speaks of mysticism as "the science of ultimates") and then comments that "it is not an opinion: it is not a philosophy. ... It is the art of establishing [a] conscious relationship with the Absolute."[174] Is mysticism a science or an art, *scientia* or *ars*? "What was formerly declared to be a 'science' has now become explicitly an 'art': but in varying the term we do not escape from the thing—behind the 'art' the 'science' necessarily lies." To Warfield, this all "looks very much like that specific philosophy which we know as Pantheism."[175] This is a theme to which Warfield returns when he looks at the problems raised by Underhill's epistemology.

Underhill's terminological confusion when she raises the medieval period presenting "as the purest examples," the practice of this innate tendency for the human spirit to be in union with the transcendental. But as Warfield notes:

> This seems to stand the whole matter on its head. It is not in virtue of their Christianity that the Christian Mystics are Mystics: Miss Underhill ... allows that their Mysticism is quite independent of their Christianity. We might better say that it is in despite of their Christianity; and that therefore Mysticism in them is modified by their Christianity just so far as their thought and practice is determined by their Christianity. They are Mystics not by virtue of what they have in common with other Christians, but by virtue of what they have in common with other Mystics.[176]

Miss Underhill cannot have it both ways. Is mysticism an art or a science? And is the innate tendency to seek union with the transcendental referring to anything distinctly Christian? If not, why involve the Christian saints as illustrative of the high water mark of the mystical impulse?

Having described Miss Underhill's attempt at defining "mysticism," Warfield now moves on to epistemological concerns. It is the pantheistic tendency, implicit to all forms of mysticism, which is the background to the fundamental epistemological problem. According to Warfield, in Underhill's *Mysticism* "there lies the positive conviction of the Mystic that there exists in himself a native spark of 'pure Being' which is and of itself divine, and that it is his part to blow this spark into a flame that he

174. Ibid., 339.
175. Ibid.
176. Ibid., 342.

may become truly himself in the consciousness that he is really God."[177] This necessarily leads to the conclusion that there "is nothing more fundamental to the whole Mystical consciousness than the conviction that what we shall see when we retreat into the 'cell of self-knowledge' is just that Reality which stands to it for God."[178] This flies in the face of everything that Warfield the Scottish Common Sense Realist held dear. Indeed, "One of the natural results of thus conceiving oneself is inevitably a certain intellectual and spiritual pride," which frequently results in "a hearty contempt for his fellow-men, who are still shut in 'by the hard crust of surface consciousness,' and who know only the 'machine-made universe presented by the cinematograph of sense.' "[179]

What is especially problematic in this regard is that "according to Miss Underhill the whole external world in which we live is not only of our own creation but is miscreated by us—being but the product of our deceiving senses; nay, each man creates an exclusive world for himself, since the sense of no two men are alike."[180] Here, Warfield responds, rather sarcastically, in words that echo the finest of Scottish Common Sense appeals to the external world as proof of its own existence:

> We may find it a pleasant exercise to speculate on what kind of a world would be involved if we had radically different senses or the world-movement proceeded in a radically different rhythm: as we may work out for example, the nature of the world in which two and two would make five and in which space would only have two or as many as four dimensions. So, holding a key in our hands, we may find a diversion in mentally picturing the changes that would be involved in the wards of the lock by the radical differences in the notches on the key. Meanwhile our senses, the stream of our consciousness, are thus and not otherwise; and that the means that the world of which we are a part, and correlated to which we are by means of our senses, and of the movement of which we are aware in the "rhythm of our consciousness," is thus and not otherwise. We may well accept the universe that is; and to be out of harmony with it is only to be intellectually, morally and spiritually mad. It is the condemnation of Mysticism that it must

177. Ibid., 345.
178. Ibid.
179. Ibid.
180. Ibid.

> begin by declaring that the world of appearance is illusion and that the rhythm of normal consciousness is a mere jangling, out of tune with reality.[181]

The best refutation of mysticism is the material world itself!

Warfield's attention now turns to another unfortunate characteristic of the mystical tendency— that the great facts of redemption are transmuted into the mere religious consciousness of the biblical authors. The mystic "has also got beyond the great redemptive acts of God by which God has intervened in the world to lay an objective basis for the salvation of sinners." In each and every one of these, "The Incarnation, the Atonement, and the rest—is seen by him to be a symbol of a subjective experience which takes place in his soul."[182] Thus, according to Warfield, "Miss Underhill ... does not so much deny the Incarnation is a historical event, as merely look by preference upon it as a symbol of inward experience."[183] This leads Warfield to conclude, "There is probably nothing in the treatment of Christianity by the Mystical writers which is more offensive than this sublimation of the great constitutive facts—in which the very heart of Christianity is to be found—into symbols of subjective transactions."[184] In Warfield's mind, the consequences of this are extremely grave:

> It is abolishing the scandal of the Cross and removing the offense of the Incarnation by the simple expedient of pushing them both out of sight. He who thinks that the importance of the Incarnation and the Atoning sacrifice as transactions in time and space is capable of "absurd exaggeration," or doubts that the Eternal Christ came into the world through the Virgin's womb, thus assuming flesh for our redemption, or that the salvation of the world depends absolutely on what happened at Calvary, has assuredly lost all sense of Christian values. He may remain a Mystic, but he has ceased to be in any intelligible sense a Christian.[185]

181. Ibid., 346.
182. Ibid., 346–47.
183. Ibid., 347.
184. Ibid.
185. Ibid., 348. Hoffecker notes that "it is clear that Warfield finds a greater affinity between mysticism and Christianity than he does between rationalism and Christianity, even though he considers both antagonistic to the fundamental principle of Christianity as he understood it." See W. Andrew Hoffecker, *Piety and the*

Thus mysticism is not only a threat to Reformed orthodoxy, it is a threat to Christianity itself.

Turning his attention to Underhill's second book, *The Mystic Way*, Warfield contends, "Having thus expounded Mysticism in its nature in the one book she simply turns in the other and says, it is just this Mysticism which what we know as Christianity really is. 'The Mystic Way' is, in other words, nothing but an elaborate attempt to explain Christianity as natural religion."[186] Unlike her previous volume, titled *Mysticism*, *The Mystic Way* does not give evidence of thoughtful and careful analysis. Instead, according to Warfield, *The Mystic Way* appears "to be the product of an impulse; to have been somewhat hastily composed; and to resemble a lawyer's brief got up for an occasion and betraying no very large-minded survey or deep consideration of its subject."[187] In this sense, "to the extent the second volume, while intended as a corollary to the first, is in actual fact a refutation of it."[188]

According to Warfield, "The thesis sustained in 'The Mystic Way' is, as we have just said, that what we know as Christianity is simply a great irruption of Mysticism. What it sets out to prove is accordingly that Jesus was only a Mystic of exceptional purity and energy."[189] Indeed, Underhill declares that Paul, John, and "all the great leaders of Christianity were just so many outstanding Mystics; and that all the phenomena which accompanied the origin of Christianity and have been thought to be supernatural in character, are just Mystical phenomena, and may be paralleled in the experiences of other Mystics and thus shown to be natural—natural, that is, to mystics."[190] Thus Underhill leaves us with natural religion and not Christianity. In her scheme, "Christianity is defined just as a Mystical movement; and that it is placed in its proper position among Mystical movements as only one of its class." Thus, there is nothing unique about Christianity, except that it is a species of the genus of mysticism. This is proven to be the case when Miss Underhill admits that this doctrine derives "not from Christ but from Plotinus."[191]

Princeton Theologians: Archibald Alexander, Charles Hodge and Benjamin Warfield (Phillipsburg: P&R Publishing, 1981), 127.

186. Ibid.
187. Ibid.
188. Ibid., 349.
189. Ibid.
190. Ibid.
191. Ibid., 354.

In this regard, Warfield is completely puzzled by Underhill's remarkable assertion that "Christian Mysticism may be set off in a class by itself," when she has but a single page earlier asserted that Christian mysticism "originated from Neoplatonic influence; that Pagan blood runs in its veins, and that its genealogy goes back to Plotinus."[192] Apparently, Underhill is, on the one hand, trying to argue that "with Jesus Christ something new came into the world, something so new that all that has been in the world before is inadequate to its explanation." Yet, on the other hand, she immediately confuses the matter by turning right around and after separating "Christian Mysticism off from all other so-called Mysticism as something ... specifically different, she cheerfully proceeds at once to mix it up again with them all."[193] She does this by arguing that Christian mysticism is simply any spiritual movement holding to the basic tenets of mysticism. Warfield is compelled to ask, is Christian mysticism in a class by itself, or is Christian mysticism simply another name for Neoplatonic mysticism, and therefore, not in a class by itself after all? It is in this context that Underhill then asserts that "Christ ceases to be the first only to become the classic expression of Christian Mysticism."[194] Warfield has had enough of the equivocation:

> Something was originated by Christ. We shall say it was Mysticism. But Mysticism obviously was not originated by Christ: it exists apart from Him, it existed before Him. But that can be remedied by recognizing all Mysticism by virtue of our agreement that Mysticism was originated by Christ, as Christian! If Christianity is just Mysticism, why of course Mysticism is Christianity, and Christianity, since Mysticism has nothing to do with him, has nothing to do with Christ.[195]

According to Warfield, then, the source of all Underhill's woes "is her determination that Christian mysticism, as it is mysticism, shall find its starting point in Christ and not in Plotinus."[196] In fact, since her very system itself admits its Neoplatonic origin, Christ is incidental to it, and thus she is forced to repeatedly equivocate by her efforts to "Christianize" Plotinus.

192. Ibid., 350.
193. Ibid., 352.
194. Ibid.
195. Ibid., 353.
196. Ibid., 355.

Given Warfield's commitment to Scottish Common Sense philosophy, mysticism does indeed represent a serious threat to Christianity itself. Reducing knowledge of God to the level of self-consciousness is to destroy the fundamental pillar of Christianity—that Christianity is a revealed religion, whose authority necessarily lies in an external revelation the Holy Scripture. By denying external authority, and looking within for a knowledge of God, the mystic inevitably tends toward pantheism and the denial of the material world. It subjugates the objective and historical events of the incarnation and resurrection to "a symbol of a subjective experience which takes place in his own soul," all anathema to Princeton orthodoxy as well as the Scottish philosophy.[197] According to Warfield, you cannot have Christ *and* Plotinus, and you cannot simply baptize natural religion. It is no wonder, then, that Miss Underhill would ascribe to Dionysius the Areopagite "the preservation of that mighty system of scaffolding which enabled the Catholic Mystics to build the towers and bulwarks of the city of God."[198] In Warfield's way of thinking, this was not the city of God that was being built. This is the fallen human spirit building the city of man based upon no external authority at all—a city built upon Plotinus rather than Christ.

CRITIQUE OF RATIONALISM

While mysticism is consistently identified as one of the two archenemies of the Princeton theology, rationalism is universally recognized as the other. For Warfield, rationalism is problematic for several reasons, all of which are related to Warfield's prior commitment to the Scottish philosophy and the inductive method. The most critical danger posed by rationalism is the attempt to move the Christian faith from that which Warfield believed to be its true epistemological foundation, the revelation of God in Jesus Christ in human history. This point becomes quite evident in Warfield's pointed criticism of rationalism in his essay,

197. Compare Warfield, "Review of *Mysticism in Christianity* by K. Fleming, and *Mysticism and Modern Life* by John Wright Buckman," 372. Here Warfield warns against "a Pantheizing anti-supernaturalistic religiousness which must not be permitted to come to us in the sheep's clothing of 'essential Christianity' on the ground that it is only another name for 'spiritual inwardness.' It is most decidedly different from that."

198. Warfield, "Christianity and Mysticism," 355.

"Christless Christianity" originally published in *The Harvard Review* in 1912.[199]

According to Warfield, there are two major components of "the old Rationalism." The first is "the assumption of the adequacy of our reason to produce of its own inalienable endowments of the whole body of religious truth which it is necessary or possible for reasonable men to embrace." The second is "the assumption of the inadequacy of history to lay a foundation of fact sufficiently assured to supply a firm basis on which the religious convictions and aspirations of reasonable men may rest."[200] The assertions that reason alone can produce "the whole body of religious truth," and that history is an inadequate foundation for Christianity, are, of course, long-standing matters of scorn by the Scottish philosophy.[201] The inevitable consequence of such rationalism, as Warfield sees it, is "the denial that Christianity ... can possibly be dependant for its existence or its power on any events or personalities in its past history."[202] In every case, Warfield contends that "the general line of argument" of the rationalist is the same. History can give us only probabilities. Religion, therefore, which requires certainties, cannot be dependent upon historical facts." And since in Warfield's conception "Jesus is at best an historical fact," the rationalist must hold, since Christianity is a religion, that it "cannot possibly be dependent upon Jesus. So far accordingly as Christianity is truly religion, it must be

199. See B. B. Warfield, "Christless Christianity," in *The Harvard Review*, V (Oct. 1912), 423–73; and reprinted in B. B. Warfield, *Christology and Criticism* (Grand Rapids: Baker Book House, 1981), 313–67.

200. Ibid., 337. Compare Warfield, "How to Get Rid of Christianity," in *The Bible Student*, I (1900), 121–27; and reprinted in Warfield, *Selected Shorter Writings*, vol. I (ed. John E. Meeter; Phillipsburg: P&R Publishing, 1980), where Warfield writes, "[Christianity] is a religion that is founded on the actual—if it is a religion of fact—if it has any historical content—it is evaporated with its history. ... Christianity is a historical religion, all of whose doctrines are facts. He who assaults the trustworthiness of the record of the intervention of God for the redemption of the world, is simply assaulting the heart of Christianity (p. 58)."

201. Indeed, James McCosh defined the characteristics of the Scottish school as diametrically opposite to that of Warfield's foe, the "old Rationalism." First, McCosh declared that Scottish Common Sense Realism "proceeds throughout by observation," and not by reason; and second, "by observation principles are discovered which are above observation, universal and external," making history essential to the discovery of truth, in contrast to the rationalist's distrust of history as the foundation for Christian faith. See James McCosh, *Realistic Philosophy: II Historical and Critical* (New York: Charles Scribner's Sons, 1887), 181–86.

202. Warfield, "Christless Christianity," 337.

independent of Jesus."[203] The result is what Warfield calls the "Christless Christianity" typical of the liberalism of his day, which as a system of ethics and morality could exist quite independently of the historical Jesus.[204]

Warfield's first line of defense is to simply remark that Butler's "Analogy" is "still extant, with its initial insistence upon probability as the guide of life, and its solid proof of the reasonableness of an historical revelation."[205] But Warfield, no doubt, realizes that merely invoking Butler's memory will not be sufficient as an apologetic against the contemporary rationalist tendency. Thus Warfield endeavors to argue *why* Christianity must be a religion grounded in history and not in reason. He does this on a number of grounds.

First, the assumption that reason itself is a sufficient ground for religion is attacked head on. "Though 'pure reason' be sufficient for the religion of pure nature, what warrants the assumption that its sufficiency is unimpaired when nature is no longer pure."[206] Warfield echoes a long-standing conviction within the Reformed tradition that fallen reason can serve only in an instrumental capacity, not as the *principium* of religion.

Second, Warfield offers a number of reasons why Christianity is a religion necessarily grounded in history. "A valid religion for sinful man includes in it, accordingly, of necessity an historical element, an actually wrought expiation for sin."[207] The fact remains that "there is a moral paradox in the forgiveness of sins which cannot be solved apart from the exhibition of an actual expiation." How can God promise to man the forgiveness of sin without a demonstration of his willingness

203. Ibid., 337–38.

204. This was a charge that Warfield would level against Charles Grandison Finney, whose own Pelagianism turned Christianity from a religion of supernatural redemption into one of ethics. Warfield quipped, "We said that God might be eliminated entirely from Finney's ethical theory without injury to it: are we not prepared now to say that He might be eliminated from it with some advantage to it." See B. B. Warfield, "The Theology of Charles Finney," in *The Princeton Theological Review*, XIX (1921), 568–619; and reprinted in B. B. Warfield, *Perfectionism*, vol. II (Grand Rapids: Baker Book House, 1981), 194.

205. Warfield, "Christless Christianity," 338. Warfield goes on, as we have previously seen, to refer the reader to the textbooks on legal evidence by Ram and Greenleaf, which will serve "to bring their philosophy down to earth," by acquainting them with the concept of reasonable doubt.

206. Ibid., 339.

207. Ibid., 340.

to provide such an expiation? As Warfield goes on to note, "An expiation, in its very nature, is not a principle but a fact, an event which takes place, if at all, in the conditions of time and space."[208] Indeed, Warfield concludes that "a Christianity without redemption—redemption in the blood of Jesus as a sacrifice for sin—is nothing less than a contradiction in terms. Precisely what Christianity means is redemption by the blood of Jesus."[209]

Third, Warfield is aware, no doubt, that the issue at stake is ultimately a question of epistemology. After contending for the need for a historical expiation from sin, Warfield must make the case that Christianity is grounded in the facts of the history of redemption. He notes that it would be a shame if people rejected God's saving act in Jesus Christ simply "because of the inability of the human mind to attain certainty with reference to matters of fact."[210] Here Warfield offers a sophisticated apologetic for the use of historical argumentation (evidential apologetics) and defends the thesis that probability arguments are not incapacitating to the Christian faith. In doing so, he clearly places himself in the long line of Scottish Common Sense philosophers.

In this regard, Warfield notes, "We deceive ourselves ... if we fancy we may distinguish in principle between historical facts as uncertain and scientific facts as certain."[211] Since we are creatures of time and space, and bound to history ourselves, are we really to believe that we "could acquire no knowledge whatever ... if uncertainty were really the mark of the historical?[212] Warfield is probably correct to locate much of the problem in the nature of the assumption that "historical facts cannot rise above probabilities." Thus, the solution is, in part, to carefully define what we do and do not mean by the use of the term "probable." According to Warfield, there are two senses in which we use the term. "As the opposite of 'demonstrative,' 'probable' refers to the nature of the ground on which the judgement of truth or reality rests." As for the second sense, "as the opposite of 'certain' it refers to the measure of assurance which the grounds on which this judgement rests are adapted to produce."[213] Since this is the case, "historical facts may be only prob-

208. Ibid.
209. Ibid., 357–58.
210. Ibid., 341.
211. Ibid.
212. Ibid.
213. Ibid., 342.

able in the one usage and not less than certain in the other." Warfield also notes:

> In point of fact, there is nothing more certain than a matter of fact: what is, certainly is; and the certainty of demonstration cannot be more sure than the certainty of the experience. It is no more sure that two and two make four, than that the two nuts which I have in each hand when brought together are four—though I arrive at my certainty in the one case *a priori* by demonstrating reasoning, and in the other *a posteriori* by actual experience. The ground of certainty in both cases is my confidence in my faculties.[214]

As Warfield reminds us, it may be argued that such confidence in my faculties applies only to present experience and not to matters of history. The critical question, then, could be framed as follows: "How can we have such certainty about matters of the past, which we ourselves did not experience?" Once again, following his Scottish forebears,[215] Warfield points out, "If what is, certainly is, then what has been, just as certainly has been; and its actuality as matter of fact is not in the least disturbed by the irrelevant circumstance that it has occurred at one point in time rather than another."[216] The fact is, according to Warfield, such events do not occur in isolation but are part of a larger context:

> Past events still live in other vibrations also, beside those which, trembling through the ether, carry their notifications to the depths of space. Everything that occurs affects everything else that occurs, and history must be conceived not merely as a series of linked chains passing side by side through time; but as one woven network covering the whole past, and running with unbroken web through the present into the illimitable future.[217]

This is an important point for Warfield. Certainly, we can only know the past in part, but this does not cripple us because "we know nothing except in part. ... But we can yet know truly where we can know only in part. And because we cannot know all the past, we must not therefore fancy that we can know nothing that is past."[218] Hence we are necessarily

214. Ibid., 342–43.
215. See McCosh's treatment of this in James McCosh, *The Scottish Philosophy* (New York: Robert Carter and Brothers, 1875), 215–16.
216. Warfield, "Christless Christianity," 343.
217. Ibid., 344.
218. Ibid., 343.

limited to "probability" when dealing with matters of fact and history.[219] Since Christianity is a religion which is grounded upon what God has done in Christ to provide for our redemption, Christianity is therefore based upon history, and in the strictest sense is probably true.

This discussion has an important bearing on the nature of the Christian faith. "Whether the origins of the Christian religion belong to this class of outstanding facts ... is merely a question of the evidence."[220] The question then turns to the nature of such evidence. "This evidence is, however, of the most compelling and varied kind. It is not merely documentary, subject to those processes of testing which we lump together under the name of criticism. It is institutional as well." Yet, "it is more than institutional. ... Christianity itself is a witness to the nature of its origins; and to Christianity must be added the whole world in its development through two thousand years."[221] Since this is the case, Christianity need not shun the historical criticism, so typical of rationalism:

> We are not fleeing from the results of historical criticism to take refuge in the argument from effects. We shall appeal, indeed, from a naturalistically biased to an unbiased historical criticism; but we shall have no difficulty in trusting the latter to give us not only an actual Jesus, but a supernatural Christ, and in Him a supernatural redemption. We are only concerned now to point out that even such a vindication of the fact-basis of Christianity on historico-critical grounds does not exhaust the evidence for it.[222]

This means that even though we are dealing with probability in the strict sense, nevertheless, when all these lines of evidence are taken

219. Herbert Hovenkamp, for example, has erroneously accused Warfield and others in the Scottish tradition of trying "to create a religion free from all doubt," as Hovenkamp puts it. See Herbert Hovenkamp, *Science and Religion in America: 1800–1860* (n.p.: University of Pennsylvania Press, 1978), x. Warfield was perfectly willing to make the case that even though Christianity was grounded in history, and therefore, in one sense "probable," the cumulative weight of the evidence renders the Christian faith "certain." Hovenkamp's failure to distinguish between *a priori* and *a posteriori* arguments for the truth of the Christian faith unfortunately confuses the matter.

220. Warfield, "Christless Christianity," 344.

221. Ibid., 344–45.

222. Ibid., 346.

together, "the facts which belong to the origins of Christianity [are] the most certain of all the facts which have occurred in the world."[223]

There are a number of specific instances in which Warfield takes direct aim at this rationalist impulse.[224] But Warfield's primary concern is with what he calls Ritschlite rationalism,[225] characterized by what Warfield describes as "general Rationalistic features." According to Warfield, this peculiar variety of rationalism amounts to a frontal attack upon not only objective authority—characteristic of all forms of rationalism—but also upon the doctrinal nature of Christianity, which is its very foundation. In addition, the Ritschlite variety of rationalism raises a number of questions about how one must deal with the history of Christianity, since as a doctrinal religion, the history of Christianity *is* a history of its doctrinal development. As Warfield sees it, Ritschlism fails on all counts.

From the outset, Warfield contends that " 'Rationalism' never is the direct product of unbelief. It is the indirect product of unbelief, among men who would fain hold their Christian profession in the face of an onset of unbelief, which they feel too weak to withstand."[226] The root of such rationalism is not intellectual but moral—an unwillingness to see that any truth claim requires defense. Thus, in Warfield's opinion, "Rationalism is, therefore, always a movement within the Christian Church: and its adherents are characterized by an attempt to save what they hold to be the essence of Christianity, by clearing it from what they deem to be accretions." This means that the rationalist impulse necessarily makes one suspicious of a Christianity dependent upon facts or

223. Ibid., 346–47. Compare Warfield's important essay, "On Faith in Its Psychological Aspects," in *The Princeton Theological Review*, xi (1911), 537–66; and reprinted in B. B. Warfield, *Studies in Theology* (Grand Rapids: Baker Book House, 1980), 313–42. Throughout this essay Warfield appeals to Scottish philosopher Sir William Hamilton. Warfield contends that we cannot believe "without adequate grounds (p. 326)," and that these grounds are necessarily connected to historical evidence, and that the role of the Holy Spirit is to provide illumination and quickening so that sinful men and women can "perceive the force and yield to the compelling power of the evidence of the trustworthiness of Jesus Christ as Saviour submitted to him in the gospel (p. 337)."

224. These are effectively surveyed in McClanahan, "Benjamin. B. Warfield: Historian of Doctrine in Defense of Orthodoxy," 452 ff.

225. See Warfield's thorough critique of Albrecht Ritschl: "Ritschl the Rationalist," in *The Princeton Theological Review*, xvii (1919), 533–84; and "Ritschl the Perfectionist," in *The Princeton Theological Review*, xviii (1920), 44–102. Repr. in B. B. Warfield, *Perfectionism*, vol. 1 (Grand Rapids: Baker Book House, 1980), 3–110.

226. Warfield, "The Latest Phase of Historical Rationalism," 591.

evidences. Thus like mysticism, rationalism always tends toward natural religion by making final appeal, not to an objective revelation, but to human reason.[227]

Warfield contends that the Ritschlite variety of rationalism is most clearly seen in an attempt to remove all metaphysical elements of Christianity, and thus nothing will be admitted "except the facts of experience." Take, for example, the fact that "the Ritschlite defines God as love. He means by this that the Christian experiences God as love, and this much he therefore knows. Beyond that, he cannot define God"; for as Warfield contends, "All question of what God is in Himself, as distinguished from what God is to us, belongs in the sphere of 'metaphysics,' and is, therefore, out of the realm of religion."[228] As Warfield understands matters, the Ritschlite does the same thing in reference to Jesus Christ, since he is forced to say nothing about him beyond "what he can verify in ... experience. For example, he can know, in such experience, nothing of Christ's preexistence, and cannot control anything told us about it by any available tests." Again, this is because "all that is outside the reach of such verification," by human experience, "belongs to the sphere of 'metaphysics,' and is, therefore, out of the realm of religion."[229] Thus if the Christian faith is to be grounded in religious experience, the close relationship between mysticism and rationalism once again becomes readily apparent. The subjective swallows up the objective, and whether it be human reason or the religious consciousness, all appeal to the authority of an objective revelation becomes an impossibility.

Another significant problem with Ritschlism, as Warfield sees it, is that contrary to its fundamental tenet—which is that we must have an undogmatic Christianity, because "theology, we are told, is killing religion"—"Christianity as it has come down to us is very far from being an undogmatic Christianity. The history of Christianity is the history of doctrine."[230] Since Christianity is by its nature a historical religion, rationalism must, therefore, deal with the problem of "what is it to do with a historical Christianity which is a decidedly doctrinal Christianity?" Here Warfield concludes, "Its task, in a word, is historically

227. Ibid.

228. Ibid., 592.

229. Ibid. Compare B. B. Warfield, "The Twentieth Century Christ," in *The Hibbert Journal*, xii (1914), 583–602, which was reprinted in B. B. Warfield, *Christology and Criticism*, 385–87.

230. Warfield, "The Latest Phase of Historical Rationalism," 592.

to explain doctrinal Christianity as corrupted Christianity; or, in other words, to explain the rise and development of doctrine as a series of accretions from without, overlying and concealing Christianity." And thus, "Ritschlism, in the very nature of the case definitely breaks down the whole tradition of Christian doctrine, from Justin Martyr down."[231]

This fact necessitates that Warfield turn his critical radar to noted historical theologians Adolf Harnack[232] and A. C. McGiffert,[233] both of whom, Warfield contends, are biased by the fundamental mistrust of dogmatic Christianity, typical of Ritschlism. This issue arises, of course, because of the difficulty raised by Warfield's belief that Christianity's doctrines *are* its fundamental facts.[234] Thus the problem with Harnack's otherwise fine work is that:

> [Harnack] certainly does not bring with him to the investigation of the teaching of Jesus, for example, a whole body of presuppositions, under the influence of which he forces his material into preconceived moulds. And he certainly does not derive his conception of Christianity from an induction from its entire phenomenal manifestation; he simply makes his reconstructed version of Jesus' Christianity the sole Christianity which he will recognize.[235]

As a consistent inductivist, Warfield is quite concerned that Harnack simply will not go where the evidence should take him. Harnack has, as a rationalist, determined what Christianity *is* before he examines any of the data. As far as Yale Professor A. C. McGiffert's "theory of the primitive church" goes, according to Warfield, McGiffert has cut off the limb on which he has been sitting. As Warfield puts it:

> He appeals to the authority of the apostles in order to destroy the authority of the apostles. This seems to us to be a most illogical

231. Ibid., 592–93.

232. Warfield reviewed each volume of Harnack's *History of Dogma* in some detail over a five-year period in the *Presbyterian and Reformed Review* from October of 1896 to October of 1900.

233. The details of McGiffert's troubles in the Northern Presbyterian church, see Lefferts A. Loetscher, *The Broadening Church: A Study of Theological Issues in the Presbyterian Church Since 1869* (Philadelphia: University of Pennsylvania Press, 1954).

234. Warfield, "The Latest Phase of Historical Rationalism," 593 ff. This point has been effectively covered by McClanahan in his fine dissertation, "B. B. Warfield: Historian of Doctrine in Defense of Orthodoxy," 452 ff.

235. B. B. Warfield, "The Essence of Christianity and the Cross of Christ,"in The Harvard *Theological Review*, vii, 1 (January, 1914), 16–46. Repr. in Warfield, *Christology and Criticism*, 414.

> proceeding. ... We cannot have two supreme standards. Either the Holy Spirit in the heart is the norm of truth and the deliverances of the apostles must be subjected to what we consider His deliverances (and then we have Mysticism cooling down into Rationalism), or else the apostolic revelation is the norm of truth, and the fancied deliverances of the Spirit in our heart must be subjected to the apostolic declarations (and then we have Protestantism).[236]

Therefore, the Ritschlite, driven by his rationalism, cannot account for the origin of Christianity, a religion grounded in what God has done in Christ, and therefore, a religion based upon history and necessarily grounded in Christian evidences. This historical basis for Christianity stands in marked contrast to Ritschlism, which attempts to ground an undogmatic ethical religion upon individual religious experience, and therefore, ultimately upon human reason. This leaves us with nothing more than natural religion. Warfield states that Ritschl has left us with a "new Naturalism, decked out in phrases borrowed from the Scriptures and Reformers, but as like their system of thought as black is to white, and called it the true doctrine of the Bible and the Reformers."[237] Ritschl is a rationalist, acting in accord with his Kantian and rationalist epistemology. To Warfield's way of thinking, any religion with its foundation in human reason—whether that be rationalism or mysticism—lacks any external authority whatsoever and robs Christianity of its claim to be the absolute religion.

A FORMIDABLE POLEMICIST

Warfield was a fierce and tenacious opponent who was always eager to bring his pen to bear when his beloved Reformed orthodoxy was threatened in any way. Whether it be Arminianism as a distinct theological system (as seen in his review of John Miley's *Systematic Theology*), or the variety of Arminianism then combining itself with revivalist elements (as seen in the work of Andrew Murray, R. A. Torrey, or Lewis Sperry Chafer), or whether it be mysticism of a sophisticated variety (as seen, for example, in the writings of Evelyn Underhill), or the rationalism of an Albrecht Ritschl, B. B. Warfield, the Princeton professor of polemical and didactic theology, was compelled to respond.

236. Warfield, "The Latest Phase of Historical Rationalism," 617–18.
237. Warfield, *Perfectionism*, vol. 1, 52.

The sheer volume of book reviews and journal articles devoted to these issues is simply amazing. Warfield brought to bear his keen mind, great breadth of knowledge, and his boundless energy. In almost every case, Warfield's concern reflects not only an unyielding defense of the Westminster Standards, but a willingness and ability to defend Scottish Common Sense epistemology and the inductive method as well. Arminianism and revivalism reflect a defective notion of sanctification when seen from the perspective of orthodox Calvinism. However, the issues raised by the mystics and rationalists are viewed by Warfield as direct challenges to Christianity itself. Any attempt to move Christianity to new epistemological footings is completely resisted and seen as a serious challenge. Warfield's philosophical sophistication is not often noted but is clearly evident in a number of cases.

Whatever one may conclude about Warfield's efforts in these matters, there is no doubt that his methodology remains remarkably consistent, whether he be working in the field of apologetics, systematic theology, or polemics. Again, there is no evidence of a "mature Warfield," whose views substantially change over time. Warfield's endeavors to respond to rationalism and mysticism should not come as a surprise, given the history of the Princeton school. But it is important to note that the topics addressed change over the course of his career. Indeed, a marked increase in hostility toward the fundamentalists rises once the Keswick movement had invaded Warfield's home turf in 1918. Warfield's hostility toward incipient fundamentalism and to what is now loosely described as "American evangelicalism" is quite remarkable in this regard. While Warfield was an effective apologist and a capable theologian, the "Lion of Princeton" was possibly most effective as a polemicist.

7

Contemporary Critics

THEOLOGICAL RANGE WARS

In his influential *Institutes of Elenctic Theology*, Francis Turretin asked, "Can the existence of God be irrefutably demonstrated against atheists?" He did not hesitate to answer, "We affirm."[1] But later voices within the Reformed tradition are not quite so confident. B. B. Warfield once remarked that Abraham Kuyper's *Principles of Sacred Theology* demonstrated an unfortunate subordination of apologetics to what the Princetonian considered to be an insignificant role. This allowed for Christianity to remain, as Warfield phrased it, "let us say it frankly—the 'great assumption.' "[2] Perhaps this was the first shot fired in what was to become a kind of theological range war within the Reformed tradition over the nature and the role of apologetics. The confidence of Turretin had given way to a truncated effort in the apologetic of Kuyper, whom otherwise Warfield greatly esteemed. The proto-presuppositionalist views of Kuyper have come to dominance in the contemporary Reformed tradition, the reason as to why Warfield's apologetic has become the subject of numerous critical evaluations. His understanding of the noetic effects of sin, of the relationship between the Holy Spirit and Christian evidences, and his conception of the relationship of faith to reason have been singled out for critical scrutiny. Some of these

1. Francis Turretin, *Institutio Theologiae Elencticae* (New York: Robert Carter, 1847), I.iii.I.

2. B. B. Warfield, "Introduction to Francis R. Beattie's *Apologetics: or the Rational Vindication of Christianity*" (1903). Repr. in B. B. Warfield, *Selected Shorter Writings*, vol. 2 (ed. John E. Meeter; Phillipsburg: P&R Publishing, 1980), 95–96. Warfield also wrote the forward to the English translation of Kuyper's *Encyclopedaedie der Heilige Godgeleerdheid*, published in 1898 under the title *Encyclopedia of Sacred Theology: Its Principles* (trans. J. Hendrik De Vries; New York: Charles Scribner's Sons, 1898). A reprint of this volume is also available under the title *Principles of Sacred Theology* (Grand Rapids: Baker Book House, 1980).

evaluations of Old Princeton and Warfield are seriously flawed, while others have done much to advance our understanding of the Princeton tradition. Often Warfield has not been granted an adequate opportunity to speak for himself since his opinions have not been sufficiently investigated. There have been defenders of Warfield to be sure,[3] but these have been few and far between, and most have not dealt with many of these specific issues. Thus there is a great need to evaluate both the historical development of the evidential apologetic at Princeton, and to set out Warfield's views in related areas.

CORNELIUS VAN TIL'S ASSESSMENT

Although the late Cornelius Van Til was himself a student at Princeton shortly after Warfield's death, and was in many ways the heir to Warfield's apologetic mantle as the professor of apologetics at Westminster Theological Seminary, Van Til largely rejected Warfield's apologetic.[4] Van Til claimed that when Warfield "attributed to 'right reason' the ability to interpret natural revelation correctly," it left Christianity appearing "only probably true."[5] Van Til even went so far as to state, "The remnants of the traditional method of apologetics that have been taken over from Romanism and Evangelicalism by Old Princeton ... must no longer be maintained."[6] Van Til argues that one of

3. See, for example, John H. Gerstner, "Warfield's Case for Biblical Inerrancy," in *God's Inerrant Word* (ed. John W. Montgomery; Minneapolis: Bethany Fellowship, 1974); and John H. Gerstner, "The Contributions of Charles Hodge, B. B. Warfield, and J. Gresham Machen," in *Challenges to Inerrancy: A Theological Response* (ed. Gordon R. Lewis and Bruce Demarest; Chicago: Moody Press, 1984), 347–81. Also see R. C. Sproul, John Gerstner, and Arthur Lindsley, *Classical Apologetics: A Rational Defense of the Christian Faith and a Critique of Presuppositional Apologetics* (Grand Rapids: Zondervan, 1984).

4. On the question of why Westminster Theological Seminary embraced the apologetic method of Van Til and rejected that of Warfield and Machen, see John R. Muether, *Cornelius Van Til: Reformed Apologist and Churchman* (Phillipsburg: P&R Publishing, 2008), 67–71; 232–34.

5. Cornelius Van Til, *The Defense of the Faith* (Phillipsburg: P&R Publishing, 1955), 264–65. Van Til is very likely referring to Warfield's comments in Warfield's "Introduction to Francis Beattie's *Apologetics*," 99–100.

6. Ibid., 299. This same sentiment is found in the writings of Warfield's esteemed contemporary, Herman Bavinck. In the prolegomena to his Reformed Dogmatics, Bavinck writes, "Protestant theologians, it must be admitted, have not always rigorously adhered to this principle [i.e., faith depends upon divine authority] and have repeatedly returned to the theory of natural theology and of the historical proofs for the truth of revelation." See Herman Bavinck, *Reformed Dogmatics, Volume*

the reasons that these remnants of Romanism must be rejected is because of Warfield's method that strove "to operate in neutral territory with the non-believer." According to Van Til, Warfield "thought that this was the only way to show the unbeliever that theism and Christianity are objectively true."[7] Van Til saw this as an unfortunate capitulation to an incipient Romanism, and even worse perhaps, "such a method" was inherently "Arminian."[8] As Van Til says elsewhere, specifically in regard to Warfield's apologetic for special revelation, "even Warfield himself ... reverts to what is virtually an Arminian view of [Scripture's] defense."[9] In the fundamental choice between Warfield and Kuyper, Van Til can state without equivocation, "I have chosen the position of Abraham Kuyper."[10]

The litany of charges Van Til brought against Warfield's apologetic methodology causes one to wonder what made Van Til reject Warfield's method so forcefully. Van Til believes Warfield uses an inherently Arminian apologetic, makes concessions to Rome, and apparently elevates human reason above divine revelation. To assume that Christians and non-Christians occupy neutral common ground is, in Van Til's way of thinking, to utterly depreciate the noetic effects of sin. If Van Til is correct, Warfield may have indeed unwittingly compromised the defense of the faith.

1: *Prolegomena* (ed. John Bolt; trans., John Vriend; Grand Rapids: Baker Academic, 2003), 512. Bavinck's lament that so many Reformed writers have adopted this method may indicate that the charge of novelty lies at Bavinck's feet, not Warfield's.

7. Ibid., 265.

8. Ibid., 279. Van Til's remarks are made in reference to Floyd E. Hamilton's *The Basis for the Christian Faith* (1927). Hamilton had been a student of William Brenton Greene, long-standing professor of apologetics at Princeton. Van Til states that Hamilton's book is representative of the Princeton apologetic. This notion that Princeton's apologetic is "Arminian" has been modified somewhat by recent defenders of Van Til. Joel R. Beeke, for example, speaks of Van Til in an article written for the centennial of Van Til's birth, as "purging non-Reformed apologetics from Reformed theology." In this case, Warfield's method is no longer called "Arminian," but is instead described as "non-Reformed." See Joel R. Beeke, "Van Til and Apologetics," in *New Horizon* (May, 1995), 6.

9. Cornelius Van Til, *The Protestant Doctrine of Scripture* (n.p.: den Dulk Foundation, 1967), 57.

10. Van Til, *The Defense of the Faith*, 265.

OTHER IMPORTANT ASSESSMENTS

Many interpreters of B. B. Warfield and the Princeton tradition have accepted Van Til's negative assessment of the Princeton apologetic to one degree or another. Jack Rogers and Donald McKim, for example, take Van Til's negative evaluation even further in their volume, *The Authority and Interpretation of the Bible*. Rogers and McKim conclude that "Warfield laid his stress not on the supernatural, but on the natural knowledge of God."[11] The authors also assert that in Warfield's conception, "philosophy preceded theology. The requirements of human reason had to be met before God could give faith."[12] Rogers and McKim claim without any qualification, Warfield "did not even acknowledge the option of an Augustinian 'faith leads to understanding' approach."[13] Such comments reflect the all too common misrepresentation of Warfield's position. Warfield himself stated the exact opposite, namely "we not only have no desire to deny, we rather wish to proclaim, the great truth involved in the watchword of the greatest of the fathers and schoolmen, *Credo ut intelligam*."[14]

Similar misrepresentations of Warfield's views are found throughout *The Authority and Interpretation of the Bible*. We are told by the authors that Warfield argued that "the Holy Spirit worked to produce acceptance of the humanly devised evidential reasons for faith."[15] We are also told that "the Holy Spirit does not produce faith for Warfield. The Spirit only made the 'faith' which was already produced in the mind by reason into 'saving faith.' "[16] We are also told that "the Bible became authoritative according to Warfield not primarily because of the Holy Spirit's witness to Jesus Christ and his message of salvation but rather because one

11. Jack B. Rogers and Donald K. McKim, *The Authority and Interpretation of the Bible* (San Francisco: Harper & Row, 1979), 328. See Jack Rogers' more balanced discussion of Warfield and Van Til's apologetic in Jack Rogers, "Van Til and Warfield on Scripture in the Westminster Confession," in *Jerusalem and Athens: Critical Discussion on the Philosophy and Apologetics of Cornelius Van Til* (ed. E. R. Geehan; Phillipsburg: P&R Publishing, 1971), 154–65. It must be duly noted, however, that Rogers and McKim do make the connection between the Princeton school and their most important predecessors, the Reformed scholastics. Van Til, in effect, overlooks this important connection by arguing for the "novelty" of the Princeton apologetic.

12. Ibid.

13. Ibid., 328.

14. B. B. Warfield, "The Right of Systematic Theology," in *Selected Shorter Writings*, vol. 2 (ed. John E. Meeter; Phillipsburg: P&R Publishers, 1980), 273.

15. Rogers and McKim, *The Authority and Interpretation of the Bible*, 330.

16. Ibid., 333.

was convinced rationally of the proofs of Scripture's divinity."[17] There are repeated references to Warfield's comments about reason,[18] with reference especially made to Warfield's remark found in the forward to Francis Beattie's *Apologetics*, that Christianity was "to reason its way to dominion." Rogers and McKim conclude, "For Warfield, reason has been left unimpaired by the Fall and its attendant sin."[19] All of these assertions are made without reference to Warfield's pervasive subjective-objective epistemological formulation, and despite Warfield's own direct statements to the contrary.[20]

A more accurate and carefully researched assessment of Warfield, though equally negative, is that reached by John C. Vander Stelt in his published Ph.D. dissertation, *Philosophy & Scripture*. Vander Stelt begins his evaluation of Warfield by noting that the Princetonian saw apologetics as more an offensive than a defensive science:

> In apologetics, Warfield was not satisfied with a mere defense and vindication of Christianity in opposition to the unbeliever's denial of it. Apologetics is, unlike an apology, not founded negatively in sin and its denial of truth. Rather it is a constructive science that has its positive origin in the "fundamental needs of the human spirit," namely to provide clear reasons for faith and to demonstrate the validity of man's knowledge of God as the ground of which theology rests. Apologetics seeks to conquer. It reasons its

17. Ibid., 333–34. These unsubstantiated assertions and *ad hominem* arguments reach their low point when the authors argue that "Warfield's concept of authority had the unfortunate practical consequence of introducing the Bible as a law book rather than as a saving good news (p. 333)." For an important correction of this misrepresentation, see W. Andrew Hoffecker, "The Devotional Life of Archibald Alexander, Charles Hodge, and Benjamin B. Warfield," in *The Westminster Theological Journal*, vol. XLII, no. 1 (Fall 1979), 124 ff; "The Relation Between the Objective and Subjective Aspects in Christian Religious Experience: A Study in the Systematic and Devotional Writings of Archibald Alexander, Charles Hodge and Benjamin B. Warfield," (Ph.D. diss.: Brown University, 1970); and *Piety and the Princeton Theologians* (Phillipsburg: P&R Publishing, 1981), especially 95 ff.

18. Ibid. See page 329 for example.

19. Ibid., 371, n. 40.

20. Paul Helseth correctly notes, the opinion that "Warfield was a rationalist whose epistemology was compromised by the assumptions of Enlightenment philosophy ... cannot be justified because Warfield's 'intellectualism' was moral rather than merely rational.' " See Paul Kjoss Helseth, *"Right Reason" and the Princeton Mind: An Unorthodox Proposal* (Phillipsburg: P&R Publishing, 2010), 71.

> way to dominion: "It thinks itself thoroughly through, attacks by not by sword, but by reasoning."[21]

In his understanding of Warfield, Vander Stelt sees the connection in Warfield's mind between the nature of apologetics and theology, with that of his anthropology and epistemology.[22] Additionally, Vander Stelt points out that for Warfield, "the basic denominator of both faith and knowledge is conviction," based upon the apprehension of evidences.[23] He concludes therefore that "Warfield's entire framework of thought in his views on apologetics and Scripture is unmistakenably intellectualistic,"[24] a view which is based upon the dualism in Warfield's thought "of his ontological and religious distinction between the supernatural and the natural."[25] Vander Stelt contends that the Scottish philosophy is inherently "semi-Arminian,"[26] and that Warfield's use of "rational apologetics, together with the implied understanding of the importance of testimonial evidences, resulted in the projection onto Scripture of a thought-pattern in which the latter," argues the author, "is conceived of first of all as a book that contains a series of infallible, propositional statements,"[27] thereby leaving us with an epistemological dualism that the author finds untenable.

CRITIQUES BY MARK NOLL AND GEORGE MARSDEN

Mark Noll and George Marsden consistently offer the most careful and balanced interpretations of the Princeton tradition, but, nevertheless, generally follow a similar negative reading of the Princeton apologetic. Mark Noll, in his volume *The Princeton Theology: 1812–1921*, contends that while the Princeton theologians "with all their hearts distrusted the Enlightenment,"[28] their enthusiastic endorsement of Scottish Common

---

21. John C. Vander Stelt, *Philosophy and Scripture: A Study in Old Princeton and Westminster Theology* (Marlton NJ: Mack Publishing Company, 1978), 167.
22. Ibid., 168.
23. Ibid., 172.
24. Ibid.
25. Ibid., 182–83.
26. Ibid., 311, 313.
27. Ibid., 311.
28. Mark A. Noll, *The Princeton Theology: 1812–1921* (Grand Rapids: Baker Book House, 1983), 11. See Noll's other fine essay documenting the wide-ranging influence of Scottish Common Sense Realism upon much of conservative theological development well into the 20th century. Mark A. Noll, "Common Sense Traditions and American Evangelical Thought: The Influence of Epistemological, Ethical and

Sense Realism ironically may have led to their own eventual seduction by Enlightenment skepticism.

> Critics of Scottish Common Sense Philosophy regularly condemn its advocates for being naive, for— that is—failing to recognize how thoroughly all human perceptions, even those of Scripture, are colored by cultural circumstances. Modern Reformed thinkers who are not Common Sense Realists are among those who insist that it is not only naive, but anti-biblical to begin a chain of reasoning with the assumption that the search for truth involves no moral preconditions in the seeker and no predetermined assumptions about what the inquiry will reveal. Some who revile Scottish Realism are moral and epistemological relativists; others believe firmly in the reality of objective truth, but do not believe it is reached by the supposedly value-free inquiries of a putatively neutral science. Both sorts of critics have had a field day with the Princeton theologians.[29]

But Noll cautions that it is, in fact, quite possible "to conclude too rapidly that the Princetonians were simply theologians of Scottish Common Sense. Influenced by this perspective as they were, they still retained the fidelity to Scripture and Reformed traditions which kept them from being entirely at the mercy of their philosophy."[30]

The possible negative influence of this philosophy can be seen in the fact that the Princetonians themselves needed to respond to the charge of capitulation to a dangerous overestimation of the neutrality of human reason and an over-intellectualization of the Christian faith. Noll points out that during Warfield's own lifetime (1895), Scottish church historian Thomas M. Lindsey criticized Warfield and the Princetonians for holding to a "purely intellectual apprehension of Scripture."[31]

Methodological Common Sense Traditions," in *American Quarterly*, 37, no. 2 (Summer 1985), 216–38.

29. Ibid., 32–33.

30. Ibid.

31. Ibid., 41. The original source for the quotation is found in Thomas M. Lindsey, "The Doctrine of Scripture: The Reformers and the Princeton School," in *The Expositor*, fifth series, vol. I (ed. William Robertson Nicoll; London: Hodder & Stoughton, 1985). Lindsey indicates that "it is the doctrine of Scripture to be found in these treatises [Charles Hodge's *Systematic Theology* and A. A. Hodge's *Commentary on the Confession of Faith*], that is to be contrasted with that of the Reformers. ... Revelation is treated as if it were concerned mainly if not entirely with the communication of knowledge, which consists of doctrines, facts and precepts (278, 282)." As Noll points out, what

In Noll's estimation, later critics of Old Princeton, such as Van Til, also rejected the "Princeton convictions concerning the natural apologetical powers of even Christians."[32] This line of criticism has been taken up by others such as Ernest Sandeen, who contends "that both historical evidence and theological reasoning show not just weaknesses, but fatal flaws in the Princeton Theology."[33] Here his focus shifts well beyond the bounds of this limited discussion to the Princeton conception of the inerrancy of the original autographic text of Scripture. He raises the argument, "How can one base the apologetic case upon the inerrancy of the autographic text of Scripture, when such a text no longer exists?"[34] As Randall Balmer and John Woodbridge have noted, these arguments against Warfield's position are in part based upon dubious assumptions and questionable historiography.[35] Nevertheless, not all are convinced that Warfield specifically, and Old Princeton generally, satisfactorily deal with the inerrancy of the original autographs and related apologetic issues. "For my part," concludes Noll, "I would like to see more evangelical concern for the Princetonians' substantive theology and their general confidence in Scriptural authority, where they most transcended the limitations of their age."[36] Yet Noll, like Van Til and others before him,

---

bothers Lindsey the most about Warfield and A. A. Hodge's view, is what Lindsey describes as "their purely intellectual idea of Scripture (p. 284)." John Frame, Van Til's successor at Westminster, apparently concurs: "Hodge also errs in the direction of a too intellectualistic concept of theology." See John M. Frame, *The Doctrine of the Knowledge of God* (Phillipsburg: P&R Publishing, 1987), 78.

32. Ibid., 42.

33. Ibid.

34. See, for example, the discussion of this in Ernest R. Sandeen, "The Princeton Theology: One Source of Biblical Literacy in American Protestantism," in *Church History*, vol. 31, no. 3 (Sept. 1962), 316 ff; and Mark S. Massa, *Charles Augustus Briggs and the Crisis of Historical Criticism* (Minneapolis: Fortress, 1990), 59–68. Massa mistakenly speaks of the "novelty" of the Princeton position (61), and describes the Princeton conception of epistemological certitude as that of "a new mathematical specificity and concreteness (p. 59)." This is quite ironic given Van Til's objection that Warfield's conception of truth left us with only "probability."

35. Randall H. Balmer, "The Princetonians, Scripture, and Recent Scholarship," in *Journal of Presbyterian History*, Vol. 60:3 (Fall 1982), 267–70; Randall H. Balmer, "The Princetonians and Scripture: A Reconsideration," in *The Westminster Theological Seminary*, vol. XLIV, no. 2 (Fall 1982), 352–65; and John D. Woodbridge, *Biblical Authority: A Critique of the Rogers/McKim Proposal* (Grand Rapids: Zondervan, 1982).

36. Noll, *The Princeton Theology*, 45.

would like to see less regard maintained "for their theological method and approach to apologetics, where they were most time-bound."[37]

In his subsequent volume on the founding of Princeton College, *Princeton and the Republic*, Noll states that while Warfield was certainly "the nation's most capable theological conservative at the end of the 19th century," Warfield's apologetic also shows the degree to which modernity had infiltrated the American intellectual scene. Noll, like virtually all of contemporary Warfield interpreters, cites Warfield's own oft-repeated words to demonstrate this contention: "Faith, in all its forms, is a conviction of truth, founded as such, of course, on evidence. ... Christianity has been placed in the world to *reason* its way to the dominion of the world."[38]

George Marsden has also written quite extensively on Warfield and the Old Princeton tradition. In an essay titled "Scotland and Philadelphia: Common Sense Philosophy from Jefferson to Westminster," Marsden contends:

> [John] Vander Stelt correctly points out the irony involved. Calvinists, who might be expected to hold that the human intellect was hopelessly blinded by the Fall, were only saying that it

37. Ibid. Noll points out that "as one who favors the Calvinism of Jonathan Edwards, which bears striking formal resemblances to that of Abraham Kuyper, I find the Princeton Theology weak on the relationship of natural and revealed theology, confused on the proper place of affected knowledge, and overly sanguine about the powers of rational apologetics (p. 44)."

38. Mark A. Noll, *Princeton and the Republic: 1768–1822* (Lawrenceville: Princeton University Press, 1989), 291. The italics are in the original. In this instance, Noll cites a virtually identical statement made by Warfield found in his "Review of Herman Bavinck's *De Zekerheid des Geloofs*." Repr. in B. B. Warfield, *Selected Shorter Writings*, vol. 2, 120–21. Several recent treatments of Presbyterian history which treat Warfield's key role in the developing Princeton Theology feature this citation as indicative of Warfield's central apologetic-theological motif—his intellectualist conception of faith. D. G. Hart cites the same statement in his fine volume on Warfield's successor at Princeton, J. Gresham Machen. Hart similarly contends, "The apparent contradiction between Princeton's trust in Common Sense and its adherence to the doctrine of universal sinfulness had little effect on these professors' assertions about the scientific character of theology." See D. G. Hart, *Defending the Faith: J. Gresham Machen and the Crisis of Conservative Protestantism in Modern America* (Baltimore: The Johns Hopkins University Press, 1994), 25. In another recent work treating the background of the fundamentalist-modernist controversy, Bradley J. Longfield cites this same quotation, listing *The Authority and Interpretation of the Bible*, by Rogers and McKim, as the source of the quotation. See Bradley J. Longfield, *The Presbyterian Controversy: Fundamentalists, Modernists, & Moderates* (New York: Oxford University Press, 1991), 44.

> was perhaps afflicted with a mild astigmatism. The corrective lens of reasonable common sense was all that was needed to lead one at least to assent to the truth of Christianity.[39]

Again, it is asserted that because of a basic commitment to Common Sense Realism, those such as Warfield who used this method did not hold to a sufficient view of the noetic damage wrought upon the fallen human race by Adam's rebellion. However, Marsden, unlike many of Warfield's interpreters, is careful to note that in Warfield's estimation, "The Holy Spirit was the agent for a change of heart." Even though Marsden points out Warfield's own assertions to this effect, he nevertheless concludes that the divine activity of God the Holy Spirit cannot be central in this scheme because "Warfield indeed wrote as though he had an unbounded confidence in the apologetic power of the rational appeal to people of common sense."[40] Marsden, following Van Til and Rogers, also cites the now well-familiar passage from Warfield's introduction to Francis Beattie's work on apologetics, that Christianity must "reason its way to dominion,"[41] as primary evidence of the Princeton tradition's misguided trust in the powers of fallen human reason.

But Marsden also notes the reason that Warfield himself gave as to why so many reject the Christian religion if truth in the Scottish conception is objective and inviolable:

> [The] common-ground approach eliminated from Warfield's apologetics the use of a venerable line of explanation for the failures of reason. In the traditions of Augustine, Calvin and Jonathan Edwards the Fall was often regarded as having so blinded the

39. George M. Marsden, "Scotland and Philadelphia: Common Sense Philosophy from Jefferson to Westminster," in *The Reformed Journal*, 29:3 (March 1979), 9. See also Marsden's discussion of these same issues as related to Warfield's successor at Princeton, J. Gresham Machen; George M. Marsden, "The New School Heritage and Presbyterian Fundamentalism," in *The Westminster Theological Seminary*, vol. XXXII (Nov. 1969), 129–47; and George M. Marsden, "J. Gresham Machen, History and Truth," in *The Westminster Theological Journal*, vol. XLII (Fall 1979), 157–75.

40. George M. Marsden, *Fundamentalism and American Culture* (New York: Oxford University Press, 1980), 115.

41. Ibid. Note that in Marsden's most recent work, the same citation from Warfield is again adduced, though Marsden speaks of Warfield this time when using the citation as "the most brilliant" Princeton polemicist during the generation after James McCosh's death. See George M. Marsden, *The Soul of the American University: From Protestant Establishment to Established Nonbelief* (New York: Oxford University Press, 1994), 213.

> human intellect that natural knowledge of God had been suppressed and therefore no one could have true understanding without receiving the eyes of faith.[42]

According to Marsden, however, the reason that non-Christians (and even some Christian theologians) reject the obvious conclusions received by intelligent apprehension— in this case the biblical evidence for supernaturalism and miracle—is because "[Warfield] saw a bias in their first principles."[43] This is a rather surprising assertion by Marsden, since after accusing Warfield of elevating "unaided reason" and ignoring the blindness to truth produced by the fall, Marsden then notes the reason which Warfield himself gave as to why non-Christians reject the truth is precisely because of their bias (i.e., their presuppositions) against the truth. Marsden concludes that Warfield's proposed solution to this problem "was not to set one worldview or set of premises against another as competing hypotheses," as in contemporary presuppositional apologetics. "Rather it was the Baconian method of setting a body of facts, objectively knowable by unbiased and dispassionate observers against the eccentric and prejudiced biases of all competing worldviews,"[44] supposedly typical of evidential apologetics. Unfortunately, Warfield's own awareness of the presuppositional biases on the part of non-Christians is not given sufficient notice.

In a later work, *The Soul of the American University* (1994), Marsden is convinced that Warfield's rejection of Abraham Kuyper's conception that "there are 'two kinds of people,' regenerate and unregenerate, and hence 'two kinds of science,' " indicates that the Princetonian saw the Amsterdamian's view as "outrageous."[45] According to Marsden, Warfield believed that "science must be an objective, unified, and cumulative enterprise. ... This belief explained Warfield's immense confidence that science would vindicate Christianity. If Christianity was

42. Ibid., 115. Compare our previous discussion of this point in chapter 4. As we have seen, Warfield clearly endorses Calvin's views on the blinding effects of sin.

43. Ibid., 116.

44. Ibid.

45. Marsden, *The Soul of the American University*, 214. Compare the similar comments made in George M. Marsden, "The Collapse of American Evangelical Academia," in *Faith and Reason* (ed. Alvin Plantinga and Nicholas Wolterstorff; Notre Dame: University of Notre Dame Press, 1983), especially 252 ff. In his *Fundamentalism and American Culture*, Marsden spoke of Warfield as being "utterly mystified," at Kuyper's formulation (115).

true, science would inevitably confirm it."[46] Marsden also draws the possible connection between Warfield, Scottish Common Sense Realism, and other American pragmatist-empiricists, such as Charles S. Peirce. "Warfield thus held essentially the same assumption about the triumph of one science for the race as other elite Protestant academics of the day. ... Common Sense philosophy and historicist pragmatism, despite their fundamental differences, were still American cousins."[47]

SCOTTISH COMMON SENSE PHILOSOPHY AND THE REFORMED TRADITION

Given this rather pervasive and negative assessment of Warfield, an evaluation of Warfield's conception of the noetic effects of sin, his understanding of the role of the Holy Spirit in the creation of saving faith, and his understanding of the relationship between faith and reason is certainly necessary. Key too is an understanding of how Common Sense Realism may have colored certain aspects of Warfield's own theology. From what sources outside the narrow Princeton circle, if any, does Warfield draw upon in the development of his own apologetic? Is there any evidence that the Princeton tradition's allegiance to the Scottish philosophy introduces an Arminian or Romanist tendency in Warfield's theology? Does it produce an intellectualist view of reason, and therefore, somehow set up an unbiblical epistemological dualism? How does this evince a supposedly flawed view of the noetic effects of sin?

Those who attempt to label Warfield's apologetic as inherently Arminian, Thomistic, or containing an incipient Romanism, are simply engaging in *ad hominem* argumentation. This can be seen very clearly, for example, in the work of Jack Rogers and Donald McKim, who assert, "Warfield overlooked Calvin's antipathy to Aristotle and Thomas Aquinas."[48] But based upon the entire Warfield *corpus*, it is difficult to

46. Ibid.

47. Ibid., 215.

48. Rogers and McKim, *The Authority and Interpretation of the Bible*, 327. See Richard A. Muller's stinging rebuke of these kinds of unsubstantiated assertions in *Christ and the Decree* (Grand Rapids: Baker Book House, 1986). As but one example, Muller notes, "Calvin's use of the language of necessity and of fourfold causality in discussing these doctrines relates his thought not only to the formulation of Augustine but also to the tradition of medieval Augustinianism. We note the relationship particularly in the Aristotelian causal structure utilized by Calvin (p. 24)." In an important essay by Thomas A. Russman, he argues that the Protestant Reformers, despite their preference for "Augustinian (Platonic) forms of foundationalism to Thomistic

seriously entertain the notion that he ever maintained an Arminian or Romanist thought at any single moment in his life. John J. Markarian's appellative for Warfield, "the very Calvinist professor," certainly stands.[49]

What about possible theological tensions within Warfield's thought? Mark Noll frames these issues in reference to the broader Princeton Tradition quite well: "Princeton's boast, if she has reason to boast at all, is her unswerving fidelity to the theology of the Reformation. These claims were not idle self-delusion."[50] While Princeton's tenacious hold to confessional Calvinism provided a high degree of theological continuity, there are dynamic elements as well. Accordingly, Noll contends that Princeton's theology was in a sense "a restatement in terms that could communicate to Victorian America ... and these *constituted modifications, even innovations*, in the history of Calvinism."[51] Therefore, Noll concludes, "If the Princeton Theology was neither as pure a reaffirmation of classical Calvinism nor internally self-consistent as its advocates or opponents thought, it still retained a remarkable consistency over the course of its remarkable life."[52] In this conception, there is an internal tension within the Princeton Theology itself; a static theological commitment to historic and confessional Calvinism which produces a conservatizing trend on the one hand, and a dynamic tension on the other, as modernity rears its ugly head in the form of the Scottish philosophy, itself a product of the Scottish Enlightenment. Noll criticizes Common Sense philosophy for stoking the impetus for "modification and innovation" away from several historic Reformed distinctions, primarily the Reformed conception of the noetic effects of sin. Thus, while the Scottish philosophy helped to shape Princeton's "biblicism and Reformed Confessionalism" it also introduced basic "tenets [which] seemed to contradict Princeton commitments to Scripture and the Reformed tradition."[53]

Virtually all contemporary interpreters of Princeton generally agree with Noll's assessment. Since the Scottish epistemology emphasizes the

---

(Aristotelian) forms," were nevertheless "foundationalists to the core." See Thomas A. Russman, " 'Reformed' Epistemology," in *Thomistic Papers*, vol. IV (Houston: Center for Thomistic Studies, 1988), 200.

49. John J. Markarian, "The Calvinistic Conception of the Biblical Revelation in the Theology of B. B. Warfield," (Ph.D. diss.: Drew University, 1963), 40.

50. Noll, *The Princeton Theology*, 39.

51. Ibid. The italics are mine.

52. Ibid., 40.

53. Ibid., 30.

objective aspects of knowing, a tension is supposedly introduced into the Princeton tradition because of the assumption of the intrinsic incompatibility of this philosophy with historic Reformed theology. It was particularly difficult to meld with the conception of the noetic effects of sin, and the monergistic work of the Holy Spirit in regeneration and illumination.

In response, then, to this widely accepted assessment of Warfield, there are four important issues which need to be developed in some detail. These offer a case for a significant re-evaluation of much of the contemporary Reformed interpretation of Warfield's apologetic methodology. First, it will be necessary to evaluate whatever connections may exist between Scottish Common Sense Realism and Reformed theology. Is there anything within the basic epistemological structure of this Scottish philosophy that is in direct conflict with historic and confessional Reformed theology? Second, it is important to examine possible antecedents underlying some of Warfield's optimistic statements regarding reason in the apologetic enterprise. As we will see, the source of this supposed Arminian and Roman tendency is not Saint Thomas and the medieval scholastic tradition, but is instead to be found in one of the very bastions of Reformed orthodoxy, the Scottish Presbyterian theologians John Dick, Thomas Chalmers, William Cunningham, and James MacGregor. Third, it is important to set out the well-established notion found in the Reformed scholastics such as Francis Turretin, regarding the ministerial, or instrumental use of reason. As we will see, there is nothing found in any of Warfield's comments about reason that point to an endorsement of reason as the *pricipium fidei*. Finally, it is important to review Warfield's all too often overlooked statements which specifically address these issues, and which in several cases stand in direct contradiction to many of the assertions made about him. If Warfield is not allowed to speak for himself, then his remarks about Christianity "reasoning its way to dominion" seem to stand alone as Warfield's definitive and systematic treatment of the subject. Since Warfield wrote occasionally and topically, rather than systematically, it is important to evaluate his assertions about faith, reason, and the role of the Holy Spirit, as they are found elsewhere in his writings.

The first point of response is to determine "what is there within the basic conceptions of Scottish Common Sense Realism that so many in the Reformed tradition found so attractive?" Paul Helm has offered an important treatment of this subject in an essay entitled "Thomas Reid,

Common Sense, and Calvinism" in which he contends that while there is no inherent connection between Scottish Common Sense Realism and Calvinism, neither is there anything to be found in [it] that is intrinsically incompatible with historic Calvinism.[54] Helm asks the critical question at the outset:

> What connection, if any, is there between this view of rationality and Calvinism? Given the existence of Calvinism (a set of propositions about God, man and the world authorized by the Christian Scriptures), what philosophical system or outlook does Calvinism entail? Or, put less strongly, what system is consistent with Calvinism? Might that system be Scottish common sense philosophy, or might common sense philosophy be one of several such systems?[55]

Helm notes that in Reid's variety of foundationalism, there is certainly a propensity toward natural theology. Reid "clearly subscribes to the program of natural theology, although there is very little in his writing that can be called an explicit argument within natural theology."[56] Even though this is the case, "anyone who reads the work of Reid cannot fail to be struck by the number of times in which he theologizes about the principles of common sense, that is, attributes the authorship of them to God."[57]

In evaluating Reid's epistemology, we must ask, "What was there, if anything, in the structure of his philosophy that made it attractive to several generations of Calvinistic theologians and apologetes?"[58] Helm identifies four specific aspects of Reid's philosophy that were attractive to various Reformed theologians:

> First, it provided a ready reply to skepticism. It was constructed by Reid with that very aim in view. ... But other versions of foundationalism also had this aim: for example, the foundationalism

54. Paul Helm, "Thomas Reid, Common Sense, and Calvinism," in *Rationality in the Calvinian Tradition* (ed. Hendrik Hart, Johan Van Der Hoeven, and Nicholas Wolterstorff; Lanham: University Press of America, 1983), 71–89.

55. Ibid., 71.

56. Ibid., 77. Note that Reid's previously unpublished lectures on natural theology have since been transcribed from student notes and subsequently published. See Thomas Reid, *Thomas Reid's Lectures on Natural Theology (1780)* (ed. Elmer Duncan; Lanham: University Press of America, 1981).

57. Ibid., 78.

58. Ibid.

> of Descartes' *Meditations*. What is distinctive about Reid's foundationalism, and a possible source of its appeal, is that the truths on which all else is built are said to be matters of common sense. That is to say, no great amount of theoretical reflection and argument is required in order to arrive at the set of foundational propositions or notions. … Further, the range, not to say the eclecticism, of Reid's foundationalism must not be forgotten. It embraced not merely certain propositions about, say, deductive reasoning and our knowledge of the external world, but also about the existence of other minds, the reasonableness of induction, memory, the existence of God, and certain propositions about morality.[59]

Thus Reid's basic conception of human knowledge gave much of the ammunition needed to oppose the destructive and skeptical epistemologies, especially those of Hume and Kant. It is also important to note that nearly 100 years later, the American intellectual climate saw a similar skepticism becoming increasingly pervasive, especially in view with the rise of romanticism and the wide-spread adoption of German anti-supernaturalism and higher criticism. D. G. Hart notes that "one might go so far as to say that within the underpinnings of Common Sense," the Princetonians, especially J. Gresham Machen, were "able to weather the storms of modern thought and offer an incisive critique of modern religion."[60] Since the Princeton theologians viewed truth as invariable and unchanging, and since they felt that orthodoxy was to be defended as a body of facts found within the Scriptures and best elaborated in the Westminster Standards, Scottish Common Sense Realism was "a natural ally for its efforts."[61] The basic epistemological framework of Reid and McCosh was, therefore, very attractive to the apologetic and polemical interests of Princeton Theological Seminary.

Paul Helm notes another important practical advantage of the Scottish epistemology. "Connected with the first … a Reidian, whether a Calvinist or not, could make the assumption, as a busy pastor or apologete, that he, his flock, and the enemies of unbelief all live in the common sense world."[62] That is, whether it be the pastor, the theologian, the lay person, or the enemy of faith, all live in the same world

59. Ibid., 78–79.

60. Darryl G. Hart, "The Princeton Mind in the Modern World," *The Westminster Theological Journal*, vol. 46 (1984), 3.

61. Ibid., 4.

62. Helm, "Thomas Reid, Common Sense and Calvinism," 79.

with the same facts, and all had the same common sense faculties, and all must use the same tests for discovering truth. Indeed, these common sense notions, which are so plain and self-evident, must themselves be disproved by those who wish to explain away the facts. This gives the advocate of Scottish Common Sense Realism a "considerable tactical advantage" since "he is able, by an appeal to common sense, to place the onus on someone who wishes to disprove one or more of these common sense notions."[63] Since "being common sense notions, they do not need proving."[64]

A third advantage of the Scottish philosophy is that it is compatible with the Baconian method of induction, without having the problems associated with a pure empiricism.[65] As Helm notes, this philosophy "is compatible with a broadly inductivist approach to the acquisition of knowledge about matters of fact."[66] There are other related advantages as well:

> Therefore, the attraction of Reid's position is that from the point of view of the exegete and expositor of Scripture it is not *obviously* rationalistic. It does not obviously dictate, in an *a priori* fashion, what individual texts and passages of the Bible must mean, in the way in which, say, Immanuel Kant does in *Religion with the Limits of Reason Alone*, nor the way the deists did in terms of their notion of "natural religion." ... A further matter that Reidianism is compatible with, if it does not actually entail it, is the dominant *a posteriori* apologetic stance of English-Speaking theology and philosophy since the end of the seventeenth century, best exemplified in the work of Paley and Butler.[67]

Despite the fact that Thomas Reid's own commitment to Calvinism was possibly "so mild as to be virtually indistinguishable from Arminianism," and that "there is no evidence that Reid adopted his common sense foundationalism, because of his Calvinism,"[68] there are others "like Witherspoon and Chalmers and J. H. Thornwell" who "were undoubtedly Calvinists" and who "adopted or retained common sense

63. Ibid.
64. Ibid.
65. See James McCosh's treatment of this in *Realistic Philosophy: Defended in a Philosophic Series* (New York: Charles Scribner's Sons, 1887), 58–77.
66. Helm, "Thomas Reid, Common Sense, and Calvinism," 80.
67. Ibid. The italics are in the original.
68. Ibid., 81.

foundationalism or features of it because of their Calvinism."[69] Helm notes that several significant Calvinists of the period, Robert Riccaltoun (1691–1769), "Rabbi" Duncan (1796–1867) and W. G. T. Shedd (1820–1894), are examples of Reformed theologians who found Reid's epistemology to be problematic, especially as it relates to natural theology. "They show that it was possible to be a philosophically alert Calvinist during the period of Reid's influence on Calvinism, without subscribing to Scottish common sense foundationalism."[70]

This raises the question then as to whether there is a necessary or logical connection between Scottish Common Sense Realism and historic Calvinism. Helm asks, does "common sense foundationalism entail ... Calvinism, or [does] Calvinism entail common sense foundationalism?"[71] Helm acknowledges the slim probability for the former notion, but "perhaps the reverse is more plausible—that Calvinism entails the truth of certain common sense propositions."[72] There are important qualifications that need to be kept in view, however, before answering the question with any finality.

> Here one has to be careful to distinguish between Calvinism entailing certain propositions which some accept on Reidist grounds, and Calvinism entailing a Reidian argument for the truth of certain common sense propositions. Calvinism may well require that certain propositions, normally accepted as true as a matter of common sense, be true without requiring them to be true because they are normally accepted as a matter of common sense. For, presumably, certain propositions also accepted as a matter of common sense must be false.[73]

Therefore, Helm concludes, "In answer to whether Calvinism entails Reidianism, or *vice-versa*, we must offer a tentative 'no.' "[74] However, and this is an important point, "maybe there is a logical relation of a lesser kind. What we might call 'full Calvinism' neither entails nor is entailed by Reidianism, yet what we might call 'Calvinistic natural

69. Ibid., 81–82.
70. Ibid., 83.
71. Ibid.
72. Ibid., 84.
73. Ibid.
74. Ibid.

theology' could be entailed by, and perhaps even entails, common sense foundationalism."[75]

Helm admits that there will be those who will be skeptical of such a possibility, and assumes for the sake of argument that such a "position is possible: one can logically be a Calvinist and yet consistently subscribe to the program of natural theology. Must one be a common sense foundationalist in order to adopt this position? The answer is no."[76] Helm finds in the apologetic efforts of Stephen Charnock (1628–1680) and John Owen (1616–1683) arguments for the existence of God, depending heavily upon such a Calvinistic conception of natural theology, yet which are not indebted to Scottish Common Sense Realism, but instead to more classical Thomistic formulations. Thus, there is no necessary connection between Common Sense and Calvinistic forms of natural theology.[77] Helm notes that "we can see that the link is at best tenuous and adventitious, and there is nothing about common sense foundationalism that makes it particularly attractive to Calvinism. Moreover there is nothing about Calvinism that requires common sense foundationalism.[78]

While this may indeed be the case, it is not correct to go to the opposite extreme and conclude that Scottish Common Sense Realism is absolutely precluded by historic Calvinism. In this regard, Helm says, "Calvinism, like the Scriptures from which it is drawn, is a theoretically undetermined affair."[79] Helm adds, "Doubtless Calvinism *rules out* certain ontologies, such as materialism and solapism, and certain epistemologies, such as total skepticism"; it does not necessarily rule out Common Sense Realism. In fact, "in the case of some of what Reid called 'first principles of necessary truths' ... the propositions of Calvinism could not be *stated* if Reid's 'logical axioms' were not observed."[80] To be sure, Reid's "arguments for the acceptance of such axioms are or ought to be convincing, much less that the axioms entail Calvinism." But Helm notes, "They are entailed by Calvinism, at least in the sense that any

75. Ibid. Helm states that "By 'Calvinistic natural theology' is meant 'schemes of natural theology held by Calvinists in a way consistent with their Calvinism.' " The possibility and desirability of this is, of course, a matter of ongoing debate within the Reformed tradition.
76. Ibid.
77. Ibid., 84–86.
78. Ibid., 86–87.
79. Ibid., 88.
80. Ibid. The italics are in the original.

intelligible and consistent set of propositions presupposes certain rules of intelligible discourse."[81]

Helm's insights are especially helpful in this regard. Although Cornelius Van Til did not discuss the role of Scottish Common Sense Realism and its influence upon Warfield's epistemology and apologetic in his published work[82]—choosing instead to charge Warfield with being an inconsistent Calvinist and somehow unduly influenced by Romanism or Arminianism—the more recent studies by Rogers and McKim, Vander Stelt, Noll, and Marsden have correctly noted the deep and abiding influence of the Scottish philosophy. There is much in this philosophy that is useful to those engaged in apologetics and polemics against anti-supernatural skepticism and subjective romanticism. Indeed, some argue that it is this commitment to Scottish Common Sense Realism that gave the Princeton tradition the philosophical framework from which to defend the faith.[83]

In addition, Paul Helm is correct when he notes that ultimately this debate is actually much broader than merely the question of the compatibility or supposed incompatibility of Calvinism and Scottish Common Sense Realism. There were undeniably orthodox Calvinists on both sides of that question. From a strictly theological perspective, however, the issue could be best understood as a question as to the validity of a Calvinistic natural theology, which allows for both a natural knowledge of God and yet remains faithful to the Reformed tradition, specifically as to the noetic effects of sin. The focus of this debate, therefore, should not be drawn as narrowly as simply pitting Old Princeton against Amsterdam as though one position were biblical and Reformed and the other was not. The debate between Warfield and Kuyper is best interpreted as part of an ongoing and long-standing debate within the broader Reformed tradition. We should not allow Van Til's "*Nein!*" to be the last word in the debate over natural theology within the Reformed tradition.

81. Ibid.

82. Van Til did apparently make this point in his classroom lectures. As one of Van Til's former students and professor of apologetics at Reformed Theological Seminary, John M. Frame, pointed out to me in personal correspondence of August 26, 1995, "In person, in his classes, Van Til frequently mentioned Warfield and all the Old Princeton men with Scottish Common Sense Realism, and that was one of the major channels of his criticism."

83. Hart, "The Princeton Mind in the Modern World," 8–11.

NATURAL THEOLOGY AND CHRISTIAN EVIDENCES

The founder of Princeton Theological Seminary, Archibald Alexander, produced his own substantial apologetic, *Evidences of the Authenticity, Inspiration and Canonical Authority of the Holy Scriptures*.[84] Alexander spent very little time discussing natural theology, choosing instead to focus his energy on the "evidences of Christianity," thereby defending revealed or supernatural religion, i.e., Holy Scripture. The reading list that Alexander produced in 1812 for the students who would attend the new seminary was very heavily indebted to the Scottish philosophy. Of the 17 works that he recommended, 9 are expositions of Scottish Common Sense Realism.[85] There is also a direct connection established between the Princeton tradition and the Scottish Presbyterians, not only as far as philosophical foundations are concerned, but especially in terms of their common understanding of the role and nature of apologetics. Although Alexander used Francis Turretin's *Institutio* as his primary text, he also considered the *Lectures on Theology* by Scottish theologian John Dick (1764–1833), to be "the best systematics in English,"[86] and even wrote the forward for the 1838 edition.[87] Dick, who was awarded the D. D. from Princeton in 1815—a mere three years after the school's founding—did not live to see his lectures published posthumously as a four-volume work. It greatly influenced two American theologians, J. H. Thornwell and R. L. Dabney, who refers to Dick's *Lectures* throughout their own widely distributed lectures on theology.[88] The way in which Dick conceptualizes natural theology and defines the role and use of reason and its relationship to Christian evidences will be instructive in evaluating Warfield's own views.

---

84. Archibald Alexander, *Evidences of the Inspiration of the Authenticity, Inspiration and Canonical Authority of the Holy Scriptures* (Philadelphia: Presbyterian Board of Publication, 1826).

85. Noll, *The Princeton Theology*, 318.

86. J. R. McIntosh, "Dick, John" in *Dictionary of Scottish Church History & Theology* (ed. Nigel Cameron; Downers Grove: InterVarsity Press, 1993), 242.

87. Donald Macleod, "Systematic Theology," in *Dictionary of Scottish Church History and Theology*, 811.

88. Ibid. Dabney's lectures in systematic theology were originally published under the title *Syllabus and Notes of the Course of Systematic and Polemic Theology Taught in Union Theological Seminary, Virginia*, sixth ed. (Richmond: Presbyterian Committee of Publication, 1927); and frequently reprinted under the title *Lectures in Systematic Theology*.

John Dick's *Lectures* are quite representative of Scottish Calvinistic discussions of natural theology. He begins his opening lecture by making a distinction between natural and supernatural theology. "By natural theology, is understood that knowledge of God which the light of nature teaches, or which is acquired by our unassisted powers, by the exercise of reason, and the suggestions of conscience."[89] Supernatural theology, on the other hand, "is the system of religion which is contained in the Holy Scriptures: and it is called supernatural, because the knowledge of it is not derived from reason, but from divine revelation."[90] Natural theology, therefore, entails the contemplation of the world around us, as men and women are "led to infer the existence of an invisible Being by whom they were created, possessed of certain perfections, the signature of which are perceived upon his works," and therefore, "from this first principle" they deduce "other doctrines of religion, as that this God governs the world."[91] We not only learn that God exists, but that we owe him our worship, we know our souls are immortal, and we learn that we will stand before him in the judgment.[92]

Much of Dick's treatment of natural theology anticipates the contemporary debate over the nature and scope of apologetics. "There is a diversity of sentiment" on this subject, and indeed "it has been disputed, not only whether these are the only articles but also whether there is such a thing as natural theology; or, in other words, whether the system ... is discoverable by unassisted reason."[93] After asking the question of whether reason and revelation are both necessary, and concluding that they are, Dick defines reason as "the intellectual and moral faculties of man, exercised without any supernatural assistance in the investigation of religion."[94] Dick states that reason can be understood in two senses: (1) as we were created in our original state, and (2) as signifying "man in his present state, when he feels the effects of the fall in all his faculties, and both his mind and conscience are defiled. It is with reason in this sense alone that we have at present to do."[95] Therefore, Dick will

89. John Dick, *Lectures on Theology* (New York: Robert Carter & Brothers, 1852), 9.
90. Ibid.
91. Ibid.
92. Ibid.
93. Ibid.
94. Ibid., 15.
95. Ibid.

proceed to discuss the role of reason with the assumption that reason is "fallen and impaired."

As with Turretin, Dick affirms that "the first principle of religion is the existence of God. ... No doubt seems to be entertained that this fundamental truth is demonstrable by reason," as seen in the works of Clarke and Paley.[96] While "nature, it is acknowledged, cries aloud in all her works that there is a God," in fact, "there was not a nation upon earth but the Jews, in which the true God was adored."[97] Dick laments that "such are the achievements of reason with respect to the first principle of religion."[98] Unassisted and fallen reason has failed to point us to God as it should: to serve and worship him, nor did it give to the nations a universal standard of morality, nor did it give sufficient arguments for the immortality of the soul, even though such a notion was widely accepted.[99] Dick concludes:

> This induction of particulars will serve to prove the insufficiency of reason to acquire the knowledge of the principles of natural theology. Let no man presume to tell us that it is sufficient, till he can point out an instance, in which, without any assistance, it has discovered and established, by satisfactory arguments, the great truths of religion. ... We have now seen how defective reason is in what may be considered to be its proper province, natural theology. If we proceed to supernatural theology, we shall find, that here it is altogether useless. It cannot make a single discovery.[100]

Unassisted reason fails miserably. As Dick notes, "Although reason could demonstrate the existence of God, and his unity, it possesses no premises from which it could infer a plurality in his nature. It is a secret which he alone could disclose."[101] What role, if any then, is reason to occupy since it has failed so miserably?

According to Dick, it is the first office of fallen reason, therefore, to judge "the evidence of religion; and while thus employed, it not only

96. Ibid., 16. See Samuel Clarke, *The Works of Samuel Clarke*, 4 vols. Repr. ed. (New York: Garland, 1978); and William Paley, *Lectures on Natural Theology* (ed. F. Le Gros Clark; London: SPCK, 1902) and *Evidences of Christianity* (London: Faulder & Clarke, 1802).
97. Ibid., 17.
98. Ibid.
99. Ibid., 16–20.
100. Ibid., 20–21.
101. Ibid., 21.

collects proofs from observation and experience in favor of the doctrines of natural theology, but examines the grounds upon which any new doctrine is said to be a divine communication."[102] While fallen reason is sufficient to serve as a "judge of evidence" of religion, it also provides another important function. "The second office of reason is to examine the contents of revelation, to ascertain the sense of the words and phrases in which it is expressed," and to "trace the relation of its parts, and to draw out in regular order the system of doctrines and duties which it teaches."[103] Therefore reason functions "as a servant," since it must be exercised "with a view to obtain a distinct idea of the import of any communication which our Creator has condescended to make of his will." This must be the case because "if we had no more understanding than the irrational animals, we should be equally incapable as they of religion."[104]

Dick contends that this conception of reason "does not constitute it a judge of religion. It is not the doctrines of religion which we submit to its test, but the evidence. Let it canvass the evidence, and proceed to settle by the laws of criticism and common sense the genuine import of revelation; but here it should stop."[105] Thus reason clearly occupies a ministerial or instrumental function, rather than a magisterial one. Reason is a servant which enables us to apprehend, evaluate, and understand supernatural revelation, but it can do nothing more. It cannot determine the content of supernatural revelation. Unassisted reason can establish the existence of God, perhaps, but the continuous failure of reason to enable us to discover God's Triune essence, our duty to serve him, our immortality, and the certainty of a final judgment, means that natural theology is insufficient to lead us to a saving knowledge of God. Natural theology must be complemented by supernatural theology.

After demonstrating the insufficiency of reason and the necessity of supernatural revelation, Dick argues that revelation is given precisely because of our sin and infirmity. Unaided and fallen reason cannot lead us to God. Since "we have proved, however, that reason is not sufficient to discover the truths of natural religion; and, consequently, that revelation was not only desirable, but necessary, to deliver men from a state

102. Ibid., 22.
103. Ibid.
104. Ibid., 23.
105. Ibid.

of ignorance."[106] Therefore, a revealed religion is necessary, and in fact, "revelation is indisputably the sole origin of the religion we profess. Without it, we should have been profoundly ignorant of the Saviour."[107] Since this revelation is given to sinners in need of a Savior, "revelation demands faith; and pure faith is an act of the mind, by which it assents to certain facts, or propositions upon the authority of testimony, without having any other evidence of truth."[108] Here again we see the imprint of Thomas Reid.

After demonstrating the necessity of revelation and setting out the ministerial role of reason in evaluating the evidence for it, Dick now turns to a lengthy series of lectures upon the "evidences of Christianity." He gives the standard survey of such evidences, including evidence of the genuineness and authenticity of the Scriptures, the arguments from miracle and fulfilled prophecy, the success of the Gospels, internal evidences for the truth of Christianity, and then finally, Dick responds to objections raised against the Christian faith.[109] He concludes, "The evidence with which revelation is accompanied, is sufficient to satisfy a candid mind. It is not indeed irresistible, that is, so overpowering that every person to whom it is presented is necessarily convinced: but it affords a rational ground for belief."[110] While there are indeed formidable objections that can be raised by "infidels," declares Dick, "our judgment should be determined by the preponderance of the evidence. If the arguments for the conclusion are superior to the arguments against it, we do not act rationally, but absurdly, when we withhold our assent."[111] Christian evidences provide us with a rational basis for faith, as well as furnishing us with defensive arguments that have far greater evidential weight and value than do those arguments raised against Christianity.

It is vital to notice that there is no discussion of the classical proofs for the existence of God. In this conception, establishing a natural theology is insufficient and does little to deal with the real point of contention between faith and unbelief, God supernaturally revealing himself to us in the person of Jesus Christ as recorded in the Scriptures. Here, then, is where fallen reason assumes its necessary, though humble

106. Ibid., 29.
107. Ibid., 30.
108. Ibid., 32.
109. Ibid., 33–110.
110. Ibid., 98.
111. Ibid., 110.

duties, since it cannot determine the content of revelation, but must judge the evidence for supernatural religion. In addition, Dick notes, "If we succeed in establishing its divine origin, we virtually disprove all other revelations, because it is obvious, that contradictory systems cannot all proceed from a Being of whom truth is an essential attribute."[112] Evidentialism seeks to establish the rational basis for Christianity as the primary apologetic task. Reason has a defensive function as well, since the religion of infidels can be attacked and demonstrated to be false. This is virtually the same conception of the task and nature of apologetics as that of B. B. Warfield, though Warfield speaks of apologetics as theological prolegomena, rather than as natural theology.

John Dick is not the only influential Scottish theologian to place great stress upon Christian evidences. Thomas Chalmers (1780–1847), while heavily dependent upon Scottish Common Sense Realism, nevertheless rejected Thomas Reid's more libertine view of the will and affirmed what Helm calls a Calvinistic variety of natural theology.[113] In his work on natural theology, Chalmers rejects *a priori* arguments such as that of Clarke,[114] but affirms *a posteriori* arguments for God's existence appealing to Thomas Reid, Dugald Stewart, and Thomas Brown for epistemological support throughout.[115] In this regard, Chalmers adopts a more favorable view toward natural theology than does John Dick or the Princetonians. But like John Dick, Chalmers also spends a great deal of time focusing on Christian evidences, devoting two volumes to the subject primarily in response to Hume's attack upon the miraculous.[116] In his own theological system, *Institutes of Theology*, Chalmers sets out virtually the same conception. Natural theology establishes the existence of God, while Christian evidences are adduced to demonstrate that Christianity possesses a supernatural revelation from God.[117]

Using Common Sense conceptions of truth throughout his work on Christian evidences, Chalmers is especially concerned to demonstrate the truthfulness of the New Testament. "They had personal access to

112. Ibid., 34.
113. Helm, "Thomas Reid, Common Sense and Calvinism," 89.
114. Thomas Chalmers, *On Natural Theology* 2 vols. (New York: Robert Carter, 1845), 99–120.
115. Ibid., 121–61.
116. Thomas Chalmers, *On the Miraculous and Internal Evidences of the Christian Revelation and the Authority of its Records*, 2 vols. (New York: Robert Carter, 1845).
117. Thomas Chalmers, *Institutes of Theology* (Edinburgh: Thomas Constable & Co., 1856), 71–243.

the messengers; and the evidences of their veracity lay before them. They were the eye and ear witnesses of those facts, which occurred at the commencement of the Christian religion and upon which its credibility rests."[118] Since we are not personally privy to these events, we must ask the critical question: "What met with their observation must have been enough to satisfy them; but we live at a distance of 2000 years, and is there enough to satisfy us?"[119]

> In laying before the reader, then, the evidence for the truth of Christianity, we do not call his mind to any singular or unprecedented exercise of its faculties. We call him to pronounce upon the credibility of written documents, which profess to have been published at a certain age, and by certain authors. The inquiry involves in it no principle which is not appealed to every day questions of ordinary criticism. To sit in judgement on the credibility of a written document, is a frequent and familiar exercise of the understanding with literary men. It is fortunate for the human mind, when so interesting a question as its religious faith can be placed under the tribunal of such evidence as it is competent to pronounce upon.[120]

Here again, we can see the stress placed upon testimony and evidence so typical of the Scottish philosophy. The human mind, even as fallen, remains competent to judge the truthfulness of these matters. Chalmers, however, does not exercise the care that John Dick had taken to develop both the powers and define the limits of fallen human reason. Yet, once this is established to his own satisfaction, Chalmers moves on to survey the standard catalog of Christian evidences, including a defense of miracles, a treatment of the value of historic evidences, the importance of eyewitness testimony, the argument from fulfilled prophecy, and then a harmonization of problem passages and apparent discrepancies.

Another important figure in the Scottish evidentialist tradition is William Cunningham (1805–61). Cunningham, a noted Free Church theologian and historian, replaced Thomas Chalmers as Principal of New College, Edinburgh, in 1847.[121] Cunningham's *Theological Lectures,*

118. Chalmers, *On the Miraculous and Internal Evidences of the Christian Revelation*, 151.
119. Ibid.
120. Ibid., 153.
121. Donald Macleod, "Cunningham, William," in *Dictionary of Scottish Church History & Theology*, 229.

published posthumously, were based upon lectures given while he served as the first professor of theology of the Free Church.

William Cunningham understood Christian evidences to be part of the first division of theology, exegetical theology. The reason Christian evidences were treated as a subset of exegetical theology, is based upon Cunningham's estimation of their importance. "The evidence that the Bible contains a revelation of God to man, or what are commonly called the evidences of Christianity," is an important part of the first division.[122] As Cunningham notes, it was commonplace to begin the treatment of the evidences for Christianity with a lecture on natural theology, which Cunningham defines as "the information that may be obtained concerning God from the natural exercise of our own powers upon ourselves and upon the objects around us."[123] Cunningham, however, does not feel the need to go into much detail on the matter because, as he states, "We could add nothing of value to what is contained in Dr. Chalmers' two volumes on Natural Theology."[124] The key issue here as Cunningham sees it is, "Can men, by the exercise of their natural faculties upon themselves, and upon other objects around them, ascertain and prove the existence of an intelligent First Cause of all things; and if so, what is the amount of the information which *in this way* may be acquired concerning him?"[125] Cunningham agrees with Dick's assertion that indeed, the existence of an all powerful Being, to whom all men and women owe obedience, can certainly be established. Cunningham notes, "The only thing practically important, so far as natural theology is concerned, is that we be able *to prove* from reason against any man who may dispute it, that there is an intelligent First Cause, who has created and governs all things."[126]

In Cunningham's next lecture, "The Insufficiency of Natural Theology," he contends that "the proof of this is not necessary as a preliminary to establishing the truth of Christianity." Thus, it is possible to demonstrate the truthfulness of Christianity solely based upon the evidences for special revelation. Indeed, "we can prove the truth of Christianity and the divine authority of the sacred Scriptures, without

122. William Cunningham, *Theological Lectures* (New York: Robert Carter & Brothers, 1878), 27.
123. Ibid., 104.
124. Ibid., 105.
125. Ibid. The italics are in the original.
126. Ibid., 105–06. Cunningham notes throughout this section that he is endeavoring to follow the general outline on this subject as set out in Turretin's *Institutio*.

either assuming or establishing the insufficiency of reason or the necessity of revelation."[127] Adopting an approach that is remarkably similar to that which Warfield himself would later advocate, Cunningham contends that "in arguing with infidels, we might supersede the discussion of this point, and, proceed at once to establish the truth of the Christian religion."[128] In other words, why labor to prove the existence of God, when this still does not deal with the question of the truthfulness of special revelation, the usual point of contention with unbelievers? Merely establishing the existence of God does not deal with the critical issue: the failure of natural theology to give a redemptive knowledge of God. In fact, the insufficiency of reason is easy to demonstrate:

> The insufficiency of reason and the necessity of revelation can be, and have been, proved from principles of reason; and the process of proving this leads to some interesting and useful speculations. The direct and proper proof from reason of the insufficiency of reason and the necessity of revelation, lies mainly in the establishment of these two positions—First, it can be proved from the light of nature and the testimony of conscience, that all men have sinned or broken God's laws; Second, it can *not* be proved from reason or the light of nature that men who have sinned against God's laws will, even upon repentance and amendment, escape punishment for their sins.[129]

Therefore Cunningham notes, "The proper ground or basis of natural theology is just the works of creation and providence,"[130] but the establishment of the truth of the Christian religion depends upon special revelation.

Sounding much like John Dick and Thomas Chalmers before him, Cunningham adopts wholesale the Scottish Common Sense conception of truth: "The evidence of sense, the evidence of consciousness, and the evidence of testimony, are recognised by all sane men as valid and certain sources of knowledge, as conveying to us information which it is our duty to receive and rest upon."[131] Natural theology is insufficient because:

127. Ibid., 115.
128. Ibid.
129. Ibid.
130. Ibid., 121.
131. Ibid.

> The truths thus discovered and established constitute what is commonly called natural theology, and the truths that are thus known, or that may be known, concerning God, are quite sufficient at least to render inexcusable those who, without any other opportunities of knowing him, do not worship and serve the true God who made heaven and earth, though they are not sufficient to guide men to salvation.[132]

While we may be able to prove the existence of God, all that this accomplishes is that it renders all without excuse. Natural theology cannot give us redemptive knowledge of God; thus natural theology alone is insufficient, even in apologetic contexts.

Next, Cunningham proceeds to discuss the relationship between natural theology and Christian evidences. "If Christianity be true, then we have in the Bible all the information which the light of nature has ever been supposed to afford us."[133] Here the limits of human reason are most clearly seen. "If the Scripture be a divine revelation, it contains information which is at least as authentic and much more full and complete, than even the clearest deductions of reason could furnish."[134] The need for additional qualifications arise at this point because when we ask the two critical questions—"Did this revelation proceed from *God*? Does the information thus conveyed to us rest upon *God's* authority?"[135]—we admit that more is involved than appears at first glance.

These questions, notes Cunningham, "plainly seem to imply that we know something about God," and that this information can be communicated from him to us through the agency of men. But these agents from God "could and did expect their claims to be believed only when they produced evidence of the truth of this position."[136] Thus, Cunningham notes, this implies that men and women must already know something of God for this to be intelligible to them. Here, then, is where we see most clearly that natural theology provides the basis for supernatural revelation.

> The proper direct evidences of a supernatural revelation, the proper proofs of a claim which a man may put forth to be received

132. Ibid., 121–22.
133. Ibid., 125.
134. Ibid.
135. Ibid.
136. Ibid., 125–26.

> as a messenger from God, commissioned to make known his will on miracles—miracles of knowledge and power—or prophecies, and what we more commonly call miracles, and not only the statement of the position to be proved, but the attempt to deduce from the miracles supposed or alleged to have been performed, an argument in support of it, *i.e.* an argument in support of the divine commission of the person by, or in connection with whom the miracles have been wrought, assume or imply that something is clearly known about God.[137]

Miracles might give us some evidence of some supreme power or supreme being, but unless there is "an admission of the fundamental principles of natural theology," which "must be in some way produced, and must exist and be in operation," men will never believe that those who perform the miracles have a "divine commission."[138] Thus, yet again we move from the insufficiency of natural theology to Christian evidences.

The following qualification must be carefully drawn. On the one hand "we must here observe that there is a great difference between asserting the necessity of an acquaintance with the fundamental principles of natural theology in making out the evidence of Christianity," and the other "asserting the right of natural theology to sit in judgement upon the *doctrines of Christianity*."[139] There are, therefore, two critical points connected with this conception of natural theology. First, though natural theology clearly demonstrates that all men and women are sinners in desperate need of redemption, it cannot tell us "whether or not, and upon what terms, sin will be forgiven."[140] Second, natural theology lays "a firm basis for the proof from miracles and otherwise, in support of a supernatural revelation."[141] Once we have established these two critical points, we can then "deduce the probability, as well as the desirableness, of a revelation," and we can show "that it is in the highest degree probable that God should have supernaturally committed to men some further information concerning himself ... than men usually have derived, or probably could derive from the unassisted use of their natural faculties."[142] Therefore, natural theology is necessary, though insufficient,

137. Ibid., 126.
138. Ibid., 127–28.
139. Ibid., 128.
140. Ibid., 129–30.
141. Ibid.
142. Ibid., 130.

and must be supplemented by special revelation, which is confirmed by Christian evidences.

When Cunningham moves on to treat Christian evidences, he makes it quite clear that the Scriptures themselves exhort all Christians to be able to give an answer for the hope that they have (1 Peter 3:15), and that ministers especially should have a firm grasp of Christian evidences. Cunningham recommends Chalmers' *On the Miraculous and Internal Evidences of the Christian Revelation, and the Authority of its Records* as "the fullest and best book on Christian evidence in the English Language."[143] The critical question with which these Christian evidences must deal is: "Were the claims of Jesus Christ and of his apostles to be received as divine messengers, specifically commissioned by God, and authorized to speak in his name, valid, or were they not?"[144] Cunningham can argue that the evidence for the truth of Christianity is overwhelming and because the case is so strong, non-Christians assume the burden of proof to prove the claims of Christ to be false.[145] Following his illustrious predecessors, Cunningham proceeds to argue for miracles (against Hume), evidence for the resurrection of Christ, fulfilled prophecy, and internal and external evidences for the truth of Christianity.[146]

Cunningham also has an important contribution to make regarding the role of the Holy Spirit in the process of confirming the truth of Holy Scripture. The Free Church theologian notes that since several writers had argued that because we can use evidences to prove to non-Christians that the Bible is indeed the Word of God, "some Popish writers have grasped at the opportunity thus afforded them of taking up the infidel cause," and have concluded therefore that the Scriptures "cannot form the basis or ground of any firm or certain persuasion."[147] In this discussion, Cunningham clearly anticipates many of the modern objections raised against the evidentialist position, and frames the question accordingly:

> The divine origin and authority of the Scriptures would therefore be said to rest upon probable evidence, not that the evidence is not sufficient to prove it, and to impose upon men without any special divine interposition an obligation to receive and act upon it as a

143. Ibid., 140.
144. Ibid., 142.
145. Ibid., 142–48.
146. Lectures XII-XXII.
147. Ibid., 322.

> truth or reality, but merely that it is not fitted of itself to produce that peculiarly full persuasion and commanding assurance which is the result of demonstration. And experience very plainly indicates that when men have only that faith and conviction of the divine origin and authority of the Bible which is just the result of the ordinary exercise of our faculties upon the rational arguments by which, as a matter of fact it is established, their persuasion of its infallible truth and divine authority does not usually seem to be very powerful and efficacious, or to produce the practical results which, in right reason, might be expected from it.[148]

If evidence is only probable in nature, how then do we arrive—as the Westminster Confession states—at the "full persuasion and assurance of the infallible truth, and divine authority thereof (I.v)"? How can probable evidence be the basis for the certainty of faith?

As stated in the Confession, Cunningham argues that this full persuasion "is the inward work of the Holy Spirit." What the Holy Spirit does is not create new evidence in which faith may be grounded, but bear witness to existing evidence, in this case the truth of Holy Scripture and the events recorded in it. "The Holy Spirit may, and does, seal this evidence and the truth it establishes upon men's understandings and hearts, so as to give them a fuller persuasion and assurance of the truth than they would otherwise possess or attain to."[149] While the evidence is objective, and therefore, technically only probably true (though it may indeed be of very high probability), Cunningham notes that only the Holy Spirit can give us this full assurance and "it is an inward work of His in our hearts, and is described as His bearing witness,"[150] that moves us from assent to the truth of the event to conviction or trust in the Savior to whom the evidences bear witness. This occurs through the Spirit's bearing witness to the objective Word itself. Thus Cunningham can assert, "There is no reason why we should regard it as implying that by a distinct intimation or explicit assertion He directly or immediately tells or assures any believer that the Scriptures are the Word of God."[151] As Cunningham sees it, God works through means, and in this case, the

148. Ibid., 326.
149. Ibid.
150. Ibid., 328.
151. Cunningham, *Theological Lectures*, 328.

means that the Holy Spirit uses is the objective evidence for the Word of God. This is also very similar to the view taken by B. B. Warfield.

While William Cunningham's co-laborer, Free Church theologian James Buchanan (1804–1870) also held similar views on apologetic methodology;[152] it is their successor, James MacGregor (1830–1894), who gives us the most interesting clue as to the source of Warfield's optimistic comments regarding Christianity "reasoning its way to dominion." MacGregor, who succeeded Buchanan as professor of systematic theology at New College, produced a three-volume work on apologetics,[153] which had been praised by Warfield on several occasions. In a review of two of the volumes of MacGregor's trilogy, Warfield spoke of MacGregor as having "great ability" and knowledge in the field, and that his work embodies "a substantial contribution to the apologetic literature of our time."[154] It is important to recall that in his essay "The Right of Systematic Theology," Warfield describes MacGregor's *The Apology for the Christian Religion*, an "eloquent book" and very approvingly quotes from the following comments in the opening page of that volume:[155]

> Christianity is *the* apologetic religion. No other religion has ever seriously set itself to the endeavor to subdue a hostile world by

152. As N. R. Needham notes, "Buchanan rejected the idea that humanity had any direct intuitive knowledge of God, arguing that theistic belief was grounded in the perception of phenomenal evidence. He admitted that the process from evidential perception to belief could be 'intuitional and spontaneous,' but held it a proper task of the apologist to press home on men 'the natural evidences for the being and perfections of God.' He also observed that apologetics normally had more to do with exposing the fallacies of unbelievers than with positively proving the truth." See N. R. Needham, "Buchanan, James," in *Dictionary of Scottish Church History & Theology* (Downers Grove: InterVarsity Press, 1993), 108. Buchanan's apologetics efforts include: *Analogy: A Guide to Truth and an Aid to Faith* (Edinburgh: T&T Clark, 1867); and *Faith in God and Modern Atheism Compared*, 2 vols. (Edinburgh: James Buchanan Jr., 1855).

153. James MacGregor, *The Apology for the Christian Religion* (Edinburgh: T&T Clark, 1891); *The Revelation of the Record* (Edinburgh: T&T Clark, 1893), and *Studies in the History of Christian Apologetics* (Edinburgh: T&T Clark, 1894). In these volumes, MacGregor sets out external evidence for the Christian faith (*The Apology for the Christian Religion*), *Revelation and the Record* is concerned with a defense of Christian supernaturalism, and *Studies in the History of Apologetics* is devoted to developing the history of apologetics in the New Testament and the first two centuries of the Christian church.

154. See B. B. Warfield, "Review of James MacGregor's *Revelation and the Record*, and *Studies in the History of Christian Apologetics*," in *The Presbyterian and Reformed Review*, vol. VIII (1897), 772–73.

155. Warfield, "The Right of Systematic Theology," 277.

> apology (from *logos*, "reason," or "reason," *ratio* vel *oratio*, 1 Pet. iii.15), to *reason* the sinful world out of worldliness into godliness. The aspect of the new religion thus appearing toward the freedom of the human soul, in addressing itself to the reason in order to reach the man in conscience and his heart, struck intelligent heathens as a presumptive evidence of truth and divinity, since reason is "the door" (John x. 1, etc.)—the *lawful* way of seeking to win and to control the manhood.[156]

While there is no way to know for sure if James MacGregor's words here serve as the source for Warfield's remark that "Christianity is to reason its way to dominion" in the forward to Francis Beattie's *Apologetics*, there is little doubt that Warfield is echoing MacGregor.[157]

This is compelling evidence that Warfield is deeply indebted to the Scottish evidentialist tradition—evidence that is not considered by his contemporary critics, several of whom have labeled him Arminian, Thomistic, or Romanist. While the connection between Warfield and MacGregor, once established, certainly does not demonstrate Warfield's evidentialism to be *the* biblical position to the exclusion of all others, it does raise additional doubts about the validity of the charge of Romanism or Arminianism (Van Til, Vander Stelt), since, if the Free Church theologians are known for anything, it is their militant opposition to Romanism and Arminianism! It also raises questions about charges of innovation (Noll) and an uncritical capitulation to the rationalism of the Scottish Enlightenment, since Princeton clearly stands within a long-standing Reformed tradition, in this case, that of the Scottish Presbyterians. Warfield's comments about reason are not

---

156. James MacGregor, *The Apology of the Christian Religion*, 9.

157. It is also interesting to note that Christoph Ernest Luthardt, under whom Warfield pursued doctoral studies, also stressed this same optimistic notion, namely that Christianity could conquer unbelief in an intellectual sense. Luthardt argued, "The progress of Christianity in history has been a triumphant one. But the progress of Christianity is that of Jesus Christ. When we say Christianity, we do in effect say Jesus Christ, for everything depends upon Him. And what Christianity means is to bow before Christ and honour Him as the only and everlasting Saviour of us all. Christianity, however, is not merely a power possessing external sovereignty, but a power exercising an inward and *spiritual authority*. Not merely the external religions, the various nations, but the entire intellectual life of mankind has been conquered and renewed thereby. With Christianity a new era dawned upon the human mind, and the whole moral and social life of our race." See Christoph Ernest Luthardt, *Apologetic Lectures on the Fundamental Truths of Christianity*, 7th ed. (trans. Sophia Taylor; Edinburgh: T&T Clark, 1909), 275–76.

drawn from Enlightenment philosophers (as Marsden contends), but from a Scottish defender of the Westminster Confession. And as David B. Calhoun points out:

> The Princetonians never allowed Scottish Common Sense Philosophy to stand by itself or to determine their theological outlook. Far more important than their philosophical views were their biblical the confessional commitments. They made their philosophy serve their theology, and not the other way around.[158]

The Scottish connection may also be evident in that Warfield himself is not interested in natural theology and theistic proofs, since Warfield is almost exclusively interested in Christian evidences, specifically the evidence for the resurrection of Christ. Following the same basic approach that both Archibald Alexander and John Dick had set forth, Warfield spends virtually all of his apologetic energies upon the defense of special or supernatural revelation (what has been treated in the Scottish tradition under the heading "Christian Evidences"), and all but ignores classical theistic argumentation, usually associated with natural theology. This mutual dependence by both the Scottish Presbyterians and the Princeton tradition upon Thomas Reid's stress on the objectivity of factual evidence as given us in the New Testament, leads to virtually identical apologetic conceptions in the efforts of Princeton and New College, Edinburgh. Therefore, any discussion of the historical context of the Princeton Apologetic is impoverished to the degree to which this important factor is overlooked.

APOLOGETIC FORERUNNERS

A third area in which a response needs to be made to Warfield's recent interpreters, is to investigate the relationship between the so-called ministerial or instrumental use of reason and special revelation, as understood in the historic Reformed tradition, specifically the Reformed scholastics, such as Francis Turretin. Before proceeding further however, it is necessary to point out that it is much more likely that Warfield develops his convictions in this area while standing squarely within the broader Reformed tradition—specifically the Scottish evidentialist conception of the insufficiency of natural theology and the stress

158. David B. Calhoun, *Princeton Seminary: The Majestic Testimony, 1869–1929* (Carlisle: Banner of Truth Trust, 1996), 414.

upon Christian evidences—than contemporary critics such as Noll and Marsden acknowledge. Since Warfield's own statements about Christianity reasoning its way to dominion are likely drawn from Scottish Presbyterian apologist James MacGregor, Warfield's own understanding of the relationship between faith and reason should be interpreted in the light of the broader Reformed understanding, rather than interpreting his comments about reason solely through the lens of the American intellectual history and the possible influence of Scottish Common Sense Reason and the Enlightenment upon that tradition. While it is certainly essential to see Warfield and Old Princeton within their historical contexts, there is an unfortunate tendency to overlook the fact that Warfield's conception of these issues is hardly novel. Instead he reflects a long-standing and widely accepted viewpoint within the Reformed tradition itself. Thus the key to understanding and interpreting Warfield on this point is through the prior formulation of the Reformed tradition, and not in light of the supposed rationalism of the Scottish Enlightenment.

It also needs to be asserted that while Warfield is most often criticized for his overly optimistic comments regarding fallen reason, he was not the only Princetonian to arrive at similar conclusions. Warfield's fellow Princeton faculty members, W. Brenton Greene,[159] C. W. Hodge,[160] and Geerhardus Vos[161] all reflect this long-standing preference for Christian evidences in light of the insufficiency of natural theology. Since Christianity is a religion of facts, and since it is the task of fallen reason to make these facts intelligible to us, as well as to marshal them against those who would reject the Christian truth claim, the role and limits of reason inevitably occupy an important place in the discussion.

As Richard A. Muller points out, the "Reformed orthodox go to some length to emphasize the biblical foundations of their claims concerning

159. W. Brenton Greene, "The Function of the Reason in Christianity," in *The Presbyterian and Reformed Review*, vol. VI (1895), 481–501. See the critical treatment of Greene's apologetic in particular and Old Princeton in general in Tim McConnel, "The Old Princeton Apologetics: Common Sense or Reformed?" in *Journal of the Evangelical Theological Society*, vol. 46, no. 4 (December 2003), 647–72.

160. C. W. Hodge, "Fact and Theory," in *A Dictionary of Christ and the Gospels*, vol. 1 (ed. James Hastings; Edinburgh: T&T Clark, 1906–08), 562–67.

161. Geerhardus Vos, "Christian Faith and the Truthfulness of Bible History," in *The Princeton Theological Review*, no. 3 (July 1906), 289–305.

the instrumental use of reason."[162] As generally understood, reason served five distinct functions:

> In the first place, reason can be used to make clear points in divine revelation, as was the case when Christ demanded of his disciples, "Have you understood all that has been said to you?" They responded, "yea" (Matt. 13:15). Second, reason must be used in discussion and argument with others, as when the Bereans compared the words of Paul with Scripture (Acts 17:11). Next, reason is necessary in the work of explication, even as Ezra and Nehemiah taught the people reasonably (Neh. 8:9). Fourth, in order to discern falsehood it was necessary to "explore the things that differ" (Phil 1:10). Finally, reason is useful to vindicate the truth from objections, as Paul himself does in the ninth chapter of Romans.[163]

Thus concludes Muller, while "fallen reason cannot be the *principium fidei* it is also clear that faith can occur only in rational creatures and that even in Scripture, rational process—both the subjective capacity and the objective light according to which concepts are formed—is integral to the life of faith."[164]

The influence of Francis Turretin upon the Princeton tradition is well documented.[165] In his *Institutio*, Turretin makes a distinction between natural and supernatural theology,[166] and argues that from natural theology, first principles of knowledge (both theoretical and practical) are deduced, and that natural theology is partly innate and acquired.[167] But while the "institution of religions in the world most clearly proves

162. Richard A. Muller, *Post-Reformation Reformed Dogmatics, Vol. 1: Prolegomena to Theology* (Grand Rapids: Baker Book House, 1987), 243.
163. Ibid.
164. Ibid.
165. Charles Eugene Edwards, "Turretin's 'Theology' " in *The Princeton Theological Review*, vol. XXVI (1928), 142–49; Timothy Phillips, *Francis Turretin's Idea of Theology and its Bearing Upon Doctrine of Scripture* (Ph.D. diss., Vanderbilt University, 1986), 9. Noll's comment, "It is possible to rate Turretin too highly as theological guide for the Princetonians ... [since] Warfield hardly refers to the Genevan at all," seems to me an overstatement. See Mark Noll, *The Princeton Theology*, 29–30. Noll admits that Charles Hodge and A. A. Hodge both patterned their own system after that of Turretin. While Warfield may not often refer to Turretin directly, as we will see, Warfield stands directly in the line of the Hodges and the Scottish evidentialists, both of whom self-consciously follow Turretin's formulations on this precise point.
166. Francis Turretin, *Institutio Theologiae Elencticae* (New York: Robert Carter, 1847), I,.ii.7.
167. Ibid., I.iii.2-4.

natural theology," nevertheless, when the question arises, "Is it by itself sufficient for salvation, and was the design of God in that revelation the salvation of those whom it is made? This we deny."[168] The revelation of God in nature is sufficient to show all men and women that God exists, but because of the effects of sin upon fallen humanity, this knowledge instead renders us without excuse.[169]

Turretin emphatically denies that human reason is "the principle and rule by which the doctrines of the Christian religion and theology" are to be measured.[170] Turretin puts the matter as follows:

> The question is not whether reason is the instrument by which or the medium through which we can be drawn to faith. For we acknowledge that reason can be both: the former indeed always and everywhere; the latter with regard to presupposed articles. Rather the question is whether the first principles from which the doctrines of faith are proved; or the foundation upon which they are built, so that we must hold to be false in things of faith what the natural light or human reason cannot comprehend. This we deny.[171]

Turretin says, "Faith is not referred ultimately to reason, so that I ought to believe because I so understand and comprehend; but to the word because God so speaks in the Scriptures," and because "the Holy Spirit directs us to the word alone."[172] Therefore, reason cannot be "the rule of religion." In this regard, Muller notes, "The weight of evidence shows Turretin to be neither a rationalist [n]or a fideist."[173]

What role, then, does reason serve? Here Turretin makes a distinction between reason as an instrument of faith and as a foundation for faith. Reason cannot in any sense be the foundation for faith (since this depends upon mysteries that reason cannot comprehend), but reason is the "instrument which the believer uses" and its office is such that "believers may work comfortably with and by it, as an instrument."[174]

---

168. Turretin, *Institutio Theologiae Elencticae*, I.iii.9–iv.4. The translation is Geiger's.
169. Ibid., I.iv.8.
170. Ibid., I.viii.1.
171. Ibid., I.viii.4.
172. Ibid., I.viii.5.
173. Richard A. Muller, "Scholasticism Protestant and Catholic: Francis Turretin on the Object and Principles of Theology," in *Church History*, vol. 55, no. 1 (March 1986), 203.
174. Turretin, *Institutio Theologiae Elencticae*, I.viii.7.

> In matters of faith reason stands not only in relation of an instrument by which, but also sometimes from a means and argument from which the theologian argues. ... Hence the same conclusion may be of faith (inasmuch as it is demonstrated by reason). Yet we must not from this infer that reason is the principle and rule by which doctrines may be measured.[175]

Turretin counsels us to avoid the two extremes of those who sin by exalting reason, regarding it as the rule of faith (i.e., the Socinians), and those who "attribute little or nothing to it."[176] The Genevan concludes that "although the human understanding is very dark, yet there still remains in some rays of natural light and certain first principles, the truth of which is unquestionable." Turretin also points out that "these first principles are true not only in nature, but also in grace and mysteries of faith. Faith, so far from destroying, on the contrary borrows them from reason and uses them to strengthen its own doctrines."[177] Therefore, "although reason and faith are of different classes (the one natural, the other supernatural), they are not however opposed, but hold a certain relation and are subordinate to each other." This means that "reason is perfected by faith and faith supposes reason, upon which are found the mysteries of grace."[178]

In Turretin's conception then, reason occupies an instrumental function, and even though corrupt and fallen, serves a role in apprehending and understanding revelation. Turretin argues that reason also serves to judge contradiction and falsehood, citing the Lutheran conception of ubiquity.[179] It is the Scriptures that exhort us to make such judgments and "the darkness of the human intellect does not hinder sound reason from judging of the truth of connections and contradictions."[180] As we have seen, this is virtually the same conception of reason as that of the Scottish evidentialists (especially John Dick), who self-consciously followed Turretin. This is largely the view held by B. B. Warfield, who stands firmly within the tradition of the Reformed scholastics.

175. Ibid., I.viii.13.
176. Ibid., I.ix.1.
177. Ibid., I.xi.5.
178. Ibid.
179. Ibid., I.x.1–2.
180. Ibid., I.x.8.

FAITH, REASON, AND THE HOLY SPIRIT

In the forward to fellow Presbyterian Francis Beattie's book *Apologetics: or the Rational Vindication of Christianity*, Warfield ironically, if not prophetically, anticipated much of the criticism that would be leveled at him by his theological descendants. Warfield's remarks about reason in this essay caused his critics to reach their negative assessment about Warfield's apologetic. A brief evaluation of Warfield's essay will determine many of Warfield's own views on these matters.

Lamenting the twin enemies of rationalism and mysticism, Warfield writes:

> The mystical tendency is showing itself in our day most markedly in a wide-spread inclination to decline Apologetics in favor of the so-called *testimonium Spiritus Sancti*. The convictions of the Christian man we are told, are not the product of reasons addressed to the intellect, but are the immediate creation of the Holy Spirit in his heart. Therefore, it is intimated, we can not only do very well without these reasons, but it is something very like sacrilege to attend to them. Apologetics, accordingly, is not merely useless, but may even become noxious, because tending to substitute a barren intellectualism for a vital faith.[181]

Ironically, many of these exact charges have now been leveled against Warfield himself.

Quickly dismissing the rationalists, since what they need is "not less Apologetics but more Apologetics,"[182] Warfield indeed seems quite perplexed about the role of apologetics proposed in the *Encyclopedia of Sacred Theology*, published by Abraham Kuyper. First, Warfield is concerned that Kuyper has adopted a mystical conception of apologetics, which in effect, results in the practical depreciation of apologetics altogether. Second, Warfield is concerned that Kuyper's understanding of theological encyclopedia is unduly confused, and may in fact amount to a departure from historic Reformed practice.

Warfield is distressed to hear the mystical conception of apologetics on "the lips of the heroes of faith," like Kuyper, "who depreciate Apologetics because they felt no need of 'reasons' to ground faith which

181. B. B. Warfield, "Introduction to Francis R. Beattie's *Apologetics*," 94.
182. Ibid.

they are sure they have received immediately from God."[183] As we have seen, the necessity of grounding the Christian faith in the evidence for special revelation, because the doctrines of Christianity are necessarily connected to the facts of revelation, is the position of much of the historic Reformed tradition. This means that Kuyper, following the mystical approach, is now identified with those who declare, "Apologetics ... will never make a Christian. Christians are made by the creative Spirit alone. And when God Almighty has implanted faith in the heart, we shall not require to seek 'reasons' to ground our conviction of the truth of the Christian religion."[184] Warfield states that this is unfortunately the union of belief and unbelief to "disparage the defenses of the Christian religion."[185] As Warfield sees it, Kuyper has been unwittingly seduced by Kant and the Enlightenment.

Second, Warfield is troubled by the fact that Abraham Kuyper demonstrates this newfound distrust of the traditional role for apologetics, since Kuyper has hidden apologetics away as "a subdivision of a subdivision," which "concerns itself only with the distinct philosophical assault on Christianity."[186] What concerns Warfield the most in this regard is that Kuyper's distrust of apologetics has led him into a self-contradictory conception of the ground of the Christian faith. Warfield concludes that in Kuyper's scheme, "something is lacking at the beginning." After placing apologetics as a subdivision of a subdivision, Kuyper also argues that "the subject of theology is the human consciousness; that in this consciousness there is implanted a *sensus divinitatis*, a *semen religionis*."[187] Thus, Kuyper has left us with a "very considerable—though certainly not a complete apologetic, which must precede and prepare the way for the 'Bibliological Group' of theological departments."[188] Warfield points out that if Kuyper argues for the "existence of a *sensus divinitatis* in man capable of producing a natural theology independently of special revelation," and then argues for "the reality of a supernatural revelation in deed and word; and as well, the reality of a supernatural preparation of the heart to receive it; before we study theology at all," has he not

183. Ibid., 95. Warfield makes a similar charge against Herman Bavinck, that he too "is a shining ornament to estimate the value of Apologetics somewhat lightly." See Warfield, "Review of Herman Bavinck's *De Zekerheid des Geloofs*," 114.

184. Ibid.

185. Ibid.

186. Ibid., 96.

187. Ibid.

188. Ibid., 97.

given an outline of the task and duties of apologetics as classically understood? Clearly then, Warfield sees Kuyper's scheme as confusing and novel, and he notes accordingly, "We cannot think it an improvement upon the ordinary *schema*."[189]

At this point, Warfield's exasperation reaches its zenith. "It is a standing matter of surprise to us that the brilliant school of Christian thinkers, on whose attitude toward Apologetics we have been animadverting, should be tempted to make little of Apologetics."[190] Since Warfield finds Kuyper's treatment of sin and regeneration in relation to science to be a "beautiful exposition," Warfield cannot understand why Kuyper does not "magnify, instead of minifying, the value of Apologetics."[191] Perhaps it is because Kuyper insists upon absolutizing "the contrast between 'the two kinds of science'—that which is the product of the thought of sinful man in his state of nature, and that which is the product of man under the regenerating grace of God."[192] While Warfield fully agrees with Kuyper that in one sense there indeed are two kinds of men, regenerate and unregenerate, what concerns Warfield is Kuyper's total absolutization of this since:

> The difference between the two is, after all, not accurately described as a difference in kind. ... Sin has not destroyed or altered in its essential nature any one of man's faculties, although—since it corrupts *homo totus*—it has affected the operations of them all. The depraved man neither thinks, nor feels, nor wills as he ought; and the products of his action as a scientific thinker cannot possibly escape the influence of this everywhere operative power.[193]

It is not Kuyper's belief that sin colors all aspects of life and knowing that Warfield protests. What Warfield rejects is Kuyper's absolutizing of the difference between Christian and non-Christians. For one thing, the regenerate man remains a sinner even after conversion, and "no new faculties have been inserted in him by regeneration; and the old faculties, common to man in all his states, have been in some measure restored to their proper functioning." Certainly the Christian and the non-Christian have different presuppositions, but to argue there are

189. Ibid.
190. Ibid., 100.
191. Ibid.
192. Ibid.
193. Ibid.

"two kinds of people, hence two kinds of science," is to draw an improper conclusion. For Warfield, the difference between the two is quantitative, not qualitative. The real difference wrought by palingenesis (new birth) should not lead us to conclude that there are really two kinds of science, a Christian science and an unregenerate science.

Thus, Warfield can conclude in this regard that the Christian, though regenerate, "does not produce a 'science' differing in kind from that produced by sinful man. ... Sinful and sinless men are, after all both men; and being both men, are fundamentally alike and know fundamentally alike."[194] Those, such as Marsden, who have observed that Warfield was perplexed by Kuyper's comment in this regard are absolutely correct. Warfield saw Kuyper's conception of the whole theological encyclopedia as confused, and therefore problematic from the outset. Warfield also thought Kuyper too innovative at this particular point, and even went so far as to note that his otherwise esteemed Dutch colleague had wedded himself too deeply with unbelief. Warfield disagreed with Kuyper's conception of an epistemological dualism drawn between the regenerate and unregenerate. And he believed that while ideally there would be one science, he also noted that any perfect science is found only in the divine mind. Fallen humanity can never attain this.[195] Because science operates on a continuum, however, Warfield states, "It is the better science that ever in the end wins the victory; and palingenetic science is the better science, and to it belongs the victory. How shall it win the victory if it declines the conflict?"[196] Here then lies the source of Warfield's perplexity, for Kuyper declines the conflict altogether. How can Christianity conquer unbelief if it refuses the fight, especially when it has all of the advantages on its side?

George Marsden certainly overstates matters when he claims that it is Kuyper who writes "from a traditional point of view,"[197] implying that Warfield is the innovator. Since Warfield writes from within a long-standing Reformed evidentialist tradition, there is really more of a question as to the degree of Kuyper's innovation, not Warfield's. By not taking due notice of the context of Warfield's review of Kuyper's theological prolegomena—the Reformed debate over natural theology and the proper structure of theological system—Marsden improperly

194. Ibid., 101.
195. Ibid., 102.
196. Ibid., 103.
197. Marsden, *The Soul of the American University*, 214.

concludes that Warfield's dismay is merely indicative of those who held "a combination of Enlightenment heritage and millennial expectation, anticipating the unification of the race on the basis of the triumph of a fully rational science,"[198] in contrast to those who hold to the Reformed understanding of the noetic effects of sin and regeneration. This is a false dichotomy. While there may be a legitimate question as to the source of Warfield's optimism in this regard, perhaps related to his postmillennial optimism, Warfield's criticism of Kuyper comes from the perspective of Reformed scholasticism and Scottish evidentialism, not Scottish rationalism.[199]

At no point in Warfield's discussion does he *ever* assert that reason serves as a kind of *principium of faith*. Warfield's comments about reason take place within the context of the in-house debate over natural theology, and faithfully follows that tradition. It must be noted that Warfield is responding to what he believes to be Kuyper's confusion on these matters. Therefore, it is quite misleading that many recent interpreters of the Princeton tradition take Warfield's remarks that "it is the distinction of Christianity that it has come into the world clothed with the mission to *reason* its way to dominion," and that "Christianity makes its appeal to right reason,"[200] as though this is all that Warfield has to say on the subject, or that his comments here are characteristic of his apologetic. The charges that Warfield is an innovator of sorts, or that he has somehow unwittingly capitulated to Enlightenment rationalism, or even worse, that he has somehow adopted an Arminian or Romanist scheme are unsupported *ad hominem* arguments.

Warfield writes in this regard:

> We are not absurdly arguing that Apologetics has in itself the power to make a man a Christian or to conquer the world to Christ. Only the Spirit of Life can communicate life to a dead soul, or can

198. Ibid., 215. It is important to note that in his treatment of this in *Fundamentalism and American Culture* (115), Marsden notes that much of the difference between Warfield, Bavinck, and Kuyper is related to differing conceptions of common ground, a better category perhaps in which to frame the overall discussion. Marsden interprets Warfield's view as "pervasive but quite limited," though Warfield himself describes the effects of sin as corrupting *homo totus*, which Warfield defines as effecting the mind, the heart, and the will. See B. B. Warfield, "Introduction to Francis Beattie's *Apologetics*," 100.

199. By making this point, I am not denying the fact that there is a legitimate debate concerning proper apologetic methodology among Reformed Christians.

200. Warfield, "Introduction to Francis Beattie's *Apologetics*," 100.

> convict the world in respect of sin, and of righteousness and judgement. We are arguing that faith is, in all its exercises alike, a form of conviction, and is therefore, necessarily grounded in evidence. And we are arguing that evidence accordingly has its part to play in the conversion of the soul; and that the systematically organized evidence which we call Apologetics similarly has its part to play in the Christianizing of the world. And we are arguing that this part is not a small part; nor is it a merely subsidiary part; nor yet a merely defensive part—as if the one end of Apologetics were to protect an isolated body of Christians from annoyance from the surrounding world, or to aid the distracted Christian to bring his head into harmony with his heart. The part that Apologetics has to play in the Christianizing of the world is rather a primary part, and it is a conquering part. It is the distinction of Christianity that it has come into the world clothed with the mission to *reason* its way to dominion.[201]

Thus Warfield's conception of the role of reason must be seen in light of this context, specifically his comments regarding the inability of apologetics to conquer the world to Christ.

As Warfield emphatically states, only the Holy Spirit gives life to the dead soul and convicts the world of sin. The Holy Spirit is the One who conquers the world for Christ, not unaided human reason. But the question necessarily arises as to how the Holy Spirit does this. Here, as Warfield had noted in some detail earlier in the essay, the Holy Spirit creates faith in the heart, not by creating faith from nothing, but by allowing the will to act upon what the mind knows to be true, yet which is otherwise sinfully suppressed.

> It is certainly not in the power of all demonstrations in the world to make a Christian. ... Faith is the gift of God; but it does not in the least follow that the faith God gives is an irrational faith, that is, a faith without grounds in right reason. It is beyond all question only the prepared heart that can fitly respond to the "reasons"; but how can even a prepared heart respond when there are no "reasons" to draw out its actions? ... The Holy Spirit does not work a blind, an ungrounded faith in the heart. What is supplied by his creative energy in working faith is not a ready-made faith, rooted

201. Warfield, "Introduction to Francis Beattie's *Apologetics*," 99.

> in nothing and clinging without reason to its object; nor yet new grounds of belief in the object presented; but just a new ability of the heart to respond to grounds of faith, sufficient in themselves, already present to the understanding. We believe in Christ because it is rational to believe in him, not though it be irrational. Accordingly, our Reformed fathers always posited in the production of faith the presence of the "*argumentum propter quod credo*," as well as the "*principium seu causa efficiens a quo ad credendum adducor*." That is to say, for the birth of faith in the soul, it is just as essential that grounds of faith should be present to the mind as that the Giver of faith should act creatively upon the heart.[202]

Therefore, in order for there to be faith present in the heart, there must be both the presence of an object of faith—in this case the contents of special revelation, specifically the person and redemptive work of Christ in whom we must believe in order to be justified—and the Holy Spirit who must perform a supernatural work, not by creating new grounds of faith, but instead, creating a new ability of the sinful heart to respond to the grounds of faith, already sufficient in themselves, and which are instrumentally apprehended by fallen reason.[203] Again, Warfield frames this in terms of his subjective-objective distinction.

When Jack Rogers and Donald McKim criticize Warfield for supposedly arguing that the "Holy Spirit does not produce faith," they apparently base their assertions on the understanding that in Warfield's scheme, the Spirit makes "faith already present in the mind by reason, into saving faith." Rogers and McKim may have, to some degree, accurately represented Warfield's view in this regard, but the implication that they draw from this, the "Holy Spirit does not produce faith for Warfield," is typical of the gross misrepresentations of Warfield's position, since Warfield emphatically states the contrary, namely that it *is* the Holy Spirit who produces faith. Those who accuse Warfield of Arminianism or Romanism likely do so because they assume that Warfield's supposed

202. Ibid. These comments are also found almost verbatim in Warfield's "Review of Herman Bavinck's *De Zekerheid des Geloofs*," 114–15.

203. As John W. Stewart points out, one of the virtues of SCSR is that it held "that a person of simple common sense could rightly discern the essence of the Scripture's message. Such a conviction was a natural extension of the Protestant principle of *sola Scriptura*." See John William Stewart, *The Tethered Theology: Biblical Criticism, Common Sense Philosophy, and the Princeton Theologians, 1812–1860*, (Ph.D. diss., The University of Michigan, 1990), 290.

appeal to right reason somehow necessitates a form of synergism in which reason is supposedly elevated over regeneration, and this, therefore, produces a kind of divine-human co-operation, since in Warfield's conception reason judges the ground for faith, the evidence for special revelation. Warfield expressly denies any form of synergism, for as he states, it is easy to "say that Christianity is attained, not by demonstrations, but by a new birth. Nothing could be more true."[204] This then leads to a second point: "How can reason judge the ground of revelation?"

If the Holy Spirit alone is responsible for faith, why does Warfield make the comments that he does about "Christianity reasoning its way to dominion"? While Warfield unequivocally asserts that we can only draw our theology from the Scriptures, nevertheless, before we can do this, "we must assure ourselves that there is a knowledge of God in the Scriptures. And before we do that, we must assure ourselves that a knowledge of God is possible for man."[205] However, the chain goes back even farther, for even:

> ... before we do that, we must assure ourselves that there is a God to know. Thus, we inevitably work back to first principles. And, in working our way back to first principles, we exhibit the indispensability of an "Apologetical Theology," which of necessity holds the place of the first among the five essential theological disciplines.[206]

This conception of apologetics is important to this discussion in several regards. It is Kuyper's failure to be clear about this that provokes Warfield's negative assessment. There is also no doubt that Warfield is echoing the Scottish Common Sense philosophers, Reid and especially McCosh, as well as the Scottish Presbyterian evidentialists, Dick, Chalmers, Cunningham, Buchanan, and MacGregor. There is an echo from Francis Turretin as well, since as Turretin had concluded, there are first principles which are true both in the light of nature, and in revealed religion.[207] It is here, then, that we see Warfield's conception of reason as occupying an instrumental function, not a magisterial role, which would leave Warfield open to a charge of rationalism.

---

204. Ibid., 98–99.
205. Ibid.
206. Ibid.
207. Turretin, *Institutio Theologiae Elencticae*, I.ix.5

It is what Warfield calls the "mystical conception" of apologetics, which piously contends that "a Christian man must take his standpoint not *above* the Scriptures, but *in* the Scriptures."[208] With this conception, Warfield can agree to a point, since as he states, one must not take their standpoint above the Scriptures. But this conception, left without qualification, begs the question. As Warfield notes, "surely [the Christian man] must *have* Scriptures, authenticated to him as such, before he can take his stand in them."[209] It is in this context then that we must see Warfield's conception of the role of reason in the dominion to be taken by Christianity. Since according to Warfield, "Faith is, in all its exercise alike, a form of conviction, and is, therefore, necessarily grounded in evidence."[210] It is because of the weight and strength of the evidential case for the ground of faith that this dominion will come. The evidences are so great that unbelievers will never be able to ultimately overcome them. This is why Christians must go on the offensive and not merely be content with defensively fending off challenges.

As Warfield sees it, the Holy Spirit works through means to create faith, in this case, the means are Christian evidences, and Christian evidences can indeed provide a sufficient basis for faith. While it is revelation that provides the foundation for faith (not reason), nevertheless, it is reason (as an instrument) that investigates the ground of special revelation, even though it cannot establish the content of that revelation. Warfield clearly stands in the line of the Reformed scholastics and Scottish evidentialists on this point.

This point also helps explain Warfield's concern that Kuyper's view minimized rather than maximized apologetics. Apologetics is to play a primary role in the "Christianizing of the world," not because Warfield exalts reason above revelation, but because Christianity "makes its appeal to right reason," and in doing so will "put all its enemies under its feet."[211] Despite all of the "tremendous energy of thought and the incredible fertility in assault which characterizes the world in its anti-Christian manifestation," it is apologetics which stands "calmly over against the world with its credentials in its hands and fears no contention of men."[212] This is why Warfield can lament, "It is a standing matter of surprise to

208. Ibid., 98. The italics are in the original.
209. Ibid.
210. Warfield, "Introduction to Francis Beattie's *Aologetics*," 100.
211. Ibid.
212. Ibid.

us that the brilliant school of Christian thinkers"—such as Abraham Kuyper—"should be tempted to make little of apologetics."[213]

Since Warfield never intended his forward to be a stand-alone systematic treatise on the relationship between faith and reason, it is important to briefly survey the Warfield corpus for additional clarification of these disputed issues. In an article on regeneration written for Johnson's *Cyclopaedia*, Warfield states that the efficient cause of regeneration is "a divine power acting supernaturally and immediately upon the soul, quickening it to spiritual life, and implanting gracious principles of action."[214] Man's response to this divine initiative (conversion), "instantly follows, as to the change of action consequent upon the change of character, and consists in repentance, faith, holy obedience, etc."[215] There can be no doubt that for the Princeton theologian, regeneration precedes faith, if not temporally, certainly causally. The efficient cause, to use the scholastic formulation, is God the Holy Spirit, and a person's response to the new birth is conversion, manifesting itself in faith and repentance. This is why Warfield can assert that apologetic arguments can convert no one. To make this assertion is not to deny that the Holy Spirit uses means to produce faith, in this case the evidence for the truth of the Christian religion.

Warfield not only asserted his conviction of the truth of the formula, *Credo ut intelligam*, but *Fides praecedit rationem* as well. His reason for affirming the truth of these formulae is because they do indeed faithfully reflect the Apostle Paul's words in 1 Corinthians—"the natural man receiveth not the things of God"—which Warfield cites as a proof-text.[216] Warfield declares, "It is only through the guidance of the Holy Ghost, dwelling within us, that we can reach to the apprehension of the deep things of God." Indeed doctrine cannot produce life: "It is the *Creator Spiritus* alone who is competent to quicken dead souls into life."[217] Here again, Warfield unequivocally asserts that faith precedes understanding,

---

213. Ibid. The debate between Warfield and Kuyper on this matter is discussed in the essay by Paul Kjoss Helseth, "B. B. Warfield on the Apologetic Nature of Christian Scholarship: An Analysis of His Solution to the Problem of the Relationship between Christianity and Culture," *Westminster Theological Journal*, vol. 62, no. 1 (Spring 2000), 101–106.
214. B. B. Warfield, "Regeneration." Repr. in *Selected Shorter Writings* (ed. John E. Meeter; Phillipsburg: P&R Publishing, 1980), 323.
215. Warfield, "Regeneration," 323.
216. Warfield, "The Right of Systematic Theology," p. 274.
217. Ibid.

and that it is the Holy Spirit alone who gives understanding of spiritual things. Reason, which investigates the ground for faith, can only occupy a ministerial or instrumental function, but apart from reason performing its humble and necessary task, there could be no faith since saving faith looks to an object: the person and work of Christ.

Warfield makes this point quite eloquently when discussing the nature of faith as found in the New Testament:

> It is, accordingly, solely from its *object* that faith derives its value. The object is uniformly the God of grace, whether conceived of broadly as the source of all life, light, and blessing, on whom man in his creature weakness is entirely dependent, or, whenever sin and the eternal welfare of the soul are in view, as the author of salvation in whom alone the hope of unworthy man can be placed. ... The *saving power* of faith resides not in itself, but in the Almighty Saviour on whom it rests. ... So little is faith conceived as containing in itself the energy or ground of salvation, that it is consistently represented as, in its *origin*, itself a gratuity from God in the prosecution of His saving work. It comes, not of one's own strength or virtue, but only to those who are chosen of God for its reception (II Thess. ii.13), and hence his gift (Eph. vi.23, cf. ii.8,9, Phil. I.29), through Christ (Acts iii.16, Phil. I.29, I Pet. I.21, cf. Heb. xii.2), by the Spirit (II Cor. iv.13, Gal. iii.2, 5); and as it is thus obtained from God (II Pet. 1.1, Jude 3, I Pet. 1.21), thanks are to be returned to God for it (Col.1.4, II Thess. 1.3). Thus, even here all boasting is excluded, and salvation is conceived in all its elements as the pure product of unalloyed grace, issuing not from, but in, good works (Eph. ii.8-12). The place of faith in the process of salvation, as biblically conceived, could scarcely, therefore, be better described than by use of the scholastic term "instrumental cause." Not in one portion of the Scriptures alone, but throughout their whole extent, it is conceived as a boon from above which comes to men, no doubt, through the channels of their own activities, but not as if it were an effect of their energies, but rather, as it has been finely phrased, as a gift which God lays in the lap of the soul.[218]

218. Warfield, "The Biblical Doctrine of Faith." Repr. in *Biblical Doctrines* (Grand Rapids: Baker Book House, 1981), 502–05. Note the discussion of faith in Warfield's "Review of Herman Bavinck's *De Zekerheid des Geloofs*," 111–17.

Here again, we find that the effectual cause is God the Holy Spirit, though men and women are certainly not passive in this process of coming to faith, since this comes "through the channels of their own activities." Thus one wonders about the propriety of taking Warfield's comments about the dominion of reason as characteristic of his total apologetic when the overall data indicates otherwise.[219]

In another important essay, "On Faith in its Psychological Aspects," Warfield treats many of the issues particularly germane to the debate. Warfield notes that faith is not an arbitrary act on the part of the subject, but it is that "mental state or act which is determined by sufficient reasons."[220] Warfield again seems to anticipate many of the criticisms that would subsequently arise:

> It, of course, does not follow that all our "beliefs," "faiths" correspond with reality. Our convictions are not infallible. When we say that "belief," "faith" is the product of evidence and is in that sense compelled consent, that is not the same as saying that consent is produced only by compelling evidence, that is, evidence which is objectively adequate. Objective adequacy and subjective effect are not exactly correlated.[221]

The problem, specifically as it relates to this debate, is not with the objective evidence but with the subjective aspects of knowing, since "the sinful heart—which is enmity towards God—is incapable of that supreme act of trust in God—or rather entrusting itself to God, its Saviour—which has absorbed into itself the term 'faith' in its Christian connotation."[222] Because of this problem, notes Warfield, many have tried to argue that faith is not "a rational act of conviction passing into

219. It is possible to argue as Noll does, that the fidelity of the Princetonians to Scripture and the Reformed confessions kept them from "being entirely at the mercy of their philosophy." See Noll, *The Princeton Theology*, 33. This may be correct to a point, but assumes that Scottish Common Sense Realism is the critical factor which seems to pull the Princetonians away from Reformed orthodoxy. This is, as we have seen, a questionable assumption on the part of Noll, since there is nothing inherent within Scottish Common Sense Realism that denies either the noetic effects of sin, or the necessity of divine illumination. In fact, it may be argued that it is those who follow Kuyper and Van Til who may indeed have adopted a novel position in these matters.

220. B. B. Warfield, "On Faith in its Psychological Aspects," reprinted in *Studies in Theology* (Grand Rapids: Baker Book House, 1981), 313.

221. Ibid., 318.

222. Ibid., 337.

confidence, resting upon adequate grounds in testimony, but an arbitrary act of sheer will, produced no one knows how."[223]

The solution to human sinfulness is given through special revelation (not as Rogers and McKim have erroneously asserted "humanly devised evidences for faith"). The Bible teaches the sinfulness of the human heart, and therefore, the impossibility of faith, unless it is "the gift of God."[224] Warfield's conception of the means to resolve this dilemma is found in a lengthy, but important treatment of the relationship between faith and the Holy Spirit:

> The mode of the divine giving of faith is represented rather as involving the creation by God the Holy Spirit of a capacity for faith under the evidence submitted. It proceeds by the divine illumination of the understanding, softening of the heart, and quickening of the will, so that the man so affected may freely and must inevitably perceive the force and yield to the compelling power of the evidence of the trustworthiness of Jesus Christ as Saviour submitted to him in the gospel. In one word the capacity for faith and the inevitable emergence in the heart of faith are attributed by the Christian revelation to that great act of God the Holy Spirit which has come in Christian theology to be called by the significant name of Regeneration. If sinful man as such is incapable of the act of faith, because he is inhabitable to the evidence on which alone such an act of confident resting on God the Saviour can repose, renewed man is equally incapable of not responding to this evidence, which is objectively compelling, by an act of sincere faith. In this highest exercise faith thus, though in a true sense the gift of God, is an equally true sense man's own act, and bears all the character of faith as it is exercised by unrenewed man in its lower manifestations.[225]

Therefore, any attempt to understand Warfield's statement "that Christianity is to reason its way to dominion," apart from his overall conception of faith, and the need for reason to investigate the ground of faith, risks in a profound sense, a misrepresentation of Warfield's position.

223. Ibid.
224. Ibid.
225. Ibid., 337–38.

CLOSER TO THE CENTER OF REFORMED TRADITION?

As a result of this re-evaluation of Warfield's apologetic, there are several conclusions that need to be made. First, Warfield stands firmly within a broadly-based historic Reformed tradition, which while affirming the possibility of natural theology on the one hand, on the other, denies its sufficiency to serve as a basis for faith. The apologetic thrust of this tradition is not focused upon the theistic proofs of so-called "classical apologetics,"[226] though the validity of these proofs are not denied. Instead the apologetic focus is directed toward Christian evidences, as both the ground for special revelation, and in response to challenges raised against Christian supernaturalism. This means that charges of innovation, Arminianism, and Romanism, often leveled against Warfield, are simply ill-founded.

Second, any evaluation of the Old Princeton apologetic is impoverished to the degree to which the discussion occurs without due recognition of the ongoing debate over natural theology and the role of Christian evidences within the broader Reformed tradition. To draw the circle of interpretation as narrow as Amsterdam versus Princeton is to cut ourselves off from much of the historical context in which the Princeton apologetic developed. While it is indeed invaluable to investigate Princeton's intellectual history, specifically the role and influence of Scottish Common Sense Realism upon Princeton's theology and apologetic, this philosophy is not the only factor which played a significant role in the development of the Princeton apologetic. Contemporary interpreters have not taken sufficient notice of the theological and apologetical antecedents within the Reformed tradition, specifically that of the Scottish Presbyterian evidentialists and the Reformed scholastics.

A third, and closely related point, is that Warfield's comments about reason have very likely been traced to the wrong source. Warfield's conception of faith, reason, and the role of the Holy Spirit are framed not in the language of the Scottish Enlightenment as many of his interpreters argue, but instead in the terms of the Scottish evidentialist tradition. Because this point has been overlooked, Warfield's conception of these doctrines have been misrepresented in several cases (as in the

226. Thus the so-called "Ligonier Apologetic" of R. C. Sproul and John Gerstner offers an approach with markedly different emphases than that of Old Princeton and the Scottish Evidentialists, though the epistemological influence of Scottish Common Sense Realism may be seen throughout. See Sproul, Gerstner, and Lindsley, *Classical Apologetics*.

case of Rogers and McKim, for example), or seen entirely through the grid of American intellectual history, resulting in the downplaying of important theological antecedents (Noll and Marsden). While it may be argued that *both* the New College theologians and the Princetonians were unduly influenced by the Scottish philosophy, and that identifying the Scottish evidentialists as one of the sources merely reinforces the argument that evidentialism is the fruit of the rejection of the classical Reformed understanding of the noetic effects of sin and the role of the Holy Spirit in producing faith. Such an argument, however, ignores the actual historical development of both traditions, specifically as they sought to oppose all forms of anti-supernaturalism, skepticism, and most of all, Enlightenment rationalism.

Fourth, such an interpretation uncritically assumes that Scottish Common Sense Realism is inherently antithetical to certain Reformed doctrines, but this must be demonstrated, not simply assumed. As Paul Helm has convincingly argued, there is nothing in the nature of Scottish Common Sense Realism which is intrinsically opposed to Calvinism. In fact, it offers an epistemological foundation for a natural theology. But what Helm overlooks perhaps, is that it not only is useful in developing a natural theology, it also serves as a means to establish the reliability of evidentiary testimony as a sufficient ground for faith. Common Sense Realism provides a philosophical basis in which to ground faith in evidence, and is therefore as important philosophically to those using Christian evidences, as it is to those trying to establish a natural theology.

Fifth, and perhaps most importantly, Warfield's views on faith, reason, and the Holy Spirit are all too often ignored or taken out or context. Not only does Warfield not deny any Reformed doctrines (including the noetic effects of sin), and while militantly affirming Reformed orthodoxy, Warfield's formulations treating these issues are in many instances more cogently framed than those of many of his critics. Warfield retains his monergism throughout, and at no point does he treat reason as a *principium fidei*. Instead, Warfield sees reason as an instrument, which investigates the ground of faith, but cannot and, indeed does not, determine the content of faith. At no point does he diminish the necessity of the Holy Spirit in the apologetic task. Since Christianity is objectively true, and therefore, based upon sufficient evidence, it has nothing to fear from unbelief and indeed can reason its way to dominion.

The time has come for a significant re-evaluation of the apologetic methodology of B. B. Warfield and Old Princeton. Indeed, the debate can no longer be framed as though it is the biblical method of Kuyper and Van Til versus the Enlightenment influenced position of Warfield. Close investigation shows that Warfield is perhaps closer to the center of the historic Reformed tradition than are many of his contemporary critics.

Bibliography

Abraham, William J. *Divine Inspiration*. New York: Oxford University Press, 1981.

Adams, Charles Kendall. *Johnson's Universal Cyclopedia*. New York: A. J. Johnson, 1893–1895

Ahlstrom, Sydney. *A Religious History of the American People*. 2 vols. New York: Image, 1975.

———. "The Scottish Philosophy and American Theology." *Church History* 24 (1955): 257–72.

———. *Theology in America: The Major Protestant Voices from Puritanism to Neo-Orthodoxy*. Indianapolis: Bobbs-Merrill Company, 1976.

Alexander, Archibald. *Evidences of the Authority, Inspiration and Canonical Authority of the Holy Scriptures*. Philadelphia: Presbyterian Board of Publication, 1836.

———. "The Idealism of Bishop Berkeley." *Presbyterian Review* 6, no. 22 (April 1885): 301–14.

Alexander, Joseph Addison. Review of John Kitto, *Cyclopædia of Biblical Literature*. *Princeton Review* 18 (October 1846): 554–568.

Allis, Oswald T. "Personal Impressions of Dr. Warfield." *Banner of Truth* 89 (Fall 1971): 10–14.

Alston, William P. *Epistemic Justification: Essays in the Theory of Knowledge*. Ithaca: Cornell University Press, 1989.

———. *Perceiving God: The Epistemology of Religious Experience*. Ithaca: Cornell University Press, 1991.

Arminius, James. *The Works of James Arminius*. 3 Vols. Translated by James Nichols and William Nichols. 1828. Repr., Grand Rapids: Baker, 1986.

Balmer, Randall, H. "The Princetonians and Scripture: A Reconsideration." *Westminster Theological Journal*, 44 (1982): 325–65.

———. "The Princetonians, Scripture, and Recent Scholarship." *Journal of Presbyterian History*, 60 (Fall 1982): 267–70.

Bamberg, Stanley W. "Our Image of Warfield Must Go." *Journal of the Evangelical Theological Society* 34, no. 2 (June 1991): 229–41.

Barker, Stephen F. and Tom L. Beauchamp. *Thomas Reid: Critical Interpretations*. Philadelphia: Philosophical Monographs, 1976.

Barr, James. *Beyond Fundamentalism*. Philadelphia: Westminster, 1984.

Bavinck, Herman. *Prolegomena*. Vol. 1 of *Reformed Dogmatics*. Edited by John Bolt. Translated by John Vriend. Grand Rapids: Baker Academic, 2003.

Beanblossom, Ronald E. "Introduction." Pages ix–ivii in *Thomas Reid's Inquiry and Essays*. Edited by Ronald E. Beanblossom and Keith Lehrer. Indianapolis: Hackett, 1983.

Beeke, Joel R. "Van Til and Apologetics." *New Horizons*, May 1995, 5–6.

Berkhof, Louis. *Introduction to Systematic Theology*. Grand Rapids: Baker, 1979.

Blaising, Craig A. "Lewis Sperry Chafer." Pages 83–96 in *Handbook of Evangelical Theologians*. Edited by Walter A. Elwell. Grand Rapids: Baker, 1993.

Bloesch, Donald. *Holy Scripture: Revelation, Inspiration & Interpretation*. Downers Grove, IL: InterVarsity Press, 1994.

Bozeman, Theodore Dwight. *Protestants in an Age of Science: The Baconian Ideal and Antebellum American Religious Thought*. Chapel Hill: University of North Carolina Press, 1977.

Breckinridge, Robert J. *The Knowledge of God, Objectively Considered*. Vol. 1 of *Theology Considered as a Science of Positive Truth, Both Inductive and Deductive*. New York: Robert Carter, 1858.

———. *The Knowledge of God, Subjectively Considered*. Vol. 2 of *Theology Considered as a Science of Positive Truth, Both Inductive and Deductive*. New York: Robert Carter & Brothers, 1859.

Broadie, Alexander. "Reid in Context." Pages 31–52 in *The Cambridge Companion to Thomas Reid*. Edited by Terrance Cuneo and René Van Woudenberg. Cambridge: Cambridge University Press, 2004.

Brown, Colin. *Miracles and the Critical Mind*. Grand Rapids: Eerdmans, 1984.

Brown, Eddie. "Murray, Andrew." *Dictionary of Scottish Church History & Theology*. Edited by Nigel M. de S. Cameron. Downers Grove, IL: InterVarsity Press, 1993.

Brown, Thomas. *Inquiry into the Relation of Cause and Effect*. Andover: M. Newman, 1822.

———. *Lectures on the Philosophy of Mind*. New York: Hallowell, Glazier, Masters and Smith, 1842.

Buchanan, James. *Analogy: A Guide to Truth and an Aid to Faith*. Edinburgh: T&T Clark, 1867.

———. *Faith in God and Modern Atheism Compared*. London: Groombridge and Sons, 1855.

Calhoun, David B. *Princeton Seminary: Faith and Learning 1812–1868*. Carlisle, PA: Banner of Truth, 1994.

———. *Princeton Seminary: The Majestic Testimony, 1869–1929*. Carlisle, PA: Banner of Truth, 1996.

Cameron, Nigel M. de S., ed. *Dictionary of Scottish Church History & Theology*. Downers Grove, IL: InterVarsity Press, 1993.

Carson, D. A. "Three Books on the Bible: A Critical Review" (review of William J. Abraham, *The Divine Inspiration of Holy Scripture*). *Journal of the Evangelical Theological Society* 26, no. 3 (September 1983): 337–67.

Chafer, Lewis Sperry. *He That Is Spiritual*. Grand Rapids: Zondervan, 1981.

———. *Systematic Theology*. 8 Vols. Dallas: Dallas Seminary Press, 1980.

Chalmers, Thomas. *Collected Works*. 25 vols. Edited by Thomas Constable. Edinburgh: Thomas Constable, 1836–42.

———. *Institutes of Theology*. 2 vols. Edinburgh: Thomas Constable, 1856.
———. *On Natural Theology*. New York: Robert Carter, 1845.
———. *On the Miraculous and Internal Evidences of the Christian Revelation and the Authority of its Records*. New York: Robert Carter, 1845.
Clark, James Kelly. *Return to Reason*. Grand Rapids: Eerdmans, 1990.
Clarke, Samuel. *The Works of Samuel Clarke*. 4 Vols. Repr., New York: Garland, 1978.
Cousar, R. W. "Benjamin Warfield: His Christology and Soteriology." Th.D. diss., University of Edinburgh, 1954.
Craig, Samuel G. "Benjamin B. Warfield." Pages xi–xlviii in *Biblical and Theological Studies*, by Benjamin B. Warfield. Edited by Samuel C. Craig. Philadelphia: Presbyterian and Reformed, 1968.
Cunningham, William. *The Reformers and the Theology of the Reformation*. Carlisle, PA: Banner of Truth, 1979.
———. *Theological Lectures*. New York: Robert Carter and Brothers, 1878.
Dabney, R. L. *Syllabus and Notes of the Course of Systematic and Polemic Theology Taught in Union Theological Seminary, Virginia*. 6th ed. Richmond, VA: Presbyterian Committee of Publication, 1927.
Davenport, Alan Wade. "Evidence and Belief, Common Sense and the Science of Mind in the Philosophy of Thomas Reid." Ph.D. diss., American University, 1987.
Davis, D. Clair. "Princeton and Inerrancy: The Nineteenth Century Philosophical Background of Contemporary Concerns." Pages 359–78 in *Inerrancy and the Church*. Edited by John D. Hannah. Chicago: Moody, 1984.
Davis, John D., ed. *A Dictionary of the Bible*. Philadelphia: Westminster, 1898.
Denny, James. *Studies in Theology: Lectures Delivered in Chicago Theological Seminary*. 1894. Repr., Grand Rapids: Baker, 1976.
DeWitt, John. "Princeton College Administrations in the Nineteenth Centuries." *Presbyterian and Reformed Review* 8 (1897): 636–82.
Dick, John. *Lectures on Theology*. New York: Robert Carter & Brothers, 1852.
Douglas, J. D. *The New International Dictionary of the Christian Church*. Grand Rapids: Zondervan, 1981.
Dowey, Edward A. *The Knowledge of God in Calvin's Theology*. New York: Columbia University Press, 1952.
Dunn, James D. G. *The Living Word*. Philadelphia: Fortress, 1988.
Edwards, Charles Eugene. "Turretin's 'Theology.'" *Princeton Theological Review* 26 (1928): 142–49.
Edwards, Paul, ed. *The Encyclopedia of Philosophy*. 8 vols. New York: Macmillan, 1967.
Ellos, William J. *Thomas Reid's Newtonian Realism*. Lanham, MD: University Press of America, 1981.
Faust, Patricia, L. *Historical Times Illustrated Encyclopedia of the Civil War*. New York: HarperCollins, 1991.
Flower, Elizabeth and Murray G. Murphey. *A History of Philosophy in America*. 2 vols. New York: Capricorn, 1977.
Frame, John M. *Apologetics to the Glory of God: An Introduction*. Phillipsburg, NJ: P&R, 1994.
———. *Cornelius Van Til: An Analysis of His Thought*. Phillipsburg, NJ: P&R, 1995.

———. *The Doctrine of the Knowledge of God*. Phillipsburg, NJ: Presbyterian and Reformed, 1987.

Frank, Douglas W. *Less Than Conquerors: How Evangelicals Entered the Twentieth Century*. Grand Rapids: Eerdmans, 1986.

Geehan, E. R., ed. *Jerusalem and Athens: Critical Discussions on the Philosophy and Apologetics of Cornelius Van Til*. Phillipsburg, NJ: Presbyterian and Reformed, 1971.

Geisler, Norman L. *Christian Apologetics*. Grand Rapids: Baker, 1976.

———, ed. *Inerrancy*. Grand Rapids: Zondervan, 1980.

Gerstner, John H. "The Contributions of Charles Hodge, B. B. Warfield and J. Gresham Machen to the Doctrine of Inspiration." Pages 347–81 in *Challenges to Inerrancy: A Theological Response*. Edited by Gordon R. Lewis and Bruce Demarest. Chicago: Moody, 1984.

———. "Scottish Realism: Kant and Darwin in the Philosophy of James McCosh." Ph.D. diss., Harvard University, 1945.

———. "Warfield's Case for Biblical Inerrancy." Pages 115–42 in *God's Inerrant Word*. Edited by John Warwick Montgomery. Minneapolis: Bethany Fellowship, 1974.

Gilson, Etienne. *Thomist Realism and the Critique of Knowledge*. Translated by Mark A. Wauck. San Francisco: Ignatius Press, 1986.

Gleason, Randall. "B. B. Warfield and Lewis Sperry Chafer on Sanctification." *Journal of the Evangelical Theological Society* 40, no. 2 (June 1997) 241–56.

Grave, S. A. "Common Sense." Pages 155–60 in vol. 2 of *The Encyclopedia of Philosophy*. 8 vols. Edited by Paul Edwards. New York: Macmillan, 1967.

———. "Reid, Thomas." Pages 118–21 in vol. 7 of *The Encyclopedia of Philosophy*. 8 vols. Edited by Paul Edwards. New York: Macmillan, 1967.

———. *The Scottish Philosophy of Common Sense*. Oxford: Clarendon, 1960.

———. "Stewart, Dugald." Pages 16–17 in vol. 8 of *The Encyclopedia of Philosophy*. 8 vols. Edited by Paul Edwards. New York: Macmillan, 1967.

Greco, John. "Reid's Reply to the Skeptic." Pages 134–55 in *The Cambridge Companion to Thomas Reid*. Edited by Terrance Cuneo and René Van Woudenberg. Cambridge: Cambridge University Press, 2004.

Greene, W. Brenton Jr. "The Function of the Reason in Christianity." *Presbyterian and Reformed Review* 6 (1895): 481–502

———. Review of Auguste Sabatier, *Outlines of a Philosophical of Religion Based on Psychology and History*. *Presbyterian and Reformed Review* 10, no. 37 (1899): 144–49.

Grenz, Stanley J. *Revisioning Evangelical Theology: A Fresh Agenda for the 21st Century*. Downers Grove, IL: InterVarsity Press, 1993.

Grier, W. J. "Benjamin Breckinridge Warfield." *Banner of Truth* 89 (Fall 1971): 3–9.

Gundlach, Bradley J. " 'B' Is for Breckinridge: Warfield's Maternal Kin." Pages 13–53 in *B. B. Warfield: Essays on His Life and Thought*. Edited by Gary L. W. Johnson. Phillipsburg, NJ: P&R, 2007.

———. "The Evolution Question at Princeton, 1845–1929." Ph.D. diss., University of Rochester, 1995.

———. "Warfield, Biblical Authority and Jim Crow." Pages 136–68 in *B. B. Warfield: Essays on His Life and Thought*. Edited by Gary L. W. Johnson. Phillipsburg, NJ: P&R, 2007.

Habermas, Gary and Anthony Flew. *Did Jesus Rise From the Dead? The Resurrection Debate*. Edited by Terry L. Miethe. San Francisco: Harper and Row, 1987.

Hamilton, James E. "Epistemology and Theology in American Methodism." *Wesleyan Theological Journal* 10 (Spring 1975): 70–79.

Hamilton, Sir William. *Discussions on Philosophy and Literature, Education and University Reform*. London: 1852.

———. *Lectures on Metaphysics and Logic*. 4 vols. Edited by H. L. Mansel and John Veitch. Edinburgh: 1859–60.

———. ["On the Philosophy of the Unconditioned"]. Review of M. V. Cousin, *Cours de Philosophie* and *Introduction à l'Histoire de la Philosophie*. *Edinburgh Review* 50 (October 1829–January 1830): 194–221.

Hannah, John D., ed. *Inerrancy and the Church*. Chicago: Moody, 1984.

Hart, Darryl G. *Defending the Faith: J. Gresham Machen and the Crisis of Conservative Protestantism in Modern America*. Baltimore: Johns Hopkins University Press, 1994.

———. "The Princeton Mind in the Modern World and the Common Sense of J. Gresham Machen." *Westminster Theological Journal* 46 (1984): 1–25.

Hart, Hendrik, Johan Van Der Hoeven and Nicholas Wolterstorff, eds. *Rationality in the Calvinian Tradition*. Lanham, MD: University Press of America, 1983.

Hastings, James, ed. *Encyclopedia of Religion and Ethics*. New York: Scribner, 1910.

———. *Dictionary of the Bible*. Edinburgh: T&T Clark, 1898

Hatch, Nathan O., and Mark A. Noll, eds. *The Bible in America: Essays in Cultural History*. New York: Oxford University Press, 1982.

Helm, Paul. "Thomas Reid, Common Sense and Calvinism." Pages 71–89 in *Rationality in the Calvinian Tradition*. Edited by Hendrik Hart, Johan Van Der Hoeven and Nicholas Wolterstorff. Lanham, MD: University Press of America, 1983.

Helseth, Paul Kjoss. "B. B. Warfield on the Apologetic Nature of Christian Scholarship: An Analysis of His Solution to the Problem of the Relationship between Christianity and Culture." *Westminster Theological Journal* 62, no. 1 (Spring 2000): 89–111.

———. "B. B. Warfield's Apologetical Appeal to 'Right Reason': Evidence of a Rather Bald Rationalism?" *The Scottish Bulletin of Evangelical Theology*, 16, no. 2 (Autumn 1998): 156–77.

———. *"Right Reason" and the Princeton Mind: An Unorthodox Proposal*. Phillipsburg, NJ: P&R, 2010.

Hirst, R. J. "Realism." Pages 77–83 in vol. 7 of *The Encyclopedia of Philosophy*. 8 vols. Edited by Paul Edwards. New York: Macmillan, 1967.

Hodge, Archibald Alexander. *Evangelical Theology*. 1890. Repr., Carlisle, PA: Banner of Truth, 1976.

———. *Life of Charles Hodge D.D. LL.D.* New York: Scribner, 1880.

———. *Outlines of Theology*. 1866. Repr., Grand Rapids: Zondervan, 1980.

———. Review of Charles Robert Morrison, *The Proofs of Christ's Resurrection: From a Lawyer's Standpoint*. *Presbyterian Review* 4, no. 13 (January 1883): 197.

Hodge, Caspar Wistar. "Fact and Theory." Pages 562–67 in vol. 1 of *A Dictionary of Christ and the Gospels*. Edited by James Hastings. Edinburgh: T&T Clark, 1906–08.

———. "The Idea of Dogmatic Theology." *Princeton Theological Review* 6 (1908): 52–82.

Hodge, Charles. *Systematic Theology*. 3 vols. Grand Rapids: Eerdmans, 1979.

———. *What is Darwinism?* 1874. Reprint edited by Mark A. Noll and David N. Livingstone. Grand Rapids: Baker, 1994.

Hoefel, Robert J. "B. B. Warfield and James Orr: A Study in Contrasting Approaches to Scripture." *Christian Scholar's Review* 16, no. 1 (September 1986): 40–52.

———. "The Doctrine of Inspiration in the Writings of James Orr and B. B. Warfield: A Study in Contrasting Approaches to Scripture." Ph.D. diss., Fuller Theological Seminary, 1983.

Hoeveler, J. David Jr. *James McCosh and the Scottish Intellectual Tradition*. Princeton: Princeton University Press, 1981.

Hoffecker, Andrew W. "The Devotional Life of Archibald Alexander, Charles Hodge and Benjamin B. Warfield." *Westminster Theological Journal* 42, no. 1 (Fall 1979): 111 ff.

———. *Piety and The Princeton Theologians*. Phillipsburg, NJ: Presbyterian and Reformed, 1981.

———. "The Relation Between the Objective and Subjective Aspects in Christian Religious Experience: A Study in the Systematic and Devotional Writings of Archibald Alexander, Charles Hodge, and Benjamin B. Warfield." Ph.D. diss., Brown University, 1970.

Horton, Robert F. "The Atonement." Pages 185–242 in *Faith and Criticism: Essays by Congregationalists*. New York: E. P. Hutton, 1893.

Hovencamp, Herbert. *Science and Religion in America: 1800–1860*. Philadelphia: University of Pennsylvania Press, 1978.

Hume, David. Letter to Thomas Reid. Repr. pages 131–32 in "Thomas Reid: The Man and His Work," by Noah Porter. Pages 118–50 in *The Story of Scottish Philosophy*. Edited by Daniel Sommer Robinson. New York: Exposition Press, 1961.

Isbell, Sherman. "MacGregor, James." In *Dictionary of Scottish Church History & Theology*. Edited by Nigel M. de S. Cameron. Downers Grove: InterVarsity Press, 1993.

Jackson, Samuel M., ed. *The New Schaff-Herzog Encyclopedia of Religious Knowledge*. 12 vols. New York: Funk and Wagnalls, 1908.

Johnson, Deryl Freeman. "The Attitudes of the Princeton Theologians Toward Darwinism and Evolution from 1859 to 1929." Ph.D. diss., University of Iowa, 1969.

Johnson, Gary L. W. "Warfield and C. A. Briggs: Their Polemics and legacy." In *B. B. Warfield: Essays on His Life and Thought*. Edited by Gary L. W. Johnson. Phillipsburg, NJ: P&R, 2007.

Jones, Charles Andrew. "Charles Hodge, The Keeper of Orthodoxy: The Method, Purpose and Meaning of His Apologetic." Ph.D. diss., Drew University, 1989.

Jones, O. M. *Empiricism and Intuitionalism in Reid's Common Sense Philosophy*. Princeton: Princeton University Press, 1927.

Kant, Immanuel. *Prolegomena to Any Future Metaphysics*. 1783. Reprint edited by Lewis White Beck. Indianapolis: Bobbs-Merrill, 1950.

Kerr, Thomson Hugh. "Warfield: The Person Behind the Theology." Lecture presented at Princeton, NJ, March 1, 1982. Edited by William O. Harris, *Princeton Seminary Bulletin* 25, no. 1 (2004): 80–93.

Krabbendam, Hendrik. "B. B. Warfield vs. G. C. Berkhouwer on Scripture." Pages 413–46 in *Inerrancy*. Edited by Norman L. Geisler. Grand Rapids: Zondervan, 1980.

Kraus, Clyde Norman. "The Principle of Authority in the Theology of B. B. Warfield, William Adams Brown, and Gerald Birney Smith." Ph.D. diss., Duke University, 1962.

Kuyper, Abraham. *Principles of Sacred Theology*. Translated by J. Hendrik De Vries. Grand Rapids: Baker, 1980.

Lecerf, Auguste. *An Introduction to Reformed Dogmatics*. Translated by Andre Schlemmer. Grand Rapids: Baker, 1981.

Letis, Theodore, P. "B. B. Warfield, Common-Sense Philosophy and Biblical Criticism." *American Presbyterians* 69, no. 3 (Fall 1991): 175–90.

———. "Brevard Childs and the Protestant Dogmaticians: A Window to a New Paradigm of Biblical Interpretation." *Churchman* 105, no. 3 (1991): 261–77.

———. "The Protestant Dogmaticians and the Late Princeton School on the Status of the Sacred Apographa." *Scottish Bulletin of Evangelical Theology* 8, no. 1 (September 1990): 16–42.

Lewis, Gordon R., and Bruce Demarest, eds. *Challenges to Inerrancy: A Theological Response*. Chicago: Moody Press, 1984.

———. *Testing Christianity's Truth Claims*. Chicago: Moody, 1976.

Lindsey, Thomas M. "The Doctrine of Scripture: The Reformers and the Princeton School." *Expositor.* Fifth Series 1 (1895): 278–93.

Lints, Richard. *The Fabric of Theology: A Prolegomena to Evangelical Theology*. Grand Rapids: Eerdmans, 1993.

———. "Two Theologies or One? Warfield and Vos on the Nature of Theology." *Westminster Theological Journal* 54, no. 2 (Fall 1992): 235–53.

Livingstone, David N. "B. B. Warfield, the Theory of Evolution and Early Fundamentalism." *Evangelical Quarterly* 58, no. 1 (January 1986): 69–83.

———. *Darwin's Forgotten Defenders: The Encounter Between Evangelical Theology and Evolutionary Thought*. Grand Rapids: Eerdmans, 1987.

———. "The Idea of Design: The Vicissitudes of a Key Concept in the Princeton Response to Darwin." *Scottish Journal of Theology* 37, no. 3 (1984): 329–57.

Livingstone, William D. "The Princeton Apologetic as Exemplified by the Work of Benjamin B. Warfield and J. Gresham Machen: A Study in American Theology 1880–1930." Ph.D. diss., Yale University, 1948.

Loetscher, Lefferts A. *The Broadening Church: A Study of Theological Issues in the Presbyterian Church Since 1869*. Philadelphia: University of Pennsylvania Press, 1957.

Longfield, Bradley J. *The Presbyterian Controversy*. New York: Oxford University Press, 1991.

Luthardt, Christoph Ernest. *The Fundamental Truths of Christianity*. 7th ed. Translated by Sophia Taylor. Edinburgh: T&T Clark, 1909.

MacGregor, James. *The Apology of the Christian Religion*. Edinburgh: T&T Clark, 1891.

———. *The Revelation and the Record*. Edinburgh: T&T Clark, 1893.

———. *Studies in the History of Christian Apologetics*. Edinburgh: T&T Clark, 1894.

Macleod, Donald. "Cunningham, William." Pages 229–31 in *Dictionary of Scottish Church History & Theology*. Edited by Nigel M. de S. Cameron. Downers Grove, IL: InterVarsity Press, 1993.

———. "Systematic Theology." Pages 809–12 in *Dictionary of Scottish Church History & Theology*. Edited by Nigel M. de S. Cameron. Downers Grove, IL: InterVarsity Press, 1993.

Markarian, John Jacob. "The Calvinistic Concept of the Biblical Revelation in the Theology of B. B. Warfield." Ph.D. diss., Drew University, 1963.

Marsden, George. "The Ambiguities of Academic Freedom." *Church History* 62, no. 2 (June 1993): 221–36.

———. "The Collapse of American Evangelical Academia." Pages 219–264 in *Faith and Rationality: Reason and Belief in God.* Edited by Alvin Plantinga and Nicholas Wolterstorff. Notre Dame: University of Notre Dame Press, 1983.

———. *Fundamentalism and American Culture*. New York: Oxford University Press, 1980.

———. "J. Gresham Machen, History, and Truth." *Westminster Theological Journal* 42, no. 1 (Fall 1979): 157–75.

———. "The New School Heritage and Presbyterian Fundamentalism." *Westminster Theological Journal* 32, no. 2 (May 1970): 129–47.

———. "Scotland and Philadelphia: Common Sense Philosophy from Jefferson to Westminster." *Reformed Journal* 29, no. 3 (March 1979): 8–12.

———. *The Soul of the American University: From Protestant Establishment to Established Nonbelief.* New York: Oxford University Press, 1994.

———. *Understanding Fundamentalism and Evangelicalism*. Grand Rapids: Eerdmans, 1991.

Massa, Mark S. *Charles Augustus Briggs and the Crisis of Historical Criticism.* Minneapolis: Fortress, 1990.

May, Henry F. *The Enlightenment in America*. New York: Oxford University Press, 1976.

McClanahan, James Samuel. "Benjamin B. Warfield: Historian of Doctrine in Defense of Orthodoxy, 1881–1921." Ph.D. diss., Union Theological Seminary in Virginia, 1988.

McConnel, Tim. "The Old Princeton Apologetics: Common Sense or Reformed?' *Journal of the Evangelical Theological Society* 46, no. 4 (December 2003): 647–72.

McCosh, James. *The Intuitions of the Mind Inductively Investigated*. New York: Robert Carter and Brothers, 1880.

———. *Realistic Philosophy Defended in a Philosophic Series*. 2 vols. New York: Scribner, 1887.

———. *The Scottish Philosophy*. New York: Robert Carter and Brothers, 1875.

McGrath, Alister. *A Passion for Truth: The Intellectual Coherence of Evangelicalism*. Downers Grove, IL: InterVarsity Press, 1996.

McIntosh, J. R. "Dick, John." Page 242 in *Dictionary of Scottish Church History & Theology*. Edited by Nigel M. de S. Cameron. Downers Grove, IL: InterVarsity Press, 1993.

Metzger, Bruce M. *The Text of the New Testament: Its Transmission, Corruption and Restoration*. New York: Oxford University Press, 1968.

Miley, John. *Systematic Theology*. 2 vols. New York: Eaton and Mains, 1892–94.

Montgomery, John W. *God's Inerrant Word*. Minneapolis: Bethany Fellowship, 1974.

———. *The Suicide of Christian Theology*. Minneapolis: Bethany Fellowship, 1975.

Moorhead, James H. "Joseph Addison Alexander: Common Sense, Romanticism and Biblical Criticism at Princeton." *Journal of Presbyterian History* 53 (1975): 51–65.

Morris, Leon. *The First and Second Epistles to the Thessalonians*. New International Commentary on the New Testament 12. Grand Rapids: Eerdmans, 1964.

Muether, John R. *Cornelius Van Til: Reformed Apologist and Churchman*. Phillipsburg, NJ: P&R, 2008.

Muller, Richard A. *Christ and the Decree: Christology and Predestination in Reformed Theology from Calvin to Perkins*. Grand Rapids: Baker, 1986.

———. *God, Creation, and Providence in the Thought of Jacob Arminius*. Grand Rapids: Baker, 1991.

———. "Grace, Election, and Contingent Choice: Arminius's Gambit and the Reformed Response." Pages 251–78 in vol. 2 of *The Grace of God, the Bondage of the Will*. Edited by Thomas R. Schreiner and Bruce A. Ware. Grand Rapids: Baker, 1995.

———. *Prolegomena to Theology*. Vol. 1 of *Post-Reformation Reformed Dogmatics*. Grand Rapids: Baker, 1987.

———. *Holy Scripture: The Cognitive Foundation of Theology*. Vol. 2 of *Post-Reformation Reformed Dogmatics*. Grand Rapids: Baker, 1993.

———. "Scholasticism Protestant and Catholic: Francis Turretin on the Object and Principles of Theology." *Church History* 55, no. 2 (March 1986): 193–205.

Murray, Iain, et al., ed. *Warfield Commemorative Issue, 1921–1971. Banner of Truth* 89 (Fall 1971).

Needham, N. R. "Buchanan, James." Pages 107–108 in *Dictionary of Scottish Church History & Theology*. Edited by Nigel M. de S. Cameron. Downers Grove, IL: InterVarsity Press, 1993.

Nelson, John O. "The Rise of the Princeton Theology." Ph.D. diss., Yale, 1935.

Nevin, Alfred. *The Encyclopedia of the Presbyterian Church in the United States of America*. Philadelphia: Presbyterian Encyclopedia Publishing, 1884.

Noll, Mark A. "B. B. Warfield." *Handbook of Evangelical Theologians*. Edited by Walter A. Elwell. Grand Rapids: Baker, 1993.

———. *Between Faith and Criticism*. San Francisco: Harper and Row, 1986.

———. "Common Sense Traditions and American Evangelical Thought: The Influence of Epistemological, Ethical and Methodological Common Sense Traditions." *American Quarterly* 37 no. 2, (Summer 1985): 216–38.

———. *Princeton and the Republic, 1768–1822: The Search for a Christian Enlightenment in the Era of William Stanhope Smith*. Princeton: Princeton University Press, 1989.

———. "The Princeton Review." *Westminster Theological Journal* 50, no. 2 (Fall 1988): 247–56.

———, ed. *The Princeton Theology, 1812–1921*. Grand Rapids: Baker, 1983.

———. *The Scandal of the Evangelical Mind*. Grand Rapids: Eerdmans, 1994.

Noll, Mark A. & David N. Livingstone. *B. B. Warfield: Evolution, Science, and Scripture*. Grand Rapids: Baker, 2000.

Ormond, Alexander T. "James McCosh as Thinker and Educator." *The Princeton Theological Review* 1, no. 3 (1903): 337–61.

Orr, James. *The Christian View of God and the World*. 3rd ed. New York: Scribner, 1897.

———. *International Standard Bible Encyclopedia*. Chicago: Howard-Severance Company, 1915.

Packer, J. I. "Is Systematic Theology a Mirage? An Introductory Discussion." Pages 117–131 in *Doing Theology in Today's World*. Edited by John Woodbridge and Thomas McComiskey. Grand Rapids: Zondervan, 1991.

Paley, William. *Evidences of Christianity*. London: Faulder and Clarke, 1802.

———. *Natural Theology*. Edited by F. Le Gros Clark. London: SPCK, 1902.

Parker, T. H. L. *Calvin's Doctrine of the Knowledge of God*. Grand Rapids: Eerdmans, 1952.

Patton, Francis L. "Benjamin Breckinridge Warfield." *Princeton Theological Review* 19 (July 1921): 229–30.

Peirce, C. S. *Collected Papers of Charles Sanders Peirce*. Vol. 5. Cambridge, MA: Harvard University Press, 1931–35.

Peterson, Richard J. "Scottish Common Sense in America. An Evaluation of its Influence." Ph.D. diss., The American University, 1963.

Phillips, Timothy R. "Francis Turretin's Idea of Theology and Its Bearing Upon His Doctrine of Scripture." Ph.D. diss., Vanderbilt University, 1986.

Pinnock, Clark H. *Tracking the Maze: Finding Our Way Through Modern Theology from an Evangelical Perspective*. San Francisco: Harper & Row, 1990.

Plantinga, Alvin. "The Foundations of Theism: A Reply." *Faith and Philosophy* 3, no. 3 (July 1986): 298–313.

———. "The Reformed Objection to Natural Theology." Pages 363–83 in *Rationality in the Calvinian Tradition*. Edited by Hendrik Hart, Johan Van Der Hoeven, and Nicholas Wolterstorff. Lanham, MD: University Press of America, 1983.

———. *Warrant and Proper Function*. Ithaca, NY: Cornell University Press, 1993.

———. *Warrant: The Current Debate*. Ithaca, NY: Cornell University Press, 1993.

Porter, Noah. "Dugald Stewart: The Man and His Work." Pages 151–89 in *The Story of Scottish Philosophy*. Edited by Daniel Sommer Robinson. New York: Exposition Press, 1961.

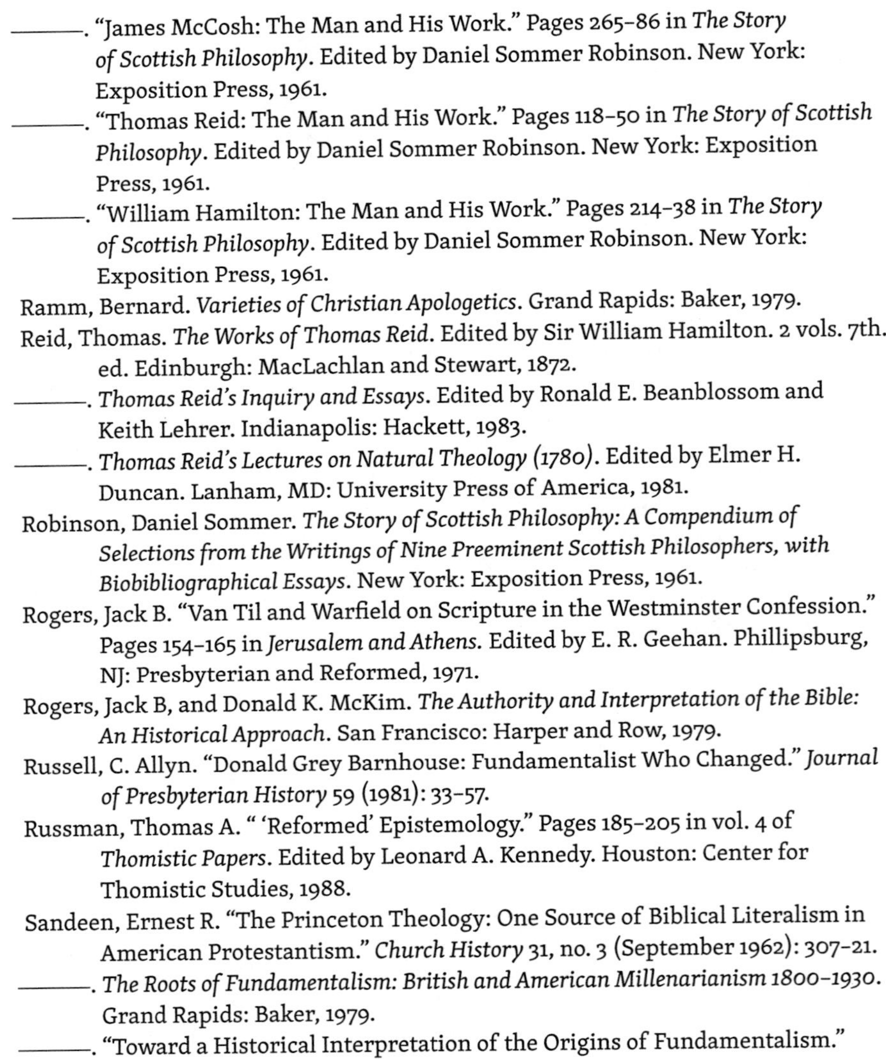

———. "James McCosh: The Man and His Work." Pages 265–86 in *The Story of Scottish Philosophy*. Edited by Daniel Sommer Robinson. New York: Exposition Press, 1961.

———. "Thomas Reid: The Man and His Work." Pages 118–50 in *The Story of Scottish Philosophy*. Edited by Daniel Sommer Robinson. New York: Exposition Press, 1961.

———. "William Hamilton: The Man and His Work." Pages 214–38 in *The Story of Scottish Philosophy*. Edited by Daniel Sommer Robinson. New York: Exposition Press, 1961.

Ramm, Bernard. *Varieties of Christian Apologetics*. Grand Rapids: Baker, 1979.

Reid, Thomas. *The Works of Thomas Reid*. Edited by Sir William Hamilton. 2 vols. 7th. ed. Edinburgh: MacLachlan and Stewart, 1872.

———. *Thomas Reid's Inquiry and Essays*. Edited by Ronald E. Beanblossom and Keith Lehrer. Indianapolis: Hackett, 1983.

———. *Thomas Reid's Lectures on Natural Theology (1780)*. Edited by Elmer H. Duncan. Lanham, MD: University Press of America, 1981.

Robinson, Daniel Sommer. *The Story of Scottish Philosophy: A Compendium of Selections from the Writings of Nine Preeminent Scottish Philosophers, with Biobibliographical Essays*. New York: Exposition Press, 1961.

Rogers, Jack B. "Van Til and Warfield on Scripture in the Westminster Confession." Pages 154–165 in *Jerusalem and Athens*. Edited by E. R. Geehan. Phillipsburg, NJ: Presbyterian and Reformed, 1971.

Rogers, Jack B, and Donald K. McKim. *The Authority and Interpretation of the Bible: An Historical Approach*. San Francisco: Harper and Row, 1979.

Russell, C. Allyn. "Donald Grey Barnhouse: Fundamentalist Who Changed." *Journal of Presbyterian History* 59 (1981): 33–57.

Russman, Thomas A. " 'Reformed' Epistemology." Pages 185–205 in vol. 4 of *Thomistic Papers*. Edited by Leonard A. Kennedy. Houston: Center for Thomistic Studies, 1988.

Sandeen, Ernest R. "The Princeton Theology: One Source of Biblical Literalism in American Protestantism." *Church History* 31, no. 3 (September 1962): 307–21.

———. *The Roots of Fundamentalism: British and American Millenarianism 1800–1930*. Grand Rapids: Baker, 1979.

———. "Toward a Historical Interpretation of the Origins of Fundamentalism." *Church History* 36, no. 1 (March 1967): 66–83.

Schaff, Phillip. *A Companion to the Greek Testament and English Version*. New York: Harper and Bros., 1882.

Sellers, Ian. "Luthardt, Christoph Ernst." In *Dictionary of the Christian Church*. Grand Rapids: Zondervan, 1981.

Seth Pringle-Pattison, Andrew. *Scottish Philosophy: A Companion of the Scottish and German Answers to Hume*. New York: Garland, 1983.

Sloane, William M. *The Life of James McCosh*. New York: Scribner, 1896.

Smith, Henry B. *Apologetics: A Course of Lectures*. New York: A. C. Armstrong & Son, 1882.

Spellman, William M. *The Latitudinarians and the Church of England, 1660–1700*. Athens, GA: University of Georgia Press, 1993.

Sproul, R. C., John H. Gerstner and Arthur Lindsley. *Classical Apologetics: A Rational Defense of the Christian Faith and a Critique of Presuppositional Apologetics*. Grand Rapids: Zondervan, 1984.

St. Amant, Penrose. "The Rise and Early Development of the Princeton School of Theology." Ph.D. diss., University of Edinburgh, 1952.

Stenson, S. H. "A History of Scottish Empiricism from 1730 to 1865." Ph.D. diss., Columbia University, 1952.

Stewart, Dugald. *Collected Works*. Edited by Sir William Hamilton. 11 vols. Edinburgh: Thomas Constable, 1854–58.

———. "Life of Thomas Reid." Pages 3–38 in vol. 1 of *Works of Thomas Reid*. 7th ed. Edited by Sir William Hamilton. Edinburgh: MacLachlan and Stewart, 1872.

Stewart, John William. "The Tethered Theology: Biblical Criticism, Common Sense Philosophy, and the Princeton Theologians, 1812–1860." Ph.D. diss., University of Michigan, 1990.

Stonehouse, Ned B. *J Gresham Machen: A Biographical Memoir*. 3rd ed. Philadelphia: Westminster Theological Seminary, 1978.

Swanton, Robert. "Warfield and Progressive Orthodoxy." *Reformed Theological Review* 23 (October 1964): 74–87.

Sykes, Stephen and John Booty. *The Study of Anglicanism*. Philadelphia: Fortress, 1988.

Thayer, Joseph. Review of B. B. Warfield, *An Introduction to the Textual Criticism of the New Testament*. *Andover Review* 8 (July–December 1887): 100–101.

Thomas, W. H. Griffith. "The Victorious Life." *Bibliotheca Sacra* 76, no. 303 (1919): 267–88.

Thorne, C. G. Jr. "Underhill, Evelyn." *The New International Dictionary of the Christian Church*. Edited by J. D. Douglas. Grand Rapids: Zondervan, 1981.

Townsend, Harvey Gates. "James McCosh: The Man and His Work." Pages 265–286 in *The Story of Scottish Philosophy*. Edited by Daniel Sommer Robinson. New York: Exposition Press, 1961.

Trembath, Kern Robert. *Evangelical Theories of Biblical Inspiration: A Review and Proposal*. New York: Oxford University Press, 1987.

Tuggy, Dale. "Reid's Philosophy of Religion." Pages 289–313 in *The Cambridge Companion to Thomas Reid*. Edited by Terrance Cuneo and René Van Woudenberg. Cambridge: Cambridge University Press, 2004.

Turretino, Francisco. *Institutio Theologiae Elencticae*. 4 vols. New York: Robert Carter, 1847.

Updike, John. *In the Beauty of the Lilies*. New York: Knopf, 1996.

van Bemmelen, Peter Maarten. "Issues in Biblical Inspiration: Sanday and Warfield." Ph.D. diss., Andrews University, 1987.

Van Til, Cornelius. *A Christian Theory of Knowledge*. Phillipsburg, NJ: Presbyterian and Reformed, 1977.

———. *The Defense of the Faith*. Phillipsburg, NJ: Presbyterian and Reformed, 1967.

———. *The Protestant Doctrine of Scripture*. n.p.: den Dulk Foundation, 1967.

Vander Stelt, John C. *Philosophy and Scripture: A Study in Old Princeton and Westminster Theology*. Marlton, NJ: Mack Publishing Company, 1978.

Vos, Arvin. *Aquinas, Calvin & Contemporary Protestant Thought*. Grand Rapids: Eerdmans, 1985.

Vos, Geerhardus. *Biblical Theology: Old and New Testaments*. Grand Rapids: Eerdmans, 1977.

———. "Christian Faith and the Truthfulness of Bible History." *Princeton Theological Review* 4, no. 3 (July 1906): 289–305.

Wallace, Daniel B. "Who's Afraid of the Holy Spirit?" *Christianity Today* 38, no. 10 (September 12, 1994).

Wallis, Wilber B. "Benjamin B. Warfield: Didactic and Polemic Theologian." *Presbyterion* 3, no. 1 (Spring 1977): 3–19; 3, no. 2 (Fall 1977): 73–94.

Warfield, Ethelbert. "Biographical Sketch of Benjamin Breckinridge Warfield." Pages v–ix in *Revelation and Inspiration.* By B. B. Warfield. Grand Rapids: Baker, 1981.

Weber, Timothy P. "The Two-Edged Sword: The Fundamentalist Use of the Bible." Pages 101–120 in *The Bible in America: Essays in Cultural History*. Edited by Nathan O. Hatch and Mark A. Noll. New York: Oxford University Press, 1982.

Wells, David F. "The Theologian's Craft." Pages 171–94 in *Doing Theology in Today's World.* Edited by John D. Woodbridge and Thomas E. McComiskey. Grand Rapids: Zondervan, 1991.

———, ed. *Reformed Theology in America: A History of its Development*. Grand Rapids: Eerdmans, 1985.

———, ed. *The Princeton Theology: Reformed Theology in America*. Grand Rapids: Baker, 1989.

Wheeler, N. M. "Uncanonical Inspiration." *Sunday School Times* 25 (January 1883): 4.

Witte, Wayne William. "John Witherspoon: An Exposition and Interpretation." Th.D. diss., Princeton Theological Seminary, 1953.

Wolterstorff, Nicholas. *Thomas Reid and the Story of Epistemology*. Cambridge: Cambridge University Press, 2001.

———. "Thomas Reid on Rationality." In *Rationality in the Calvinian Tradition.* Edited by Hendrik Hart, Johan Van Der Hoeven and Nicholas Wolterstorff. Lanham, MD: University Press of America, 1983.

Woodbridge, John D. *Biblical Authority: A Critique of the Rogers/McKim Proposal.* Grand Rapids: Zondervan, 1982.

Woodbridge, John D., and Randy Balmer. "The Princetonians and Biblical Authority: An Assessment of the Ernest Sandeen Proposal." Pages 251–79 in *Scripture and Truth.* Edited by John Woodbridge and D. A. Carson. Grand Rapids: Zondervan, 1983.

Woodbridge, John D., and Thomas Edward McComiskey. *Doing Theology in Today's World*. Grand Rapids: Zondervan, 1991.

Zaspel, Fred G. *The Theology of B. B. Warfield: A Systematic Summary*. Wheaton, IL: Crossway, 2010.

The Works of Benjamin Breckinridge Warfield

B. B. Warfield was a prolific author. Any attempt to easily classify his published works is daunting since the total number of books, articles, and reviews number well over one thousand. In addition, many of these books, articles, and reviews have been variously Repr.. In the interest of establishing continuity, I will follow the method of categorization set out in John E. Meeter and Roger Nicole, *A Bibliography of Benjamin Breckinridge Warfield, 1851–1921*. Phillipsburg: Presbyterian and Reformed, 1974. This volume includes all of Warfield's published (and some unpublished) materials in chronological format, including a helpful numbering system, an alphabetical index and a topical index.

Abbreviations

BD *Biblical Doctrines*
BS *Biblical Studies*
BTS *Biblical and Theological Studies*
CA *Calvin and Augustine*
CC *Christology and Criticism*
CaCa *Calvin and Calvinism*
CR *Critical Reviews*
ERE *Encyclopedia of Religion and Ethics*
IAB *Inspiration and Authority of the Bible*
IN *Inspiration* (co-authored with A. A. Hodge)
ISBE *International Standard Bible Encyclopedia*
JBL *Journal of Biblical Literature*
JUC *Johnson's Universal Cyclopedia*
NSHERK *New Schaff-Herzog Encyclopedia of Religious Knowledge*
P *The Presbyterian*
PE *Perfectionism.*
PJ *The Presbyterian Journal*
PM *The Presbyterian Messenger*
PQ *The Presbyterian Quarterly*
PR *Presbyterian Review*
PRR *Presbyterian and Reformed Review*
PTR *Princeton Theological Review*
PWC *Person and Work of Christ*
RI *Revelation and Inspiration*
SP *Studies in Perfectionism*
ST *Studies in Theology*
STA *Studies in Tertullian and Augustine*
SSW *Selected Shorter Writings*

Books and Pamphlets with Separate Imprints Listed Alphabetically

Biblical Doctrines. Grand Rapids: Baker, 1981.

Biblical and Theological Studies. Philadelphia: Presbyterian & Reformed, 1968.
Calvin and Augustine. Philadelphia: Presbyterian & Reformed, 1956.
Calvin and Calvinism. Grand Rapids: Baker, 1981.
Christology and Criticism. Grand Rapids: Baker, 1981.
Critical Reviews. Grand Rapids: Baker, 1981.
The Divine Origin of the Bible. Philadelphia: Presbyterian Board of Publication, 1882.
Warfield, B. B., and A. A. Hodge. *Inspiration*. Edited by Roger Nicole. Grand Rapids: Baker, 1979.
The Inspiration and Authority of the Bible. Phillipsburg, NJ: Presbyterian & Reformed, 1948.
An Introduction to the Textual Criticism of the New Testament. London: Hodder and Stoughton, 1886.
Perfectionism. 2 vols. Grand Rapids: Baker, 1981.
The Person and Work of Christ. Phillipsburg: Presbyterian and Reformed, 1950.
The Plan of Salvation. Grand Rapids: Eerdmans, 1980.
Revelation and Inspiration. Grand Rapids: Baker, 1981.
The Saviour of the World. New York: Hodder and Stoughton, 1914.
Selected Shorter Writings of Benjamin B. Warfield. Edited by John E. Meeter. 2 vols. Philadelphia: Presbyterian and Reformed, 1980.
Studies in Perfectionism. Phillipsburg, NJ: Presbyterian and Reformed, 1958.
Studies in Tertullian and Augustine. Grand Rapids: Baker, 1981.
Studies in Theology. Grand Rapids: Baker, 1981.
Syllabus on the Canon of the New Testament. Pittsburgh, 1881.
Syllabus on the Special Introduction to the Catholic Epistles. Pittsburgh: W. W. Waters, 1883.

Articles or Other Individual Contributions to Dictionaries, Periodicals and Other Volumes with More Than One Author

"Agnosticism." In *NSHERK*. Repr. in vol. 1 of *SSW:* 34–36.
"Albrecht Ritschl and His Doctrine of Christian Perfection." *PTR* 17, no. 4 (October 1919): 533–84. Repr. in *SP*.
"Apologetics." In *NSHERK*. Repr. in *ST:* 3–21.
"Augustine's Doctrine of the Knowledge and Authority." *PTR* 5, no. 3 (July–October, 1907): 353–97. Repr. in *STA* and *CA*.
"In Behalf of Evangelical Religion." *P*, September 23, 1920, 20. Repr. in vol. 1 of *SSW*.
"A Calm View of the Freedmen's Case." *The Church at Home and Abroad* 1 (January 1887). Repr. in vol. 2 of *SSW:* 735–742
"Calvinism." Pages 17–25 in vol. 2 of *JUC*. Originally written by A. A. Hodge and revised by Warfield.
"Calvinism." In *NSHERK*. Repr. in *CaCa* and *CA:* 287–303.
"Calvin's Doctrine of the Creation." *PTR* 13, no. 2 (April 1915): 190–255. Repr. in *CaCa*.
"Calvin's Doctrine of the Knowledge of God." *PTR* 7, no. 2 (April 1909): 219–325. Repr. in *CaCa* and *CA*.
"The Christ that Paul Preached." *Expositor*, Eighth series 15 (February 1918). Repr. in *BD* and *PWC:* 73–90.

"Christian Evidences: How Affected by Recent Criticisms." *Homiletic Review* 16 (August 1888). Repr. in vol. 2 of *SSW*: 124–31.

"Christianity the Truth." *BD* 3 (January 1901). Repr. in vol. 2 of *SSW*: 213–18.

"Christless Christianity." *Harvard Theological Review* 5 (October 1912): 423–73. Repr. in *CC* and *PWC*.

"The Century's Progress in Biblical Knowledge." *Homiletic Review* 39 (March 1900). Repr. in vol. 2 of *SSW*: 3–13.

"Darwin's Arguments against Christianity and Against Religion." *Homiletic Review* 17 (January 1889). Repr. in vol. 2 of *SSW*: 132–41.

"Dr. Hodge as a Teacher of Exegesis." In *The Life of Charles Hodge*. By A. A. Hodge. New York: Scribner, 1880. Repr. in vol. 1 of *SSW*.

"Drawing the Color Line." *The Independent* 40 (July 5, 1888). Repr. In vol. 2 of *SSW*: 743–50.

"The Essence of Christianity and the Cross of Christ." *Harvard Theological Review* 7, no. 4 (October 1914): 538–94. Repr. in *CC* and *PWC*.

"Faith." In *Dictionary of the Bible*. Edited by James Hastings. Edinburgh: T&T Clark, 1898. Repr. in *BD* and *BTS*.

"The Genuineness of Mark 16:9–20." *Sunday School Times* 24 (December 1882): 755 ff.

"God." In *Dictionary of the Bible*. Edited by John Davis. Philadelphia: Westminster, 1898. Repr. in *ST*.

"The Greek Testament of Westcott and Hort." *PR* 3, no. 10 (April 1882): 325–56.

"How to Get Rid of Christianity." *BS* 1 (March 1900). Repr. in vol. 1 of *SSW*: 51–60.

"The Idea of Systematic Theology." *PRR* 7, no. 26 (April 1896): 243–71. Repr. in *ST*.

"The Indispensableness of Systematic Theology to the Preacher." *Homiletic Review* 33 (February 1897). Repr. in vol. 2 of *SSW*: 280–88.

Warfield and A. A. Hodge. "Inspiration." *PR* 2, no. 6 (April 1881): 225–60. Repr. in *IN*.

"Inspiration." In *ISBE*. Repr. in *RI* and *IAB*.

"Inspiration and Criticism." Pittsburgh: n.p., 1880. Repr. in *RI* and *IAB*.

"The Inspiration of the Bible." *Bibliotheca Sacra* 51, no. 204 (October 1894): 610–40. Repr. in *RI* and *IAB*.

Introduction to *Apologetics*, by Francis Beattie. Richmond, VA: Presbyterian Committee of Publications, 1903. Repr. in vol. 2 of *SSW*.

" 'It Says:,' 'Scripture Says:,' 'God Says:' " *PRR* 10, no. 39 (July 1899): 472–510. Repr. in *RI* and *IAB*.

"Jesus Christ, the Propitiation for the Whole World." *Expositor*, Eighth series 21 (April 1921). Repr. in vol. 1 of *SSW*: 167–77.

"John Calvin the Theologian." *Minutes and Proceedings of the Ninth General Council of the Alliance of Reformed Churches in New York.* Edited by G. Mathews. London: Office of the Alliance, 1909. Repr. in *CA*.

"The Latest Phase of Historical Rationalism." *PQ* 9 (January, April 1895). Repr. in *ST*: 591–600.

"The Millennium and the Apocalypse." *PTR* 2, no. 4 (October, 1904): 599–617. Repr. in *BD*.

"Oberlin Perfectionism." *PTR* 19 (January–October 1921): 1–63; 225–88; 451–93; 568–619. Repr. in vol. 2 of *SP* and *PE*.

"James McCosh, D.D., L.L.D., and William Greenough Thayer Shedd, D.D., L.L.D." *PRR* 6, no. 21 (1895): 123–24.
"On the Antiquity and Unity of the Human Race." *PTR* 9, no. 1 (January 1911): 1–25. Repr. in *ST* and *BTS*.
"On Faith in its Psychological Aspects." *PTR* 9, no. 4 (October 1911): 537–66. Repr. in *ST* and *BTS*.
"Our Seminary Curriculum." *P*, September 15, 1909, 7–8. Repr. in *BTS* 11 (October 1909) and vol. 1 of *SSW*: 369–373.
"Personal Recollections of Princeton Undergraduate Life IV: The Coming of Dr. McCosh." *Princeton Alumni Weekly* 26–28 (April 12 and 19, 1916).
"*The Question of Miracles*." *BD* 7 (March-June, 1903). Repr. in vol. 2 of *SSW*: 167–204.
"The Real Problem of Inspiration." *PRR* 4, no. 14 (April 1893): 177–221. Repr. in *RI* and *IAB*.
"Recent Reconstructions of Theology from the Point of View of Systematic Theology." *Homiletic Review* 35 (March 1898). Repr. in vol. 2 of *SSW*: 289–99.
"Regeneration." In vol. 7 of *JUC*. Repr. in vol. 2 of *SSW*.
"The Resurrection of Christ a Historical Fact." *Journal of Christian Philosophy* 3 (April 1884). Repr. in vol. 1 of *SSW*: 178–92.
"Revelation." In *ISBE*. Repr. in *RI* and *IAB*.
"The Right of Systematic Theology." *PRR* 7, no. 27 (July 1896): 412–58. Repr. in vol. 2 of *SSW*.
"The Task and Method of Systematic Theology." *American Journal of Theology* 14 (April 1910): 192–233. Repr. in *ST*.
"Theology a Science." *BD* 1 (January 1900). Repr. in vol. 2 of *SSW*: 207–12.
"The Twentieth Century Christ." *Hibbert Journal* 12 (April 1914). Repr. in *CC* and *PWC*: 189–208
" 'The Victorious Life.' " *PTR* 16 (July 1918): 321–73. Repr. in vol. 2 of *SP* and *Pe*.
"What is Calvinism?" *P*, March 2, 1904, 6–7. Repr. in vol. 1 of *SSW*.

Book Reviews

Bavinck, Herman. *De Zekerheid des Geloofs*. Kampen: 1901. *PTR* 1 (January 1903). Repr. in vol. 2 of *SSW*: 106–123.
Bois, Henri. *Le Dogme Grec*. Paris: 1893. *PRR* 6 (October 1895): 782.
Buckman, J. W. *Mysticism and Modern Life*. New York: 1915. *PTR* 14 (April 1916). Repr. in *CR*: 366–72.
Chafer, L. S. *He That is Spiritual*. New York: 1918. *PTR* 8 (April 1919): 322–27.
Chandler, Arthur. *The Spirit of Man*. London: 1891. *PRR* 3 (July 1892): 586 ff.
Faith and Criticism [Congregational Essays]. London: 1893. *PRR* 5 (April 1894): 354–57.
Fleming, W. K. *Mysticism in Christianity*. New York: 1913. *PTR* 14 (April 1916). Repr. in *CR*: 343–48.
Gerhart, Emanuel V. *Institutes of the Christian Religion*. New York: 1891. *PRR* 2 (October 1891): 716 ff.
Horton, Robert F. *Inspiration and the Bible*. 2nd ed. London: 1888. *PR* 10 (1889): 324 ff.
MacGregor, James. *The Revelation and the Record*. Edinburgh: 1893. *PRR* 8 (October 1897): 772 ff.

MacGregor, James. *Studies in the History of Christian Apologetics*. Edinburgh: 1894. *PRR* 8 (October 1897): 772 ff.
John Miley, *Systematic Theology*, vol. 1. New York: 1892. *Magazine of Christian Literature* 8 (April 1893). Repr. in vol. 2 of *SSW*: 308–13.
Miley, John. *Systematic Theology*, vol. 2. New York: 1894. *Magazine of Christian Literature* 12 (February 1895). Repr. in vol. 2 of *SSW*: 314–20.
Murray, Andrew. *The Spirit of Christ*. London: 1888. *PR* 10 (April 1889): 334 ff.
Sabatier, Auguste. *The Doctrine of the Atonement and Its Historical Evolution*. London: 1904. *PTR* 3 (July 1905). Repr. in *CR*: 106–11.
Strauss, D. F. *The Life of Jesus*. London: 1892. *PRR* 5 (July 1894): 512 ff.
Torrey, R. A. *What the Bible Teaches*. Chicago: 1898. *PRR* 10 (July 1899): 562–64.
Underhill, Evelyn. *Mysticism*. London: 1911. *PTR* 12 (January 1914). Repr. in *CR*: 334–56.
Underhill, Evelyn. *The Mystic Way*. London: 1913. *PTR* 12 (January 1914). Repr. in *CR*: 334–56.
Underhill, Evelyn. *Immanence*. London: 1912. *PTR* 12 (January 1914). Repr. in *CR*: 334–56.
Underhill, Evelyn. *The Miracles of Our Lady Saint Mary*. New York: 1906. *PTR* 12 (January 1914). Repr. in *CR*: 334–56.

Subject and Author Index

Scripture Index

Old Testament

New Testament